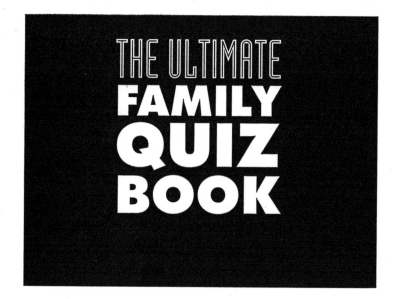

THE ULTIMATE FAMILY QUIZ BOOK

GEORGE BEAL AND CLIVE TROTT

CARTOONS BY
MIKE WREN

TED SMART

First published in 1998 by Sebastian Kelly
11 Bardfield Centre
Great Bardfield
Essex CM7 4SL

24681097531

This edition produced for the Book People Ltd
Hall Wood Avenue, Haydock, St. Helens
WA11 9UL

ISBN 1 84081 097 1

Editor: Clive Gifford
Editorial Assistant: Lynne French
Cover Design: In©
Production: Ian Paulyn

THE ULTIMATE
FAMILY
QUIZ
BOOK

Contents

Quiz Sessions

Children's Quizzes

This book is divided into quiz sessions for both adults and children. The quiz sessions contain 10 quizzes of 15 questions each. The sessions are divided into the following categories of questions, icons for which can be found on the opposite page:

General Knowledge
Science
Natural History
Geography
English Language
Sport
History
Cinema and TV
Popular Music
Literature

The children's section contains 40 quizzes each with 15 questions. The children's quizzes contain questions from the following categories:

General Knowledge
Science and Maths
Natural History
Geography
English
History

General Knowledge

Science

Natural History

Geography

English Language

Sport

History

Cinema and TV

Popular Music

Literature

SESSION 1
QUIZ 1

1. Where is Traitors' Gate?
2. St Matthew is the patron saint of whom?
3. In a pack of cards, which way does the King of Hearts look; to his left, or to his right?
4. What is a Peach Melba?
5. What is sauce lyonnaise?
6. What is taramasalata?
7. What nationality was Brother Jonathan?
8. What is known as the 'devil's bedpost'?
9. What are croutons?
10. What was the name of the early Australian coach and mail company?
11. St Michael is the patron saint of whom?
12. If you go back 20 years or so, who would measure something in picas?
13. The jolly swagman went 'Waltzing Matilda'. What was a matilda?
14. Can you eat acorns?
15. St Nicholas is the patron saint of whom?

ANSWERS

1. The Tower of London. 2. Accountants and bankers. 3. To his right. 4. Peach halves with ice-cream and raspberry sauce. 5. A sauce with white wine and onions. 6. A Greek 'dip' dish of smoked-fish or roe paste with olive oil, etc. 7. An American. 8. The four of clubs playing-card. 9. Small pieces of toast fried in butter. 10. Cobb and Co. 11. Grocers. 12. A printer. A pica is one-sixth of an inch. 13. The swagman's roll containing his blanket. 14. Yes, but they are better served up as food for pigs. 15. Children.

SESSION 1
QUIZ 2

• •

1. What is chalcedony?
2. A lightning conductor was invented by which American statesman in 1752?
3. Edward Bevan invented an ingenious window-blind, and patented it in 1769. What was it?
4. What can be measured in joules?
5. What is an aqueduct?
6. What is putty made of?
7. What does a micrometer measure?
8. What is a hovercraft?
9. James Hargreaves invented a machine for the textile industry in 1764. What was it?
10. Daniel Rutherford discovered one of the most important of gases in 1772. What was it?
11. Which gem was produced artificially in 1955?
12. The study and art of printing is called what?
13. Calcium carbonate is more familiarly known as what?
14. What kind of clock was invented in 1656 by Christian Huygens?
15. Sir John Harington designed and installed what sanitary device in 1589?

SESSION 1
QUIZ 3

1. Fireflies are nocturnal beetles. True or false?
2. Is the blackberry a member of the rose family?
3. A group of hares is called: (a) a down (b) a harrow (c) a brace?
4. The largest-known sea anemone measures: (a) 30 cms (1 ft) (b) 60 cms (2 ft) (c) 1 metre (3 ft)?
5. What is another name for the blackberry?
6. What kind of animal could be described as a Karakul?
7. In one day, a mole can burrow: (a) 25 metres (b) 50 metres (c) 100 metres?
8. What is another name for sorrel?
9. A mongoose is a mammal whose favourite food is what?
10. What is the name given to the largest European deer?
11. Wheat is really a special kind of grass. True or false?
12. What is a mango?
13. A cosset is a young lamb. True or false?
14. What is a group of antelope called?
15. What is cuckoo-spit?

ANSWERS

1. True. 2. Yes. 3. A down. 4. 60 cms. 5. The bramble. 6. A breed of sheep. 7. (c) 100 metres. 8. Dock. 9. Snakes. 10. The elk. 11. Yes. 12. A tropical tree with fleshy, melon-like fruit. 13. True. 14. A herd or a troop. 15. A froth made by the froghopper insect.

SESSION 1
QUIZ 4

• •

1. In which country is the River Ebro?
2. Can you name all of the former 'Ridings' in Yorkshire?
3. What is the name of the city formerly called Danzig?
4. Where and what is 'Scotland Yard'?
5. In which country would you find the town of Bruges?
6. Where and what is 'Tiffany's'?
7. Saint Pierre and Miquelon, off Newfoundland, belongs to which country?
8. Where is the Dogger Bank?
9. Where is Capitol Hill?
10. The Brenner Pass, through the Alps, helps connect which two countries?
11. What is the capital of Argentina?
12. Monapia was the ancient name for which island?
13. Until 1974, Bangladesh was part of which country?
14. What is the status of the Maldive Islands?
15. Which city is on the River Senne?

ANSWERS

1. Spain. 2. Three. North, East, West. 3. Gdansk. 4. Headquarters of the Metropolitan Police in London. 5. Belgium. 6. It's an expensive jeweller's in New York. 7. France. 8. In the North Sea. 9. Washington, DC. 10. Austria and Italy. 11. Buenos Aires. 12. The Isle of Man. 13. Pakistan. 14. They are an island republic. 15. Brussels.

SESSION 1
QUIZ 5

1. In cockney rhyming slang, what does 'Cain and Abel' mean?
2. What does 'cack-handed' mean?
3. What, in Australia, was or is a 'brumby'?
4. What is the difference between the words 'alter' and 'altar'?
5. What is meant by the slang, 'Ackers'?
6. What is wrong with this sentence: He was not all together pleased at the news?
7. What is the boot of a car called in the United States?
8. What is the name for someone who studies birds?
9. What is a diphthong?
10. What are examples of diphthongs?
11. What is a bowler hat called in America?
12. What does an American mean by a 'teeter-totter'?
13. What is the name for someone who studies the art of clock-making?
14. Which single word means both 'more than one leaf' and 'departs'?
15. What would one be if one were described as a 'county' person?

ANSWERS

1. Table. 2. Originally, left-handed, but later, just plain clumsy. 3. An untamed wild horse. 4. 'Alter' means 'to change' and 'altar' is a block or table used in church services. 5. Money. 6. It should read: He was not altogether pleased at the news. 7. The trunk. 8. Ornithologist. 9. Two vowels pronounced together so as to make a new, combined sound. 10. OU as in 'house', OI as in 'hoist', 11. A derby hat. 12. A seesaw. 13. Horologist. 14. Leaves. 15. Ostentatiously upper-class.

SESSION 1
QUIZ 6

•   •

1. In which sport would you find, Fenders, Mothers, Sheets and Reefs?
2. Who is the only man to have played both Cricket and Rugby Union for England at ful international level?
3. Which member of the Royal Family has won an Olympic Medal?
4. Which player traditionally throws the ball in at a Rugby Union line out?
5. In snooker, if there are two reds left and I clear the table gaining the maximum points available, how many points have I scored?
6. Who are the only team from outside the USA to win Baseball's World Series?
7. Who won the 1997 Grand National Steeplechase?
8. Who won the 1997 Coca Cola Cup?
9. With which team did Nigel Mansell make his Formula One debut?
10. Who was captain of the victorious England Cricket team for the 1997 Sharjah one day tournament?
11. On which English race course is the Derby run?
12. How many Gold medals did Michelle Smith win for Eire, in the 1996 Olympic Games?
13. Who captained the South African cricket team in 1998?
14. Which team did Chelsea beat to win the 1998 European Cup Winners Cup Final?
15. By what name are Bradford's Rugby league team known?

ANSWERS

1. Sailing. 2. Alistair Highall. 3. The Princess Royal (Princess Anne). 4. The Hooker. 5. 43. 6. The Toronto Blue Jays. 7. Lord Galeen. 8. Leicester City. 9. Lotus. 10. Adam Hollioake. 11. Epsom. 12. Three. 13. Hansie Cronje. 14. Stuttgart. 15. The Bulls.

SESSION 1
QUIZ 7

• •

1. Who was Lady Jane Grey?
2. What was the name of the socialist society founded by George Bernard Shaw and Sidney and Beatrice Webb?
3. What did the name *Baader-Meinhof* refer to in the 1960's?
4. What was the Ottoman Empire?
5. Who did Kaiser Wilhelm II dismiss in 1890, an event that became known as, 'dropping the pilot'?
6. What momentous event occurred off the Falkland Islands, in 1914?
7. Who was Dag Hammarskjöld?
8. What was started by the British attack on Rommel's line on 23rd October, 1942?
9. What is a Cypriot?
10. Which famous British statesman died on 24th January, 1965?
11. What disaster overtook the Grand Hotel, Brighton, during a Conservative Party conference in 1984?
12. Constantine II (1964-1967) was the last monarch of which country?
13. What did Admiral Horthy become in 1920?
14. Who was Chiang Kai-shek?
15. King Edward VII opened which major museum at South Kensington on 26th June, 1909?

ANSWERS

1. Queen of England for only nine days in 1553. 2. The Fabian Society. 3. A name given to some anarchistic young people, who staged terrorist activities. 4. The empire of Turkey founded by Othman in the 13th century. 5. Bismarck. 6. The German Battleship fleet was sunk. 7. Secretary-General of the United Nations until he was killed in a plane crash in 1961. 8. The Battle of El Alamein. 9. A citizen of the Republic of Cyprus. 10. Sir Winston Churchill. 11. An IRA bomb was detonated. 12. Greece. 13. Regent of Hungary. 14. The last non-communist leader of China. 15. The Victoria and Albert.

SESSION 1
QUIZ 8

• •

1. Which famous actor starred in both *Some Like It Hot* and *The Odd Couple*?
2. Who starred in the film *Tom Jones*?
3. In which film did Sylvester Stallone play in goal while Pele and Michael Caine were on the pitch?
4. Who shared the lead with Maggie Smith in the film *A Room with a View*?
5. Who starred in the film *The Sound of Music*?
6. This ex-member of Monty Python directed films like *Brazil* and *The Fisher King*. Who is he?
7. Which well-known actress played herself in *Airport 75*?
8. Jeff and Beau Bridge's father appeared in many films including *Airplane*. What is his name?
9. Terence Stamp, Anthony Newley and Laurence Harvey all turned down a part in the 1966 film which made Michael Caine a star. What was the film?
10. Which movie star's real name was Frank James Cooper?
11. The cartoon show, *Top Cat*, was based on which old T.V. Show?
12. Who starred in the film *On the Waterfront?*
13. Brothers, Jake and Elwood, liked which kind of music?
14. Name two film stars who have been married at least eight times.
15. Who starred in the film *The Heiress?*

ANSWERS

1. Jack Lemmon. 2. Albert Finney. 3. Escape To Victory. 4. Denholm Elliot. 5. Julie Andrews. 6. Terry Gilliam. 7. Gloria Swanson. 8. Lloyd Bridges. 9. *Alfie.* 10. Gary Cooper. 11. *Sgt. Bilko.* 12. Marlon Brando, Lee J. Cobb, Karl Malden. 13. Blues Music, they were *The Blues Brothers.* 14. Zsa Zsa Gabor, Georgia Holt, Stan Laurel, Mickey Rooney, Lana Turner. 15. Olivia de Havilland.

SESSION 1
QUIZ 9

• •

1. Which 1970's pop icon had alter-egos known as Ziggy Stardust and Aladdin Sane?
2. Name the controversial lead singer with Pulp?
3. Who won the Best Male Artist Award in the 1998 BRITs?
4. In 1988 who sang, 'Don't worry, be happy'?
5. Who covered, The artist formerly known as Prince's hit, 'Kiss', with The Art of Noise?
6. Which band did Phil Oakey front in the late seventies and eighties?
7. Who were 'Walking on Sunshine', when they won the 1997 Eurovision Song Contest with, 'Love Shine a Light'?
8. With which band was TV Presenter Jools Holland the keyboard player?
9. Who replaced Gary Moore as lead guitarist of Thin Lizzy in the early 1980s?
10. If Paul Weller was the lead singer and Bruce Foxton was the bassist, who was the drummer?
11. Who, in 1998, performed the 'Ballad of Tom Jones'?
12. By what name is Harry Webb better known?
13. The heavy metal band Saxon have never had a top ten hit. True or false?
14. Who had a number 7 hit with, 'Shout It To The Top' in October 1984?
15. Which major international female artist started her career as lead singer of the Sugarcubes?

ANSWERS

1. David Bowie 2. Jarvis Cocker 3. Finley Quaye 4. Bobby McFerrin 5. Tom Jones 6. Human League 7. Katrina and the Waves 8. Squeeze 9. Snowy White (Hard) 10. Rick Buckler, The Jam (Hard) 11. Space 12. Cliff Richard 13. True 14. The Style Council 15. Bjork

18

SESSION 1
QUIZ 10

• •

1. *The Corn Is Green* is a play written by which man who spoke no English until he was eight?
2. 'Abandon hope, you who enter here.' Where does this phrase originate?
3. Shakespeare wrote: 'Which like the toad, ugly and venomous,' how did he continue?
4. Complete the proverb: 'Actions speak...'
5. Who was Violet Elizabeth Bott?
6. Who wrote *Tropic of Capricorn?*
7. The author of *Frankenstein* was married to the poet, Percy Bysshe Shelley. What was her name?
8. Who wrote *The Naked and the Dead?*
9. Complete these book titles: *The ------- and the Hearth, The Man in the ---- Mask* and *The ------ of the Baskervilles.*
10. 'A little learning is a dangerous thing' is the beginning of a poem by whom?
11. In which boys' paper did the stories of *Tom Merry & Co.* appear?
12. In which Shakespeare play does 'Sebastian' appear?
13. Who wrote stories of Uncle Remus and Brer Rabbit?
14. 'It is an ancient Mariner,/And he stoppeth one of three' is the beginning of a poem by whom?
15. 'Wackford Squeers' appears in which Dickens novel?

SESSION 2
Quiz 1

• •

1. What is a phobia?
2. What is the medical condition called 'myopia'?
3. What did Sir Walter Raleigh discover in Trinidad in 1595?
4. What is a satellite?
5. What colour is the gem called aquamarine?
6. The patella is another name for which bone?
7. What is measured in knots?
8. What is a Bofors?
9. What instrument did Adolphe Sax invent?
10. What does a thermometer measure?
11. What is the study of the chemistry of living organisms called?
12. Which is the second largest planet?
13. What is phosphor bronze?
14. In early times, what sort of weapon was a trident?
15. In later times, what was a Trident?

ANSWERS

1. A fear, aversion or hatred. 2. Shortsightedness. 3. The Great Pitch Lake, the world's largest deposit of asphalt. 4. A small body, such as a moon, which orbits a planet. 5. A pale, bluish green. 6. The kneecap. 7. Speed. (Knots are often used for the speed of ships and aircraft). 8. An anti-aircraft gun. 9. The saxophone. 10. Temperature. 11. Biochemistry. 12. Saturn. 13. An alloy of copper, tin, zinc and phosphorus. 14. A three-pronged spear. 15. A ballistic missile.

SESSION 2
Quiz 2

• •

1. What is a baboon?
2. The leek is a plant relative of the lily. True or false?
3. What is a yak?
4. What is variously called the bêche-de-mer, the trepang or sea-slug?
5. What is a tuatara?
6. What is an abalone?
7. What sort of animal is a Bedlington?
8. Which very large animal has one, or sometimes two, horns on its snout?
9. What is an aphid?
10. What is another name for the endive?
11. What is a chamois?
12. A prairie-dog is; (a) a kind of wolf (b) a kind of ground squirrel (c) a small cat?
13. The peach is a member of the rose family. Yes or no?
14. What is dangerous about the Anopheles mosquito?
15. Could you take a mud-puppy for a walk?

ANSWERS

1. A large type of monkey, found in Africa. 2. True. 3. A kind of Tibetan wild cattle. 4. The sea-cucumber (not a vegetable), highly prized as a delicacy by the Chinese. 5. It's a small reptile from New Zealand with a spine on its back. 6. It's an edible shellfish, sometimes called the sea-ear. 7. A breed of dog. 8. The rhinoceros. 9. It's another name for the greenfly. 10. Chicory. 11. The goat-antelope of Europe. 12. (b) a kind of ground-squirrel. 13. Yes. 14. It carries and spreads the disease of malaria. 15. No. It's a kind of salamander.

SESSION 2
Quiz 3

• •

1. Kampuchea is now the official name of which country?
2. Which important American city stands on the Potomac river?
3. Where and what is the Serpentine?
4. Where is Ruritania?
5. The original building for one of the world's largest museums was called Montague House, London. What is it called now?
6. What is the commonest name for a pub in Britain?
7. What, in earlier times, was the main industry of Paternoster Row, London?
8. Which are the Low Countries?
9. If you 'crossed the Rubicon' where would you be?
10. Where are the Cheviot Hills? Southern or Northern England?
11. Which is the largest railway station in the United Kingdom?
12, Where is the River Kwai (made famous by the book about its bridge)?
13. Where in the world do they speak Tamil?
14. What is the capital of Algeria?
15. There is a 'Tin Pan Alley' in both London and New York. What is it?

ANSWERS

1. Cambodia. 2. Washington. 3. It's a lake in Hyde Park, London. 4. It doesn't exist. It's fictional! 5. The British Museum. 6. The Red Lion. 7. Bookselling and publishing. 8. Belgium, the Netherlands and Luxembourg. 9. Italy. 10. Northern England. 11. Clapham Junction. 12. In Thailand. 13. Southern India and Sri Lanka. 14. Algiers. 15. The area given over to publishers and writers of popular music.

• •

1. Can you name two words, sounding alike, which mean the same as this pair: twisted/kind of grain?
2. Which word, starting with M, means 'boring' or 'dull'?
3. Which word, beginning with O, means 'atrocious' or 'scandalous'?
4. Finish the proverb: 'Great oaks from...'
5. 'Nether' and 'nethermost' were old ways of saying what?
6. What does 'vamoose' mean?
7. What is the difference between the prefixes 'ante' and 'anti'?
8. What is the female version of 'baron'?
9. What is the female version of 'masseur'?
10. What was a 'broad arrow'?
11. What is a jabot?
12. What is the name for someone who studies the nerves?
13. What was meant by the old word 'deem'?
14. What, originally, was a Thug?
15. Can you name a four-letter word for terror or fright?

ANSWERS

1. Wry/rye. 2. Monotonous. 3. Outrageous. 4. '...little acorns grow'. 5. Lower and lowest. 6. 'Go – fast!' 7. The first means 'before' and the second means 'against'. 8. Baroness. 9. Masseuse. 10. A government mark stencilled on to stores and property. 11. A lace front for a dress or shirt. 12. Neurologist. 13. Think or believe. 14. An Indian devotee of the goddess Kali, who killed travellers. 15. Fear.

SESSION 2
Quiz 5

• •

1. At which sport does Jane Sixsmith represent England?
2. Which former England Centre led Newcastle to the Division One title in 1998 as their Director of Rugby?
3. What is the minimum number of darts required to complete a leg from 501?
4. If I score 'Was-a-ri' in Judo, how many points have I scored?
5. Name the two Williams drivers for the 1998 Formula One season.
6. For which rally team did Colin McRae drive in 1997 & 1998?
7. Is 'The Oaks' a race for colts or fillies?
8. Who was the longest-serving England cricket captain?
9. Name Arsenal's highest ever scorer.
10. In the 1970s Brian Jacks rose to national fame due to the 'Superstars' television programme, but in which sport did he actually compete for Great Britain at international level?
11. Who was BBC TV personality of the year in 1996?
12. What incident in a German tennis tournament, meant that Monica Seles was injured and out of tennis for over a year?
13. Which European city hosts the games of the American football team known as 'Galaxy'?
14. Up until 1998 who sponsored the World Professional Snooker Championship?
15. In the Euro 96' match between Germany and England, what was the score after extra time?

ANSWERS

1. Hockey. 2. Rob Andrew. 3. Nine. 4. Half. 5. Heinz Harold Frentzen and Jacques Villeneuve. 6. Subaru. 7. Fillies. 8. Mike Atherton. 9. Ian Wright. 10. Judo. 11. Jonathan Edwards. 12. She was stabbed, on court, by a fan of Steffi Graf. 13. Frankfurt. 14. Embassy. 15. 1-1.

SESSION 2
Quiz 6

• •

1. Which famous London market moved from central London to a more southerly site in 1974?
2. What was the Munich Agreement of 1938?
3. Who was murdered by the Bolsheviks at Ekaterinburg in July, 1918?
4. What was the better-known name of the Russian revolutionary, Lev Davidovich Bronstein?
5. What was the Berlin Airlift?
6. What did Athelstan, King of Mercia, become in A.D. 927?
7. Where and what was Wessex?
8. Who were rescued from the Altmark ship, off Norway, in 1940?
9. The Prime Minister, Margaret Thatcher, visited which Eastern European country in March, 1987?
10. Who was Franklin Delano Roosevelt?
11. Vichy, France, was the headquarters of what during WW2?
12. Who was Ernest Bevin?
13. What was the better-known name of Joseph Vissarionovich Djugashvili?
14. In 1853, the *Wellingtonia gigantea* was discovered in California. What was it?
15. Which London department store opened on 15th March, 1909?

ANSWERS

1. Covent Garden. 2. A meeting between Hitler, Neville Chamberlain, Mussolini and Daladier. 3. The whole Russian royal family. 4. Leo Trotsky. 5. A method of ferrying supplies by air into Berlin when it was blockaded in 1948. 6. King of England (Wessex and Mercia). 7. One of the old kingdoms of England before A.D.808. Wessex included the counties of Hampshire, Dorset, Wiltshire and Somerset. 8. British prisoners of war. 9. The Soviet Union. 10. He was the 32nd American president. 11. Pétain's puppet government. 12. A trade union leader and politician. 13. Stalin. 14. The largest tree in the world. 15. Selfridges.

25

SESSION 2

Quiz 7

• •

1. Who starred in the silent film *Sherlock, Jr.?*
2. Which comic provided the voice of the genie in Disney's first *Aladdin?*
3. Who starred in the film *Forty Ninth Parallel?*
4. How many episodes were there in the 1914 serial film *The Exploits of Elaine?*
5. Who received an Oscar for his creation of Wallace and Gromit?
6. Who starred in the film *Blow Up?*
7. Who starred in the film *The Private Life of Henry VIII?*
8. From which film did the song 'A Couple of Swells' come?
9. Who starred in the film *The Lavender Hill Mob?*
10. Who starred in the films *The Deer Hunter* and *Cape Fear?*
11. In which film did Katharine Hepburn and Spencer Tracy star as husband-and-wife lawyers?
12. Who commenced each episode of a TV series with the words 'Good Evening, All?'
13. Which leader of the Labour Party played himself in *Rockets Galore?*
14. Omar Sharif is famed in a field other than acting. What is it?
15. Which American Senator played himself in *The Candidate?*

ANSWERS

1. Buster Keaton. 2. Robin Williams. 3. Leslie Howard, Raymond Massey, Laurence Olivier. 4. Fourteen. 5. Nick Park. 6. David Hemmings, Sarah Miles. 7. Charles Laughton. 8. *Easter Parade*, 1948. 9. Alec Guinness, Stanley Holloway. 10. Robert De Niro. 11. *Adam's Rib* (1949). 12. P.C. Dixon, played by Jack Warner. 13. Michael Foot. 14. He is a champion bridge-player. 15. Hubert Humphrey.

SESSION 2
Quiz 8

• •

1. Which 1985 film, starring David Bowie and Patsy Kensit, flopped disastrously?
2. Elvis Presley's first UK hit reached number 2 in May 1956. Name the song?
3. All Saints had their first hit in March 1998. What was the song?
4. What band does Jarvis Cocker front?
5. Who reached number one in 1965 with, 'Tears', and has had top ten hits with, 'Love Is Like A violin', 'The River', and 'Promises'?
6. In Nov 1980, Motorhead reached number 15 in the UK with what song?
7. In 1989, Stock, Aitkin and Waterman teamed up with, The Christians, Holly Johnson, Paul McCartney and Gerry Marsden to record which song for charity?
8. In 1981, Soft Cell reached number 1 with, 'Tainted love'. Name the band's debut album released in the same year?
9. Which song, first released in 1957, took 29 years, 42 days to reach number 1 in Dec 1986?
10. Which all-girl band sang 'Viva forever'?
11. Which British band released their debut album, Rattus Norvegicus in 1977?
12. Pink Floyd have only had one UK number 1 single. Name the song?
13. Janet Jackson has never had a UK number 1. True or false?
14. Name one of Rolf Harris's top twenty hits other than his number 1 single, 'Two Little Boys'?
15: Who was the blonde in Blondie?

ANSWERS

27

SESSION 2
Quiz 9

• •

1. Who wrote the play *Pygmalion?*
2. The character 'Pip' appears in which book by Charles Dickens?
3. Who said: 'Dr Livingstone, I presume?'
4. Which famous children's books did Frances Hodgson Burnett write?
5. What line follows, 'There is a Lady sweet and kind, Was never face so pleased my mind;'
6. What line follows, 'And did those feet in ancient time'
7. 'All men are created equal.' Where does this phrase originate?
8. What did Thomas Moore think 'A little learning' was?
9. 'Ayesha' is a character in which famous book?
10. Who, on his desert island, said, 'I am monarch of all I survey', according to William Cowper?
11. 'All the world's a stage, and all the men and women merely players.' Where does this phrase originate?
12. Who created 'Batman'?
13. Who created the gentleman cracksman 'Blackshirt'?
14. Who wrote *Catch 22?*
15. According to Noël Coward, who go out in the noon-day sun?

ANSWERS

1. George Bernard Shaw. 2. *Great Expectations.* 3. Sir Henry Morton Stanley. 4. *The Secret Garden; Little Lord Fauntleroy.* 5. 'I did but see her passing by, And yet I love her till I die'. 6. 'Walk upon England's mountains green?' 7. The American Declaration of Independence. 8. A dangerous thing. 9. *She.* 10. Alexander Selkirk. 11. Shakespeare's *As You Like It.* 12. Bob Kane. 13. Bruce Graeme. 14. Joseph Heller. 15. Mad dogs and Englishmen.

28

SESSION 2
Quiz 10

· ·

1. Before decimalisation, our coinage used the letters £, s and d. What did they mean?
2. Which word beginning with ante- means 'before marriage'?
3. Who is the patron saint of teachers?
4. Which anniversary does a pearl wedding celebrate?
5. What, in medieval times, was a groat?
6. What is ravioli?
7. Who was George Cadbury?
8. Who, in ancient times, were Shem, Ham and Japheth?
9. Who, or what, is the Old Lady of Threadneedle Street?
10. In what groups does one find a squadron?
11. What is kohlrabi?
12. The name of which famous nurse is concealed by the anagram Flit on, cheering angel?
13. Who in the world would be called a 'Jock'?
14. In a pack of cards, which way does the Queen of Spades look: to her left, or to her right?
15. What are the religious followers of Nanak called?

ANSWERS

1. The '£' sign is the Latin letter L for *libra*, pound. The 's' is for *soldi*, shillings, and 'd' for *denarius*, penny. 2. Antenuptial. 3. St Gregory. 4. The thirtieth. 5. Any thick, silver coin. 6. Small pasta cases with a savoury filling. 7. A businessman and philanthropist from the famous chocolate firm. 8. The sons of Noah. 9. The Bank of England. 10. Aircraft, ships, soldiers. 11. A variety of cabbage, but much like a turnip. 12. Florence Nightingale. 13. A Scotsman. 14. To her right. 15. Sikhs.

SESSION 3
QUIZ 1

- -

1. Which is the world's largest amphibian?
2. 'George', a male mandrill (baboon) in the London Zoo, died aged (a) 40 years, (b) 45 years or (c) 48 years?
3. *Homo erectus pekinensis* was an example of whose ancestors?
4. What domestic animal could be described as a Siamese?
5. Which creature can jump one hundred times its length?
6. What is a mangel-wurzel?
7. A female horse aged four or under is called a what?
8. What fox-faced monkey-like small creatures are found almost entirely in Madagascar?
9. What is a firefly?
10. A rabbit can run at 35 miles an hour. True or false?
11. What is peculiar about the teeth of a rodent?
12. What kind of animal could be described as a Cotswold?
13. What is an oak-apple?
14. The macaw is a member of which expressive bird family?
15. What kind of animal is said to bell?

ANSWERS

1. The giant salamander, found in China and Japan, can be six feet long.
2. 40 years. 3. Mankind. It was an early example of man found in China.
4. A cat. 5. The flea. 6. A kind of beet used as animal food. 7. A filly.
8. The lemurs. 9. A small beetle which is able to make flashing signals at night. 10. True. 11. They never stop growing. 12. A breed of sheep.
13. It's a small round protuberance caused by an insect's nest on an oak.
14. The parrots. 15. A deer.

SESSION 3
QUIZ 2

• •

1. Where is the Gower Peninsula?
2. Where is the Clifton Suspension Bridge?
3. Where in England would you find the River Coquet?
4. Norfolk Island forms part of which country?
5. Which major city is on the River Avon?
6. Where is the Golden Gate Bridge?
7. The official name '*Eire*' refers to which country?
8. Where is 'Sunset Boulevard'?
9. What is the modern name for the Sandwich Islands?
10. In what city is Piccadilly Railway Station?
11. 'New Holland' was an early name for which country?
12. To which country do St Pierre and Miquelon belong?
13. '*España*' refers to which country?
14. Where in the world would you find Bondi Beach?
15. In which county are the Quantock Hills?

ANSWERS

1. South Wales, west of Swansea. 2. In Bristol, over the River Avon. 3. In Northumberland. 4. Australia. 5. Bristol. 6. In San Francisco, USA. 7. The Irish Republic. 8. Los Angeles. 9. Hawaii. 10. Manchester. 11. Australia. 12. France. 13. Spain. 14. Sydney, Australia. 15. Somerset.

SESSION 3
QUIZ 3

1. What is the difference between 'kerb' and 'curb'?
2. What is one doing if one 'comes the old soldier'?
3. Harry was an aged man, although his wife was only aged 50. How is the word 'aged' pronounced?
4. What is the meaning of 'chutzpah'?
5. A waldgravine was (a) a former noblewoman in Germany, (b) an extinct type of wolf or (c) an engraver of tombstones.
6. What article of clothing is a 'deerstalker'?
7. What is the British equivalent of Zip codes?
8. What is a proscenium?
9. What does 'He didn't do a hand's turn' mean?
10. Can you make an anagram out of 'golden land'?
11. An 'apartment' to an American is what to an Englishman?
12. What happens if you are 'between the devil and the deep blue sea'?
13. A begum is (a) a kind of West Indian dance, (b) an African witch-doctor or (c) a Muslim princess.
14. What do Americans call trousers?
15. Complete this simile: 'Good in parts, like the...'

ANSWERS

1. A kerb is the edge of the pavement, and curb means to 'restrain or check'.
2. Wheedling or persuading. 3. The first is pronounced 'ayjid' and the second 'ayjd'. 4. It's a Yiddish word meaning 'effrontery' or 'cheek'. 5. (a) a former noblewoman in Germany. 6. A hat, as used by Sherlock Holmes.
7. Postcodes. 8. The arch at the front of a theatre's stage. 9. He did no work. 10. Old England. 11. A flat. 12. You're faced with a choice between two equally unpleasant options. 13. (c) a Muslim princess. 14. Pants.
15. '...Curate's egg'.

32

SESSION 3
QUIZ 4

• •

1. For which Formula One team did Nigel Mansell win the World Drivers' Championship?
2. For which County Cricket team did Brian Lara play in the 1997 & 1998 seasons?
3. Who were Rugby Union Division One champions in the 1996/97 season?
4. Apart from Manchester United and Arsenal, up until 1999, which was the only other team to have won the Premier League?
5. Who is the only British Olympian to have won Gold Medals in three consecutive Olympic Games?
6. Name Denver's American football team.
7. Which British swimmer won the 100m Breaststroke Gold Medal in the 1980 Olympic Games?
8. With which club did Bobby Moore end his professional playing career?
9. By which name was wrestler Shirley Crabtree better known?
10. Who was the first British boxer in the 20th century to win a World Heavyweight title?
11. One of the most successful skiers of the 1990s was Alberto Tomba, what nationality is he?
12. Which sport do Birchfield Harriers take part in?
13. Who won the Golden Boot in the 1986 World Cup finals?
14. Who sponsored the 1998 Rugby League Challenge Cup Final?
15. Who won the 1997 British Touring Car Championship?

ANSWERS

1. Williams. 2. Warwickshire. 3. Wasps. 4. Blackburn Rovers. 5. Steven Redgrave. 6. Broncos. 7. Duncan Goodhew. 8. Fulham. 9. Big Daddy. 10. Lennox Lewis. 11 Italian. 12. Athletics. 13. Gary Lineker. 14. Silk Cut. 15. Alain Menu.

33

1. Who is the current Duke of Cornwall?
2. What was the Diet of Worms of 1521?
3. 11 people were killed in St Peter's Fields, Manchester in 1819. What was it called?
4. In which country is the Democratic Party a major political unit?
5. Which Italian poet raised an army and seized Fiume in 1919?
6. What happened on 6th June, 1944, in Northern France?
7. Where in England did Julius Caesar first set foot?
8. Which large island country in the Indian Ocean was annexed by France in 1896?
9. How many ships were there in the Spanish Armada? (a) 329 (b) 1,029 (c) 129
10. The slavery-abolitionist John Brown made a raid at Harper's Ferry in the United States in 1859. What was the result?
11. Who was Eamon De Valéra?
12. Who was Alexander the Great?
13. What major governing authority was abolished in England in 1986?
14. Who became leader of the Conservative Party on 10th February, 1975?
15. Following the death of King Edward VII on 6th May, 1910, who became king?

ANSWERS

1. Prince Charles. 2. A meeting of leaders of the Holy Roman Empire to outlaw Luther and his teachings. 3. The Peterloo Massacre. 4. The United States. 5. Gabriele D'Annunzio. 6. The D-Day landings. 7. Deal, Kent. 8. Madagascar. 9. (c) 129. 10. He was captured and hanged. 11. President of the Irish Republic (1959-73). 12. King of Macedonia (356BC-323BC) and conqueror of much of the world then known. 13. The Greater London Authority (GLC). 14. Margaret Thatcher. 15. King George V.

• •

1. What was the name of the frog who compered *The Muppet Show?*
2. Who starred in the film *Ghost?*
3. Who starred in the film *Brighton Rock?*
4. From which stage show did the song 'Send in the Clowns' come?
5. Who directed the films *M.A.S.H.* and *The Player?*
6. Who starred in the film *Women in Love?*
7. Who starred in the film *Singin' in the Rain?*
8. Which singer's voice is heard in the cartoon film *The Lion King?*
9. Who or what was 'Flipper'?
10. Whose name was originally John Charlton Carter?
11. Who was the first British actor to win an Oscar?
12. Which film star first became famous for his role in the T.V. show *Moonlighting?*
13. Who starred in the silent 1924 film *The Thief of Bagdad?*
14. Who starred in the film *State Secret?*
15. Who was the first British actress to win an Oscar?

ANSWERS

1. Kermit. 2. Whoopi Goldberg. 3. Richard Attenborough. 4. *A Little Night Music.* 5. Robert Altman. 6. Alan Bates, Glenda Jackson. 7. Gene Kelly. 8. Elton John. 9. A dolphin. 10. Charlton Heston. 11. George Arliss, who appeared in *Disraeli* in 1929. 12. Bruce Willis. 13. Douglas Fairbanks. 14. Douglas Fairbanks Jnr, Jack Hawkins 15. Vivien Leigh, who appeared in *Gone With the Wind* in 1939.

SESSION 3
QUIZ 7

• •

1. Which British band were on 'Hope Street in 1995?
2. Which Australian singer collaborated with Nick Cave to reach number 11 with, 'Where The Wild Roses Grow'?
3. For the 1998 World Cup, two songs with the words 'Top Of The World' were released in support of the England football team. The official version was performed by England United, who performed the other?
4. Ronan is the lead singer with which Irish boy band?
5. Chris Rea has had only one UK top ten hit. Name the song?
6. Which former Australian soap star's debut single was 'Torn'?
7. Which 1970's pop icon, played Che Guevara in the stage production of Evita, rode a 'Silver Dream Racer', and mutinied on the Bounty?
8. The Eurythmics have only had one UK number 1, name the song?
9. Who was the original lead singer with Generation X?
10. With which double A-side single did Jasper Carrott have his only chart success, reaching number 5 in August 1975?
11. Who reached number 3 in the UK with, 'My Best Friend's Girl', in 1978 and number 5 with, 'Drive' in 1984?
12. In 1997, the four piece band Aqua topped the charts with 'The Barbie Song'. What nationality are they?
13. Name the 1987 song taken to number 12 in the UK by Glen Hoddle and Chris Waddle?
14. 'Mad' Richard Ashcroft is the vocalist with which UK Album chart-topping band?
15. In 1998 which two bands held a concert in Belfast to support the, 'Yes', campaign for the referendum on the Good Friday peace agreement?

ANSWERS

15. U2 & Ash
Roundabout 11. The Cars 12. Danish 13. 'Diamond Lights' 14. The Verve
Angel (playing with my heart)' 9. Billy Idol 10. Funky Moped/Magic
Road To Hell' 6. Natalie Imbruglia 7. David Essex 8. 'There Must Be An
1. The Levellers 2. Kylie Minogue 3. Chumbawamba 4. Boyzone 5. 'The

36

SESSION 3
QUIZ 8

● ●

1. Who was 'Michael Henchard' in the novel *The Mayor of Casterbridge?*
2. Who created the fictional character 'Count Dracula'?
3. What is the main subject of novels by Dick Francis?
4. De Morgan wrote: 'Great fleas have...' Can you complete the phrase?
5. 'Natty Bumppo' is a character created by which American author?
6. Who wrote *Lisa of Lambeth?*
7. Which writer used the letter 'Q' as a pseudonym?
8. 'The best laid plans of mice and men.' Where does this phrase originate?
9. The character 'Quilp' appears in which book by Charles Dickens?
10. Who wrote *The Lord of the Rings?*
11. Who wrote *The Mask of Dimitrios?*
12. 'Mike Hammer' was a fictional hero devised by whom?
13. Who was James Boswell?
14. Complete the proverb: 'Dead men...'
15. Anna Sewell wrote the book *Black Beauty.* Who or what was 'Black Beauty'?

ANSWERS

1. He was the Mayor. 2. Bram Stoker. 3. Suspense and detective novels featuring horse-racing. 4. 'Little fleas upon their backs to bite 'em.' 5. J. Fenimore Cooper. 6. W. Somerset Maugham. 7. Sir Arthur Quiller-Couch. 8. Robert Burns: *To a Mouse.* 9. *The Old Curiosity Shop.* 10. J.R.R. Tolkien. 11. Eric Ambler. 12. Mickey Spillane. 13. Friend and fellow-traveller of Dr Samuel Johnson. 14. '...tell no tales.' 15. A horse.

SESSION 3
QUIZ 9

1. Who wrote the play *Cavalcade?*
2. What is a rollmop?
3. According to the 'language of flowers', what does the asphodel signify?
4. Which anniversary does a sapphire wedding celebrate?
5. St David is the patron saint of what?
6. What is the Purple Heart?
7. What is hock?
8. Who, with his wife, was expelled from the Garden of Eden?
9. Rice paper isn't made from rice. What is it made from?
10. What is meant by 'Dutch courage'?
11. Who was the Father of English Poetry?
12. Which anniversary does an emerald wedding celebrate?
13. What kind of food is baclava?
14. According to the 'language of flowers', what does the honeysuckle signify?
15. Poseidon is another name for Neptune. True or false?

ANSWERS

1. Noël Coward. 2. A herring fillet rolled up with onion and pickled. 3. My regret follows you to the grave. 4. The forty-fifth. 5. Wales. 6. An American decoration awarded to soldiers wounded in battle. 7. A white Rhine wine. 8. Adam and Eve. 9. The pith of a plant. 10. Courage with the aid of strong liquor. 11. Geoffrey Chaucer. 12. The fifty-fifth. 13. Pastry filled with nuts and honey. 14. Generous and devoted attention. 15. True.

SESSION 3
QUIZ 10

. . . .

1. What is agoraphobia?
2. What kind of signal was sent across the Atlantic for the first time in 1901?
3. What did the French clock-maker Antoine Redier invent in 1847?
4. What object in the sky is called Io and is 3,632 kilometres in diameter?
5. What did Percy Shaw of Yorkshire invent in 1934, which is seen on roads all over the world?
6. What is a capstan?
7. Rubella is a disease, also called what?
8. Water vapour is usually called what?
9. What gemstone is found in the Cairngorm Mountains of Scotland?
10. How many sides has an octagon?
11. What are the two digits used in the binary system of calculation?
12. What is gum arabic?
13. A high degree of mechanisation in industry is called what?
14. Which is longer, a metre or a yard?
15. What is a catamaran?

ANSWERS

1. Fear of open spaces. 2. Radio signals. 3. The first alarm clock. 4. Jupiter's third-largest moon. 5. Cats' eyes. 6. A winding device used aboard ship for hauling in a cable or rope. 7. German measles. 8. Steam. 9. The cairngorm. It's a yellowish stone. 10. Eight. 11. 0 and 1. 12. An adhesive obtained from acacia trees. 13. Automation. 14. A metre. 15. A vessel for sailing, with two hulls.

SESSION 4
QUIZ 1

1. Where in Britain would you find an example of a bascule bridge?
2. Where in the world would you find the Gabba cricket ground?
3. Dacia is the old name for which country?
4. Where is the Isle of Thanet?
5. Where and what is Stonehenge?
6. Which city is on the Liffey river?
7. In which country would you find the Black Forest?
8. Where and what is Plinlimmon?
9. In which English county would you find the River Blackwater?
10. Where would you find the Leaning Tower?
11. In which city would you find Connolly railway station?
12. The Simplon Tunnel is between which two countries?
13. The American president James Monroe gave his name to which capital city?
14. In which American city would you find the Liberty Bell?
15. Which is the longest bridge in Britain?

I'm <u>free</u>, I'm <u>free</u>!

ANSWERS

1. Tower Bridge, London. 2. Brisbane, Australia. 3. Romania. 4. In Kent. It is separated from the rest of the county by the River Stour. 5. An ancient group of assembled large stones near Salisbury. 6. Dublin. 7. Germany. 8. A mountain in Wales. 9. Essex. 10. Pisa, Northern Italy. 11. Dublin. 12. Switzerland and Italy. 13. Monrovia, capital of Liberia. 14. Philadelphia. 15. The Humber Bridge, over the River Humber.

?!' SESSION 4
QUIZ 2

● ●

1. If someone said you were 'wet behind the ears', what would it mean?
2. To what object did the Earl of Chesterfield give his name?
3. What is the meaning of 'nefarious'?
4. In cockney rhyming slang, what does 'pen and ink' mean?
5. What is the skirting board in a room called in the United States?
6. What is a 'black maria'?
7. What speak, 'louder than words'?
8. What does 'feasible' mean: (a) able to be done (b) possible (c) probable?
9. What is the name for someone who studies reptiles?
10. Which word means a metal and guided?
11. Which word means mimic or ape?
12. If you were 'green about the gills' what would you be like?
13. What is a kimono?
14. What was 'Durst' an old way of saying?
15. What is the name for someone who studies animals?

ANSWERS

1. That you were lacking in experience. 2. A kind of sofa or couch.
3. Extremely wicked. 4. Stink. 5. The base board. 6. A police van.
7. Actions. 8. (a) able to be done. 9. Herpetologist. 10. Lead. 11. Imitate.
12. As if you were going to be sick. 13. A kind of robe, fastened with a
sash. 14. Dared. 15. Zoologist.

41

SESSION 4
QUIZ 3

• •

1. Where do Surrey County Cricket Club play the majority of their home games?
2. Name Phoenix's NBA Basketball team?
3. Which football team was Eric Morecambe renowned for supporting?
4. How many players are there in a Polo team?
5. Who was England's top scorer in the 1992 Olympic Hockey tournament?
6. Who scored a hat-trick against England in the 1992 European Championships?
7. Name Houston's American football team.
8. Which British cyclist who won a gold medal at the 1992 Olympic Games on a radical graphite and carbon-fibre bike?
9. Who won the 1998 Rugby League Challenge Cup?
10. In Rugby Union what can you do inside your own 22, but not outside, unless it's a penalty?
11. Which two football teams play each other in the Edinburgh derby match?
12. What sport do the Manchester Giants play?
13. For which Formula One team did James Hunt win the World Drivers' Championship?
14. What was the score in the 1998 FA Cup final, when Arsenal defeated Newcastle to take the Cup and League double?
15. Which heavyweight boxer is nicknamed, 'The Real Deal'?

ANSWERS

1. The Oval. 2. The Suns. 3. Luton Town. 4. Four. 5. Sean Kerley.
6. Marco Van Basten. 7. Oilers. 8. Chris Boardman. 9. Sheffield Eagles.
10. Kick the ball, 'out on the full', (i.e. into touch without bouncing).
11. Heart of Midlothian & Hibernian. 12. Basketball. 13. McLaren.
14. 2-0. 15. Evander Holyfield.

SESSION 4
QUIZ 4

• •

1. President McKinley of the United States died on 14th September 1901, following what?
2. Which head of state in North America was executed in 1867?
3. Who is Valéry Giscard d'Estaing?
4. Who was Attila?
5. Which English monarch once had tea with Hitler?
6. Who was assassinated in Delhi, India, on 20th January, 1948?
7. On 1st April, 1965, the Greater London Council replaced what?
8. In what year did food rationing end?
9. Zanzibar and Pemba were ceded to Britain by Germany in 1890 in exchange for which North Sea island?
10. London and Paris were linked in 1891 by which new device?
11. Which newspaper proprietor was found dead in the sea off Tenerife in 1991?
12. Which Nazi leader landed by parachute near Glasgow, on 10th May, 1941?
13. Which Frenchman was pardoned and his prison sentence quashed in July, 1906?
14. England, had a dictator in the 1650s. Who was he?
15. How did Cardinal Wolsey die in 1530?

ANSWERS

1. Being shot and wounded eight days earlier. 2. Maximilian, Emperor of Mexico. 3. A former president of France. 4. King of the Huns. 5. Edward VIII (after his abdication). 6. Mahatma Gandhi. 7. The London County Council (LCC). 8. 1954. 9. Heligoland. 10. The public telephone. 11. Robert Maxwell. 12. Rudolf Hess, Hitler's deputy. 13. Alfred Dreyfus. 14. Oliver Cromwell. 15. After being taken ill on a journey from York to London.

• •

1. Which TV sitcom features a dog called Eddie and a home help called Daphne?
2. From which musical play comes the song 'Ol' Man River'?
3. Who wrote the song 'I've Got You Under My Skin'?
4. Who starred as T.E. Lawrence in the epic *Lawrence Of Arabia?*
5. Who is Shirley MacLaine's brother?
6. *Thelma And Louise* starred which two famous actresses?
7. Which film featured John Gordon Sinclair as a boy who loses his place on the school football team to a girl?
8. Whose epitaph is: 'On the whole, I'd rather be in Philadelphia'?
9. Which actress's Oscar acceptance speech included the famous phrase, 'You like me, you really like me?'
10. Jodie Foster won an Oscar for her role in the film *The Accused.* What was the other film she won a best actress Oscar for?
11. What film featured a search for a toy only known as 'Rosebud'?
12. What Vietnam film featured helicopters attacking to the music 'The Ride Of The Valkyries'?
13. Dooley Wilson, as 'Sam' sang what in the film *Casablanca?*
14. Which Sci-Fi film, based on a book by Frank Herbert, featured Sting?
15. In which film did Paul Newman star as a pool player?

ANSWERS

1. *Frasier.* 2. *Show Boat.* 3. Cole Porter. 4. Peter O'Toole. 5. Warren Beatty. 6. Susan Sarandon and Gina Davis. 7. *Gregory's Girl.* 8. W.C. Fields. 9. Sally Fields. 10. *Silence Of The Lambs.* 11. *Citizen Kane.* 12. *Apocalypse Now.* 13. 'As Time Goes By.' 14. *Dune.* 15. *The Hustler.*

SESSION 4
QUIZ 6

• •

1. Which British entertainer had top ten hits in the 1950's with, 'Singing The Blues', 'Butterfingers', 'Water Water', and 'Little White Bull'?
2. Which band recorded, 'Three Lions', with David Baddiel and Frank Skinner for Euro 96 and the 1998 World Cup?
3. In 1976, which international singing star had her first UK hit reaching number 7 with, 'Jolene'?
4. Of which progressive rock band was Fish the original lead singer?
5. In 1998, which US teen band was made up of, Taylor, Isaac and Zac?
6. What does the M stand for in the band name, M People?
7. In which seventies teeny bop band would you have found, 'Les and Woody', singing, 'Shang-a-lang' and, 'Give A Little Love, Take A Little Love'?
8. According to Cornershop, what does, everybody need a bosom for?
9. From which British city do heavy rockers Saxon originate?
10. In 1997 & 1998 who topped the Album charts with, 'Urban Hymns'?
11. A.J., Howie, Nick, Kevin and Brian, make up which US boy band?
12. Name Jimi Hendrix's only UK number one?
13. Which group has had the most weeks on the UK chart in any one year?
14. Which midlands group had 6 number ones in the early 1970's including, 'Skweeze Me Pleeze Me', Coz I Luv You', and, 'Mama Weer All Crazee Now'?
15. Metallica's, 'Hero Of The Day', is dedicated to Motorhead's Lemmy. True or false?

ANSWERS

1. Tommy Steele 2. Lightning Seeds 3. Dolly Parton 4. Marillion 5. Hanson 6. Manchester 7. Bay City Rollers 8. A pillow 9. Barnsley 10. The Verve 11. Backstreet Boys 12. Voodoo Chile (slight return) 13. Oasis (134 in 1996) 14. Slade 15. True

SESSION 4
QUIZ 7

● ●

1. Who wrote *Autobiography of a Super-tramp?*
2. 'Banquo' appears in which play by Shakespeare?
3. 'The better part of valour is discretion.' Where does this phrase originate?
4. Under what name did Patrick Dannay and Manfred B. Lee write?
5. Who wrote *Tom Brown's Schooldays?*
6. What line follows 'Where the bee sucks, there suck I:'?
7. Who wrote *Confessions of an English Opium-Eater?*
8. Stories about Lord Snooty and his pals appeared in which publication?
9. Who, reputedly, said, 'Youth is wasted on the young'?
10. Andrew Lang wrote a series of 'Fairy Books'. How were they distinguished?
11. Complete the proverb: 'Don't change horses...'
12. Who wrote *The Rime of the Ancient Mariner?*
13. 'When angry, count four; when very angry...' Complete Mark Twain's famous line.
14. Who wrote *The Ipcress File?*
15. What was the main occupation of John Betjeman?

ANSWERS

1. William Henry Davies. 2. *Macbeth.* 3. Shakespeare's *Henry IV.* 4. Ellery Queen. 5. Thomas Hughes. 6. 'In a cowslip's bell I lie'. 7 Thomas de Quincey. 8. *The Beano.* 9. George Bernard Shaw. 10. By colours: thus, *The Green Fairy Book, The Yellow Fairy Book,* etc. 11. '...in midstream'. 12. Samuel Taylor Coleridge. 13. Swear. 14. Len Deighton. 15. Writing poetry.

SESSION 4
QUIZ 8

• •

1. St Francis de Sales is the patron saint of whom?
2. What kind of stew comes from Lancashire?
3. What were 'dundrearies'?
4. What kind of food item comes from Chelsea?
5. What kind of food is a garibaldi?
6. In cooking, what does en croûte mean?
7. From where does the popular pub name, 'The Pig and Whistle' come?
8. What are Quakers?
9. If you were a printer, how many points would make an inch?
10. If your birthday was April 5th, what star sign would you be?
11. What is a Christian Scientist?
12. What is the Talmud?
13. In wartime, what was a WAAF?
14. What is a kebab?
15. What is Bezique?

ANSWERS

1. Authors and journalists. 2. Hot pot. 3. Long side-whiskers favoured in Victorian times. 4. A bun. 5. A kind of biscuit with a layer of currants. 6. Cooked in a pastry crust. 7. It was originally the Old English piggen wassail, a bucket from which drinkers filled their own mugs. 8. Followers of a belief put forward by George Fox, who rejected rites and creeds. 9. Twelve. 10. Aries. 11. Someone who believes that healing can be achieved by religious faith. 12. An encyclopaedia of Jewish laws. 13. A member of the Women's Auxiliary Air Force. 14. Vegetables, meats, etc., cooked on a skewer. 15. A card-game which originated in France.

SESSION 4
QUIZ 9

. . . .

1. What sort of device was a Lee-Enfield?
2. Edwin Land invented what kind of camera in 1947?
3. Where in the body is the Achilles tendon?
4. What machine tool did Henry Maudslay invent in 1800?
5. What important electrical device was invented in 1825 by William Sturgeon?
6. Speaking of the weather, what is meant by 'precipitation'?
7. Which has most calories: margarine or butter?
8. What is autophobia?
9. "Mr Watson, come here, I want you." was the first message in 1876 by whom?
10. What is the process of eating, digesting and assimilating food called?
11. What is a camera obscura?
12. Platinum takes its name from the Spanish word *platina*, meaning silver. True or false?
13. The science which studies the history of the Earth's crust is called what?
14. What is the study of the science of light called?
15. Between which planets is the asteroid belt situated?

ANSWERS

• •

1. What would you find in an apiary?
2. What kind of animal could be called a Suffolk Punch?
3. What is a group of hedgehogs called?
4. What is a bird of paradise?
5. What is a capuchin?
6. What is a gosling?
7. What is a prehensile tail?
8. Where would you find the eyes of a snail?
9. The barn owl's night vision is much better than ours. Is it
    (a) twice as good or (b) a hundred
10. What is another name for alfalfa?
11. What is a kipper?
12. Apart from being the name of a domestic animal, what
    else is called a 'cat'?
13. Which animal lives in a warren?
14. What is hemlock?
15. Which cat-like animal with tufted ears once roamed wild
    in Europe?

ANSWERS

1. Bees. 2. A horse. 3. An array. 4. A bird with gorgeous plumage, found in New Guinea. 5. A species of monkey found in South America. 6. A young goose. 7. One which is capable of wrapping itself around objects. 8. At the tip of its 'horns'. 9. A hundred times as good. 10. Lucerne. 11. A herring, split open and cured. 12. A kind of boat. 13. A rabbit. 14. A poison obtained from a plant of the same name. 15. The lynx.

SESSION 5
QUIZ 1

1. The name of which bird is associated with silliness?
2. What is the name of the adjustable spanner invented by Charles Moncke?
3. What's wrong with this sentence: One should always carry an umbrella when you go out walking here?
4. Can you name two words which sound alike and mean the same as this pair: band of singers/24 sheets of paper?
5. What exactly is a zealot?
6. What does 'Q.E.D.' mean?
7. What is the meaning of 'edifice'?
8. Name two words, sounding alike, which mean the following: use needle and thread/plant seeds.
9. In cockney rhyming slang, what does 'half-inch' mean?
10. If Fred 'went bananas' what happened?
11. If you took umbrage, would it be poisonous?
12. What's the plural of 'axis'?
13. If your surname is Clark, what might you be nicknamed?
14. How should the following sentence read: 'Help! I will drown and no one shall save me.'?
15. What does 'catchpenny' mean?

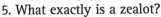

ANSWERS

1. Cuckoo. 2. A 'monkey wrench', named after the inventor. 3. It should read: One should always carry an umbrella when one goes out walking here. 4. Choir/quire. 5. A rather fanatical follower, enthusiast or fan. 6. 'Quod erat demonstrandum': that which was to be proved. 7. A building. 8. Sew/sow. 9. Pinch. 10. He got wildly angry. 11. No, it only means 'to feel resentment'. 12. Axes. 13. Nobby. 14. Help! I shall drown and no one will save me. 15. Cheap, trivial.

SESSION 5
QUIZ 2

• •

1. Name Queens Park Rangers' home ground.
2. Name Pittsburgh's American football team.
3. What do Skoal Bandit, Zakspeed and Lotus have in common?
4. Name the British adventurer who led the successful Thrust II supersonic land speed record attempt.
5. What sport do Poole Pirates take part in?
6. What nationality was Greg Rusedski at birth?
7. Which sport played in the southern hemisphere is a cross between Rugby, American football and Gaelic football, with teams such as the Essendon Bombers and Footscray Bulldogs?
8. Where do the 'Broncos' English Rugby League team come from?
9. In Cricket, a batsman may only score a maximum of 30 leg byes in any one innings. True or false?
10. Who was the first person to break the four-minute mile?
11. What sport do the Cardiff Devils play?
12. Ice Dance champions Torvill and Dean are associated most with which piece of music?
13. The 'Buccaneers' American football team come from which US city?
14. Name West Bromwich Albion's football ground?
15. Name the five disciplines in the modern pentathlon?

ANSWERS

1. Loftus Road. 2. The Steelers. 3. They are all ex-Formula One teams. 4. Richard Noble. 5. Speedway. 6. Canadian. 7. Australian Rules Football. 8. London. 9. False. 10. Roger Bannister. 11. Ice Hockey. 12. Bolero by Ravel. 13. Tampa Bay. 14. The Hawthorns. 15. Fencing, Swimming, Shooting, Running and Horse Riding.

SESSION 5
QUIZ 3

• •

1. Who was leader of the Labour Party immediately before Tony Blair?
2. What was the Field of the Cloth of Gold?
3. Which company opened the first supermarket in Britain, at Manor Park, East London, in 1947?
4. Which motoring organisation was started on 29th June, 1905?
5. Which American general was known as 'Old Blood and Guts'?
6. Who was Mr Five-Per-Cent?
7. Who was Simón Bolivar?
8. What happened in the Falkland Islands on 2nd April 1982?
9. Who was assassinated in Dallas in 1963?
10. King Edward III established which famous Order of chivalry in 1348?
11. Which commercial radio station began operating in October, 1973?
12. Where and what was Bechuanaland?
13. Millions of rabbits in Britain died in 1953 as a result of what?
14. Who was Jean Batten?
15. In what year did Columbus make his first major voyage?

ANSWERS

1. John Smith. 2. A plain in Picardy, France, where Henry VIII met Francis I of France in 1520. 3. The London Co-operative Society (The Co-Op). 4. The Automobile Association. 5. General George Patton. 6. Calouste Gulbenkian, oil millionaire. 7. A revolutionary in South America, known as 'The Liberator'. 8. They were invaded by Argentina. 9. President John Kennedy. 10. The Order of the Garter. 11. LBC – The London Broadcasting Company. 12. A country in Southern Africa, now called Botswana. 13. The spreading of the disease of myxomatosis. 14. A New Zealander who flew solo from England to Australia. 15. 1492.

52

SESSION 5
QUIZ 4

• •

1. From which film and stage show did the song 'Climb Every Mountain' come?
2. Who starred in the film *Goldfinger?*
3. Which famous actress turned down the female lead in *Gone With The Wind?*
4. Who starred in the film *Victim?*
5. Which was the first musical film with its own score?
6. The star of *Little Caesar* was born in Bucharest as Emmanuel Goldenberg. Who is he?
7. Sir John Pratt, the British diplomat, had a famous film-actor-brother. Who was he?
8. Which movie star's real name was Jane Alice Peters?
9. Who starred in the 1943 film *Shadow of a Doubt?*
10. Who starred in the film *The Baby and the Battleship?*
11. Who starred in the film *The Producers?*
12. Which two famous actors turned down the lead role in *The Godfather* that eventually went to Al Pacino?
13. Who played Bonnie in the film *Bonnie and Clyde?*
14. Which famous American comedian was born in England at Eltham, Kent?
15. Who starred in the film *Blade Runner?*

ANSWERS

1. *The Sound of Music.* 2 Sean Connery, Honor Blackman. 3. Bette Davis. 4 Dirk Bogarde. 5 *The Broadway Melody*, 1929. 6 Edward G. Robinson. 7. Boris Karloff, whose real name was William Henry Pratt. 8 Carole Lombard. 9. Joseph Cotten. 10 John Mills, Richard Attenborough. 11 Zero Mostel, Gene Wilder. 12. Robert Redford and Warren Beatty. 13. Faye Dunaway. 14 Bob Hope. 15 Harrison Ford.

SESSION 5

QUIZ 5

● ●

1. Blockbuster's Bob Holness started life as a session musician and played saxophone on Gerry Rafferty's 1978 hit, 'Baker Street'. True or false?
2. Courtney Love is lead singer of which American band?
3. Name Donna Summers only UK number 1 hit?
4. Vanessa Mae reached number 16 in Jan 1995 with, 'Toccata And Fugue'. What instrument does she play?
5. Which US soul singer recorded the original, 'Alphabet Song', for the children series, Sesame Street?
6. '(Sittin' On) The Dock Of The Bay' was the only UK top 10 hit for which US vocalist?
7. Name Hot Chocolate's lead vocalist?
8. In which year did Bucks Fizz win the Eurovision Song Contest?
9. In which UK county does Rod Stewart have his main residence?
10. Falco is the only Austrian to top the UK chart. Which fellow Austrian was he paying tribute to, in his number 1 hit song?
11. Who reached number 1 in July 1972 with, 'Schools Out'?
12. Who was lead singer with 1980's chart toppers, Culture Club?
13. Which singer, real name Gloria Fajardo, owns 2 Cuban Hotels, lives in Miami, has a daughter called Emily and broke her back in a bus crash in 1990?
14. What do the songs, 'Back Home', 'This Time We'll Get It Right', and 'World In Motion', have in common?
15. True or False, Barry Manilow has only had 1 UK top 10 hit?

ANSWERS

1. False 2. Hole 3. 'I Feel Love'. 4. Violin 5. Luther Vandross 6. Otis Redding 7. Errol Brown 8. 1981 9. Essex 10. Mozart 11. Alice Cooper 12. Boy George 13. Gloria Estefan 14. England World Cup football songs 15. True (I Wanna do it with you, Number 8, 1982)

54

SESSION 5
QUIZ 6

• •

1. Complete the proverb: 'Clothes do not...'
2. What had John Debrett and John Burke in common?
3. What was the most famous book from the author of *Kidnapped* and *The Black Arrow?*
4. Who wrote the play *The Playboy of the Western World?*
5. 'Breathes there a man, with soul so dead,/Who never to himself hath said,' is the beginning of a poem by whom?
6. Who wrote the verse *Matilda* (told such awful lies)?
7. Who was the leading character in the novel *1984?*
8. *Pamela* was whose first novel?
9. 'Blood is thicker than water'. Where does this phrase originate?
10. What historical novel did Henryk Sienkiewicz write?
11. Complete the proverb: 'Accidents will happen...'
12. Who were the Houyhnhnms in *Gulliver's Travels?*
13. Who said, 'Father, I cannot tell a lie. I did it with my little hatchet'?
14. Who wrote the novel *An American Tragedy?*
15. Who, in Russia, occupied a place similar to that of Shakespeare in England?

ANSWERS

1. '...make the man'. 2. They both produced books of reference on the Peerage. 3. *Treasure Island.* 4. J.M. Synge. 5. Hilaire Belloc. 6. Sir Walter Scott. 7. 'Winston Smith'. 8. Samuel Richardson. 9. John Ray: *English Proverbs* (1670). 10. *Quo Vadis.* 11. '...in the best-regulated families'. 12. A noble race of horses who ruled humans. 13. George Washington (according to Mark Twain). 14. Theodore Dreiser. 15. Alexander Pushkin.

SESSION 5
QUIZ 7

• •

1. Which anniversary does a crystal wedding celebrate?
2. Who was the original Johnnie Walker of Scotch whisky fame?
3. What is Canasta?
4. St Jerome is the patron saint of whom?
5. St Elizabeth of Hungary is the patron saint of whom?
6. What are 'devils on horseback'?
7. Which country's national assembly is called Congress?
8. Which are Europe's Latin languages?
9. If your surname is 'White', what might your nickname be?
10. According to the 'language of flowers', what does the quince signify?
11. St Luke is the patron saint of whom?
12. What is Islam?
13. What is a thick cream of lemon juice, lemon peel, eggs, sugar and butter called?
14. Which word, beginning with ante- means 'to date, before true time'?
15. Two 16th-century German painters, father and son, had the same name. Who were they?

ANSWERS

1. The fifteenth. 2. John Walker, an Ayrshire man, who bought a grocery business in Kilmarnock in 1820. 3. A card-game of the rummy family. 4. Librarians. 5. Bakers. 6. Prunes stuffed with chutney and grilled, or fried rolled up in bacon. 7. The United States. 8. Italian, French, Spanish, Catalan, Portuguese, Romanian. 9. Snowy or Knocker. 10. Temptation. 11. Doctors. 12. The religion founded by Muhammad 1,300 years ago. 13. Lemon curd. 14. Antedate. 15. Hans Holbein, the Elder and the Younger.

SESSION 5
QUIZ 8

• •

1. What did Erno Rubik invent in 1975?
2. What vehicle was first built in 1936 by Ferdinand Porsche in Germany?
3. What kind of animals would a zoologist study?
4. Which object in the sky is called Ganymede and is 5,276 kilometres in diameter?
5. Which of the planets is nearest the Sun?
6. How many carats are there in pure gold?
7. What metal is the main constituent of steel?
8. How many sides has a polygon?
9. Bronze is an alloy of which two metals?
10. How long is a cubit?
11. What is an optician?
12. The Zeppelin built in 1900 was the first successful example of what kind of craft?
13. Which object in the sky is called Titania and is about 1,580 kilometres in diameter?
14. What is the chemical symbol for Copper?
15. A substance which destroys bacteria and prevents their growth is called a what?

ANSWERS

1. The Rubik cube. 2. The Volkswagen Beetle car. 3. All. 4. It is Jupiter's largest moon. 5. Mercury. 6. 24. 7. Iron. 8. Three or more sides (it's a many-sided figure). 9. Copper and tin. 10. 18 inches. 11. Someone who makes and sells optical equipment. 12. The first rigid dirigible airship. 13. It is the largest of the moons of Uranus. 14. Cu. 15. Antiseptic.

SESSION 5
QUIZ 9

· ·

1. Oats are really a special kind of grass. True or false?
2. A female horse aged five or more is called what?
3. What is a bandicoot?
4. What is a ptarmigan?
5. A pomeranian is a breed of dog. True or false?
6. A capybara is related to the guinea-pig. True or false?
7. What breed of animal could be called a Shetland?
8. How do bats sleep?
9. Which animal lives in a drey?
10. What is a bilberry?
11. What is a mandrake?
12. What kind of animal could be termed a Thoroughbred?
13. What kind of animal is said to bellow?
14. What is a sardine?
15. How many humps does a Bactrian camel have?

ANSWERS

SESSION 5

QUIZ 10

• •

1. Where in the world would you find Central Park?
2. Which capital city stands on the River Vltava?
3. Dartmoor Prison was built in 1806 for what purpose?
4. What is Van Diemen's Land called today?
5. Where is St Mark's Cathedral?
6. Where in the world would you find a Magyar?
7. What, in England, was the Fosse Way?
8. To which country does Martinique belong?
9. Where is Balmoral Castle?
10. Upstream from Oxford, what is the River Thames known as?
11. Lake Titicaca is found in which two South American countries?
12. Where would you find people speaking Afrikaans?
13. Which city is on the Scottish River Tay?
14. The official name 'Deutschland' refers to which country?
15. Victoria railway stations may be found in three cities in the world. Which?

ANSWERS

1. New York City. 2. Prague. 3. To hold French prisoners-of-war. 4. Tasmania. 5. Venice. 6. Hungary. 7. A Roman road stretching from the south coast of Devon to Grimsby. 8. France. 9. On the River Dee, Scotland. 10. The Isis. 11. Peru and Bolivia. 12. South Africa. 13. Dundee. 14. Germany. 15. London, Manchester and Bombay, the Firth of Tay.

SESSION 6
QUIZ 1

1. Colin Jackson is famous for which athletics event?
2. If I was playing Stapleford rules, what sport would I be playing?
3. In which county is Headingley cricket ground?
4. Which snooker player is nicknamed 'The Whirlwind'?
5. Which snooker player gained the nickname, 'The Hurricane'?
6. Who managed Leeds United to a UEFA Cup place in the 1997/98 season?
7. Name Atlanta's Baseball team.
8. Which jump jockey holds the record for the most winners in a season?
9. Which British squash player finally ousted Jansher Khan as world number one in 1998?
10. In Cricket, and excluding the wicket keeper, which fielding position is usually nearest the bat?
11. How high is the net on a tennis court: 2ft 6ins, 3ft or 3ft 4ins?
12. How old was Stephen Hendry when he became Snooker's world number one?
13. Name the three events in equestrian three-day eventing?
14. In which European country was the sport of Handball invented?
15. By what name was the USA's Olympic Basketball team known in the 1996 Olympic Games?

ANSWERS

1. 110m Hurdles. 2. Golf. 3. Yorkshire. 4. Jimmy White. 5. Alex Higgins. 6. George Graham. 7. The Braves. 8. Tony McCoy. 9. Peter Nichol. 10. Silly point. 11. 3ft. 12. 20. 13. Dressage, Cross Country & Show Jumping. 14. Germany. 15. The Dream Team.

SESSION 6
QUIZ 2

● ●

1. What event took place in St Paul's Cathedral in July, 1981, and was seen by 700 million T.V. viewers?
2. In which year did the Gunpowder Plot take place?
3. The island of Réunion became a colony of which country in 1764?
4. Oliver Cromwell, although he became England's Head of State, was not King. What was he called?
5. Who was Alfred the Great?
6. What part of Rome became a sovereign state in 1929?
7. Who was the last Danish king of England?
8. What 'British' character was invented by John Arbuthnot in 1712.
9. Which famous magazine went on sale for the first time on 1st October, 1938?
10. In very early times, what was the status of Sussex, Essex and Kent?
11. The followers of John Wycliffe, the 14th century religious reformer, were called what?
12. Who was Chester Arthur?
13. Which British award for bravery was instituted on 23rd September, 1940?
14. What, politically speaking, was 'the Axis' before the Second World War?
15. In 1889, Lord Rosebery was elected chairman of which new London authority?

ANSWERS

1. Prince Charles and Lady Diana Spencer were married. 2. 1605. 3. France. 4. The Lord Protector. 5. The King of Wessex who resisted the Danes. 6. The Vatican City. 7. Hardicanute (1019-1042). 8. John Bull. 9. Picture Post. 10. They were kingdoms of England before A.D. 808. 11. Lollards. 12. 21st American president. 13. The George Cross. 14. The alliance between Germany, Italy and (later) Japan in WW2. 15. The London County Council.

SESSION 6
QUIZ 3

• •

1. What creature was the star of the *Free Willy* series of movies?
2. English gentleman and actor David Niven was born in which country?
3. Ruby Keeler, Mary Pickford, Norma Shearer and Fay Wray were not American born. From which country did they originally come?
4. Who starred in the film *Brief Encounter?*
5. Which was the first Mickey Mouse cartoon?
6. What was unusual about the film *Becky Sharp* released in 1935?
7. What morning show has been hosted by Chris Evans, Mark Little and Keith Chegwin?
8. Stanley Baker, Jack Hawkins, Michael Caine starred together in which African war film?
9. Who starred in the film *Doctor in the House?*
10. Who starred in the film *Crocodile Dundee?*
11. Michael Douglas had an affair with which actress in the film *Fatal Attraction?*
12. The Bond films were based on books written by which author?
13. Who starred in the film *The Outlaw Josey Wales?*
14. Who played the leading role in the three film versions of *The Thirty-Nine Steps?*
15. Which film has been re-made more times than any other?

ANSWERS

1. A killer whale. 2 In Scotland. 3. Canada. 4. Trevor Howard and Celia Johnson. 5. *Steamboat Willie,* 1928. 6. It was the first in three-colour Technicolor. 7. *The Big Breakfast.* 8. *Zulu.* 9. Dirk Bogarde, Kenneth More, James Robertson Justice. 10. Paul Hogan, Linda Kozlowski. 11. Glenn Close. 12. Ian Fleming. 13. Clint Eastwood. 14. 1935: Robert Donat; 1959: Kenneth More, 1978: Robert Powell. 15. *Cinderella.*

SESSION 6
QUIZ 4

1. In 1998 Jazzy Jeff and The Fresh Prince released a single called, 'Lovely Day'. By what name is, The Fresh Prince better known?
2. Which country did A-Ha come from?
3. What was the surname of Matt and Luke from Bros?
4. What is Blur's home town?
5. What was Blondie's first number 1 hit?
6. Who in the 1970's had top ten hits with, 'Billy Don't Be A Hero' and 'The Night Chicago Died'?
7. Which Peter was a founder member of Genesis?
8. 'You Can't Hurry Love', was the first solo UK number 1 for which male singer and drummer?
9. In Which Movie did Madonna sing, 'Another Suitcase In Another Hall'?
10. Name Meatloaf's only UK Number 1?
11. Who sang the duet with Tina Turner, 'It Takes Two', which reached number 5 in Nov 1990?
12. In 1984 Prince starred in a semi-autobiographical film of what name?
13. Who had a top ten hit in Nov 1987 with 'Letter From America'?
14. Gladys Knight sang the theme song for which Bond film?
15. What links Derek And The Dominoes, The Yardbirds, Cream and Blind Faith?

ANSWERS

1. Will Smith 2. Norway 3. Goss 4. Colchester 5. 'Heart of Glass' 6. Paper Lace 7. Gabriel 8. Phil Collins 9. Evita 10. 'I'd do anything for love', (But I won't do that)' 11. Rod Stewart 12. Purple Rain 13. The Proclaimers 14. Licence To Kill 15. Eric Clapton played guitar in all four bands.

SESSION 6
QUIZ 5

. . . .

1. Who wrote *The Guns of Navarone*?
2. 'The boy stood on the burning deck.' Where does this phrase originate?
3. Which of the following is not an author: Dickens, Molière, Goethe, Tchaikovsky?
4. Who created the fictional aristocratic detective 'Lord Peter Wimsey'?
5. *The Adventures of Huckleberry Finn* was written by whom?
6. Who wrote *The Informer*?
7. With which Arab ruler are the *Arabian Nights* much associated?
8. 'If I should die, think only this of me:' is the beginning of a poem by whom?
9. Who wrote the book *Utopia* in 1516?
10. Who was Thomas Carlyle?
11. 'Brevity is the soul of wit.' Where does this phrase originate?
12. What is a euphemism?
13. 'Professor George Edward Challenger' appears as a character in which book by Arthur Conan Doyle?
14. 'To lose one parent, Mr Worthing, may be regarded as a misfortune. To lose both looks like...' Can you finish the line?
15. Who spoke the above lines, in what play?

SESSION 6
QUIZ 6

•••••••••••••••••••••••••••••••••••••

1. If your surname is 'Murphy', what might your nickname be?
2. What is Scientology?
3. Who was the first Pope?
4. How did worsted get its name?
5. What is prosciutto?
6. Who was James Earl Carter?
7. St Eloi is the patron saint of whom?
8. St Genesius is the patron saint of whom?
9. What is vermouth?
10. What is Shintoism?
11. To the ancient Greeks and Romans who was Apollo?
12. Who was the original 'Angry Young Man'?
13. How did teddy-bears receive their name?
14. If you were born on Good Friday or Christmas Day, what special power might you have?
15. If a foreign car displayed the letters RO, what would its country of origin be?

ANSWERS

1. Spud. 2. A set of ideas put forward by a science-fiction writer, L. Ron Hubbard in the 1950s. 3. St Peter. 4. It was originally made in Worstead, Norfolk. 5. Finely-cured uncooked ham, often smoked. 6. Former US president Jimmy Carter. 7. Jewellers. 8. Actors. 9. A wine-based drink flavoured with herbs. 10. A Japanese form of Buddhism. 11. The god of music and poetry. 12. John Osborne. 13. It was named after the American president, Theodore 'Teddy' Roosevelt. 14. The power of seeing and commanding spirits! 15. Romania.

• •

1. The flying fox is not a fox at all. What is it?
2. What sort of animal is called a terrier?
3. The lettuce is a member of the daisy family. Yes or no?
4. Can you name the very common, small, grey, many-legged garden creature sometimes called a 'leatherjacket'?
5. What is the wild Australian 'teddy-bear' called?
6. What sort of animal is a Rottweiler?
7. Parsley is a plant relative of the carrot. Yes or no?
8. Birds have more neck-bones than giraffes. True or false?
9. What is a clove?
10. Is it true that Scandinavian lemmings commit mass suicide?
11. Is it true that lemmings are rodents, like rabbits and mice?
12. What is a cayuse?
13. Which animal lives in a hive?
14. What is a tamarind?
15. What is a tamarisk?

ANSWERS

1. A bat. 2. Various breeds of dogs. 3. Yes. 4. Woodlouse. 5. The koala. 6. A breed of dog. 7. Yes. 8. True. 9. The flower-bud of the clove tree, dried and used as a spice. 10. No. It's a myth. 11. True. 12. An American term for a poor horse. 13. A bee. 14. A tropical tree which has pods filled with sweet, reddish-black pulp. 15. A small tree or shrub which grows in salt deserts or by the seashore.

SESSION 6
QUIZ 8

• •

1. What did Ladislao Biro invent in 1933?
2. What machine first saw service in 1961 and was built by Unimation?
3. If something is cupreous, what does it contain?
4. What colour is a ruby?
5. What is graphite?
6. What is a facsimile?
7. Sir Joseph Swan demonstrated the use of a modern lighting object in 1878. What was it?
8. What did Samuel Morse invent in 1837?
9. How many days are there in a year?
10. Who invented the jet engine?
11. Isaac Newton discovered what in 1687?
12. What element does the chemical symbol K represent?
13. What is controlled by a rheostat?
14. What is gastritis?
15. What is 'nickel silver'?

ANSWERS

1. The ballpoint pen. 2. An early form of chemistry, much given to errors.
3. Copper. 4. Red. 5. A form of carbon, sometimes called black-lead.
6. An exact copy of a picture or other flat-surface pattern. 7. The filament
electric lamp. 8. The Morse code. 9. 365 (366 in leap years). 10. Frank
Whittle. 11. The force of gravity. 12. Potassium. 13. Electric current.
14. Inflammation of the stomach lining. 15. An alloy of copper, nickel
and zinc.

SESSION 6
QUIZ 9

• •

1. Is there really such a place as 'Timbuktu'? If so, where is it?
2. In which city would you find the Gare du Nord railway station?
3. In which city would you find Grand Central railway station?
4. To which country do the Canary Islands belong?
5. Where is Hans Christian Andersen's memorial, the Little Mermaid, located?
6. Which cathedral in Britain has three spires?
7. Which submarine first sailed under the Arctic ice-cap?
8. Where did the coconut originate?
9. Where is the Chamber of Horrors?
10. Where is Exmoor?
11. What is the second highest mountain in the world?
12. The Republic of Benin is in which continent?
13. Which city is on the River Hooghly?
14. Nyasaland is a country now called what?
15. The volcano Popocatepetl is in which country?

_____

ANSWERS

1. Yes. It is in the Mali Republic, Northern Africa. 2. Paris. 3. New York. 4. Spain. 5. In Copenhagen harbour. 6. Lichfield Cathedral. 7. The Nautilus. 8. Polynesia. 9. It's part of the Madame Tussauds waxwork show in London. 10. Somerset. 11. K2. 12. Africa. 13. Calcutta. 14. Malawi. 15. Mexico.

SESSION 6
QUIZ 10

• •

1. What have been called 'the Devil's Picture Books'?
2. What is a split infinitive?
3. In the theatrical world what is an 'angel'?
4. What does the Latin 'ad hoc' mean?
5. What is the singular form of the word 'graffiti'?
6. Who were 'the great unwashed'?
7. What are gym shoes often known as in the United States?
8. Americans refer to this item of clothing as an undershirt. What do we call it?
9. Can you name two words sounding alike which mean the same as this pair: remain/heavy measurer?
10. How much does a 'stitch in time' save?
11. What is a 'lady bountiful'?
12. Is a babu (a) a kind of monkey, (b) an Indian clerk or (c) an American child?
13. Complete this simile: 'To blush like a...'
14. What does 'machiavellian' mean?
15. What is a 'chanticleer'?

ANSWERS

1. Playing-cards. 2. The insertion of an adverb between the word 'to' and a verb. As 'to boldly go where no man went before'. 3. Someone who invests money in a production. 4. 'For this special purpose'. 5. Graffito. 6. An early and snobbish term for the working class. 7. Sneakers. 8. A vest. 9. Wait/weight. 10. Nine. 11. A local female benefactor who wishes to achieve acclaim. 12. (b) an Indian clerk. 13. 'Schoolgirl'. 14. Unscrupulous, devious, perfidious. 15. A cock.

SESSION 7
QUIZ 1

• •

1. What did Britain buy 176,602 shares of on 25th October, 1875?
2. 31 people lost their lives in a fire at which London underground station in November 1987?
3. What famous mutiny, aboard which ship, took place off Tonga on 28th April, 1789?
4. What headgear for men came into general use in about 1884?
5. Who was Warren Harding?
6. Which is the oldest royal residence in Britain?
7. At the Battle of Ashdown, in A.D. 871, the Danes were defeated by forces under which famous king?
8. Who was the last English monarch to lead his troops in battle?
9. Who was Woodrow Wilson?
10. Which former general became President of the French Fifth Republic in 1959?
11. Who was Madame de Pompadour?
12. What did the Boers in South Africa begin in December, 1835?
13. Who was the last monarch of Germany?
14. Who discovered the Pacific Ocean?
15. Who was the last monarch of Portugal?

ERM...
CHARGE?

ANSWERS

1. Shares in the Suez Canal. 2. Kings Cross. 3. The Bounty. 4. The straw boater. 5. He was 29th American president. 6. Windsor Castle. 7. King Alfred. 8. King George II at Dettingen in 1743. 9. He was the 28th American president. 10. Charles de Gaulle. 11. The mistress of King Louis XV of France. 12. The 'Great Trek' northward from Cape Colony. 13. Wilhelm II (1888-1918). 14. Francisco Pizarro in 1513. 15. Manoel II.

SESSION 7
QUIZ 2

• •

1. Mark Hamill played which character in the film *Star Wars?*
2. Tom Cruise starred in a film based on a John Grisham novel. What was the film?
3. This cute alien was desperate to 'phone home'. What was his name?
4. Who starred in the film *Annie Hall?*
5. Who starred in the film *Hobson's Choice?*
6. Who starred in the film *Duck Soup?*
7. What is unusual about the 1995 film *Toy Story?*
8. From which film and stage show did the song 'Consider Yourself' come?
9. Who starred in the film *The Day of the Triffids?*
10. Who starred in the film *Passport to Pimlico?*
11. Who starred in the original film *To Be or Not to Be?*
12. Which movie star's real name was Frances Gumm?
13. How did the Marx Brothers acquire their names?
14. For which film did Oliver Stone win a best director Oscar in 1986?
15. From which film and stage show did the song 'Diamonds Are a Girl's Best Friend' come?

ANSWERS

1. Luke Skywalker. 2. *The Firm.* 3. *E.T. The Extra-Terrestrial.* 4. Woody Allen and Diane Keaton. 5. Charles Laughton, Brenda de Banzie, John Mills. 6. The four Marx brothers. 7. It is entirely computed-generated. 8. *Oliver!* 9. Howard Keel. 10. Stanley Holloway, Margaret Rutherford. 11. Jack Benny. 12. Judy Garland. 13. They were taken from a comic strip called 'Mager's Monks'. 14. *Platoon.* 15. *Gentlemen Prefer Blondes.*

SESSION 7
QUIZ 3

● ●

1. Which band recorded the albums 'In Utero' and 'Nevermind'?
2. Who recorded the Album, 'No Jacket Required'?
3. What was the first UK top ten hit for Elton John?
4. Who is the only Conservative Prime Minister to have a UK top ten hit?
5. Hawkwind have only had one top ten hit, name it?
6. Which British artist has had the highest total of weeks on the UK chart?
7. Which non-British or American act has totalled the highest number of weeks on the UK chart?
8. In Sept 1996 the Cardigans reached number 21 with, 'Lovefool'. From what album did the track come?
9. In September 1996, Mariah Carey reached number 3 with, 'Endless Love'. Which male soul singer dueted with her on this track?
10. Which band have a lead singer called Cerys and recorded the album, 'International Velvet'?
11. What nationality were Boney M?
12. Who recorded the albums, 'Meddle and 'Wish You Were Here'?
13. In December 1993 Chaka Demus and Pliers had a number one hit with, 'Twist And Shout', who recorded the original?
14. Which American southern boogie band had hits with 'Sweet Home Alabama' and 'Freebird'?
15. Midge Ure was formerly vocalist with which 80's New Romantic band?

ANSWERS

1. Nirvana 2. Phil Collins 3. Your Song 4. Ted Heath 5. 'Silver Machine' 6. Cliff Richard 7. ABBA 8. First Band On The Moon 9. Luther Vandross 10. Catotonia 11. Jamaican and German 12. Pink Floyd 13. Brian Poole and The Tremeloes 14. Lynyrd Skynyrd 15. Ultravox

SESSION 7
QUIZ 4

· ·

1. The character 'Porthos' appears in which famous book?
2. Complete the proverb: 'The devil take...'
3. What sort of creatures were (a) Babar, (b) Tarka and (c) Orlando?
4. 'The buck stops here'. Where does this phrase originate?
5. Who wrote *South Riding?*
6. Who created the fictional character 'The Baron', also called 'John Mannering'?
7. Who wrote *Ivanhoe?*
8. Who wrote *The Diary of a Nobody?*
9. By what name was children's author Charles Lutwidge Dodgson better known?
10. In which novel by one of the Brontë sisters does 'Cathy Earnshaw' appear?
11. Complete the proverb: 'Cast not your pearls...'
12. Who wrote *Rebecca?*
13. Who created the character 'Harry Palmer', although he is never named in the books about him?
14. Complete this line by Shakespeare: 'Friends, Romans, countrymen...'
15. Complete the proverb: 'The course of true love...'

ANSWERS

1. *The Three Musketeers.* 2. '...the hindmost'. 3. (a) an elephant (b) an otter (c) a cat. 4. From a notice on the desk of President Truman. 5. Winifred Holtby. 6. John Creasey as 'Anthony Morton'. 7. Sir Walter Scott. 8. George Grossmith. 9. Lewis Carroll. 10. *Wuthering Heights.* 11. '...before swine. 12. Daphne du Maurier. 13. Len Deighton. The name was only used in the films. 14. '...lend me your ears'. 15. '...never did run smooth'.

73

• •

1. What does circa or c. in connection with dates mean?
2. In ancient times, what were centaurs believed to be?
3. What is a brandysnap?
4. The Palladium in London is a variety theatre. Isn't this a Latin name?
5. What was meant by 'my old Dutch'?
6. Which word, beginning with post- means 'after dinner'?
7. Who in the world would be called a 'Limey'?
8. Who or what was Big Bertha?
9. What, applied to a person, is a 'ham'?
10. Which politician is known as 'Tarzan'?
11. Who painted the picture of a stag entitled 'Monarch of the Glen'?
12. What is an éclair?
13. The Scales represent which sign of the Zodiac?
14. Which anniversary does a cotton wedding celebrate?
15. What is an ambassador?

ANSWERS

1. About or around. 2. A race of beings half-horse, half-man. 3. A thin crisp biscuit flavoured with ginger and brandy. 4. Yes, but the original was a temple or image of the goddess Pallas. 5. A cockney expression, meaning 'my wife'. 6. Postprandial. 7. An Englishman. 8. A large gun trained on Paris during WWI. 9. An actor with more enthusiasm than ability. 10. Michael Heseltine. 11. Sir Edwin Landseer. 12. A long, light pastry with cream filling and chocolate sauce. 13. Libra. 14. The first. 15. A diplomatic envoy who represents his own head of state in a foreign country.

SESSION 7
QUIZ 6

● ●

1. The science and technology of nuclear studies is called what?
2. The study of minerals is called what?
3. How many fluid ounces are equivalent to one litre?
4. Glass is mainly composed of what?
5. What is the name given to the outer layer of skin?
6. Euclid, the Greek mathematician, is known as the father of what?
7. How long does it take light from the sun to reach the earth?
8. What everyday igniting device was invented by John Walker in 1827?
9. The first artificial dye was created in 1856 by Sir William Perkins. What colour was it?
10. How many moons does Uranus have: (a) 6, (b) 5 or (c) 4?
11. In 1926 Erik Rotheim made the first gas-propelled spray-can. It was the ancestor of what?
12. After he invented the electric battery in 1800, how did Count Alexander Volta's name become known?
13. In 1675 John Flamsteed became the first man in what job?
14. What are the four dimensions?
15. In litres, what is the capacity of the human lungs?

ANSWERS

1. Nucleonics. 2. Mineralogy. 3. 35.2. 4. Sand. 5. The epidermis.
6. Geometry. 7. About eight minutes. 8. The friction match. 9. Mauve.
10. Five. 11. The aerosol. 12. The electric measure of force, or volt, was
named after him. 13. Astronomer Royal. 14. Width, depth, length and
time. 15. Five litres.

SESSION 7

QUIZ 7

. . . .

1. What does the word 'dinosaur' mean?
2. What is a freesia?
3. What is a tunny?
4. A coatimundi is a type of raccoon. True or false?
5. What's the name of a fox's home?
6. What kind of animal could be called a percheron?
7. What is cotoneaster?
8. What is cochineal?
9. What is a group of geese called?
10. What sort of animal is called an Aberdeen Angus?
11. What is an aspen?
12. What sort of fruit is the gean?
13. Which animal is the deadly enemy of snakes and rats?
14. Vanilla is a member of the orchid family. Yes or no?
15. Which elephant has the largest ears: African or Indian?

ANSWERS

1. 'Huge' or 'terrible' lizard. 2. A plant of the Iris family, grown in South Africa. 3. Another name for a tuna fish. 4. True. 5. An earth. 6. A breed of horse. 7. A tree or shrub related to the hawthorn. 8. A red dyestuff made from the pulverised bodies of the Coccus insect. 9. A gaggle. 10. A breed of cattle. 11. A forest tree, also known as the trembling poplar. 12. The wild cherry. 13. The mongoose. 14. Yes. 15. African.

76

• •

1. Where is the Statue of Liberty?
2. Where and what is Stromboli?
3. Which is the world's largest church?
4. Where is the Great Barrier Reef?
5. Where would you find the Kremlin?
6. What is the highest point in Australia?
7. Where in the world do they speak Catalan?
8. Where is Transylvania?
9. 'Eesti' refers to which country?
10. Anvers is another name for which Belgian city?
11. What was previously known as Angora?
12. Which is Britain's largest lake?
13. What, in England, was Ermine Street?
14. The shamrock is the national symbol of which country?
15. Which city is on the Tiber?

ANSWERS

1. On Liberty Island, New York Harbor, USA. 2. An active volcano in Italy. 3. St Peter's, Rome. 4. Off the coast of Queensland, Australia. 5. Moscow, Russia. 6. Mount Kosciusko, 2,228 m. 7. In Catalonia, Spain. 8. Romania. 9. Estonia. 10. Antwerp. 11. Ankara, Turkey. 12. Loch Lomond, Scotland. 13. A Roman road, stretching from Beachy Head to York. 14. Ireland. 15. Rome.

SESSION 7
QUIZ 9

• •

1. Why is our 'funnybone' so called?
2. What is an 'ocker'?
3. What is the name for someone who studies coins and medals?
4. To what living thing did Leonard Fuchs, the German botanist, gave his name?
5. What is a 'drongo', and how did the term originate?
6. What do we mean by the expression 'to play gooseberry'?
7. 'Draw, O Caesar, erase a coward.' What is unusual about this sentence?
8. To what kind of dog did Spain give its name?
9. Which word can mean beautiful or a market?
10. A doxy is: (a) a kind of flower, (b) a breed of dog or (c) a woman of low character?
11. What is the difference between 'allusion' and 'illusion'?
12. If you were totally lumbered, what would have happened?
13. In cockney rhyming slang, what does 'daisy roots' mean?
14. What is 'to essay' an ancient way of saying?
15. Is a doge: (a) a Venetian magistrate (b) a French breed of poodle (c) a kind of judo?

ANSWERS

1. Its correct name is the humerus. 2. An Australian know-it-all. 3. Numismatist. 4. The fuchsia plant. 5. Australian slang for a persistent failure, named after a racehorse of a similar nature. 6. To be an unwelcome third person when two people want to be alone. 7. It's a palindrome. It reads the same, letter for letter, backwards and forwards. 8. The spaniel. 9. Fair. 10. (c) a woman of low character. 11. An 'allusion' is a suggestion or reference to something; an 'illusion' is a false impression. 12. You would have been completely put upon, or taken advantage of. 13. Boots. 14. To attempt or try. 15. (a) a Venetian magistrate.

78

SESSION 7
QUIZ 10

• •

1. If I was sitting on the 'Strip', watching the 'Christmas Tree' and revving my 'Rail', what sport would I be taking part in?
2. Which football team play at Maine Road?
3. Who captained Essex County Cricket team during the 1994 season?
4. In American Football how many points are awarded for a 'Safety'?
5. What are the three disciplines in a Triathlon?
6. If Stoke City were playing a home derby match, who would they be playing?
7. Who won the 1994 women's Rugby World Cup?
8. In which month is the Kentucky Derby run?
9. Who provided the engines for the 1998 McLaren Formula One team?
10. What do the initials MCC stand for?
11. How wide is a discus throwing circle: 2.5m, 2.7m or 3.1m?
12. Which sport was the subject of the Popplewell Report in 1985?
13. What do the initials BBBC stand for?
14. In 1990 the horse Mr Frisk set a record time in which major race?
15. In which major sporting championship does the winner receive a, 'Green Jacket?

ANSWERS

SESSION 8
QUIZ 1

• •

1. Who starred in the film *Independence Day?*
2. What films featured ewoks, droids and the Millenium Falcon spaceship?
3. Who's debut feature as a director was the film *Duel?*
4. Who starred in the film *Richard III?*
5. Who starred in the film *It's a Wonderful Life?*
6. Who starred in the film *Jaws?*
7. Which is the newest BBC radio station?
8. Three films with the words 'Shanghai', 'Rome', 'Orient' in their titles, all end with the same word. What is the word?
9. George Lansbury, a former leader of the Labour Party, had a film-actress granddaughter. Who is she?
10. Stepin Fetchit took his name from a racehorse. What was his real name?
11. Which T.V. sci-fi series featured characters including Villa, Servalan and ORAC?
12. Which controversial late night show was hosted by Terry Christian?
13. Who starred in the film *Chinatown?*
14. Which Oscar-winning actress is now a Labour M.P.?
15. Which sports commentator was replaced by Sue Barker as host of *A Question Of Sport?*

ANSWERS

1. Will Smith, Bill Pullman, Jeff Goldblum, Mary McDonnell. 2. *Star Wars.* 3. Steven Spielberg. 4. Sir Ian McKellen. 5. James Stewart, Donna Reed, Lionel Barrymore. 6. Roy Scheider, Robert Shaw, Richard Dreyfuss. 7. Radio Five. 8. Express. 9. Angela Lansbury. 10. Lincoln Theodore Monroe Andrew Perry. 11. *Blake's Seven.* 12. *The Word.* 13. Jack Nicholson, Faye Dunaway. 14. Glenda Jackson. 15. David Coleman.

SESSION 8
QUIZ 2

1. In March 1980, The Jam entered the chart at number one with which song?
2. Which member of Take That, left the band to pursue a solo career in July 1995?
3. 'You're The One That I Want', and 'Summer Nights' were singles taken from which 1978 movie?
4. 'With A Little Help From My friends', has been taken to number one by two different acts, name them?
5. Which group recorded the albums, 'A Day At The Races' and, 'A Night At The Opera'?
6. Who recorded the albums, 'Hergest Ridge' and 'Tubular bells'?
7. What nationality is Brian Adams?
8. Which group recorded the album, 'Carry On Up the Charts'?
9. Which group produced their 'Greatest Hits' before their 'Arrival' album?
10. Who were the voices behind, Derek and Clive?
11. What was Take That's, final single?
12. Which Beatle became a Travelling Wilbury?
13. Which brothers featured heavily on the soundtrack to the film, 'Saturday Night Fever'?
14. 'Whisky In The Jar', was the first UK top ten hit for which Irish band?
15. Which 50's & 60's singing star, father of Kim, had hits with, 'A Teenager In Love', 'Sea Of Love', and 'Rubber Ball'?

ANSWERS

SESSION 8

QUIZ 3

• •

1. 'Sir Percy Blakeney' appears in which famous book?
2. Who wrote *The Forsythe Saga*?
3. 'The child is father of the man.' Where does this phrase originate?
4. Complete the proverb: 'Beauty is in...'
5. Which playwright, a contemporary of Shakespeare, was killed in a pub brawl?
6. Who wrote *The Woman in White*?
7. Who, according to the opening line of the book, was born in 1632 in York?
8. 'David Balfour' appears in which book by R.L. Stevenson?
9. 'Captain Ahab' appears in which adventure story by Herman Melville?
10. Who created the female James Bond 'Modesty Blaise'?
11. Who wrote *Puck of Pook's Hill*?
12. Of which well-known book was Boris Pasternak the author?
13. 'Holden Caulfield' is a character in which book by J.D. Salinger?
14. What line follows, 'Ye mariners of England'?
15. Who was the Bard of Avon?

SESSION 8
QUIZ 4

• •

1. Who is the patron saint of travellers?
2. Who, or what, is 'Ernie'?
3. What is cannelloni?
4. What is a bisque?
5. What is haggis?
6. Who painted landscapes of the Suffolk countryside?
7. Which anniversary does a lace wedding celebrate?
8. What is a bruxelloise?
9. Moses was the leader of which nation?
10. What does the name of the city Philadelphia mean?
11. What is meant by 'Dutch gold'?
12. What is consommé?
13. What kind of food item comes from Worcester?
14. What is the name of the young girl who plays a leading part in *Peter Pan*?
15. How does the Archbishop of York sign himself?

ANSWERS

1. St Christopher. 2. The Electronic Random Number Indicator Equipment for drawing Premium Bonds. 3. Thin rolls of pasta stuffed with meat or vegetables. 4. A creamy soup. 5. A Scottish dish made with the heart, lungs and liver of a sheep or calf. 6. John Constable. 7. The thirteenth. 8. A French sauce for asparagus. 9. Israel. 10. City of brotherly love. 11. An alloy of copper and zinc. 12. Clear meat soup. 13. Sauce. 14. Wendy. 15. His Christian name followed by Ebor.

SESSION 8
QUIZ 5

• •

1. How fast is the earth orbiting the sun?
2. Cartography is the science of what?
3. What did Alberto Santos-Dumont build and operate in 1898?
4. What happens to phosphorus on contact with the air?
5. The scientific study of seas and oceans is called what?
6. What kind of animals would a lepidopterist study?
7. A dodecagon has how many sides?
8. Pneumonia is a disease which affects which part of your body?
9. What does a microscope do?
10. Richard Trevithick built a coach driven by what sort of power in 1801?
11. The Dead Sea contains about (a) 25% (b) 40% (c) 12% salts?
12. The science of the study of the body and its parts is called what?
13. Which is the largest tree in the world?
14. What is the colour of chlorophyll?
15. How much of an iceberg is below the surface: 25%, 45% or 85%?

ANSWERS

1. 107,200 kilometres per hour. 2. Maps and map-making. 3. A cylindrical balloon with a gasoline engine. 4. It bursts into flame. 5. Oceanography. 6. Butterflies and moths. 7. Twelve. 8. Lungs. 9. Magnifies small objects. 10. Steam. 11. 25%. 12. Anatomy. 13. A sequoia in California is over 80 metres tall and has a girth of 30 metres. 14. Green. 15. 85%.

SESSION 8
QUIZ 6

• •

1. Cinnamon is a member of the laurel family. Yes or no?
2. A giant panda is a bear-like creature which feeds almost entirely on what?
3. What kind of animal is said to coo?
4. A fritillary is (a) a butterfly, (b) a kind of lily?
5. The evergreen shrub Camellia is a relative of the tea plant. True or false?
6. What is an asp?
7. What is a jackdaw?
8. A mandrill is a member of which animal family?
9. What sort of animal is called a Charolais?
10. What is the name given to a fox's tail?
11. What is the record life-span of the domestic cat: (a) 28 years, (b) 36 years or (c) 40 years.
12. Grampus is a name given to a sea mammal usually called what?
13. The elder is a member of the honeysuckle family. Yes or no?
14. An egret is (a) a kind of heron, (b) the name for a young eagle.
15. Bamboo is a kind of grass. Yes or no?

ANSWERS

1. Yes. 2. Bamboo shoots. 3. A dove. 4. Both are true! 5. True. 6. It's a general term for a venomous snake. 7. A species of crow. 8. Baboons. 9. A breed of cattle. 10. A brush. 11. 36 years. 12. A whale or a dolphin. 13. Yes. 14. It's a kind of heron. 15. Yes.

85

• •

1. Who was the first sovereign to live at Buckingham Palace?
2. Where is the Vale of the White Horse?
3. Why is the Vale of the White Horse so called?
4. In which city is the Doge's Palace?
5. What country was the republic of Slovakia formerly part of?
6. What is the Pennine Chain?
7. Which city is on the River Orwell?
8. Byzantium is an ancient name for which city?
9. Where are the Scilly Isles?
10. The Cenotaph stands in Whitehall in London. What does 'cenotaph' mean?
11. In which city would you find Paddington railway station?
12. Where is the Golden Temple?
13. Which cathedral has the world's tallest spire?
14. Where in the world would you find the people called Lapps?
15. On which stretch of water does the Swiss city of Lausanne stand?

ANSWERS

1. Queen Victoria. 2. A valley in Oxfordshire. 3. Because it carries the image of a white horse where the turf is cut away to reveal the chalk beneath. 4. Venice. 5. Czechoslovakia. 6. A mountain range in the Midlands and North of England. 7. Ipswich. 8. Istanbul. 9. Off Land's End, Cornwall. 10. An empty tomb. 11. London. 12. Amritsar, India. 13. Ulm Cathedral, Germany. 14. In Lapland, which is spread across Norway, Sweden and Finland. 15. Lake Geneva.

• •

1. 'Verily' was an old way of saying what?
2. What slang term would an American use to describe a pimple?
3. Why are British policemen sometimes called 'bobbies'?
4. What does an American call a clothes-peg?
5. What is odd about the names 'sea-lion' and 'sea-horse'?
6. If you were 'in the doghouse', what would it mean?
7. What is unusual about the sentence 'King, are you glad you are king'?
8. What is the difference between 'bizarre' and 'bazaar'?
9. What is the difference between 'averse' and 'adverse'?
10. A baby's nappy is called what in the US?
11. What, in earlier times, was an 'argosy'?
12. What would a lorry in the United States be called?
13. What exactly is a 'glutton'?
14. Which word, starting with P, means ardent or zealous?
15. Which word means both 'a cash register' and 'to cultivate land'.

ANSWERS

1. Truly. 2. He'd call it a 'zit'. 3. Because they were started at the suggestion of Sir Robert (Bob) Peel. 4. A clothes-pin. 5. A sea-lion isn't a lion, and a sea-horse isn't a horse. 6. You would be in disgrace. 7. It's a palindrome. It reads the same, word for word, backwards and forwards. 8. The first means 'odd or unusual' and the second 'a type of market'. 9. The first means 'opposed, or disinclined' and the second 'hostile, contrary'. 10. A diaper. 11. A large merchant ship. 12. A truck. 13. Apart from the popular 'greedy-person', it is an animal also known as the wolverine. 14. Passionate. 15. Till.

SESSION 8
QUIZ 9

1. Which county cricket team has its home at Old Trafford?
2. In 1994, which country hosted the Winter Olympics?
3. By which name is Rugby Union's William Henry Hare better known?
4. If I were to 'Serve, Dig, Spike or Set', what sport would I be playing?
5. In equestrianism, which rider with the first name Nick, won the World Cup in 1995?
6. Alison Fisher is one of the leading female exponents of which sport?
7. In which country did Pele finish his professional playing career?
8. What does 'PB' against a runner's time indicate?
9. Who, before Lynford Christie, last won an Olympic 100m gold medal for Britain?
10. What was ex-England hooker Brian Moore's occupation when not on the Rugby pitch?
11. What is the highest possible 'Out' shot in darts?
12. Name the home city for 'The 49ers', American Football team.
13. How many players are there in a Gaelic Football team?
14. How old was Brian Clough when he finished his playing career; 29, 31, 34 or 38?
15. Where is the Leander Rowing Club based?

ANSWERS

1. Lancashire. 2. Norway. 3. Dusty. 4. Volleyball. 5. Nick Skelton. 6. Snooker. 7. USA. 8. Personal Best. 9. Alan Wells. 10. Solicitor. 11. 170. 12. San Francisco. 13. 15. 14. 29. 15. Henley-on-Thames.

SESSION 8
QUIZ 10

1. Following an earthquake in London in 1580, how many people died? (a) none (b) 2 (c) 43.
2. In March, 1938, what was renamed 'Ostmark' as part of the German Reich?
3. Who was Benjamin Harrison?
4. Who was the last monarch of Italy?
5. Which French prime minister was reputed to have slept fully clothed?
6. Where and what was Northumbria?
7. The People's Palace was opened by Queen Victoria in 1887. Where was it?
8. What was the Weimar Republic?
9. What happened in August, 1914, so starting World War I?
10. Bosnia and Herzegovina was annexed by which country in 1908?
11. What body of men did Louis-Philippe of France found in North Africa in 1831?
12. When did the Channel Islands become part of England?
13. Which British monarch was bigamously married?
14. Of whom or what was St Pancras the patron saint?
15. The first issue of the *Daily News* newspaper appeared on 21st January, 1846. Who was the editor?

ANSWERS

1. (b) 2. 2. Austria. 3. He was the 23rd American president. 4. Humbert II (1946). 5. Georges Clemenceau. 6. One of the old kingdoms of England before A.D.808. 7. At Mile End, in the East End of London. 8. The first German republic, set up after WWI, and abolished in 1933 by Adolf Hitler. 9. Germany invaded Belgium. 10. Austria-Hungary. 11. The French Foreign Legion. 12. They didn't, and they don't. As part of Normandy, the islanders were the people who conquered the English! 13. King George IV. 14. Children. 15. Charles Dickens.

SESSION 9
QUIZ 1

● ●

1. St Winifred's School Choir reached number one in 1980 with which song?
2. 'Golden Brown' was a hit for which band?
3. What did Italian model Sabrina, sing about in 1988?
4. With which movie theme did the Central Band of the Royal Air Force reach number 18 in 1955?
5. What was the Rolling Stones' first UK number one?
6. 'Lucille' and 'Coward of the County', were number one hits for which Country and Western singer?
7. Don Mclean's 'American Pie', was his only UK number one. True or false?
8. What nationality is Manfred Mann?
9. Barry Manilow has only had one UK top ten hit. True or false?
10. Which TV Rat had a hit in 1984, with, 'Love Me Tender'?
11. Under what name did Manfred Mann release singles after 1973?
12. Who had hits in the late 1960's with, 'Californian Dreamin'', 'Monday, Monday' and 'Dedicated To The One I Love'?
13. Where is Doors singer Jim Morrison buried?
14. Who had a number 4 hit with 'I Love Rock 'n' Roll' in April 1982?
15. Was Jethro Tull a singer or a band?

ANSWERS

1. 'No one quite like Grandma'. 2. The Stranglers. 3. 'Boys, Boys, Boys' (Summer-time love). 4. 'Dambusters March'. 5. 'It's all over now'. 6. Kenny Rogers. 7. False (It went to number two). 8. South African. 9. True. 10. Roland Rat. 11. Manfred Mann's Earth Band. 12. Mamas and the Papas 13. Paris. 14. Joan Jet and the Blackhearts 15. A band.

SESSION 9
QUIZ 2

· ·

1. Who was Omar Khayyam?
2. Whose biographical book was *The Moon's a Balloon?*
3. Who wrote *Lost Horizon?*
4. What, according to Tennyson, are more than coronets?
5. Who is 'hero' in Shakespeare's play *Much Ado About Nothing?*
6. R. Austin Freeman's books featured the world's premier scientific detective. What was his name?
7. In which novel by W. Somerset Maugham does the character 'William Carey' appear?
8. Who said, on arriving at New York Customs: 'I have nothing to declare but my genius'?
9. Lovelace wrote: 'I could not love thee, dear, so much...' What follows?
10. Who wrote *The African Queen?*
11. 'Day breaks on England down the Kentish hills', is the beginning of a poem by whom?
12. 'The course of true love never did run smooth'. Where does this phrase originate?
13. How does Cleopatra kill herself in *Antony and Cleopatra?*
14. Who wrote *Lady Chatterley's Lover?*
15. Which novels use the French Revolution as a background?

ANSWERS

1. A Persian poet and mathematician. 2. David Niven's. 3. James Hilton. 4. Kind hearts. 5. Hero, who is a female character! 6. Dr Thorndyke. 7. *Of Human Bondage.* 8. Oscar Wilde. 9. 'Lov'd I not honour more.' 10. C.S. Forrester. 11. James Elroy Flecker. 12. Shakespeare's *A Midsummer Night's Dream.* 13. By snake-bite. She places an asp to her bosom. 14. D.H. Lawrence. 15. Dickens's *A Tale of Two Cities,* Orczy's *The Scarlet Pimpernel.*

SESSION 9
QUIZ 3

. . . .

1. What are 'angels on horseback'?
2. Who was Sir Frank Brangwyn?
3. What is the name given to the male reproductive organ of a plant?
4. What had Shakespeare and George Washington in common?
5. What is a flapjack?
6. St Dunstan is the patron saint of whom?
7. A jeroboam is a measure of wine equivalent to how many bottles?
8. What is colcannon?
9. Who is the patron saint of Norway?
10. What are profiteroles?
11. In a pack of cards, which way does the Queen of Clubs look: to her left, or to her right?
12. Who is the reigning monarch of Japan?
13. Eros is another name for Cupid. True or false?
14. Rule by the people as a whole is called what?
15. What is a 'Scotch woodcock'?

ANSWERS

1. Oysters wrapped in bacon. 2. Artist, illustrator and designer. 3. The stamen. 4. They were both redheads. 5. A kind of broad, flat, pancake. 6. Blacksmiths. 7. Four. 8. An Irish dish of mashed potatoes and cabbage with butter. 9. St Olaf. 10. Small puffs of choux pastry, filled with cream and covered in chocolate sauce. 11. To her left. 12. Emperor Akihito. 13. True. 14. Democracy. 15. Eggs and anchovies on toast.

SESSION 9
QUIZ 4

• •

1. Where on the body would you find your occiput?
2. If your doctor told you that you had coryza, what would you be suffering from?
3. What would you use a drosometer to measure?
4. What, in ancient times, was the Philosophers' Stone?
5. What did the Russian Venera 9 space probe do?
6. What does an ammeter measure?
7. The scapula is another name for which bone?
8. What poison was used to kill the Ancient Greek thinker Socrates?
9. What colour is a topaz?
10. What does a theodolite measure?
11. Pewter is an alloy of which two metals?
12. Corundum is a mineral which produces which precious stones?
13. What colour is the stone called lapis lazuli?
14. Who was Louis Brennan?
15. A better name for frozen dew is what?

ANSWERS

1. The back of your head. 2. The common cold. 3. Dew. 4. A mythical stone fabled to have the power of turning base metal into gold. 5. Orbited Venus. 6. Electric current. 7. The shoulder-blade. 8. Hemlock. 9. Yellowish or bluish, although it is sometimes without colour. 10. Angles. It is used by surveyors. 11. Tin and lead. 12. Sapphires and rubies. 13. Blue with veins of gold. 14. Inventor of the monorail. 15. Frost.

93

SESSION 9
QUIZ 5

• •

1. How do we get cocoa?
2. A group of crows is called (a) a crowd (b) a murder.
3. What is a capercailzie?
4. What was a quagga?
5. What is a custard-apple?
6. What is a hazel-nut?
7. Where would you find a Red Admiral; (a) at sea (b) on a flagpole (c) in your garden?
8. Where did the cucumber originate?
9. What is an aloe?
10. What sort of animal is an ounce?
11. Freshwater eels are all born in one place. Where?
12. What is an anaconda?
13. What's the record life-span of the domestic dog: (a) 28 years, (b) 30 years or (c) 32 years?
14. Which, of all the mammals, produces the largest baby?
15. What kind of animal could be described as a Hampshire?

ANSWERS

1. It's the seed of the cacao tree, ground and powdered. 2. A murder. 3. It's a large type of grouse. 4. A type of zebra. 5. A fruit with soft flesh grown in the West Indies, America and Asia. 6. The fruit of the hazel-nut bush or tree. 7. (c) In your garden. 8. Southern Asia. 9. A plant which produces a bitter-tasting substance used in medicine. 10. A snow leopard. 11. The Sargasso Sea in the Atlantic. 12. A large South American snake. 13. 28 years. 14. The blue whale. 15. A breed of sheep.

94

SESSION 9
QUIZ 6

• •

1. Which is the world's smallest continent?
2. Where is the original Waterloo?
3. Hokkaido is an island, part of which country?
4. What is the capital of Jordan?
5. What is the West African country, Upper Volta, now known as?
6. On which stretch of water does Geneva stand?
7. In what country are the ruined remains of the ancient city of Troy?
8. Where in the world would you find a Maori?
9. What do the Parisians call their underground railway system?
10. Heligoland once belonged to Britain and formerly to Denmark. To which country does it belong now?
11. In which city would you be likely to find a gondola?
12. Which is the highest mountain peak in England?
13. The leek is a national symbol of which country?
14. The Belgian Congo is a country now called what?
15. What was the DDR?

ANSWERS

SESSION 9

QUIZ 7

. . . .

1. What does 're-invent the wheel' mean?
2. What word, beginning with F, means copy or replica?
3. If you 'nail your colours to the mast', what does it mean?
4. Can you name two words, sounding alike, which mean the same as these phrases: grain used for food/instalment story?
5. What is a hustler, in its American sense?
6. What does the Yiddish word 'schlock' mean?
7. What weapon was named after the French town of Bayonne?
8. If you suffered from phobophobia, what would you fear?
9. What do Americans call a 'drawing pin'?
10. What is the name for words which have the same (or similar) meanings, like brief/short, difficult/hard and sly/cunning?
11. If you spent your free time doing the same thing as if you were working, what would people say you were doing?
12. Why is a 'mantelpiece' so called?
13. What is a 'pastiche'?
14. What is the male version of a 'heroine'?
15. Can you name two words, sounding similar, which mean the same as this pair: wildebeest/original.

ANSWERS

1. To do something which is already well known or established.
2. Facsimile. 3. You make clear your view and refuse to surrender.
4. Cereal/serial. 5. Someone who lives on his wits. 6. Something of inferior quality. 7. The bayonet. 8. Fear! 9. A thumb tack. 10. Synonyms. 11. Taking a busman's holiday. 12. It was used for placing mantles or cloaks to dry by the fire. 13. A work of art of literature made up from other sources. 14. Hero. 15. Gnu/new.

SESSION 9
QUIZ 8

• •

1. Which football club is generally accepted as the oldest in England?
2. Peter Shilton played his 1000th league game with which club?
3. Kendo is the ancient Japanese art of what?
4. A cricket umpire holds both arms straight up above his head to indicate what?
5. How often is the US Masters golf tournament held?
6. Which county did former England cricket captain Tony Greig also lead?
7. By joining, which country will turn the Five Nations Rugby Union tournament into the 'Six Nations'?
8. For what feat will the gymnast Nadia Comaneci always be remembered?
9. What is the name of New Orleans American football team?
10. In the Tour de France what does the green jersey signify?
11. In Golf, what is the term for one under par at a hole?
12. What sport do the Scottish Claymores play?
13. If you were at Goodison Park or Anfield which city would you be in?
14. Who won the 1998 Rugby Union Women's World Cup?
15. For which Italian side did 'Gazza', play?

ANSWERS

1. Notts County. 2. Leyton Orient. 3. Sword fighting. 4. Six runs. 5. Every year. 6. Sussex. 7. Italy. 8. The first perfect 10 score in a major competition. 9. The Saints. 10. Points Leader. 11. Birdie. 12. American Football. 13. Liverpool. 14. New Zealand. 15. Lazio.

SESSION 9
QUIZ 9

• •

1. Francisco Pizarro, the Spanish conqueror, overcame which people, and where, in 1533?
2. What century-long event ended after the English were defeated at Castillon in 1453?
3. Who was Richard Cobden?
4. In October, 1822, Dom Pedro became Emperor of which South American country?
5. If a country was ruled entirely by its nobility, it would be called what?
6. In Birkenhead the first of a system of transport was started in August 1860. What was it?
7. What is the surname of the Queen?
8. Which bridge was opened on 4th September 1964?
9. Who, in the 15th century, was Lambert Simnel?
10. Which venerable figure, a philosopher and member of the Order of Merit, was imprisoned in 1961?
11. What were the Pre-Raphaelites?
12. Who were the Brylcreem Boys?
13. Which English monarch was never crowned?
14. On 14th January, in both 1205 and 1814, what were held on the river Thames?
15. In which city in 1921 did a mutiny take place on a Russian battleship?

_____

ANSWERS

1. The Incas of Peru. 2. The Hundred Years' War. 3. English advocate of Free Trade. 4. Brazil. 5. An aristocracy. 6. The first British tram service. 7. The Queen has no surname, but is a member of the House of Windsor. 8. The Forth Bridge. 9. An impostor and pretender to the English throne. 10. Bertrand Russell. 11. A group of young British artists in the 19th century who wanted art to be realistic. 12. Young RAF officers in WW2. 13. Edward VIII. 14. Frost fairs when the river froze over. 15. Kronstadt.

SESSION 9

QUIZ 10

• •

1. What was film star Herbie?
2. Who is the actor-nephew of the film director Sir Carol Reed?
3. Who starred in the film *Dances With Wolves?*
4. How many musical items were included in the film *Fantasia?*
5. Which T.V. sitcom features characters called Ross, Chandler and Phoebe?
6. Which rock band provided soundtrack music for the film *Flash Gordon?*
7. Who starred in the film *The Sting?*
8. Who starred in the 1993 film *The Fugitive?*
9. What happened to the 1942 movie *Yankee Doodle Dandy* in 1985?
10. Which movie star's real name was Roy Scherer?
11. Whose sister Jeanne appeared with him in the film *Yankee Doodle Dandy?*
12. What was unusual about the 1932 Czech film *Extase?*
13. Who starred in the film *The Hospital?*
14. *In Murder on the Orient Express,* who played the role of Hercule Poirot?
15. Which B-movie featured salad vegetables intent on murder?

ANSWERS

1. A VW Beetle car. 2. Oliver Reed. 3. Kevin Costner, Mary McDonnell. 4. Eight. 5. *Friends.* 6. Queen. 7. Paul Newman, Robert Redford. 8. Harrison Ford. 9. It was computer-converted to full colour. 10. Rock Hudson. 11. James Cagney's. 12. It featured actress Hedy Lamarr in the nude. 13. George C. Scott, Diana Rigg. 14. Albert Finney. 15. *Attack Of The Killer Tomatoes.*

1. What did the fictional character 'Phileas Fogg' achieve?
2. 'Who would true valour see,/Let him come hither' is the beginning of a poem by whom?
3. Who wrote *The Water-Babies*?
4. Who said, 'It is impossible for an Englishman to open his mouth, without making some other Englishman despise him.'?
5. Who wrote the words to *Cherry Ripe* and *Gather Ye Rosebuds*?
6. Who wrote the original story of *The Wizard of Oz?*
7. 'James Gatz' is a character in which book by F. Scott Fitzgerald?
8. Who wrote the mystery story *The Franchise Affair?*
9. 'Hamelin Town's in Brunswick/By famous Hanover city;' is the beginning of a poem by whom?
10. Who wrote the play *Who's Afraid of Virginia Woolf?*
11. Which famous children's book did Beatrix Potter write?
12. The character 'Mrs Proudie' appears in which famous book?
13. Who wrote *Room at the Top?*
14. Which character in Dickens was always waiting for something to turn up?
15. The character 'Rochester' appears in which famous book?

ANSWERS

1. He went Round the World in Eighty Days. 2. John Bunyan. 3. Charles Kingsley. 4. George Bernard Shaw, in Pygmalion. 5. Robert Herrick, poet. 6. L. Frank Baum. 7. The Great Gatsby. 8. Josephine Tey. 9. Robert Browning. 10. Edward Albee. 11. The Tale of Peter Rabbit. 12. Barchester Towers. 13. John Braine. 14. Mr Micawber. 15. Jane Eyre.

• •

1. If something is served à la maître d'hôtel, how is it prepared?
2. Osiris was a god of ancient Egypt. What was his domain?
3. What is pesto?
4. What is a sassenach?
5. What is a doughnut?
6. Which French drink has a strong anise taste?
7. Which anniversary does a china wedding celebrate?
8. Who was the Beast of Bolsover?
9. Who was Edith Cavell?
10. Who, in a music-hall song, went to Crewe in mistake for Birmingham?
11. From which musical play did the song 'Some Day My Heart Will Awake' come?
12. What is saltimbocca?
13. Which of British stamps were the first to be perforated?
14. Who was the Boston Strangler?
15. 'Shear you sheep in May.... (what's the next line in the verse?)

ANSWERS

1. Served plain with parsley garnish. 2. The underworld. 3. A sauce of basil, garlic, pine nuts, olive oil and cheese. 4. An Englishman, according to the Scots language. 5. Sweetened dough, fried in fat. 6. Absinthe. 7. The twentieth. 8. Dennis Skinner, MP. 9. British nurse, executed by the Germans in WWI. 10. Marie Lloyd. 11. *King's Rhapsody*. 12. An Italian dish of veal, ham and cheese. 13. The Penny Red of 1854. 14. Albert de Salvo. 15. 'And shear them all away.'

SESSION 10
QUIZ 3

1. Who has been called 'the Father of Chemistry'?
2. A drug which makes a patient insensitive to pain, touch or temperature is called a what?
3. Which famous American bridge was designed by John Roebling but completed by his son in 1886?
4. When iron oxidises, what is formed?
5. What system has replaced the carburettor in many modern cars?
6. What is a more familiar word for the umbilicus?
7. What is opsomania?
8. What is xenophobia?
9. What happens to your eyes if you sneeze?
10. For what do we use our olfactory sense?
11. What is measured by an ampère?
12. What is speleology?
13. What was the Caravelle, and where did it come from?
14. Who invented the photocopier (xerography) in 1948?
15. In London, the station 2LO began what in 1922?

ANSWERS

SESSION 10
QUIZ 4

• •

1. Apes have one special difference from monkeys. What is it?
2. What kind of animal is said to meow?
3. Where did the pomegranate originate?
4. What domestic animal could be described as a Burmese?
5. What was remarkable about the skeleton of Piltdown Man, found in Sussex?
6. The antlers of young deer are covered in what?
7. What is a tapir?
8. If a bee stings you, how will it affect the bee?
9. A freshwater lobster is called what?
10. What sort of animal is an ocelot?
11. What, on a horse, is a hock?
12. Animals which suckle their young are called what?
13. Has an earwig anything to do with ears?
14. What is a group of budgerigars called?
15. What is yarrow or milfoil?

ANSWERS

1. Apes have no tails. 2. A cat. 3. Persia. 4. A cat. 5. It was a fake. 6. Velvet. 7. A smallish creature with a flexible nose. 8. The bee loses its sting, and dies. 9. A crayfish. 10. A wild American cat like a small leopard. 11. The ankle. 12. Mammals. 13. Nothing whatsoever. 14. A chatter. 15. A perennial meadow plant with very small, daisy-like flowers arranged in clusters.

SESSION 10
QUIZ 5

. . . .

1. Which is the largest county in England?
2. What is peculiar about the door of No. 10 Downing Street?
3. Where and what is Fontainebleau?
4. What is the French-speaking principality on the Mediterranean Sea called?
5. What is a native of Monaco called?
6. Prehistoric remains abound in the Eildon Hills in Britain. Where are these hills?
7. Which city is on the River Amstel?
8. Where and what is the Matterhorn?
9. On which river does Lisbon stand?
10. What would you find at West Point in the USA?
11. What is the capital of Ethiopia?
12. The Suez Canal is named after the town of Suez, but what town lies at the other end of the canal?
13. Where in the world would you find a Liverpudlian?
14. What would you expect to find in Wall Street, New York?
15. To which country does Réunion belong?

ANSWERS

1. North Yorkshire. 2. It cannot be opened from the outside. 3. A chateau not far from Paris, used as the summer residence for the French President. 4. Monaco. 5. A Monegasque. 6. Roxburgh, Scotland. 7. Amsterdam. 8. A famous mountain in Italy and Switzerland. 9. The Tagus. 10. The US Military Academy. 11. Addis Ababa. 12. Port Said. 13. In Liverpool. 14. Offices of financiers, brokers and bankers. 15. France.

SESSION 10
QUIZ 6

1. Name two words, sounding alike, which mean the same as this pair: atmosphere/one who inherits.
2. It'll be alright on the night. What's wrong with this sentence?
3. Pagoda is a Chinese word for an Eastern temple. True or false?
4. What does dependent mean?
5. What does dependant mean?
6. Finish the proverb: 'Advice most needed is...'
7. Which word beginning with B can mean frontier or border?
8. Why were milliners so called?
9. What is the meaning of 'opulent'?
10. What is the plural of 'talisman'?
11. What is a female 'peacock' called?
12. A yegg is: (a) an American safe-breaker, (b) a young Scottish calf or (c) a kind of hiccup?
13. What is the connection between the word 'salary' and an everyday cooking ingredient?
14. What would it mean if you 'got a flea in your ear'?
15. How was the word ouija (for a ouija board) derived?

ANSWERS

1. Air/heir. 2. The word 'alright'; It should be 'all right'. 3. No, it's a Portuguese word, probably derived from an Eastern one. 4. Relying upon, as in 'dependent upon whether I shall succeed'. 5. One who depends upon another. 6. '...least heeded'. 7. Boundary. 8. Makers of ladies' hats usually followed Milan fashions. 9. Wealthy and showy. 10. Talismans. 11. Peahen. 12. (a). 13. The word 'salary' comes from 'salt' which was the Roman legionaries' pay. 14. That you were scolded or told off. 15. It was invented from the French and German words for 'yes', oui and ja.

SESSION 10

QUIZ 7

1. What was American footballer William Perry's nickname?
2. David Bedford is associated with which sport?
3. Where was the 1986 Football World Cup held?
4. What is the nickname of Wigan's Rugby League team?
5. Whilst playing which sport did Prince Charles break his arm?
6. Which Pam was Martina Navratilova's doubles partner?
7. What sport do the Boston Red Socks play?
8. Who was the first person to have been in charge of both England and Australia's football teams?
9. Which city hosted the 1972 Olympic Games?
10. Who was the first overseas manager to win the FA Cup?
11. Bob Nudd was World Champion at which sport?
12. Who was the first man to win the Embassy World Snooker Championship twice?
13. What was Mohammed Ali's original name?
14. Mick the Miller was a champion at which sport?
15. Which controversial British athlete reputedly tripped Mary Decker in the 1984 Olympics?

ANSWERS

1. The Fridge. 2. Athletics. 3. Mexico. 4. Warriors. 5. Polo. 6. Shriver. 7. Baseball. 8. Terry Venables. 9. Munich. 10. Ruud Gullit. 11. Angling. 12. Steve Davis. 13. Cassius Clay. 14. Greyhound Racing. 15. Zola Budd.

SESSION 10
QUIZ 8

• •

1. Parliament passed the Stamp Act in 1765 to tax which group of people?
2. Who was Dwight David Eisenhower?
3. Who was Jomo Kenyatta?
4. Who or what were the Fenians?
5. What, politically, do Americans run for and Britons stand for?
6. Who was the first English king able to sign his name?
7. What were the Nuremberg Laws?
8. Where and what was Mercia?
9. Richard II was the first English king to do what, in 1399?
10. What document, drafted by Thomas Jefferson, was carried by the American Congress on 4th July, 1776?
11. Who wrote *The Decline and Fall of the Roman Empire?*
12. Which country in the Himalayas was conquered by the Gurkhas in 1768?
13. What was the Berlin Wall?
14. What sculpture did Étienne Falconet complete in 1763?
15. What innovation was part of the journey on the Glasgow-London night express on 2nd April, 1873?

ANSWERS

1. The American Colonists. 2. He was the 34th American president. 3. President of Kenya. 4. An anti-British secret society of Irishmen founded in New York in 1858. 5. Congress and Parliament. 6. Richard II. 7. German laws enacted in 1935, outlawing the Jews. 8. One of the kingdoms of England before A.D.808. 9. Abdicate. 10. The Declaration of Independence. 11. Edward Gibbon. 12. Nepal. 13. A wall erected to prevent East Germans from escaping to the West. 14. Pygmalion and Galathea. 15. The first sleeping-car was introduced.

SESSION 10
QUIZ 9

• •

1. Who starred in the film *The Dam Busters?*
2. To what song did the boys finally strip in *The Full Monty?*
3. Who starred in the film *One Flew Over the Cuckoo's Nest?*
4. Who starred in the film *The Wizard of Oz?*
5. In which film did Rex Harrison and Audrey Hepburn co-star?
6. In *Spice: The Movie,* who starred as the Spice Girls' manager?
7. From which film and stage show did the song 'Happy Talk' come?
8. Who starred in the film *Robin Hood, Prince of Thieves?*
9. In Monty Python's *Life Of Brian,* which python played Brian?
10. Exactly how many parts did Alec Guinness play in the film Kind Hearts and Coronets?
11. Which T.V. character lived at 23 Railway Cuttings, East Cheam?
12. What would you find at 84, Charing Cross Road?
13. Which father and daughter appeared in *Tiger Bay* and *The Truth About Spring?*
14. Who was America's Sweetheart?
15. From which film and stage show did the song 'Hopelessly Devoted to You' come?

ANSWERS

1. Michael Redgrave. 2. You Can Leave Your Hat On. 3. Jack Nicholson, Louise Fletcher. 4. Judy Garland. 5. My Fair Lady. 6. Richard E. Grant. 7. South Pacific. 8. Kevin Costner. 9. Graham Chapman. 10. Eight. 11. Tony Hancock in *Hancock's Half Hour.* 12. A bookshop. 13. Sir John and Hayley Mills. 14. Mary Pickford. 15. *Grease.*

SESSION 10
QUIZ 10

. . . .

1. Billy Joel has only had one UK number one written about his then wife, Christine Brinkley. What was the song called?
2. Name Jean Michel Jarre's only UK top ten hit?
3. Tammy Wynette appeared with which British band on the number 2 hit, 'Justified And Ancient'?
4. Huey Lewis is Jerry Lee Lewis' Nephew. True or false?
5. Who reached number one in 1975 with, 'Make Me Smile, (Come Up And See Me)'?
6. Who is the lead singer of Guns N' Roses?
7. Who has had top ten hits with, 'Come On You Reds', 'We're Gonna Do It Again', 'Move Move Move (The Red Tribe)'?
8. Which song, released around the time of his death was Elvis Presley's last UK number 1?
9. Who was the long time singing partner of Paul Simon?
10. Jimmy Sommerville started his career as lead vocalist with which band?
11. Edwin Collins was the lead singer with which 1980's band?
12. What was the Spice Girls first album called?
13. Which influential bands' members included Mo Tucker, Sterling Morrison and Lou Reed?
14. In which film did David Bowie appear alongside a cast of Jim Henson puppets?
15. Who recorded the album, 'What's The Story, Morning Glory'?

ANSWERS

1. 'Uptown Girl' 2. 'Oxygene (part iv)' 3. The KLF 4. False 5. Steve Harley and Cockney Rebel 6. Axel Rose 7. Manchester United Football Club 8. 'Way Down' 9. Art Garfunkel 10. The Communards 11. Orange Juice 12. Spice 13. Velvet Underground 14. Labyrinth 15. Oasis

1. What is meant by a 'ballpark figure'?
2. What does it signify when eight bells are sounded at sea?
3. St Anthony is the patron saint of whom?
4. Which anniversary does a steel wedding celebrate?
5. To the ancient Romans, who was Cupid?
6. What did Alexander of Macedon and Alfred, King of England, have in common?
7. What is another name for the 'Abominable Snowman'?
8. Who in the world would be called 'Digger'?
9. What did Oscar Wilde's Lady Windermere carry?
10. What kind of food is an Oval Osborne?
11. In a pack of cards, which way does the Jack of Clubs look: to his left, or to his right?
12. The Twins represent which sign of the Zodiac?
13. What does 'Going Dutch' mean?
14. What is a tartare sauce?
15. The lemon-sole is not a sole, but a relative of what?

ANSWERS

1. A rough estimate. 2. The end of a watch of four hours. 3. Grave-diggers. 4. The eleventh. 5. The god of love. 6. They were both known by the title 'The Great'. 7. The Yeti. 8. An Australian. 9. A fan. 10. A kind of biscuit. 11. To his right. 12. Gemini. 13. Each person paying for themselves at a meal. 14. A mayonnaise dressing with chopped pickles, olives, capers etc. 15. The plaice.

SESSION 11
QUIZ 2

• •

1. Why might one 'get a lift' from what Elisha Otis invented in 1853?
2. The biological study of cells and their functions is called what?
3. What was, or is, a blimp?
4. What nationality was the astronomer Copernicus?
5. What makes up just over 27% of the Earth's crust?
6. What was a ZX81 an early example of?
7. When is Halley's Comet likely to be seen from Earth again: 2062, 2012, 2001?
8. Cupronickel is an alloy of which two metals?
9. What important communication line was laid across the ocean in 1858?
10. What is a taxidermist?
11. Will two magnets with their North poles facing attract or repel?
12. Which is longer, one and a half kilometres or a mile?
13. What colour is a moonstone?
14. What does a speedometer measure?
15. Who were the two Sir William Braggs?

ANSWERS

1. It was the passenger elevator. 2. Cytology. 3. A non-rigid balloon or airship. 4. Polish. 5. Silicon. 6. Home computer. 7. 2062. 8. Copper and nickel. 9. The transatlantic cable. 10. A person practised in the art of preparing, stuffing and mounting skins. 11. Repel. 12. A mile. 13. White. 14. Speed. 15. Physicists, father and son.

111

SESSION 11

QUIZ 3

• •

1. How far can a frog jump?
2. What is a mite?
3. Which is the world's largest crab? Does it measure (a) 30 cms across (b) 25 cms across (c) 20 cms across?
4. What kind of animal is said to bray?
5. What ape is known to local people as 'man of the forest'?
6. What is unusual about the lungfish?
7. Which is the largest bird in the world?
8. What is chicory?
9. What sort of flavour does a Blenheim Orange have?
10. What kind of animal is said to 'low'?
11. What is pepper?
12. How high can a flea jump approximately: (a) 12.5 cms (b) 15 cms (c) 20 cms?
13. What does the name 'dachshund' mean?
14. How many bones are there in a swan's neck: (a) 12 (b) 23 (c) 32?
15. What is a Keeshond?

ANSWERS

1. About 3 metres. 2. In the animal sense, a very tiny spider-like creature. 3. 30 cms across. It's the giant spider crab of Japan. 4. An ass or donkey. 5. The orang-utan. 6. It is able to breathe air. 7. The ostrich. 8. A plant whose leaves are used in salads, and whose roots are ground to mix with coffee. 9. Apple flavour - it's an apple! 10. A cow. 11. The pungent dried berries of the pepper plant, usually powdered. 12. 20 cms. 13. Badger-hound. 14. (b) 23. 15. A breed of dog.

SESSION 11
QUIZ 4

• •

1. How many states are there in Australia?
2. Where and what is Dunkery Beacon?
3. What is the capital of the Ukraine?
4. Cologne is a city now known by another name. What is that name?
5. The Gold Coast is the old name for which country?
6. To which real river did the song 'Ol' Man River' refer?
7. Where in England would you find the Farne Islands?
8. If a car displayed the letters TR, what would be its country of origin?
9. Verulamium was the name given by the Romans to what?
10. In which London street would you find the Hilton and Dorchester hotels and Grosvenor House?
11. Where and what is 'The Pentagon'?
12. Which country regards 'Land of My Fathers' as its anthem?
13. Where and what is the Mull of Kintyre?
14. What is meant by the Six Counties?
15. What is the capital of Thailand?

ANSWERS

1. Eight. 2. The highest point on Exmoor. 3. Kiev. 4. Köln. 5. Ghana. 6. The Mississippi. 7. They are 17 small islands off the Northumberland coast. 8. Turkey. 9. St Albans. 10. Park Lane. 11. The US military headquarters at Alexandria, Virginia. 12. Wales. 13. A headland in western Scotland. 14. It is a name sometimes used to describe Northern Ireland. 15. Bangkok.

· ·

1. What is the name for someone who studies the stars?
2. What would be your condition if you found yourself in 'Queer Street'?
3. To what did a watchmaker, Christopher Pinchbeck give his name?
4. What does an American call a jumble sale?
5. What does the word 'sceptic' mean?
6. What does 'pro tem.' stand for?
7. What was a 'doughboy'?
8. Which word, beginning with R, means to dwell or to inhabit?
9. What, in the United States, is a 'hobo'?
10. What is another name for an American 'dime'?
11. What is the name for someone who studies handwriting?
12. What is the meaning of 'larboard'?
13. What is a 'highball', as known to Americans?
14. What was a 'spiv'?
15. Where would you be if you were in an American 'hoosegow'?

ANSWERS

1. Astronomer. 2. You'd be in financial difficulties. 3. The alloy, pinchbeck. 4. A rummage sale. 5. Someone who disbelieves you. 6. 'Pro tempore': for the time being. 7. An American soldier. 8. Reside. 9. A tramp, or someone who moves around looking for a way to live or work. 10. Ten cents. 11. Graphologist. 12. It is the old word for the port side, or left-hand side, of a ship. 13. A whisky-and-soda. 14. In wartime and soon after, a man who made money without really working. 15. In jail.

SESSION 11
QUIZ 6

. . . .

1. Name Minnesota's American Football team.
2. Who sponsors the traditional curtain raiser to Wimbledon, at Queens Club?
3. How many players are there in a Ryder Cup team?
4. How many hulls does a catamaran have?
5. With which sport do you associate Tony Jarrett?
6. Which sport did Nigel Mansell move to after leaving Formula One?
7. Who sponsored Jaguar's successful challenge at Le Mans?
8. Name the odd one out: Pike, Chub, Roach, Pouting.
9. What nationality is tennis player Gabriel Sabatini?
10. Which football team plays its home games at The Valley?
11. Who was the first man to defeat Frank Bruno in a world title fight?
12. In which sport are players awarded Brownlow Medals?
13. Who was man-of-the-match in the 1998 England v South Africa test at Headingley?
14. Which tennis player has won more women's singles titles than any other, and in 1984 set the longest winning streak of 74 victories?
15. For which Club did England star Graeme Le Saux play during the 1997/98 season?

ANSWERS

1. Vikings. 2. Stella Artois. 3. Twelve. 4. Two. 5. Athletics (110m Hurdles). 6. Indy Car Racing. 7. Silk Cut. 8. Pouting is a sea fish. 9. Argentinian. 10. Charlton Athletic. 11. Tim Witherspoon. 12. Australian Rules Football. 13. Mark Butcher. 14. Martina Navratilova. 15. Chelsea.

SESSION 11
QUIZ 7

• •

1. What was CND, launched in 1958?
2. The Treaty of Paris was signed in 1763. What was its purpose?
3. Which of King Henry VIII's wives outlived him?
4. In 1964 rival gangs of young people began rioting and making disturbances at seaside towns. What did they call themselves?
5. The Rotherhithe tunnel under the Thames was opened in: (a) 1830 (b) 1843 (c) 1850?
6. In Delhi, India, on 1st January, 1877, Queen Victoria was proclaimed what?
7. When King William IV died in 1837, who succeeded him to the throne?
8. Who became commander-in-chief of the American forces in 1775?
9. What were the Huguenots?
10. Which London authority was abolished in 1988?
11. Women campaigners for the vote were known as what in 1906?
12. What caused 43 people to be killed in north-eastern England in 1916?
13. Who was Perkin Warbeck?
14. When were Premium Bonds first introduced: (a) 1956 (b) 1960 (c) 1970?
15. The Atlantic Charter was issued by Churchill and Roosevelt in 1941. What did it proclaim?

ANSWERS

SESSION 11
QUIZ 8

• •

1. Who starred in the 1927 silent film *Sunrise?*
2. From which film and stage show did the song 'I Could Have Danced All Night' come?
3. Who starred in the film *Modern Times?*
4. Name the only film outing for George Lazenby as James Bond?
5. Which actor turned down three major parts that made Humphrey Bogart famous, including the lead role in *Casablanca?*
6. Who starred in the film *The Night of the Hunter?*
7. Name the T.V. comedy set around a hapless unit of the Home Guard in World War 2?
8. Who starred in the film *An American in Paris?*
9. Who starred in the film *M*A*S*H?*
10. Who was Batman in the film *Batman Forever?*
11. Who played The Penguin in the film *Batman Returns?*
12. Which long-running television show featues a pub called 'The Rover's Return'?
13. Which series of films set in a rowdy girls' school starred Alastair Sim?
14. Who starred in the film *All That Heaven Allows?*
15. In which film did the furry creatures called mogwais appear?

ANSWERS

SESSION 11

QUIZ 9

• •

1. Rod Stewart's, 'Sailing', was used for a BBC TV series about which ship?
2. Which American singer's first UK number one was, 'Only The Lonely'
3. What nationality are folk singers, Foster and Allen?
4. The Moody Blues are best known for their song, 'Nights In White Satin', but what was their only UK number 1 single?
5. Which band asked us to 'Rock The Casbah' and wondered, 'Should I Stay Or Should I Go'?
6. Which three piece band were Ginger Baker and Jack Bruce members of?
7. With which band did Liza Minnelli collaborate on her 1989, 'Results', album?
8. Mother and Son band, Lieutenant Pigeon reached number 1 in September 1972, with which song?
9. What nationality were the band, Kraftwerk?
10. In July 1982, Wavelength, recorded their only hit, 'Hurry Home'. What major event was the inspiration for the song?
11. In 1980 Marti Webb reached number 3 with, 'Take That Look Off Your Face'. From which musical did the song come?
12. Which Foo Fighter was originally the drummer in Nirvana?
13. Paul Young's debut solo hit reached number 1 in June 1983. Name the song?
14. Who was the lead vocalist with the Undertones?
15. Which US female vocal group was always reputed to be Prince Charles' favourite Pop act?

ANSWERS

1. HMS Ark Royal 2. Roy Orbison 3. Irish 4. 'Go Now' 5. The Clash 6. Cream 7. The Pet Shop Boys 8. 'Mouldy Old Dough' 9. German 10. The Falklands War 11. Tell Me On A Sunday 12. Dave Grohl 13. 'Wherever I Lay My Hat (That's My Home)' 14. Fergal Sharkey 15. The Three Degrees

118

SESSION 11

QUIZ 10

● ●

1. Who wrote *Anna of the Five Towns?*
2. Who said: 'Give me a lever long enough, and I will move the World.'
3. Who wrote *The Manchurian Candidate?*
4. In which Shakespeare play does 'Proteus' appear?
5. Which famous children's book did Kenneth Grahame write?
6. 'I must go down to the sea again...' Can you recite the next line of Masefield's poem?
7. Who wrote *A Dance to the Music of Time?*
8. Don't count your chickens before they are hatched. Where does this phrase originate?
9. Who wrote *All Quiet on the Western Front?*
10. What line follows 'Listen, my children, and you shall hear'?
11. Who wrote *Tom Jones?*
12. *No Orchids for Miss Blandish* was written by whom?
13. 'Sidney Carton' is a character in which book by Charles Dickens?
14. What were the words that would open Ali Baba's magic cave?
15. According to Alexander Pope, in what does 'Hope springs eternal'?

ANSWERS

1. Arnold Bennett. 2. Archimedes. 3. Richard Condon. 4. *Two Gentlemen of Verona.* 5. *The Wind in the Willows.* 6. 'To the lonely sea and the sky.' 7. Anthony Powell. 8. *Don Quixote,* by Cervantes. 9. Erich Maria Remarque. 10. 'Of the midnight ride of Paul Revere.' 11. Henry Fielding. 12. James Hadley Chase. 13. *A Tale of Two Cities.* 14. 'Open sesame.' 15. The human breast.

SESSION 12
Quiz 1

• •

1. What is gunpowder?
2. The blue dye called indigo comes from what?
3. What, in WW2, was a Stuka?
4. The study of the processes of life in animals and plants is called what?
5. What was first built from a stack of zinc and copper discs sandwiched between cardboard discs soaked in acid?
6. What is the art and practice of cultivating the land called?
7. Radio waves are reflected back to Earth by what?
8. What is an antidote?
9. What is an alloy?
10. What illuminating experience first occurred in London in 1810?
11. Hydrocyanic acid is also called what?
12. Which is the smallest planet?
13. The sternum is another name for which bone?
14. Who was Anthony Fokker?
15. What can an insulator not do?

ANSWERS

1. A mixture of 75% saltpetre, 15% charcoal powder and 10% sulphur. 2. The indigo plant. 3. A German dive-bombing aircraft. 4. Physiology. 5. First electrical battery. 6. Agriculture. 7. The Heaviside Layer. 8. A substance which counteracts the effect of a poison. 9. A metal made of a mixture of two or more metals. 10. The first electric lamp. 11. Prussic acid. 12. Pluto. 13. The breast-bone. 14. Dutch aircraft designer. 15. Conduct electricity.

SESSION 12
Quiz 2

• •

1. Which is the original native to Britain, the grey or the red squirrel?
2. The harvestman is a spider-like creature with very long legs. True or false?
3. What is another name for the thrift plant?
4. What kind of animal is said to whinny?
5. Which dog is sometimes called an alsatian?
6. A chipmunk is a (a) a type of squirrel (b) a kind of ape.
7. What are capers?
8. What kind of animal is said to hoot?
9. What is a globe artichoke?
10. What is an albatross?
11. About how many kinds of poisonous snake are there?
12. Are there such things as sea serpents?
13. What is the only venomous snake native to Britain?
14. What is a sloe?
15. Does a centipede have a hundred legs?

ANSWERS

1. The red squirrel. 2. True. 3. The sea pink. 4. A horse. 5. The German Shepherd. 6. (a) a type of squirrel. 7. Pickled flower-buds of a bush found in Sicily, used for flavouring. 8. An owl. 9. A plant with scaly leaves which have edible bases. 10. Large seabirds, of which there are about a dozen species. 11. About 200. 12. Yes. A number of large snakes live in the sea; usually they about 3 metres long. 13. The viper, or adder. 14. The fruit of the blackthorn. 15. No. The number varies, but it never reaches a hundred!

SESSION 12
Quiz 3

• •

1. Cawnpore is a former name for which city?
2. Where in the world would you find a Dyak?
3. 'Oxon' is another name for where?
4. The maple is the national symbol of which country?
5. Which English city is known familiarly as 'Brum'?
6. How many 'Royal Boroughs' are there in Britain, and what are their names?
7. Where and what is Watling Street?
8. Which country owns Easter Island?
9. Which city is on the River Foyle?
10. In which country can the Sphinx be found?
11. Where is Port Sunlight, and what made it famous?
12. In the United States, what is Amtrak?
13. Saint Lazare railway station will be found in which city?
14. Where is the Shwe Dagon Pagoda?
15. What is the capital of Canada?

ANSWERS

1. Kanpur. 2. Borneo. 3. The county of Oxfordshire. 4. Canada. 5. Birmingham. 6. Four. Kensington and Chelsea, Kingston-upon-Thames, Windsor and Carnarvon. 7. A Roman road extending from London to Shrewsbury. 8. Chile. 9. Derry (Londonderry). 10. Egypt. 11. It's on Merseyside and is famed as the headquarters of soap manufacturers, Lever Brothers. 12. The passenger rail system. 13. Paris. 14. Rangoon, Burma. 15. Ottawa.

122

• •

1. What is a 'moonlighter'?
2. If an American offered to 'come by', what would you expect him to do?
3. What's the plural of 'dwarf'?
4. Whose motto is 'Be Prepared'?
5. What is meant by the word 'unwitting'?
6. To an American, what is a 'John Hancock'?
7. What would you get in America if you asked for a 'vest'?
8. What should you ask for if you were looking for a toilet in America?
9. What, according to the magazine *Private Eye*, are 'hackettes'?
10. What is a consonant?
11. What is a vowel?
12. In European politics, what does the acronym CAP stand for?
13. What kind of flower was named after its grower, Dr Alexander Garden?
14. How did the word 'fan', meaning an enthusiast, come into being?
15. What does the old-fashioned term 'To fare' mean?

ANSWERS

1. Occupants of premises who depart during the night to avoid paying debts or dues. 2. Call on you. 3. Dwarfs. 4. The Scouts. 5. Unknowing, ignorant. 6. A signature. 7. A waistcoat. 8. The rest-room. 9. Woman journalists. 10. Any letter of the alphabet which is not a vowel. 11. The alphabetical letters a, e, i, o, u. Also, sometimes, y and w. 12. Common Agricultural Policy. 13. The gardenia. 14. It is short for fanatic. 15. To travel.

SESSION 12
Quiz 5

• •

1. In which city is the annual World Professional Snooker Championship held?
2. Who captained the Scottish Rugby Union team during it's 1990 Grand Slam victory?
3. Which race was won 14 times by Mike Hailwood?
4. Which Chinese game involves 144 tiles divided into six suits?
5. In which sport do you refer to the pitch as a Gridiron?
6. What is the maximum score possible in one game of Ten Pin Bowling?
7. In which sport would you compete for the Air Canada Silver Broom?
8. Which sport features banderillas, veronicas, muletas and picadors?
9. Which is larger: the United States or British golf ball?
10. How many hits are allowed on one side of the net in Volleyball?
11. June Croft is associated with which sport?
12. How many lanes are there in an Olympic-sized swimming pool?
13. Which stick and ball game uses the largest pitch?
14. By what name is footballer Edson Arantes do Nascimento better known?
15. Which is the first 'Classic' of the English Horse racing season?

ANSWERS

1. Sheffield. 2. David Sole. 3. Isle of Man TT. 4. Mah Jong. 5. American Football. 6. 300. 7. Curling. 8. Bull Fighting. 9. US. 10. Three. 11. Swimming. 12. Eight. 13. Polo. 14. Pele. 15. The 1000 Guineas.

124

SESSION 12
Quiz 6

• •

1. Which famous ship, sunk in 1545, was lifted from the seabed in 1982?
2. Which queen was discovered to be bald at the time of her execution?
3. What was laid beneath the sea between Dover and Calais in 1850?
4. Who was Lyndon Baines Johnson?
5. Under what name is the former Elizabeth Bowes-Lyon now known?
6. What have these people in common: Julius Caesar; Abraham Lincoln; Mahatma Gandhi?
7. What instrument of destruction was invented in 1777 by David Bushnell?
8. What office did Archbishop Makarios assume in December 1959?
9. Who in the English parliament led the campaign against the slave trade?
10. What did Albert Schweitzer found in Lambaréné, French Equatorial Africa?
11. May Day became a Bank Holiday in which year?
12. The first British colour supplement was published by what newspaper in 1962?
13. The Dorset labourers in Tolpuddle, Dorset, were punished for what action?
14. When was the last time we had an earthquake in Britain?
15. Who was Roald Amundsen?

ANSWERS

1. The Mary Rose. 2. Mary, Queen of Scots in 1587. 3. The first submarine telegraph cable. 4. He was the 36th American president. 5. The Queen Mother. 6. They were all assassinated. 7. The torpedo. 8. He became the first president of Cyprus. 9. William Wilberforce. 10. A hospital to combat sleeping sickness and leprosy. 11. 1978. 12. *The Sunday Times*. 13. Forming a trade union. 14. In 1984, on 19th July, in Gwynedd. 15. Norwegian explorer who was first to reach the South Pole.

125

SESSION 12
Quiz 7

• •

1. What was the name of the first James Bond film to feature Pierce Brosnan in the lead role?
2. Who starred in the film *The Way to the Stars*?
3. Who, in the movies, was the 'Brazilian Bombshell'?
4. Who starred in the film *Northwest Frontier*?
5. Who starred in the film *If...*?
6. Which T.V. programme, featuring 'Scottie' and 'Bones', was set in space and became a long series of major films?
7. From which film and stage show did the song 'Some Enchanted Evening' come?
8. Who starred in the film *The Guns of Navarone*?
9. What was controversial about the 1915 silent movie *The Birth of a Nation*?
10. Which two brothers acted in the film *The Falcon's Brother*?
11. Which famous cartoon cat was always trying to eat 'Tweetie-Pie'?
12. What was unusual about the language used in the 1965 film *Incubus,* starring William Shatner?
13. From which film and stage show did the song 'I Got Rhythm' come?
14. Which T.V. cop show featured a bald detective played by Telly Savalas?
15. Who starred in the film Mildred Pierce?

ANSWERS

1. *Goldeneye.* 2. John Mills. 3. Carmen Miranda. 4. Kenneth More, Lauren Bacall. 5. Malcolm McDowall, David Wood, Richard Warwick. 6. *Star Trek.* 7. *South Pacific.* 8. Gregory Peck, David Niven. 9. It featured the Ku Klux Klan. 10. George Sanders and Tom Conway. 11. Sylvester. 12. It was Esperanto. 13. *Girl Crazy.* 14. *Kojak.* 15. Joan Crawford.

SESSION 12
Quiz 8

• •

1. In 1989 who recorded the album, 'Like A Prayer'?
2. Who was the lead singer with Tubeway Army? E)
3. In 1992, Witney Houston reached number 1 with, 'I Will Always Love You', from which movie does the song come?
4. Who in the 1970's had top 10 hits with, 'Love Is Life', 'You Sexy Thing' and 'So You Win Again'?
5. Who reached number 1 in December 1986 with, 'Caravan Of Love'?
6. In 1991, Iron Maiden had their first UK number 1 with, 'Bring your Daughter To The Slaughter', but what was their first top ten hit?
7. Name Michael Jackson's sister who has had a top ten hit with 'The Best Things In Life Are Free'?
8. Which band's biggest-selling album was 'Pills, Thrills And Bellyaches'?
9. In 1957, Harry Belafonte reached number one with, 'Mary's Boy Child'. Who recorded a cover version in 1978 which also reached number 1?
10. In 1994 Whigfield went straight in at number 1 with which song?
11. 'Ballroom Blitz', 'Blockbuster' and 'Teenage Rampage', were all hits for which 1970s UK band?
12. From which album do Shakespeare's Sister's hits, 'Stay', 'You're History', and 'I Don't Care', come?
13. Who hit number one in 1992 with Ebeneeezer Goode?
14. Who had hits in the 1970's, with his brothers, his sister and on his own, recording songs such as, 'Puppy Love', 'Crazy Horses', and Young Love?
15. Who hit number 4 in 1982 with, 'Maid of Orleans'?

ANSWERS

1. Madonna. 2. Gary Numan. 3. The Bodyguard. 4. Hot Chocolate. 5. The Housemartins. 6. 'Run To The Hills'. 7. Janet Jackson. 8. Happy Mondays. 9. Boney M. 10. 'Saturday Night'. 11.Sweet 12. 'Hormonally Yours' 13. Shamen 14. Donny Osmond 15. Orchestral Manoeuvres in the Dark

127

SESSION 12

Quiz 9

. . . .

1. Who was Sir Max Beerbohm?
2. The character 'Caliban' appears in which Shakespeare play?
3. What was truly remarkable about the American author Helen Adams Keller?
4. Arthur Mee was the editor of a famous reference work. What was it called?
5. Who wrote *Lorna Doone?*
6. Complete the proverb: 'Brevity is...'
7. 'Yet each man kills the thing he loves.' From where does this phrase originate?
8. In which Shakespeare play does 'Regan' appear?
9. Name the two main characters who sailed aboard the Hispaniola.
10. 'And did those feet in ancient time/Walk upon England's mountains green?' is the beginning of a poem by whom?
11. In which book by Evelyn Waugh does 'Guy Crouchback' appear?
12. In which part of England is the novel *Lorna Doone* based?
13. In what languages did these authors write: (a) Dante (b) Maxim Gorki (c) Betjeman (d) André Gide?
14. Who wrote *The Good Companions?*
15. Who first employed the word 'sleuth', to mean a detective?

ANSWERS

1. A critic and caricaturist. 2. *The Tempest.* 3. She was blind and deaf. 4. *The Children's Encyclopaedia.* 5. R. D Blackmore. 6. ...the soul of wit. 7. Oscar Wilde: *The Ballad of Reading Gaol.* 8. *King Lear.* 9. Long John Silver and Jim Hawkins. 10. William Blake. 11. *Men at Arms.* 12. Exmoor. 13. (a) Italian (b) Russian (c) English (d) French. 14. J.B. Priestley. 15. The author, Angus Bethune Reach, in his book, *Clement Lorimer,* used the expression 'sleuthhound', in 1848.

● ●

1. What famous landmark stands on the site of Tyburn Tree in London?
2. Westminster Abbey is over 166 metres long. Yes or no?
3. What group of people are found in an orchestra?
4. What is meant by 'Dutch nightingales'?
5. What can be grouped into fleets?
6. In what place do Jewish people worship?
7. What is ratatouille?
8. The goat represents which sign of the Zodiac?
9. What is mornay?
10. According to the 'language of flowers', what do oak leaves signify?
11. In which year did Britain join the EEC?
12. Whose statue stands in front of Wesley's Chapel in City Road, London?
13. What kind of food product is aioli?
14. What is chow mein?
15. Samson, a judge of Israel, possessed what great gift?

ANSWERS

1. Marble Arch. 2. Yes. 3. Musicians. 4. Frogs. 5. Ships, cars, birds. 6. A synagogue. 7. A vegetable stew containing tomatoes, aubergines, peppers, etc. 8. Capricorn. 9. A cream sauce with cheese flavouring. 10. Bravery. 11. 1972. 12. John Wesley. 13. Garlic mayonnaise. 14. Fried noodles. 15. Enormous strength.

• •

1. What kind of animal is a kite?
2. What is a shaddock?
3. How big is a newly-born kangaroo?
4. What is an amphibian?
5. What is a gudgeon?
6. How much do the world's heaviest coconuts weigh?
7. What is a John Dory?
8. A group of badgers is called (a) a bark (b) a sete?
9. How big is Britain's largest ant: (a) about half an inch, (b) about a third of an inch or (c) about a quarter of an inch?
10. What is a group of leopards called?
11. Can any mammals lay eggs?
12. What kind of animal could be described as a Cheviot?
13. What was originally called the love apple?
14. A zebu is a kind of zebra. True or false?
15. The brush-tailed rat-kangaroo is a rodent found in Africa. True or false?

ANSWERS

1. A hawk. 2. A fruit related to the orange and lemon, and resembling the grapefruit. 3. About two centimetres long. 4. A creature which needs to return to water to breed, such as frogs, toads, salamanders. 5. An easily-caught freshwater fish, like a small carp. 6. 18Kg. 7. A fish of the mackerel family. 8. A sete. 9. About a third of an inch. 10. A leap. 11. Yes, the platypus and the spiny anteater or echidna. 12. A breed of sheep. 13. The tomato. 14. False. It's a kind of African domestic cattle. 15. False. It's a marsupial found in Australia.

SESSION 13
QUIZ 2

• •

1. What does the Monument in London commemorate?
2. Whose country retreat is the house called Chequers?
3. Where in the world do they speak Swahili?
4. On which stretch of water does Chicago stand?
5. Which river forms part of the border between England and Scotland?
6. Where in the world do they speak Faroese?
7. Where and what is Mount Etna?
8. Where is the Palace of Topkapi?
9. What was known in early times as 'Cathay'?
10. What have the county of Surrey, the country of Jamaica and the county of Yorkshire in common?
11. Where and what was Mercia?
12. Sauchiehall Street is in which British city?
13. The Chiltern Hills spread over two counties. Which are they?
14. Which river forms a border between Devon and Cornwall?
15. Which country regards 'Scots Wha Hae' as its anthem?

ANSWERS

1. The place where the Great Fire started. 2. The Prime Minister. 3. East Africa. 4. Lake Michigan. 5. The Tweed. 6. The Faroe Islands, between Scotland and Norway. 7. An active volcano in Italy. 8. In Istanbul, Turkey. It is now a museum. 9. China. 10. They all have cities called Kingston. 11. An ancient kingdom of Britain, in what is now the Midlands. 12. Glasgow. 13. Oxfordshire, Buckinghamshire. 14. The Tamar. 15. Scotland.

131

• •

1. What does the phrase, 'Apple-pie order' mean?
2. What's wrong with this sentence: Our cat always licks it's paws after a meal?
3. If you were playing checkers in America, what would you be doing?
4. What is the name for someone who studies mankind?
5. What is the name for someone who studies or collects postage-stamps?
6. What is the difference between adventitious and adventurous?
7. A peon is (a) a flower (b) a labourer in Spain (c) a comedian.
8. What does 'carry a torch' mean?
9. What would it mean if you 'cast pearls before swine'?
10. A 'shambles' is a real mess, but what was it originally?
11. What modern term replaces the word, 'Methinks'?
12. What does 'compos mentis' mean?
13. What is a 'ham', theatrically-speaking?
14. What does 'Twain' mean?
15. What is a 'chipolata'?

ANSWERS

1. Everything neat and in its place. 2. It should read: Our cat always licks its paws after a meal. 3. You'd be playing draughts. 4. Anthropologist. 5. Philatelist. 6. The first means 'accidental' and the second means 'venturesome'. 7. (b). 8. To be in love with someone. 9. That you offered something of value to someone who could not understand its value. 10. A butcher's slaughterhouse. 11. I think. 12. Sane, in one's right mind. 13. An actor who overacts, and lacks real ability. 14. Two. 15. A small sausage.

132

SESSION 13
QUIZ 4

• •

1. Who is the only man to have won World Titles at both motor cycle and car racing?
2. Which sporting figure re-enacted Hannibal's crossing of the Alps for charity?
3. Which football club formerly played their home games at The Baseball Ground?
4. With which team did Damon Hill begin his Formula One career?
5. Who was the, 'Crafty Cockney', winner of the World Professional Darts Championship in 1980?
6. Which US baseball star married Marilyn Monroe?
7. Which sporting star was kidnapped in 1983, never to be seen again?
8. Which team always leads the Olympic parade?
9. What is New Zealand's Rugby League team known as?
10. In which sport are the balls made of crystallate?
11. In which sport would you compete for a Lonsdale Belt?
12. Which sports commentator had a Private Eye column named after him for his amusing commentary mistakes?
13. Which steeplechase course contains the notorious hazards, The Chair and Beachers Brook?
14. Which two disciplines are common to both men's and women's gymnastics?
15. Which is the only city to have hosted the Commonwealth Games twice?

ANSWERS

1. John Surtees. 2. Ian Botham. 3. Derby County. 4. Williams. 5. Eric Bristow. 6. Joe DiMaggio. 7. Shergar. 8. Greece. 9. The Kiwis. 10. Snooker. 11. Boxing. 12. David Coleman. 13. The Grand National course at Aintree. 14. Floor and Vaulting horse. 15. Edinburgh.

SESSION 13
QUIZ 5

1. Who was William McKinley?
2. What street conveyance appeared in London for the first time in 1861?
3. Of which country was King Farouk the sovereign from 1936?
4. Which monarch this century was almost sixty when he was crowned?
5. To be in prison is sometimes referred to as being 'in the clink'. Why?
6. What was unique about the founding of the town of Jamestown in Virginia?
7. What kind of performer was Charles Blondin?
8. Where and when did the Great Fire of London start?
9. Which famous consort of an English King sold oranges outside the Theatre Royal in London?
10. When was the state of war (World War 2) with Germany formally declared at an end?
11. Which famous black leader was assassinated on 4th April 1968, in Memphis, Tennessee?
12. Which pianist became the first Prime Minister of the new state of Poland after the First World War?
13. What did 75,000 Londoners die of during 1665?
14. Which major newspaper closed down for almost a year in 1978?
15. The Kingdom of Serbs, Croats and Slovenes was established in 1919. What was it eventually called?

ANSWERS

1. He was the 25th American president. 2. Trams. 3. Egypt. 4. King Edward VII. 5. In early times, there was a prison in Southwark called The Clink Prison. 6. It was the first permanent English colony on the American mainland. 7. A rope walker who crossed Niagara Falls. 8. At a baker's in Pudding Lane, in 1666. 9. Nell Gwynn. 10. 9th July, 1951. 11. Martin Luther King. 12. Ignace Jan Paderewski. 13. The Great Plague. 14. *The Times*. 15. Yugoslavia.

134

SESSION 13
QUIZ 6

• •

1. Which film star began her career in Czechoslovakia under the name 'Hedy Kiesler'?
2. Which T.V. show was created by Gene Roddenberry?
3. Who starred in the film *The Courtneys of Curzon Street?*
4. Who starred in the film *The Bank Dick?*
5. Who starred in the 1969 film *Goodbye, Mr Chips?*
6. Which film actor was known as 'The Duke'?
7. Who starred in the film *North by Northwest?*
8. Which controversial cartoon series features characters called Kyle, Kenny, Stan and Cartman?
9. What T.V. programme is abbreviated to the letters *TOTP?*
10. Who starred in the film *Lawrence of Arabia?*
11. Who played 'Dorothy Michaels' in the film *Tootsie?*
12. From which film and stage show did the song 'If I Ruled the World' come?
13. Who turned down the role of Indiana Jones in *Raiders of the Lost Ark?*
14. Who starred in the silent film *Safety Last?*
15. What did actress Frances McDormand do in 1996?

ANSWERS

1. Hedy Lamarr. 2. *Star Trek.* 3. Anna Neagle, Michael Wilding. 4. W.C. Fields. 5. Peter O'Toole, Petula Clark. 6. John Wayne. 7. Cary Grant, Eva Marie Saint. 8. *South Park.* 9. *Top Of The Pops.* 10. Peter O'Toole, Alec Guinness, Anthony Quinn, Jack Hawkins, Omar Sharif. 11. Dustin Hoffman. 12. *Pickwick.* 13.Tom Selleck. 14. Harold Lloyd. 15. Win a best actress Oscar for her role in *Fargo.*

135

SESSION 13
QUIZ 7

. . . .

1. Who recorded the theme song for the 1988 Los Angeles Olympics?
2. Who released, Vindaloo in support of the English fotball team in 1998?
3. In the mid 70's David Soul had a string of top ten hits. TV viewers were more familiar with him as whom?
4. Can you name the lead singer of Madness?
5. In the early 1970's Judy Collins entered the UK chart 8 times with the same song. Name the song?
6. Where do the band Del Amitri come from?
7. In 1979 the Dickies reached number 7 with a cover of a children's TV programme theme song. What was the song?
8. What was the Doors' only UK top ten hit?
9. Which band had hits with 'Hombug' and 'A Whiter Shade Of Pale?'
10. Which band's first album was 'Pablo Honey'?
11. Who entered, 'Ooh Aah...Just A Little Bit', in the 1996 Eurovision Song Contest?
12. Who entered the chart in June 1998 with, 'Lost In Space'?
13. In 1988, a beer commercial gave The Hollies their second UK number 1. Can you name the song?
14. What was Michael Jackson's first solo UK number 1?
15. In 1981, Joe Dolce had his one and only UK hit which reached number one. What was the song?

ANSWERS

1. Whitney Houston (one moment in time). 2. Fat Les. 3. Hutch (Starsky & Hutch). 4. Suggs. 5. Amazing Grace. 6. Scotland. 7. The Banana Splits. 8. 'Light My Fire'. 9. Procul Harum. 10. Radiohead. 11. Gina G 12. Lighthouse Family 13. He ain't heavy, he's my brother 14. 'One Day In Your Life'. 15. 'Shaddap you face'.

136

SESSION 13
QUIZ 8

• •

1. Sir John Tenniel was the illustrator of which children's books?
2. In which Shakespeare play does 'Titania' appear?
3. Complete the proverb: 'Ask no questions...'
4. 'Farewell to the Land where the gloom of my glory' is the beginning of a poem by whom?
5. 'Svengali' appears in which play by George Du Maurier?
6. Who wrote Jitterbug Perfume and Even Cowgirls Get The Blues?
7. 'Oh East is East, and West is West, and never the twain shall meet.' From where does this phrase come?
8. In which Shakespeare play does 'Rosalind' appear?
9. Who had nothing to offer but 'blood, toil; tears and sweat'?
10. Complete the proverb: 'Catch not at the shadow...'
11. Complete the proverb: 'Books and friends should be...'
12. Who wrote Rumpole of the Bailey?
13. Complete the proverb: 'Better an egg today...'
14. When thrown to the lions, who was spared because of his previous kindness?
15. Who wrote The Darling Buds of May?

ANSWERS

1. *Alice's Adventures in Wonderland* and *Through the Looking Glass*. 2. *A Midsummer Night's Dream*. 3. '...and be told no lies'. 4. Lord Byron. 5. Trilby. 6. Tim Robbins. 7. Kipling, *The Ballad of East and West*. 8. *As You Like It*. 9. Winston Churchill. 10. '...and lose the substance'. 11. '...few but good'. 12. John Mortimer. 13. '...than a hen tomorrow'. 14. Androcles. 15. H.E. Bates.

• •

1. Who did Margaret Thatcher follow as leader of the Conservative party?
2. Who is the patron saint of tax-collectors?
3. What is a Chateaubriand?
4. Which word, beginning with post- means 'after death?'
5. How much was a pennyweight?
6. What is a Battenburg?
7. Which theatre in London was originally called the Waldorf?
8. What is lasagne?
9. Friday is named after Frigga, the German goddess of married love. True or false?
10. What is the word for a group of angels?
11. Of what group does one find a posse?
12. Which herb looks like parsley but has a slight taste of aniseed?
13. Who was the painter of the famous *Laughing Cavalier?*
14. Who is the patron saint of scholars?
15. In which city, apart from London, would you find Soho?

ANSWERS

1. Ted Heath. 2. St Matthew. 3. A thick grilled fillet steak. 4. Post-mortem. 5. 24 grains. 6. A cake with squares of pink and yellow sponge. 7. The Strand. 8. Flat pasta cooked with tomatoes, cheese or meat. 9. True. 10. A host. 11. Cowboys, constables, police. 12. Chervil. 13. The Dutch portrait painter, Frans Hals. 14. St Bridget. 15. Birmingham.

SESSION 13
QUIZ 10

• •

1. The phonograph was invented by Edison, but who invented the gramophone?
2. What event was the Bell X1 connected with?
3. Aerophobia is (a) a fear of draughts (b) a fear of flying.
4. Phonetics is the study of what?
5. What is gun-metal?
6. Who is regarded as the pioneer of modern computers?
7. The science of the study of animal life is called what?
8. What does Eureka! mean?
9. What was a V2?
10. Herpetology is the study of what?
11. Which of the following kinds of energy source is renewable : coal; oil; gas; wind?
12. Aeronautics is the study of what?
13. What was pioneered by Joseph Lister?
14. What was broadcast by radio for the first time in 1900?
15. What is hypochondria?

ANSWERS

1. Emile Berliner, who invented a recorder/player of flat discs. 2. Breaking the sound barrier. 3. It's both. 4. Speech and the sounds made by the voice. 5. An alloy of copper, tin and zinc. 6. Charles Babbage. 7. Zoology. 8. I have found it! 9. A long-distance weapon in the form of a rocket. 10. Reptiles. 11. Wind. 12. Aircraft and flying. 13. Antiseptic surgery. 14. The human voice. 15. An abnormal belief that one is ill, usually with an imaginary illness.

• •

1. In the old days, lawbreakers were hanged at Tyburn Tree, London. What marks the spot now?
2. What is the current name of the country formerly known as Tripolitania?
3. What is the Indian name for India?
4. Where in Britain is the Isle of Sheppey?
5. What is the mistral?
6. Who, in 1859, first crossed Niagara Falls on a tightrope?
7. Who usually lives at No. 11 Downing Street, London?
8. Which is the largest gulf in the world?
9. The Alps cover land areas in which five countries?
10. Ashby-de-la-Zouch, according to a once-popular song, is a little English town by the sea. Is that true?
11. Where is the Bridge of Sighs?
12. How many countries are members of the United Nations: (a) 185, (b) 197 or (c) 301?
13. What was the old name for the Republic of Vanuatu in the Pacific?
14. Which is the largest forest in Britain?
15. The Mont Cenis Pass is between which two countries?

ANSWERS

1. Marble Arch. 2. Libya. 3. Bharat. 4. In the Thames Estuary. 5. A cold dry N.W. wind that blows down the Rhône valley to the Mediterranean coast of France. 6. Blondin. 7. Usually, the Chancellor of the Exchequer. 8. The Gulf of Mexico. 9. Switzerland, Austria, France, Italy and Yugoslavia. 10. No! It's in Leicestershire, quite a long way from the coast. 11. Venice. 12. (a) 185. 13. The New Hebrides. 14. Kielder Forest, Northumberland. 15. France and Italy.

● ●

1. If you 'weigh anchor', what are you doing?
2. A British soldier would go to the NAAFI. Where would an American soldier go?
3. What, in earlier times, was an article of clothing called a boa?
4. What is an android?
5. What is an 'ebb tide'?
6. What is a chaparral?
7. What is a twill?
8. What is a twerp?
9. What would 'pencil' have meant in the eighteenth century?
10. What is a moron?
11. What is a clique?
12. What is 'flim-flam'?
13. What is cavalry?
14. What do 'aught' and 'ought' mean?
15. Pogonophobia is a fear of what?

ANSWERS

1. Raising the anchor from the water, ready to sail away. 2. The PX or post exchange. 3. A scarf of feathers. 4. A robot in human form 5. A receding tide. 6. A dense, tangled, brushwood. 7. A woven fabric showing diagonal lines. 8. A slang term for someone contemptible: either stupid, a cad, or both. 9. Brush. 10. A feeble-minded person. 11. An exclusive group of persons. 12. A trick or deception, also idle meaningless talk. 13. A group of horse-soldiers. 14. Anything. 15. Beards.

SESSION 14
QUIZ 3

● ●

1. What did Virginia Wade's 1977 and Boris Becker's 1985, Wimbledon victories have in common?
2. Which sport's ruling body is based at the Hurlingham Club in London?
3. From which city do the, 'Bears' American football team come?
4. Which sport do the Peterborough Pirates play?
5. Who was the manager of Manchester United at the time of the Munich air crash?
6. Who said, 'I float like a butterfly and sting like a bee'?
7. Which football team are known as the Hatters?
8. At which sport did David Steele captain England?
9. Which athlete was stripped of his 100m Olympic Gold medal in 1988, for failing a drugs test?
10. Which show jumper will be best remembered for being liberal with his use of the 'V' Sign?
11. Which sporting entrepreneur sold his leisure clubs to a brewery and bought a major interest in the sporting activities of Hull?
12. Which sport is played on a diamond?
13. Who beat Manchester United in the 1979 FA Cup Final, winning 3-2, with the winning goal coming in the 89th minute?
14. Name the large balloon-shaped sail used when sailing with the wind?
15. In which sport do you aim to score, using a, 'cannon' or an, 'in-off', with the red, white or spot white?

ANSWERS

SESSION 14
QUIZ 4

● ●

1. Who were the Chindits?
2. In 1947, what did Prince Philip become?
3. Which northern Australian city was bombed by the Japanese in 1942?
4. Who or what in Spain was the Falange?
5. What happened to Cardinal Karol Wojtyla on 16th October, 1978?
6. Which queen bathed every three months, 'whether she needed to or not'?
7. How did Sir Francis Drake die?
8. Which building in Stratford-upon-Avon was destroyed by fire in 1926?
8. What was Aleksei Leonov the first to do?
9. Which British political party came to an end in 1990?
10. What was the Maginot Line?
11. What did Benito Mussolini found in 1917?
12. Which American city became the 'Motor Capital' of the world from 1903 onwards?
13. Who or what was the Klu Klux Klan?
14. George Carey is Archbishop of Canterbury. How many preceded him?
15. Was Rotten Row, London every really rotten?

ANSWERS

SESSION 14

QUIZ 5

. . . .

1. Who starred in the film *Lassie Come Home?*
2. In the film *Too Much Too Soon*, Errol Flynn played the part of another real actor. Who?
3. Who was known as 'the First Lady of the Screen'?
4. From which film and stage show did the song 'If I Were a Rich Man' come?
5. What naughty word did Emma Dunn utter in the 1932 US film *Blessed Event?*
6. Who starred in the film *Yankee Doodle Dandy?*
7. Who kissed 16-year-old Petula Clark in the 1949 film *Don't Ever Leave Me?*
8. Who starred in the film *Carmen Jones?*
9. Who turned down the role of Ghandi in the film of the same name?
10. Who starred in the remake of *The Avengers?*
11. Who was born Israel Baline in 1888 in Temun, Siberia?
12. Who starred in the 1996 film *Twister?*
13. Which film featured a selection of ghosts and a giant dough man terrorising a city?
14. Who starred in the film *Enter The Dragon?*
15. Who hosts the TV series, *Have I got news for you?*

ANSWERS

1. Roddy McDowell, Dame May Whitty, Elsa Lanchester, Edmund Gwenn. 2. John Barrymore. 3. Norma Shearer. 4. Fiddler on the Roof. 5. Damn. 6. James Cagney. 7. Jimmy Hanley. 8. Dorothy Dandridge, Pearl Bailey, Harry Belafonte. 9. Sir Alec Guinness. 10. Uma Thurman, Ralph Fiennes. 11. Irving Berlin. 12. Helen Hunt, Bill Paxton. 13. *Ghostbusters.* 14. Bruce Lee. 15. Angus Deayton.

SESSION 14
QUIZ 6

1. Which ex-member of Yazoo released the album 'Alf'?
2. For what was Mungo Jerry's number one hit, 'In The Summer Time' used for in the summer of 1996?
3. Complete the missing band member: 'Crosby, Stills, Nash and...'?
4. Who recorded England's official song for Italia '90 (World in Motion)?
5. With which song did the New Seekers reach number one in December 1971?
6. Who said "ullo John got a new motor?', in 1984?
7. Who had number one hits in the 60's with 'Apache', 'Telstar', and 'Foot Tapper'?
8. Who sang the 'Leader of the Pack' in 1965?
9. In the mid 1990's who topped the charts with 'Oh Carolina', and 'Boombastic'?
10. Who featured on the re-recording of Smokie's 'Living Next Door To Alice' in May 1995?
11. With which song did Buddy Holly achieve his only UK number 1 single?
12. Which band reached number 1 with 'Rock Around The Clock' in 1955?
13. Which band did Kurt Cobain front?
14. Skunk Anansie have had a string of hits in the UK. Their name derives from Jamaican folk lore. What creature is a Skunk Anansie?
15. Which part of the UK do Runrig come from?

ANSWERS

1. Alison Moyet. 2. Anti Drink Drive commercial. 3. Young (Neil Young). 4. New Order (Englandneworder). 5. 'I'd Like To Teach The World To Sing (In Perfect Harmony). 6. Alexei Sayle. 7. The Shadows. 8. The Shangri-las. 9. Shaggy. 10. Roy Chubby Brown. 11. 'It Doesn't Matter Any More'. 12. Bill Haley and the Comets 13. Nirvana. 14. A Spider. 15. Scotland.

SESSION 14
QUIZ 7

• •

1. Who wrote *The Faerie Queene?*
2. *The Magus* and *The Collector* are books by which British author?
3. *The Halfpenny Marvel* was a boys' weekly, introducing a famous detective in its first issue. Who?
4. In which Shakespeare play does 'Prospero' appear?
5. 'Doctor Aziz' appears in which book by E.M. Forster?
6. Who adopted a pen-name made up of the word 'yes' in French and Russian?
7. Who wrote *The L-Shaped Room?*
8. Complete the proverb: 'A bad workman always...'
9. *David Copperfield* was the favourite book of which author?
10. Who said, 'a woman is only a woman, but a good cigar is a smoke'?
11. What was the better-known pseudonym of Samuel Langhorne Clemens?
12. 'The female of the species is more deadly than the male.' Where does this phrase originate?
13. 'Inspector Bucket' appears in which book by Charles Dickens?
14. 'Bottom' is a character from which Shakespeare play?
15. Who wrote the play *Death of a Salesman?*

ANSWERS

1. Edmund Spenser. 2. John Fowles. 3. 'Sexton Blake'. 4. *The Tempest.* 5. *A Passage to India.* 6. Ouida. 7. Lynne Reid Banks. 8. '...blames his tools.' 9. Charles Dickens, who wrote it! 10. Rudyard Kipling. 11. Mark Twain. 12. *The Female of the Species* (Kipling). 13. *Bleak House.* 14. *A Midsummer Night's Dream.* 15. Arthur Miller.

● ●

1. What is a madeleine?
2. St Peter is the patron saint of whom?
3. Who was Alexander the Great?
4. What is kedgeree?
5. From the gastronomic point of view, what is a legume?
6. St Cecilia is the patron saint of whom?
7. St Stephen is the patron saint of whom?
8. What is bouillabaisse?
9. Which is London's largest park?
10. What is toad in the hole?
11. What do O.J. Simpson's initials stand for?
12. St David is the patron saint of whom?
13. Who was the 'Brown Bomber'?
14. What is Albert sauce?
15. What is sauerkraut?

ANSWERS

1. A small, shell-shaped, sponge cake. 2. Fishermen. 3. A Macedonian soldier and conqueror who reached India. 4. A dish of rice, fish and hard-boiled eggs. 5. Peas, beans and lentils. 6. Singers and musicians. 7. Bricklayers. 8. A thick soup made with different kinds of fish. 9. Richmond, Surrey. 10. Sausages baked in batter. 11. Orenthal James. 12. Poets. 13. Joe Louis, heavyweight boxer. 14. A sauce made with cream, butter, horse-radish, mustard and vinegar. 15. Pickled cabbage.

SESSION 14
QUIZ 9

· ·

1. What colour is a sapphire?
2. What is a monomaniac?
3. Seismology is the study of what?
4. What is argon?
5. Palaeontology is the study of what?
6. What is nychtophobia?
7. In which country is it believed that gunpowder was invented?
8. Who was Archimedes?
9. What is Alpha Centauri?
10. What is a masochist?
11. What is the name of the nearest star?
12. Who invented the miner's safety-lamp?
13. What does 'dirigible' mean?
14. What substance is fermented to make alcohol?
15. What is impetigo?

ANSWERS

1. Blue. 2. Someone who has an enormous liking for one subject. 3. Earthquakes. 4. A gas, of which the atmosphere contains about 1%. 5. Animal and plant fossils. 6. A fear of the dark. 7. China. 8. Greek mathematician. 9. The third brightest star in the sky. 10. Someone who derives pleasure from being ill-treated or hurt by others. 11. Proxima Centauri. 12. Sir Humphry Davy. 13. The word means 'something that can be directed', and is normally used as a name for an airship or navigable balloon. 14. Sugar. 15. A contagious skin disease, mainly of the face and hands.

• •

1. The potato is a member of the nightshade family. Yes or no?
2. What is a herbivore?
3. A copperhead is a type of (a) rattlesnake (b) eagle?
4. A dik-dik is a small East African bird. True or false?
5. What is the correct name for the insect called 'daddy-long-legs'?
6. What was the dodo?
7. What is a cassowary?
8. What large animal is usually found in large African rivers, and whose name means 'river-horse'?
9. What sort of animal is a Dandie Dinmont?
10. What is a calabash?
11. What is an insectivore?
12. What sort of animal is a schnauzer?
13. What is the general name given to creatures like snakes, lizards, crocodiles and tortoises?
14. What sort of animal is a saluki?
15. What is a cucumber?

ANSWERS

1. Yes. 2. A plant-eating animal. 3. (a) a rattlesnake. 4. False. It's a small antelope. 5. The crane-fly. 6. An extinct flightless bird once found on Mauritius. 7. A large, flightless bird of Australia, similar to the ostrich and emu, but smaller. 8. The hippopotamus. 9. A breed of dog. 10. A large, melon-shaped fruit of the calabash tree. 11. An insect-eating mammal, like a mole or a shrew. 12. A breed of dog. 13. Reptiles. 14. A breed of dog. 15. The fruit of a creeping plant with bristly lobed leaves.

SESSION 15
QUIZ 1

1. What word, beginning with C, can mean dogma or doctrine?
2. To an American, what is a 'hunky'?
3. What does 'to wax' mean?
4. What does 'to wane' mean?
5. The city of Damascus gave its name to what?
6. What does 'ten bucks' mean to an American?
7. What is the name for someone who studies plants?
8. If your surname is Miller, what might you be nicknamed?
9. Can you make a one-word anagram out of 'no more stars'?
10. What, in the United States, is a 'mortician'?
11. What is wrong with the phrase, 'One should always do his best'?
12. What do the initials WMO mean?
13. What was, or is, a 'grass widow'?
14. Who or what was a 'quisling'?
15. What do Americans call pants?

No, not quizling darling...

ANSWERS

1. Creed. 2. A foreigner, especially one from middle Europe. 3. To grow or increase. 4. To shrink or decrease in size. 5. The cloth called 'damask'. 6. Ten dollars. 7. Botanist. 8. Dusty. 9. Astronomer. 10. An undertaker. 11. It should read, 'One should always do one's best'. 12. World Meteorological Organisation. 13. A woman whose husband is much occupied outside and apart from the domestic scene. 14. A wartime traitor (after Vidkun Quisling, the Norwegian traitor). 15. You'd ask for underpants.

SESSION 15
QUIZ 2

1. From which country does Tae Kwon Do originate?
2. Name the four competition swimming strokes?
3. How many players are there in a Water Polo team?
4. Who was the youngest man ever to win a singles title at Wimbledon?
5. What is the height of a Badminton net; 4ft 9ins, 5ft 1in, 5ft 4ins or 5ft 9ins?
6. In TT motorcycle racing, what does TT stand for?
7. Name Detroit's American football team?
8. In Rugby Union, how many players are linked together in a scrum?
9. Who was the English goalkeeper who could not stop the 'Hand of God'?
10. In show jumping how many faults are awarded for a refusal?
11. Over which course is the Champion Hurdle run?
12. What is the shortest men's high hurdle distance in the Olympic Games?
13. In which sport would you take part in sprints and pursuits, on a track, marked with a Red Printer's line, a Stagers line and a Blue band?
14. In which sport would you compete in the Biennial World Championships in slalom, tricks and jumps events?
15. Malcolm Cooper is a British double Olympic Gold medallist at which sport?

ANSWERS

1. Korea. 2. Freestyle, Butterfly, Breaststroke, Backstroke. 3. Seven. 4. Boris Becker. 5. 5ft 1in. 6. Tourist Trophy. 7. Detroit Lions. 8. 16. 9. Peter Shilton. 10. Three. 11. Cheltenham. 12. 110m. 13. Cycling. 14. Water Skiing. 15. Small Bore Rifle Shooting.

SESSION 15

QUIZ 3

1. What opened between Paddington and Farringdon Street, London, on 10th January, 1863?
2. Who were Eva Duarte Péron and Maria Estela Péron?
3. Who was the original Nosey Parker?
4. Pizarro founded which major city in Peru in 1535?
5. In 1982, the destroyer HMS Sheffield was sunk by an Exocet missile fired by which nation?
6. Who were the greatest political enemies of late 19th-century England?
7. Which was the first monarch of the House of Tudor?
8. Which public figure made her first journey by rail on 13th June, 1842?
9. Which British prime minister was awarded the Nobel Prize for Literature?
10. What happened at Chernobyl, USSR, in April, 1986?
11. In 1972, 40,000 British Asians were expelled from which East African country and by whom?
12. Who was Engelbert Dollfuss, and how did he meet his end?
13. Who was Grover Cleveland?
14. When did Eva Perón of Argentina die?
15. Which was the first state of the USA.

ANSWERS

1. The world's first underground railway. 2. First and second wives of the Argentine general and president, Juan Domingo Péron. 3. Matthew Parker, Archbishop of Canterbury, (1504-1575). 4. Lima. 5. Argentina. 6. Benjamin Disraeli and William Gladstone. 7. Henry VII. 8. Queen Victoria. 9. Sir Winston Churchill. 10. A devastating accident occurred in the nuclear reactor there. 11. From Uganda by President Idi Amin. 12. The last pre-war Austrian Chancellor; he was murdered by the Nazis. 13. He was the 22nd American president. 14. 1952. 15. Delaware.

152

SESSION 15
QUIZ 4

1. Who starred in the film *Invasion of the Body Snatchers?*
2. Which four sister actresses appeared in the film *The Story of Alexander Graham Bell?*
3. Which American drama about oil barons included Sue Ellen, Bobby and Miss Ellie among its cast?
4. Who starred in the film *Badlands?*
5. Which movie was based on the life of middleweight boxer Jake La Motta?
6. Who played Hutch in *Starsky And Hutch?*
7. Who starred in the film *Grease?*
8. Which was the first British film to win an Oscar?
9. Who starred in the film *Double Indemnity?*
10. Which football hardman starred in the 1998 film *Lock, Stock and Two Smoking Barrels?*
11. Who starred in the film *Lethal Weapon?*
12. Who starred in the 1925 silent film *The Big Parade?*
13. What famous T.V. doctor did both Tom Baker and Jon Pertwee play?
14. Which movie star was the 'Girl With the Million-Dollar Legs?'
15. What was the name of the 8ft tall yellow canary in the T.V. show *Sesame Street?*

ANSWERS

1. Donald Sutherland, Brooke Adams, Leonard Nimoy, Jeff Goldblum.
2. Polly Ann, Georgianna, Loretta Young, and Elizabeth Jane Young, better known as Sally Blane. 3. *Dallas*. 4. Martin Sheen and Sissy Spacek. 5. *Raging Bull*. 6. David Soul. 7. John Travolta, Olivia Newton-John. 8. *The Private Life of Henry VIII*, in 1934. 9. Fred MacMurray, Barbara Stanwyck. 10. Vinnie Jones. 11. Mel Gibson, Danny Glover. 12. John Gilbert. 13. Dr. Who. 14. Betty Grable. 15. Big Bird.

SESSION 15

QUIZ 5

• •

1. Queens', 'Bohemian Rhapsody' was at number 1 for longer than any other single in the UK. True or false?
2. Who in the 1970's, did the, 'The Jukebox Jive', with their, 'Sugar Baby Love'?
3. With whom did Elton John record his first UK number 1, 'Don't Go Breaking My Heart'?
4. What nationality are The Crash test dummies?
5. Who reached number 3 in February 1980 with, 'Turning Japanese'?
6. Which band won a 'Brit' award, then handed it back when it was discovered that they mimed all their records?
7. Which group rescheduled their 1998 UK tour for tax reasons?
8. China Crisis only had one UK top ten hit, name the song?
9. Which band features Peter Buck as its lead guitarist?
10. With whom did UB40 record their number one hit, 'I Got You Babe'?
11. The Thompson Twins were a duo. True or false?
12. Which Beatle had hits in the early 1970's with, 'It Don't Come Easy', Back Off Boogaloo' and 'You're Sixteen'?
13. Whose songs include 'Tangled Up In Blue', 'All Along The Watchtower' and 'Masters Of War?
14. Who reached number one in 1992 with. 'Deeply Dippy'?
15. Which Welshman had top ten hits in 1981, with, 'This Old House', 'Green Door', and 'You Drive Me Crazy?

ANSWERS

SESSION 15

QUIZ 6

• •

1. 'I wandered lonely as a cloud' is the beginning of a poem by whom?
2. By what name is Jean-Baptiste Poquelin better known?
3. 'For fools rush in where angels fear to tread.' Where does this phrase originate?
4. What was the name of the capital of King Arthur's kingdom?
5. Who wrote the play *The School for Scandal*?
6. Complete Shelley's line: 'If winter comes, can .... be far behind?'
7. Who wrote *Love in a Cold Climate*?
8. Who wrote *The Grapes of Wrath*?
9. Who wrote *Breakfast at Tiffany's*?
10. According to Tennyson, 'In Spring a young man's fancy' does what?
11. The character 'Mrs Doasyouwouldbedoneby' appears in which famous story?
12. Which was Shakespeare's last play?
13. What had John Evelyn in common with Samuel Pepys?
14. Who created the villain 'Dr Fu Manchu'?
15. Who wrote *My Idea Of Fun*?

ANSWERS

1. William Wordsworth. 2. Molière. 3. *An Essay on Criticism*. (Pope). 4. Camelot. 5. Richard Brinsley Sheridan. 6. Spring. 7. Nancy Mitford. 8. John Steinbeck. 9. Truman Capote. 10. Lightly turns to thoughts of love'. 11. *The Water Babies*. 12. Henry VIII, written with the assistance of John Fletcher. 13. They were both diarists. 14. Sax Rohmer. 15. Will Self.

SESSION 15
QUIZ 7

• •

1. According to the 'language of flowers', what does the snowdrop signify?
2. Who is the patron saint of television?
3. What is euchre?
4. What is coleslaw?
5. What kind of food item comes from Melton Mowbray?
6. In the year 1752, what date followed 2nd September?
7. What is an agnostic?
8. What instrument did Niccolo Paganini play?
9. Which anniversary does a silk and fine linen wedding celebrate?
10. What is a referendum?
11. What is the Koran?
12. What is a male swan called?
13. Who, or what, in London, is the 'Old Bill'?
14. What is Dogget's 'Coat and Badge'?
15. To the ancient Romans, who was Jupiter?

ANSWERS

1. Hope. 2. St Clare. 3. A card game. 4. A cabbage salad. 5. Meat pies. 6. 14th September. The calendar had changed and 11 days were omitted. 7. Someone who believes that man cannot know whether God exists or not. 8. The violin. 9. The twelfth. 10. A national vote on a particular issue. 11. The sacred book of Islam. 12. A cob. 13. The Metropolitan Police. 14. A prize annually awarded to Thames watermen. 15. The god ruling all gods and men.

SESSION 15
QUIZ 8

• •

1. What is horticulture?
2. A protusion, or rupture in a weak place on the body is called a what?
3. Who invented nylon?
4. What is the study of all living things?
5. Which head of state in Israel was a biochemist?
6. The scientific study of crystals is called what?
7. What is beryl?
8. What is antimony?
9. What name is given to the shape of an ordinary round tin can?
10. Who invented instant coffee?
11. As a measure, how long is a hand?
12. What is metrology?
13. The Pole Star or North Star is sometimes called what?
14. What electrical communication system was invented in 1839?
15. What sort of shuttle was invented for the weaving industry by John Kay in 1733?

ANSWERS

1. The art of gardening. 2. Hernia. 3. Wallace H. Carothers. 4. Biology. 5. Chaim Weizmann. 6. Crystallography. 7. A precious stone: varieties of it are emerald and aquamarine. 8. A hard, brittle element of metallic appearance. 9. Cylinder. 10. The Nestlé Company of Switzerland in 1937. 11. 10 cms. 12. The science of weights and measures. 13. Polaris. 14. The telegraph. 15. A flying shuttle.

SESSION 15
QUIZ 9

• •

1. Which is Britain's largest meat-eating wild animal?
2. What is an adder?
3. What is the name given to pouched animals?
4. A condor is a type of (a) puma (b) vulture?
5. A female donkey is called (a) a jenny (b) a jill (c) a doe?
6. What animal is the domestic form of the polecat?
7. Rye is really a special kind of grass. True or false?
8. A dog sweats through its paws. True or false?
9. What is a sea-horse?
10. What is a group of bears called?
11. What is the tallest animal of all?
12. What sort of animal is a pointer?
13. What is, or was, a unicorn?
14. What sort of animal is a tigon?
15. The onion is a member of the lily family. Yes or no?

ANSWERS

1. The badger. 2. Another name for the viper. 3. Marsupials. 4. A type of vulture. 5. A jenny. 6. The ferret. 7. True. 8. True. 9. A small fish with a prehensile tail and a head something like that of horse. 10. A sloth. 11. The giraffe. 12. A dog. 13. It never existed, but was believed to be a horse-like animal with a single horn on its forehead. 14. The offspring of a lion and a tigress. 15. Yes.

SESSION 15

QUIZ 10

• •

1. Where is the Orange River?
2. Where and what is Manhattan?
3. Which is Scotland's longest river?
4. The daffodil is the national symbol for which country?
5. The chrysanthemum is the national symbol for which country?
6. Lusitania is the old name for what?
7. England has two Newcastles. One is 'upon Tyne'. What is the other?
8. What is the old country of Bohemia now called?
9. Burma is now called what?
10. Where and what was Lyonesse?
11. Where and what was Bernicia?
12. Where does the River Thames rise?
13. What is the capital of Iceland?
14. What is the name of the underground railway system in Rome?
15. Where would you find an Elephant and Castle?

ANSWERS

1. South Africa. 2. It's an island at the centre of New York City. 3. The Tay. 4. Wales. 5. Japan. 6. Portugal. 7. Newcastle-under-Lyme. 8. Staffordshire. 8. The Czech Republic. 9. Myanmar. 10. A mythical 'lost' land connecting Cornwall and the Scilly Isles. 11. An ancient kingdom in northern England between the Tyne and the Forth. 12. In the Cotswold Hills. 13. Reykjavik. 14. La Metropolitana. 15. In South London; it's a major junction, and formerly the name of a pub.

159

SESSION 16
QUIZ 1

1. In Luge Tobogganing do competitors travel feet or head first?
2. Name Boston's NBA Basketball team?
3. What is the aim of a Puissance show jumping event?
4. Who is the youngest man ever to play football for England at full international level?
5. In cricket what was originally in Dorset Square, then where Marylebone station currently stands and is now in St John's Wood?
6. In Rounders, what is awarded if the bowler delivers three 'no-balls'?
7. At which sporting event would you have a 'Barrel Man', hold a 'Cinch', have a 'Hang-up' and sit in a 'Shute box'?
8. At which racetrack is the 2000 Guineas run?
9. Name the variant of Lawn Bowls predominantly played in the North of England?
10. What is the official distance for a Marathon?
11. Name Maclaren's two drivers for the 1998 season?
12. What is the sport of Modern Pentathlon supposed to be mimicking?
13. Over which course is the Prix de l'Arc de Triomphe run?
14. Name Toronto's Baseball team?
15. Which footballer was credited with the 'Hand of God' in the 1986 World Cup?

ANSWERS

1. Feet first. 2. Celtics. 3. To jump higher than anyone else. 4. Michael Owen. 5. Lord's Cricket Ground. 6. Half-Rounder. 7. Rodeo. 8. Newmarket. 9. Crown Green Bowls. 10. 26miles 385yds (42.2km). 11. Mikka Hakkinen & David Coulthard. 12. The journey of a Kings messenger through enemy territory. 13. Longchamps. 14. Blue Jays. 15. Diego Maradona.

SESSION 16
QUIZ 2

• •

1. Who was the last monarch of Russia?
2. The disputes in Cyprus are largely due to the quarrels between which two peoples?
3. What disaster caused the Tay Bridge, Scotland, to collapse in December, 1879?
4. How long did King Edward VIII reign: (a) 10 months (b) 7 months (c) 14 months?
5. The foundation stone of which great bank was laid in August, 1732?
6. What mode of transport came to London in 1836?
7. What, in 1858, was the Miracle of Lourdes?
8. In 1856, the trekking Boers in South Africa set up an independent republic called what?
9. A German banker, whose first names were Meyer Amschel, founded a famous company in Frankfurt. What was his surname?
10. In 1894, what innovation in shipping routes was opened in Lancashire?
11. Which national newspaper did Sir Arthur Pearson found in 1900?
12. Who were the Desert Rats?
13. Who was the legendary Prester John?
14. Which daily newspaper went on sale in 1896 at a price of fid (a halfpenny)?
15. What was the Black Hole of Calcutta?

ANSWERS

1. Nicholas II. 2. Greeks and Turks. 3. A tornado struck the area, and 75 people were killed. 4. (a) 10 months. 5. The Bank of England. 6. Steam trains, from London Bridge to Deptford. 7. When St Bernadette is believed to have had a vision of the Virgin. 8. Transvaal. 9. Rothschild. 10. The Manchester Ship Canal. 11. *The Daily Express.* 12. The British 7th Armoured Division in North Africa. 13. A Christian priest and king. 14. *The Daily Mail.* 15. In 1756, the Nawab of Bengal imprisoned 146 people in a tiny cellar, and only 23 survived the night.

SESSION 16
QUIZ 3

• •

1. From which stage show did the song 'I'm Forever Blowing Bubbles' come?
2. What film starred Will Smith and Tommy Lee Jones as alien hunters?
3. Who starred in the film *The Godfather*?
4. How much did Jim Rockford charge as a private investigator in *The Rockford Files*?
5. Who starred in the film *Red River*?
6. From which film and stage show did the song 'Indian Love Call' come?
7. If it was Friday and five o'clock, what used to be on BBC TV?
8. What was noteworthy about the 1926 silent film *The Black Pirate*?
9. From which film and stage show did the song 'It Ain't Necessarily So' come?
10. What part did Jerry Lacey play in the film *Play It Again, Sam*?
11. Who starred in the film *The Card*?
12. Which movie star was 'The Hunk'?
13. What or who was 'Genevieve' in the film of the same name?
14. In which Disney film did two dogs share spaghetti at an Italian café?
15. Who directed the film *Mississippi Burning*?

ANSWERS

1. The US production, *The Passing Show of 1918*. 2. *Men In Black*. 3. Marlon Brando. 4. 200 dollars a day plus expenses. 5. John Wayne, Montgomery Clift. 6. *Rose Marie*. 7. *Crackerjack*. 8. It was in Technicolor. 9. *Porgy and Bess*. 10. Humphrey Bogart. 11. Alec Guinness. 12. Victor Mature. 13. A vintage car. 14. *The Lady And The Tramp*. 15. Alan Parker.

SESSION 16
QUIZ 4

• •

1. What nationality is singer Bjork?
2. Who's top ten hit's include, 'Animal Nitrate', 'Metal Mickey' and 'Film Star'?
3. Who reached number 1 in the 1960's with, 'Make It Easy On Yourself' and 'The Sun Ain't Gonna Shine anymore'?
4. Simon Le Bon was lead singer with which New Romantic band'?
5. Barbara Streisand's number 1 hit, 'Evergreen', was the theme song from which film?
6. Which band did John Lydon (Aka Johnny Rotten) form after the break up of the Sex Pistols?
7. American band, The Presidents of the United States of America, once played the Democratic convention in support of the real President, Bill Clinton. True or false?
8. Bobby 'Boris' Pickett and the Crypt-Kickers reached number 3 in 1973 with which tongue-in-cheek horror song?
9. Which Michael Jackson video did Lenny Henry record a spoof of for the BBC in 1983?
10. Who reached number 2 in 1970 and number 8 in 1991 with, 'All Right Now'?
11. Who sang, 'Things Can Only Get Better', in 1994?
12. Which cockney singer had top ten hits in the 1960's with, 'A picture Of You', 'That's What Love Will Do' and 'It Only Took A Minute'?
13. Who recorded, 'Who Killed Bambi', on the flip side of the Sex Pistol's, 'Silly Thing'?
14. 'The Bomb! (These Sounds Fall Into My Mind)' was a number 5 hit in 1995 for which Producer/artist/group?
15. Smokey Robinson reached number 1 in 1981 with, 'Being With You'. He had previously held that position with, 'Tears Of A Clown', as the front man of which band?

ANSWERS

1. Icelandic. 2. Suede. 3. The Walker Brothers. 4. Duran Duran. 5. 'A Star Is Born'. 6. Public Image Ltd. 7. True. 8. 'Monster Mash'. 9. 'Thriller' 10. Free. 11 . D:Ream 12. Joe Brown (and the Bruvvers) 13. Tenpole Tudor 14. The Bucketheads (Kenny Gonzales). 15. Smokey Robinson and the Miracles

163

SESSION 16
QUIZ 5

1. 'When I consider how my life is spent' is the beginning of a poem by whom?
2. Who wrote *Gigi*?
3. Whose autobiography is entitled *Life on the Mississippi*?
4. Who wrote *Farewell, My Lovely*?
5. Complete the proverb: 'Cut your coat...'
6. Which children's book did Richard Adams write?
7. 'Bilbo Baggins' is a character in which two books?
8. Which poet wrote *A Shropshire Lad*?
9. Who wrote the classic novel *Madame Bovary*?
10. How did Lord Acton complete this line: 'Power tends to corrupt, and absolute power .....
11. Who originated the phrase, 'Big Brother is watching you'
12. Which novel by Charles Dickens was left unfinished?
13. What was the occupation of Johann Christoph Friedrich von Schiller?
14. The character 'Sexton Blake' had an American counterpart. Name him.
15. Complete the line, 'Laugh, and the world laughs with you, weep...'

ANSWERS

1. John Milton. 2. Colette. 3. Mark Twain's. 4. Raymond Chandler. 5. '...according to your cloth'. 6. *Watership Down*. 7. *The Hobbit* and *Lord of the Rings*. 8. A.E. Housman. 9. Gustave Flaubert. 10. ...corrupts absolutely. 11. George Orwell in his book *1984*. 12. *The Mystery of Edwin Drood*. 13. He was a German playwright and poet. 14. Nick Carter. 15. 'and you weep alone'.

● ●

1. What is couscous?
2. Who is the reigning monarch of Spain?
3. St Agatha is the patron saint of whom?
4. The American cartoonist Chester Gould conceived which character?
5. Which day is the Muslim Sabbath?
6. A Frenchman referring to 'trèfles, carreaux, piques, et coeurs' would be speaking of what?
7. According to the 'language of flowers', what does the veronica signify?
8. Sir William Alexander Smith founded what boys' organisation?
9. Some extra books to the Bible are called the Apocrypha. How many are there?
10. Whose capital is Edinburgh (apart from Scotland!)?
11. What is nougat?
12. What does the Beaufort Scale measure?
13. Who was 'Tricky Dicky'?
14. Which tribal chieftain in Europe became president and later, king of his country?
15. What is a prune?

ANSWERS

1. A cereal dish of cracked grain or semolina. 2. Juan Carlos. 3. Nurses. 4. Dick Tracy. 5. Friday. 6. The suits of playing-cards. 7. Fidelity. 8. The Boys' Brigade. 9. Fifteen (all Old Testament). 10. Tristan da Cunha. 11. A sweetmeat, of a sweet paste filled with chopped nuts. 12. Wind. 13. US President Richard Nixon. 14. Zog of Albania. 15. A dried plum.

165

SESSION 16
QUIZ 7

1. An expert in codes and ciphers would be called what?
2. What important navigational device did John Bird invent in 1757?
3. What is an insecticide?
4. Who was Sir Richard Arkwright?
5. How many moons does the planet Jupiter have; (a) 12 (b) 10 (c) 8?
6. What did Henry Ford invent which helped build his Model T Ford more quickly and cheaply?
7. What is a vacuum?
8. What is the difference between a biretta and a beretta?
9. What was the name of the first manned spacecraft?
10. What is the name for a unit of heat?
11. In which year did Marie Curie win a Nobel Prize?
12. Christopher Latham Sholes invented what was called 'a literary piano' in 1870. What was it?
13. What is 'white metal'?
14. What odourless, inflammable gas was discovered in 1766 by Henry Cavendish?
15. What is Canopus?

ANSWERS

1. A cryptologist. 2. The sextant. 3. A substance which kills insects. 4. Inventor and industrial leader. 5. Twelve. 6. The modern production assembly line. 7. A space containing absolutely nothing. 8. The first is a cap worn by a priest, and the second is a small pistol. 9. Vostok 1. 10. A therm. 11. 1911. 12. The first practical typewriter. 13. An alloy of lead, tin, antimony and copper. 14. Hydrogen. 15. The second brightest star in the sky.

SESSION 16
QUIZ 8

· ·

1. What is a wallaby?
2. What kind of animal is said to grunt?
3. Rice is really a special kind of grass. True or false?
4. What is a juniper?
5. Which of the following animals belongs to the Equidae family; zebra, wild ass or pony?
6. What is an octopus?
7. Which is the world's most poisonous snake?
8. Is it true that elephants are afraid of mice?
9. What kind of animal is said to caw?
10. What is a locust?
11. Which bird has the widest wing-spread known as a span?
12. What is another name for veronica?
13. What sort of animal is a Sealyham?
14. What is the name of the dog- or fox-like wild creatures similar to wolves?
15. What was a cockatrice?

ANSWERS

1. A kind of small kangaroo. 2. A pig. 3. True. 4. An evergreen shrub or tree with sharp, prickle-pointed leaves. 5. The horse. 6. An eight-legged sea creature. 7. The tiger snake, a kind of cobra, found in Australia. 8. No. 9. A crow. 10. The word is used for two quite different things; an insect like a large grasshopper, and a vegetable called the locust-bean. 11. The albatross, whose spread is about 3-4 metres. 12. Speedwell. 13. A breed of dog. 14. Jackals. 15. A mythical monster in the form of a serpent.

SESSION 16
QUIZ 9

• •

1. How many Scilly Isles are there; 14, 40 or 140?
2. On which river does New Orleans stand?
3. What did Florentine navigator, Amerigo Vespucci, gave his name to?
4. What is the capital of Afghanistan?
5. Which town lies at the very centre of Australia?
6. The Great St Bernard Pass is between which two countries?
7. Where in the world do they speak Navajo?
8. Where in the world would you find the Catacombs?
9. What exactly are the Catacombs?
10. Which Belgian city stands where the River Schelde flows into the sea?
11. To whom do the Virgin Islands belong?
12. Which city is on the Rio de la Plata river?
13. What, in London, is known as the 'Ally Pally'?
14. Where would you find Hadrian's Wall?
15. What is the highest mountain in Britain?

ANSWERS

1. About 140. 2. The Mississippi. 3. America. 4. Kabul. 5. Alice Springs. 6. Switzerland and Italy. 7. In the US amongst the largest Indian tribe. 8. In Rome. 9. Underground passages with shelves for tombs. 10. Antwerp. 11. There are two groups: one American and the other British. 12. Buenos Aires. 13. Alexandra Palace, in the north of London. 14. At the north of England, by the Scottish border. 15. Ben Nevis in Scotland.

• •

1. What does an American mean by a 'faucet'?
2. How many sides does a polygon have?
3. What's the male version of a 'sorceress'?
4. What is a back-bencher?
5. What is the plural of 'roof'?
6. What does the old word 'Tarry' mean?
7. Which word has replaced 'Wont'?
8. What are the two meanings of digest?
9. 'Any one of us could be right'. 'Anyone of us could be right'. Which of these two sentences is correct?
10. What do the initials, RAC stand for?
11. What is the phrase, 'Live on, Time, emit no evil' an example of?
12. What was a zoot-suit?
13. What would you do with a 'black velvet'?
14. What does an American call a 'dinner jacket'?
15. A leading person in sport is named after what playing-card?

ANSWERS

1. A tap. 2. Many. 3. Sorcerer. 4. An MP who has no official government post. 5. Roofs. 6. Linger. 7. Habit, as in 'as is my wont'. 8. (a) a noun meaning a summary (b) a verb meaning to assimilate. 9. The first one. 10. Royal Automobile Club. 11. A palindrome (a word or phrase which reads the same backwards and forwards). 12. A former high-fashion suit with a long coat and tight trousers. 13. Drink it. It's a mixture of stout and champagne. 14. A tuxedo. 15. Ace.

SESSION 17
QUIZ 1

1. Which European country overthrew its monarchy and became a republic on 5th October, 1910?
2. Gold diggers in Ballarat, Australia, died in a clash with troops in 1854. What was the conflict called?
3. During the last war, what was an 'Anderson'?
4. What started in California in 1848?
5. The early Roman historian Flavius Josephus, wrote a history of which people?
6. Who was married at the Château de Candé, Touraine, on 3rd June, 1937?
7. Who was Aristophanes?
8. The cousin of the American president Theodore Roosevelt also became president. Who was he?
9. Who was Yuri Alekseyevich Gagarin?
10. What was unique about HMS Dreadnought, launched by the Queen in 1960?
11. Which English queen is said to have had six fingers on one hand?
12. Which queen of England was bald at the age of 31?
13. On 2nd July, 1858, Disraeli and Gladstone felt unwell in House of Commons. Why?
14. What did the Jameson Raid into the Transvaal on 29 December, 1895 lead to?
15. What is the Bayeux Tapestry?

ANSWERS

1. Portugal. 2. The Eureka Stockade. 3. An air raid shelter. 4. The Gold Rush. 5. The Jews. 6. The Duke of Windsor and Wallis Simpson. 7. A Greek playwright and poet. 8. Franklin Delano Roosevelt. 9. A pioneer Russian cosmonaut. 10. It was Britain's first nuclear submarine. 11. Anne Boleyn. 12. Queen Elizabeth I. 13. They were overcome by the terrible smell from the River Thames. 14. The outbreak of the Boer War. 15. A long, embroidered cloth telling the story of the Norman Conquest.

SESSION 17
QUIZ 2

1. Who directed and starred in the film *Citizen Kane?*
2. What British city was *The Full Monty* set in?
3. Who starred in the film *The Colditz Story?*
4. In which cartoon film is the kingdom of Pepperland attacked by the Blue Meanies?
5. Which game show host coined the catchphrases, 'Nice to see you, to see you nice' and 'Let's have a look at the old scoreboard'?
6. What show starred the 'Fonz' and Mr Cunningham?
7. Who starred in the film *The African Queen?*
8. Who played Princess Leah in the Star Wars trilogy?
9. From which film and stage show did the song 'Oh, What a Beautiful Mornin' come?
10. Who won the best actress Oscar for her role in *Dead Man Walking?*
11. The part of a famous film comedian was played by Buddy Doyle in *The Great Ziegfeld.* Who?
12. From which film and stage show did the song 'Ol' Man River' come?
13. Which actor needed to lose his dirty raincoat to star in *A Woman Under the Influence?*
14. What film featured a malevolent computer called HAL?
15. The part of which actress was played by Faye Dunaway in Mommie Dearest?

ANSWERS

1. Orson Welles. 2. Sheffield. 3. John Mills. 4. *The Yellow Submarine.*
5. Bruce Forsythe. 6. *Happy Days.* 7. Humphrey Bogart, Katharine Hepburn. 8. Carrie Fisher. 9. Oklahoma! 10. Susan Sarandon. 11. Eddie Cantor. 12. *Show Boat.* 13. Peter Falk. 14. *2001: A Space Odyssey.*
15. Joan Crawford.

SESSION 17
QUIZ 3

1. Which Cockneys had top ten hits with, 'Rabbit', 'Ain't No Pleasing You', and 'Snooker Loopy'?
2. Who recorded the album, 'Mr Bad Guy'?
3. Who recorded the album, 'Joshua Tree'?
4. Which feline band had top ten hits with, 'Runaway Boys', and 'Rock This Town'?
5. What type of music did, The Specials, The Beat, and Selector, play?
6. In 1998 which band implored Scotland's football team, 'Don't Come Home Too Soon'?
7. What was Madness's first top ten hit?
8. Which Hawaiian reached number 1 in Jun 1988 with, 'Nothing's Gonna Change My Love For You'?
9. What is the best selling single of all time?
10. The Bluebells reached number 1 with which song over 8 years after it's first release?
11. Which group recorded 11 number 1 hits in a row between 1963-1966?
12. What nationality is heavyweight singer Demis Roussos?
13. Who was the lead vocalist with Roxy Music?
14. Which band was Ozzy Osbourne the lead singer of?
15. In 1982 Musical Youth reached number 1 with, 'Pass The Dutchie'. What is a 'Dutchie'?

ANSWERS

1. Chas & Dave. 2. Freddie Mercury. 3. U2. 4. The Stray Cats. 5. Ska
6. Del Amitri 7. 'One Step Beyond'. 8. Glen Medeiros. 9. 'Candle In The
Wind 97' (Elton John). 10. 'Young At Heart'. 11. The Beatles. 12. Greek.
13. Brian Ferry. 14. Black Sabbath. 15. A Jamaican cooking pot.

SESSION 17
QUIZ 4

• •

1. Complete the proverb: 'Circumstances...'
2. William Harrison Ainsworth wrote many books with titles like *Jack Sheppard* and *Windsor Castle*. Name two more.
3. 'Margot Beste-Chetwynde' appears in which book by Evelyn Waugh?
4. 'He thought he saw an Elephant,/That practised on a fife:' is the beginning of a poem by whom?
5. *A Journey to the Centre of the Earth* was written by which author?
6. Who wrote The Red Badge of Courage?
7. In which Shakespeare play does the 'Duke Orsino' appear?
8. What was the name of the fictional Australian mixed race detective?
9. What line follows, 'Shall I compare thee to a summer's day?'
10. Who wrote *1984?*
11. Who wrote *Black Narcissus?*
12. Who created 'Philip Trent', appearing in the book *Trent's Last Case?*
13 For what form of verse was this author also famed?
14. What line follows, 'Tiger! Tiger! burning bright'?
15. What line follows, 'The rich man in his castle'?

ANSWERS

1. '...after cases.' 2. *Guy Fawkes, The Tower of London, Old St Paul's.*
3. *Decline and Fall.* 4. Lewis Carroll. 5. Jules Verne. 6. Stephen Crane.
7. *Twelfth Night.* 8. Inspector Napoleon Bonaparte. 9. 'Thou art more lovely and more temperate.' 10. George Orwell. 11. Rumer Godden.
12. E.C. Bentley. 13. The invention of the nonsense rhymes called 'clerihews'. 14. 'In the forests of the night'. 15. 'The poor man at his gate'.

173

• •

1. A German referring to 'Herzen, Schellen, Grün und Eicheln' would be speaking of what?
2. What Italian artist was also an architect, philosopher, poet, composer, sculptor and mathematician?
3. To what did Buncombe, North Carolina, give its name?
4. Mercury is another name for the messenger of the gods Hermes. True or false?
5. What did Catherine II of Russia and Peter I of Russia have in common?
6. How old is the card game of Whist?
7. Which is the holy city of Hindus?
8. If something is held 'in camera', what does it mean?
9. What is béarnaise?
10. What is the Devil's Picture-book?
11. Composed of what group does one find a bevy?
12. Who was Sir Stafford Cripps?
13. What animal's name do the Chinese give to the year 1999?
14. Thursday is named after Thor, the German god of thunder. True or false?
15. Sunday is named after the Sun. True or false?

ANSWERS

1. German playing-cards with Hearts, Bells, Leaves and Acorns as suits. 2. Leonardo da Vinci. 3. Bunkum, or nonsense. 4. True. 5. They were both known by the title 'The Great'. 6. It dates from the eighteenth century. 7. Benares. 8. With the public as a whole excluded. 9. A sauce made with egg-yolks, butter, shallots, tarragon and vinegar. 10. A pack of playing-cards. 11. Girls, beauty, larks, quails, swans. 12. British Labour statesman and Chancellor of the Exchequer. 13. The year of the Hare. 14. True. 15. True.

SESSION 17
QUIZ 6

• •

1. What was the Tin Lizzie, introduced in the USA in 1908?
2. What is oreology?
3. Pneumatic machines are driven by what?
4. The study of living things in relation to their environment is called what?
5. What was, or is, a quadrant?
6. What is agate?
7. What is anthrax?
8. Nitrogen is the main constituent of air. True or false?
9. The science relating to the flow of fluids is called what?
10. What was the aircraft called which had a rotary wing and was flown before the first helicopter?
11. An advanced system of electric lighting was invented in 1840 by Sir William Grove. What was it?
12. What device, valuable to miners, did Sir Humphry Davy invent in 1815?
13. The study of matter and energy is called what?
14. Joseph Priestley discovered one of the most important of gases in 1774. What was it?
15. The condensing steam engine was invented by which famous Scotsman in 1765?

ANSWERS

1. The Ford Model T. 2. The scientific study of mountains. 3. Compressed gases, often air. 4. Ecology. 5. An instrument for measuring the altitude of heavenly bodies. 6. A hard silica. 7. A bacterial disease of cattle which can be passed to man. 8. True. 9. Hydraulics. 10. The autogyro or autogiro. 11. The incandescent electric light. 12. The miner's safety lamp. 13. Physics. 14. Oxygen. 15. James Watt.

SESSION 17
QUIZ 7

• •

1. A male horse aged five or more is called a what?
2. What do ruminant animals do?
3. What is a cuttlefish?
4. A group of rhinoceroses is called a crash, a ring or a horn?
5. What sort of animal is a Corgi?
6. What is another name for the heartsease?
7. What is a yew?
8. Would a green rag upset a bull if you waved it?
9. What record does the humming-bird, about 5cms long, hold?
10. What is sesame?
11. The capybara is the largest rodent in the world, and comes from...?
12. A group of partridges is called (a) a covey (b) a pride.
13. What film cartoon character chased Tweetie-Pie?
14. What sort of animal is a caracal?
15. What is scarlet pimpernel?

ANSWERS

1. A stallion. 2. Chew the cud. 3. A mollusc able to squirt a dense sepia-coloured fluid. 4. A crash. 5. A breed of dog. 6. The wild pansy. 7. An evergreen tree often used as a garden hedge. 8. No more than a red one. Bulls are colour-blind. 9. It's the world's smallest bird. 10. A plant whose seeds are used for making oils, or for food. 11. South America. 12. A covey. 13. Sylvester, the cat. 14. A wild cat known as the Persian lynx. 15. A small wild plant of the primrose family with scarlet flowers.

SESSION 17

QUIZ 8

• •

1. Which city is on the Tigris river?
2. Which is the world's largest waterfall?
3. What is the Sirocco?
4. 'Auld Reekie' is a familiar name for which city?
5. Which is the largest island in the world?
6. What would you find at Princeton, Dartmoor, in Devon?
7. What is British Honduras now called?
8. What mysterious objects are to be found on Easter Island in the Pacific?
9. Caledonia was the name given by the Romans to what?
10. What was known to the Romans as 'Cambria'?
11. Which is the tallest building in Britain?
12. Where in the world would you find a Mancunian?
13. What is the Dardanelles?
14. After Paris, which is the largest French-speaking city?
15. Canton is a former name for which Chinese city?

ANSWERS

1. Baghdad. 2. Boyoma Falls, Congo. 3. A hot wind which blows from the Sahara over the North Mediterranean coasts. 4. Edinburgh. 5. Greenland. 6. Dartmoor Prison. 7. Belize. 8. Huge stone statues of human heads. 9. Scotland. 10. Wales. 11. Canary Wharf Tower, in east London. 12. In Manchester. 13. A narrow strait in Turkey which divides Europe and Asia. 14. Montreal, Canada. 15. Guangzhou.

• •

1. What is a quid pro quo?
2. Can you name two words sounding alike which mean the same as this pair of phrases: song of praise/male of 'her'?
3. Can you make a Gilbert and Sullivan title out of the anagram 'name for ship'?
4. What were 'bright young things'?
5. What is the meaning of 'prognosticate'?
6. In American English, what is a shnook?
7. A limousine is a kind of car, but what does the word actually mean?
8. What happens if 'you cut off your nose to spite your face'?
9. What does an American mean by a 'realtor'?
10. What does the word 'pianoforte' mean?
11. What is the difference between a scholar and a pupil?
12. A valise, to an American, is what to a Briton?
13. What is a tram called in the United States?
14. What was a 'gentleman's gentleman'?
15. How did the word 'lampoon' originate?

ANSWERS

1. 'Something for something'; a kind of retaliation. 2. Hymn/him. 3. *HMS Pinafore*. 4. Upper-class socialites of the 1920s and 1930s. 5. To foretell. 6. Someone completely put upon, and totally naïve. 7. A cloak. 8. You do something in anger which is actually going to do you more harm. 9. An estate agent. 10. A piano, but the word originally means 'soft and strong'. 11. A scholar is a learned person; a pupil is someone being taught. 12. A suitcase. 13. A streetcar. 14. A high-class valet. 15. From the Old French word 'lampon', meaning a kind of drinking song.

SESSION 17

QUIZ 10

• •

1. How many players are there on an, 'Aussie Rules' football team?
2. How long is an American football pitch?
3. On what surface is the game of, 'Bandy', played?
4. Which is usually smaller, a Rugby League ball or a Rugby Union ball?
5. Which sport would I be taking part in if I were competing in, The Scottish Six Days Trial?
6. Starting in Paris, where does the world famous rally finish?
7. Where do the, 'Mets', Baseball team come from?
8. Over which course is the St Leger run?
9. Which Arsenal Goalkeeper missed the 1973 FA Cup Final, due to a broken leg, and later became a commentator first on the BBC, then ITV?
10. Wayne Gretzky having scored more than 2000 points in under 850 games, is regarded as one of the greatest exponents of which sport?
11. In Netball what do the initials WD stand for?
12. In the mid-1980s, the Birmingham super prix was raced, Monte Carlo style around the streets of the city. What class of cars were raced?
13. When was the MCC founded; 1787, 1790, 1801 or 1821?
14. How many players are there in an outdoor Field Hockey team?
15. How heavy is a Hammer in athletics; 12lb, 14lb, 16lb or 18lb?

ANSWERS

1. Eighteen. 2. 100yds. 3. Ice. 4. Rugby League Ball. 5. Motorcycle Trials Riding. 6. Dakar. 7. New York. 8. Doncaster. 9. Bob Wilson. 10. Ice Hockey. 11. Wing Defence. 12. Formula 3000. 13. 1787. 14. Eleven. 15. 16lb.

SESSION 18
QUIZ 1

• •

1. Who starred in the film *The Blue Lamp?*
2. Who was the female lead in the film *Top Gun?*
3. Which film actress was born in Brussels, and was the daughter of a Dutch baroness?
4. When were the Oscars first held: 1928, 1932 or 1936?
5. From which film and stage show did the song 'America' come?
6. What was the first programme to be shown on Channel 4?
7. What is wrong with the cartoon film character Gerald McBoing Boing?
8. Who starred in the film *Mission Impossible?*
9. From which film and stage show did the song 'Big Spender' come?
10. Who starred in the 1939 film *The Four Feathers?*
11. Which American 'black-face' singer was born in St Petersburg?
12. Who is Emilio Estevez's father?
13. Name the ex-Blue Peter presenter who hosted 'The Money Programme'?
14. Who starred in the film *Show Boat?*
15. Who was Dick Dastardly's canine sidekick?

ANSWERS

SESSION 18
QUIZ 2

• •

1. Where did the band, The Long Pigs, get their name?
2. Who reached number 1 in 1957 with, 'Great Balls Of Fire'?
3. John Lennon reached number 1 in July 1969 with, 'Give Peace A Chance'. Under the name of which band did he record the song?
4. In 1984 who sang, 'Girls Just Want To Have Fun'?
5. In August 1992 K.D. Lang recorded, 'Crying', which reached number 13. With whom did she record the song?
6. Jamiroquai entered the top 10 with, 'Stillness In Time', in which year?
7. Which British band had top ten hits in the 1980's with, 'Ghosts' and 'I Second That Emotion'?
8. Which was the first Beatle to have a solo number 1?
9. Rolf Harris's number 1 hit, 'Two little boys', was released in 1969. When was the song written; 1903, 1921, 1950 or 1968?
10. Name INXS's lead singer who tragically died in 1997?
11. With which band did Stephen Jones reach number 3 in 1996 singing, 'You're Gorgeous'?
12. In the Beatles, which instrument did Paul McCartney usually play?
13. If Sting was the Bassist, and Andy Summers was the guitarist, who was the drummer?
14. Who was the lead singer with Punk band The Damned?
15. Who performed the lead vocals on the Sex Pistols', 'No One Is Innocent' which reached number 7 in July 1978?

ANSWERS

1. The term used by cannibals to describe human flesh. 2. Jerry Lee Lewis. 3. The Plastic Ono band. 4. Cyndi Lauper. 5. Roy Orbison. 6. 1995. 7. Japan 8. George Harrison. 9. 1903. 10. Michael Hutchence. 11. Baby Bird. 12. Bass Guitar. 3. Stuart Copeland. 14. Dave Vanian. 15. Ronnie Biggs.

SESSION 18
QUIZ 3

• •

1. Who wrote *The Scarlet Letter?*
2. 'Clyde Griffiths' was the leading character in which book by Theodore Dreiser?
3. Who created the fictional detective 'Inspector French'?
4. Who created the fictional gentleman adventurer 'Bulldog Drummond'?
5. Complete the line: 'O what a tangled web we weave, when first we...'
6. Complete Browning's line: 'God's in his heaven...'
7. Who was Sir John Betjeman?
8. Who wrote the poem *The Dong with a Luminous Nose?*
9. Who was the young heroine found in Eleanor Hodgman Porter's children's books?
10. The character 'Mr Pecksniff' appears in which book by Charles Dickens?
11. In which Shakespeare play does the character 'Portia' appear?
12. Which famous children's book did Arthur Ransome write?
13. What was mysterious about the diary of Samuel Pepys?
14. Where and what was 'Shangri-la'?
15. The character 'Dolly Varden' appears in which famous book?

ANSWERS

1. Nathaniel Hawthorne. 2. *An American Tragedy.* 3. Freeman Wills Crofts. 4. H.C. McNeile. 5. '...practise to deceive.' According to Sir Walter Scott. 6. 'All's right with the world.' 7. English writer and poet laureate. 8. Edward Lear. 9. Pollyanna. 10. *Martin Chuzzlewit.* 11. *The Merchant of Venice.* 12. *Swallows and Amazons.* 13. It was written in a special code and not deciphered until 1825. 14. An ideal community, featured in the book *Lost Horizon,* by James Hilton. 15. *Barnaby Rudge.*

• •

1. In a pack of cards, which way does the Jack of Diamonds look, to his left, or to his right?
2. What is a vol au vent?
3. Which close relative of the onion has a similar, but more delicate flavour?
4. Which anniversary does a golden wedding celebrate?
5. What is the sixth sign of the Zodiac?
6. What, as a game, is Chemin de Fer?
7. Which anniversary does an iron or sugar-candy wedding celebrate?
8. What was a 'doughboy'?
9. What was a 'mae-west'?
10. Who in the world would be called a 'Pom' or 'Pommie'?
11. The crab represents which sign of the Zodiac?
12. What is the Society of Friends?
13. St Jude is the patron saint of what?
14. What is a macaroon?
15. Which word, beginning with post- means 'someone who studies after graduating'.

ANSWERS

1. To his left. 2. Very light puff pastry with room for a filling. 3. The leek. 4. The fiftieth. 5. Virgo. 6. A card game, mainly for gamblers. 7. The sixth. 8. An American soldier. 9. An inflatable life-jacket. 10. An Englishman, according to an Australian. 11. Cancer. 12. Another name for the Quakers. 13. Lost causes. 14. A sweet biscuit made with almonds. 15. Postgraduate.

SESSION 18
QUIZ 5

• •

1. In 1891, two Frenchmen decided to place the engine of their motor-car in what new position?
2. In 1913, Nathaniel Wales invented a now-indispensable kitchen storage device. What was it?
3. Brass is an alloy of which two metals?
4. Biology is the study of what?
5. What does 'argentine' mean?
6. The science and technology of extracting metals from their ores is called what?
7. With what device are Paul Nipkow and John Logie Baird associated?
8. George Graham invented a device for regulating clocks in 1721. What was it?
9. Alfred Nobel, who founded the Peace Prizes, invented what in 1866?
10. What does WWW stand for?
11. Duralumin is an alloy of which three metals?
12. What is ammonia?
13. What did Samuel Colt invent in1836?
14. What machine for easier travel took its modern form in 1878?
15. In Roman numerals, what is D?

ANSWERS

SESSION 18
QUIZ 6

• •

1. Is it possible for a bird to have teeth?
2. What kind of animal could be described as a Yorkshire White?
3. What is an onager?
4. Which creature lives in an eyrie?
5. What is another name for the filbert?
6. What is an alligator?
7. What is a crab-apple?
8. What is a spaniel?
9. What is the name for an insect-eating animal covered with sharp spines?
10. What is a prawn?
11. What is vanilla?
12. What is a mussel?
13. What is a polliwog?
14. What is a bittern?
15. What kind of animal could be described as a Large White?

ANSWERS

1. No modern bird does, but the prehistoric bird-like Archaeopteryx certainly had teeth. 2. A breed of pig. 3. The wild ass of Central Asia. 4. An eagle. 5. The hazelnut. 6. A crocodile-like reptile mainly found in America. 7. A small, wild, bitter apple. 8. A breed of dog. 9. A hedgehog. 10. A shrimp-like crustacean. 11. A flavouring substance obtained from the pods of a Mexican climbing orchid. 12. A shellfish, still highly prized as food. 13. A tadpole. 14. A bird similar to the heron family but with a shorter neck. 15. A breed of pig.

• •

1. What is the United States' busiest airport?
2. What is Britain's second most populous city?
3. Havana is the capital of which country?
4. Aix-la-Chapelle is the French name for the German city of...?
5. Where in the world would you find Buenos Aires?
6. 'België' or 'Belgique' refers to which country?
7. In New York City, streets are divided into East and West by what avenue?
8. The rose is the national symbol for which country?
9. Which city is on the River Seine?
10. What would you expect to find in The Temple, London?
11. Which English county, having been 'abolished', is now 'alive' again?
12. What is the country of Siam now called?
13. What is the Wash, and where is it?
14. What is the tallest structure in the United Kingdom?
15. What is the Bosphorus?

ANSWERS

1. O'Hare Airport. 2. Birmingham. 3. Cuba. 4. Aachen. 5. Argentina. 6. Belgium. 7. Fifth Avenue. 8. England. 9. Paris. 10. Lawyers' offices. 11. Rutlandshire. 12. Thailand. 13. A large, shallow bay on the coast of Norfolk and Lincolnshire. 14. The IBA mast in Lincolnshire. 15. A narrow strait which joins the Black Sea to the Sea of Marmora.

SESSION 18

QUIZ 8

1. What was 'parlous' an old way of saying?
2. If you 'led someone up the garden path', what would it mean?
3. A sepoy is (a) a cuttle-fish (b) an Indian soldier (c) a kind of skin disease.
4. A matelot is (a) a sailor (b) a skin eruption (c) a thin carpet?
5. What does ad.lib. stand for?
6. What well-known drink was originally called 'usquebaugh'?
7. What is another word for gnome or goblin?
8. If you were asked to act in loco parentis, what would you have to do?
9. What does 'I trow' mean?
10. Which word can mean both 'sound of a clock' and 'a type of flea or nit'?
11. What is a 'beefeater'?
12. While we in Britain 'form a queue', what do Americans do?
13. What is a series of misfortunes better known as?
14. What does 'p.m.' stand for?
15. If, in earlier times, you 'took the King's shilling', what did you do?

ANSWERS

1. Perilous or dangerous. 2. That you caused them to believe something untrue. 3. (b) an Indian soldier. 4. (a) a sailor. 5. Ad libitum: 'at your pleasure'. 6. Whisky. 7. Elf. 8. Act as a parent to someone. 9. I believe. 10. Tick. 11. A member of the Yeomen of the Guard who attend state functions. 12. Make a line. 13. A chapter of accidents. 14. 'Post meridian' after midday. 15. You enlisted in the Army.

SESSION 18

QUIZ 9

. . . .

1. In Lawn Bowls what is the target ball known as?
2. In which country did the sport of Petanque originate?
3. Which equestrian sport is broken down into, Trotting and Pacing events, where the drivers sit on lightweight carts and the horses are not permitted to gallop?
4. Where is the King George VI Chase run?
5. How many players are there in an outdoor Handball team?
6. Who was the bowler that was hit for six sixes by Sir Garfield Sobers in one over?
7. What is the diameter of a netball net; 15ins, 16ins, 17ins or 18ins?
8. In which sport would you use a half-butt, a spider and an extended spider?
9. Which football team plays its home games at Upton Park?
10. At the Olympics, in which sport would you compete in the Trap and Skeet events?
11. In Judo, which is higher; an Orange, Blue or Green belt?
12. If Sabre and Foil are two of the disciplines, what is the third?
13. What wood is a cricket bat traditionally made from?
14. From which sport does the phrase, 'take a raincheck', come?
15. What is the maximum number of jumps to be negotiated, in the show jumping phase of a three-day event?

ANSWERS

1. The Jack. 2. France. 3. Harness Racing. 4. Kempton Park. 5. Eleven. 6. Derek Nash. 7. 15ins. 8. Snooker. 9. West Ham United. 10. Clay Target shooting. 11. Blue. 12. Épée (Fencing). 13. Willow. 14. Baseball. 15. 12.

SESSION 18
QUIZ 10

• •

1. Who were the Plantaganets?
2. Which group of people was set legally free in the British Empire in August, 1834?
3. How many kingdoms in England were there before A.D. 808 ?
4. Who was the last English monarch to die in battle?
5. In the Monte Bello islands, 1952, the first British experiment of what kind of object took place?
6. Which ex-movie actor became the 40th US president?
7. At the second Battle of Ypres, 1915, what deadly weapon was used for the first time?
8. Which famous steamship made her maiden voyage in April, 1838?
9. What, in connection with the motor-car, was begun on 1st January, 1904?
10. Who was taken hostage in Beirut in January, 1987?
11. Which country did the United States bomb in 1986 in retaliation for terrorist activities?
12. Who was the first king of the Israelites?
13. What historical event took place in the United States from 1861–1865?
14. Who was called 'the wisest fool in Christendom'?
15. In what year did the first motor-bus appear in London: (a) 1880 (b) 1899 (c) 1901?

ANSWERS

1. A line of English kings from Henry II to Richard III. 2. Slaves. 3. Nine. 4. King Richard III, in 1485. 5. The first British atomic device. 6. Ronald Reagan. 7. Chlorine poison gas. 8. The Great Western. 9. The issue of licences and number plates. 10. Terry Waite. 11. Libya. 12. King Saul. 13. The American Civil War. 14. King James VI of Scotland/James I of England. 15. (b) 1899.

189

SESSION 19

QUIZ 1

1. What was Madonna's first UK number one hit?
2. Who had top ten hits with 'Lovin Things' and 'Ob-la-di Ob-la-da'?
3. In 1975 who sang 'Love Me Love My Dog'?
4. Who had top ten hits with 'Runaway', 'Hey Little Girl' and 'Little Town Flirt'?
5. Who released the album 'Don't Look Back' in 1978?
6. Who was the lead singer and rhythm guitarist with The Shadows?
7. Terry Hall sang with The Specials before forming which group?
8. As a spin-off single from which TV series did, Paul Shane and the Yellowcoats reach number 36 in 1981?
9. Who performed the theme to the Bond film, Live And Let Die?
10. Who released the album 'New Boots And Panties'?
11. Who was the lead singer with The Clash?
12. Who was 'Glad All Over' to be number one in 1963, but were in 'Bits And Pieces' to only make number two in 1964?
13. Charles and Eddie reached number one with which song in 1992?
14. Who recorded the album 'Penthouse and Pavement'?
15. Who had hits in 1991 with 'Promise Me', 'Holding On' and 'Woman To Woman'?

ANSWERS

1. 'Into The Groove'. 2. Marmalade. 3. Peter Shelly. 4. Del Shannon. 5. Boston. 6. Bruce Welch. 7. Fun Boy Three. 8. Hi-De-Hi. 9. Paul McCartney. 10. Ian Dury and the Blockheads. 11. Joe Strummer. 12. Dave Clark Five. 13. 'Would I Lie To You.' 14. Heaven 17. 15. Beverley Craven.

SESSION 19
QUIZ 2

• •

1. 'I will arise and go now, and go to Innisfree,' is the beginning of a poem by whom?
2. Who wrote *The Informer*?
3. Who wrote the book *John Halifax, Gentleman*, which appeared in 1857?
4. 'Lizzie Borden took an axe....' What did she do then?
5. Complete the proverb: 'The child is father...'
6. According to Samuel Johnson, what is Patriotism?
7. Who were Athos and Aramis?
8. 'I must go down to the seas again' begins a poem by whom?
9. Who wrote *The Pumpkin Eater*?
10. Who created the ex-convict and cracksman character 'Boston Blackie'?
11. Complete the proverb: 'Between two stools...'
12. Who wrote *The Pilgrim's Progress*?
13. What was unusual about the character 'Rebecca' in the book of that name?
14. Who wrote *Don Quixote*?
15. What line follows, 'When icicles hang by the wall,'?

ANSWERS

1. W. B. Yeats. 2. Liam O'Flaherty. 3. Mrs Craik, also known as Dinah Maria Mulock. 4. 'And gave her mother forty whacks'. 5. '...to the man'. 6. The last refuge of a scoundrel. 7. Two of the Three Musketeers. 8. John Masefield. 9. Penelope Mortimer. 10. Jack Boyle. 11. '...you fall to the ground'. 12. John Bunyan. 13. She never appears. 14. Miguel de Cervantes. 15. 'And Dick the shepherd blows his nail'.

SESSION 19
QUIZ 3

1. What food is junket?
2. Which anniversary does a silver wedding celebrate?
3. What do the initials a.m. stand for?
4. Who was the great love of Dante Alighieri?
5. Who ranks higher, a marquess or an earl?
6. What group of objects is described as a flotilla?
7. What is a dolma?
8. What was, or is, an Annie Oakley?
9. What is scrumpy?
10. Which anniversary does an ivory wedding celebrate?
11. What group of objects can be described as a crew?
12. What kind of food item comes from Banbury?
13. Who was Britain's monarch before Queen Elizabeth II?
14. What group is often described as a fifteen?
15. Who was Konrad Adenauer?

ANSWERS

1. Curds, mixed with cream, sweetened and flavoured. 2. The twenty-fifth. 3. ante meridian. 4. Beatrice. 5. A marquess. 6. Ships. 7. A vine or cabbage leaf with savoury stuffing. 8. A free ticket for a circus or theatre. 9. Cider made from small, sweet apples. 10. The fourteenth. 11. Sailors or aircraft staff. 12. Cake. A kind of mince pie. 13. George VI. 14. A rugby team. 15. A German statesman.

192

SESSION 19
QUIZ 4

1. What is a circumference?
2. The tibia is another name for which bone?
3. What machine with remarkable powers of balance was invented in 1852 by Léon Foucault?
4. What is the name of a negatively-charged particle that exists in an atom?
5. Sterling silver is pure silver plus a tiny percentage of what?
6. What is pharmacology?
7. What kind of instrument is a bowie?
8. Toxicology is the study of what?
9. How many planets are there?
10. What kind of animals would a hippologist study?
11. Iodine takes its name from the Greek word iodes, meaning violet. True or false?
12. Astronomy is the study of what?
13. What is claustrophobia?
14. What is the name given to very high-pitched sounds above 20,000 khz?
15. What is an airship?

ANSWERS

1. The distance all the way round a circle. 2. The shin-bone. 3. The gyroscope. 4. Electron. 5. Copper. 6. The science of drugs. 7. A knife. 8. Poisons. 9. Nine. 10. Horses. 11. True. 12. The stars. 13. Fear of confined spaces. 14. Ultrasound. 15. A power-driven dirigible aircraft, lighter than air.

SESSION 19
QUIZ 5

1. Is it true that an ostrich will stick its head in the sand when in danger?
2. To what plant did the botanist Leonard Fuchs give his name?
3. What is chlorophyll?
4. What is the alligator pear also known as?
5. Which fish has a curling, prehensile tail?
6. What sort of animal is a pug?
7. A pinniped is a paddle-footed animal. Can you name one example?
8. What is a guava?
9. A kid is (a) any young creature (b) a young goat.
10. Brachiosaurus, a dinosaur, weighed about 75 tonnes when alive. Is this a record?
11. What is a shrike?
12. Where does an animal live if it is arboreal?
13. Mulberry leaves are the favourite food of which insect?
14. What are animals with backbones called?
15. The rhesus is found in India, where it is very destructive. It is a member of what animal family?

ANSWERS

1. No. It's untrue. 2. The fuchsia. 3. The green colouring matter in plants. 4. The avocado. 5. The sea horse. 6. A breed of dog. 7. Seals, sealions, walruses. 8. A tropical plant with yellow, pear-shaped fruit. 9. A young goat. 10. Yes. 11. A bird with a hooked bill, short wings and a long tail. 12. In trees. 13. The silkworm, the caterpillar of the silkmoth. 14. Vertebrates. 15. Monkeys.

194

SESSION 19
QUIZ 6

•••••••••••••••••••••••••••••••••

1. Which Mediterranean island lies close to a smaller island called Gozo?
2. In which city would you find Red Square?
3. Which country's name means 'land of silver'?
4. The St Gotthard Tunnel, Switzerland, is remarkable as what?
5. Where in the world do they speak Tagalog?
6. What is Stansted?
7. The name 'Iberia' refers to which area?
8. Copenhagen is the capital of which country?
9. Where in the world do they speak Pidgin?
10. Where and what is Santorini?
11. The official name 'Ísland' refers to which country?
12. What is the capital city of Norway?
13. What are 'antipodes'?
14. What is the capital of Uruguay?
15. Where in England is 'The Golden Mile'?

ANSWERS

1. Malta. 2. Moscow. 3. Argentina. 4. The world's longest road tunnel. 5. The Philippines. 6. London's third airport. 7. The Spanish and Portuguese peninsula. 8. Denmark. 9. New Guinea and the surrounding islands. 10. An active volcano in Crete. 11. Iceland. 12. Oslo. 13. Any two places on opposite sides of the Earth. 14. Montevideo. 15. Blackpool.

• •

1. In American English, what is a prat?
2. What is the female version of 'colt'?
3. What is the difference between 'already' and 'all ready'?
4. It will be a real problem if you upset this vehicle! Name the vehicle.
5. What does an American mean by 'suspenders'?
6. What is a bandana?
7. The city of Florence gave its name to which coin?
8. To what material did the town of Mosul give its name?
9. What would you ask for in the United States, if you wanted to buy a pair of tights?
10. What is the name for someone who studies fish?
11. How many objects are in a 'baker's dozen'?
12. If you were 'like putty' in someone's hands, what would you be?
13. What does the rhyming slang 'Lord Mayor' mean?
14. What is the name for someone who studies codes and ciphers?
15. What is Interlingua?

ANSWERS

1. The buttocks or bottom. Hence pratfall in the theatre. 2. Filly. 3. The first means 'before', and by the time mentioned' and the second, 'everyone ready'. 4. The apple-cart. 5. Braces. 6. A large coloured handkerchief of silk or cotton. 7. The florin. 8. Muslin. 9. Pantie hose. 10. Ichthyologist. 11. 13. 12. Easily influenced. 13. Swear. 14. Cryptologist. 15. An artificial language.

SESSION 19
QUIZ 8

•••••••••••••••••••••••••••••••••••••

1. Over which course is the Whitbread Gold Cup run?
2. What is the second most expensive property in the British version of Monopoly?
3. Who won the British Open Golf Tournament in 1985?
4. In Rugby, who feeds the ball in to the scrum?
5. For which sport is Joe Montana famous?
6. Which football team play at, 'The Dell'?
7. Where do the Seahawks American Football team come from?
8. Over which course is the Grand National run?
9. What sport do the Sheffield Eagles play?
10. How many players are there in a Netball team?
11. How high is a Volleyball net; 2.22m, 2.32m, 2.40m or 2.43m?
12. With what sport do you associate Miguel Indurain?
13. In Rallying, why was the Audi Quattro revolutionary?
14. Where do surfers in the UK congregate to, 'Ride the bore'?
15. What CC, are the majority of Speedway motorcycles?

ANSWERS

1. Sandown Park. 2. Park Lane. 3. Sandy Lyle. 4. Scrum Half.
5. American Football. 6. Southampton. 7. Seattle. 8. Aintree. 9. Rugby League. 10. Seven. 11. 2.43m. 12. Cycling (especially the Tour de France). 13. First Rally car with permanent four-wheel drive. 14. The River Severn. 15. Two hundred.

197

SESSION 19
QUIZ 9

• •

1. What is the C.I.A.?
2. What historic tragic event took place in Marseilles in October 1934?
3. On 4th November, 1605, who was arrested in the vaults of the Houses of Parliament?
4. Which king acceded to the throne of England on Boxing Day, 1135?
5. In 1931, the United States adopted what as its national anthem?
6. Which ship left England in December 1787 under the command of Captain William Bligh?
7. Who arrived back in Spain from America in 1493?
8. Who was the only English pope?
9. Who was the last Saxon king of England?
10. Who was St Augustine?
11. Which large museum in London opened in 1759?
12. What took the place of the *Daily Herald*, which ceased publication on 14th September, 1964?
13. Wat Tyler and John Ball were leaders of what rebellion in 1381?
14. Who was Harry S. Truman?
15. What happened to the Shah of Iran in 1979?

ANSWERS

SESSION 19
QUIZ 10

• •

1. What was memorable in the film *A Night to Remember?*
2. Who starred in the film *The Graduate?*
3. Which three movie stars received their first screen kisses when aged 14?
4. Which actor won an Oscar in a film in which he never spoke?
5. Who played the sadistic dentist in *Little Shop Of Horrors?*
6. From which stage show did the song 'I'm Just Wild About Harry' come?
7. In early children's television, who was 'Little Weed'?
8. *Gregory's Girl* was a film made by which British director?
9. Who starred in the 1938 film *The Adventures of Robin Hood?*
10. Which story of two composers netted director Milos Forman his second best director Oscar?
11. From which film and stage show did the song 'Sixteen Going on Seventeen' come?
12. What T.V. show featured a Boston bar where, 'everybody knows your name'?
13. Who starred in the film *Beverly Hills Cop?*
14. Who wrote the book on which the film *The Godfather* was based?
15. From which film and stage show did the song 'Stranger in Paradise' come?

ANSWERS

1. Who wrote *The Lord of the Flies?*
2. Complete the proverb: 'The darkest hour...'
3. Who wrote *The Seven Pillars of Wisdom?*
4. Complete the proverb: 'Distance lends...'
5. Who wrote *The Horse Whisperer?*
6. Who wrote *Schindler's Ark?*
7. The twin brothers Peter and Anthony Shaffer are famed as what?
8. 'All animals are equal, but some animals are more equal than others'. Where does this phrase originate?
9. The fictional character 'The Saint' was created by whom?
10. Who wrote *The Hitchhikers' Guide To The Galaxy?*
11. Complete the proverb: 'Don't have too many...'
12. Who wrote *Crime and Punishment?*
13. What, according to Bulwer Lytton, 'is mightier than the sword'?
14. Complete the proverb: 'Cleanliness is...'
15. Frederick Marryat wrote a story along the lines of the Swiss Family Robinson. It was called...?

ANSWERS

1. William Golding. 2. '...is that before the dawn'. 3. T.E. Lawrence. 4. '...enchantment to the view'. 5. Nicholas Evans. 6. Thomas Keneally. 7. Novelists and playwrights. 8. *Animal Farm* (Orwell). 9. Leslie Charteris. 10. Douglas Adams. 11. '...irons in the fire'. 12. Feodor Mikhailovich Dostoyevsky. 13. The pen. 14. '...next to godliness'. 15. Masterman Ready.

SESSION 20
QUIZ 2

• •

1. What was called an 'Albert'?
2. The Bull represents which sign of the Zodiac?
3. Who composed 'The Planets'?
4. Rule by officialdom is called what?
5. According to the 'language of flowers', what does the bay leaf signify?
6. In a pack of cards, which way does the Jack of Hearts look, to his left, or to his right?
7. St Sebastian is the patron saint of whom?
8. Is a pantechnicon a large van?
9. Who was the first-ever murder victim?
10. St Isidore is the patron saint of whom?
11. Which word, beginning with post- means 'those coming after'?
12. Who is the reigning monarch in Denmark?
13. St Apollonia is the patron saint of whom?
14. Which anniversary does a paper wedding celebrate?
15. What is black pudding?

ANSWERS

1. A heavy type of watch chain. 2. Taurus. 3. Gustave Holst. 4. A bureaucracy. 5. 'I change but in death'. 6. To his left. 7. Athletes. 8. It is now, but originally it was a building housing artistic works in Belgrave Square, London. 9. Abel, who was murdered by his brother, Cain. 10. Farmers. 11. Posterity. 12. Queen Margaret II. 13. Dentists. 14. The second. 15. A kind of sausage made from pigs' blood.

201

SESSION 20
QUIZ 3

• •

1. The study and treatment of diseases of the mind is called what?
2. The science and study of radioactive materials is called what?
3. 'Muscular rheumatism' is also called what?
4. What kinds of animal would an ichthyologist study?
5. What does a seismometer measure?
6. What is Sirius?
7. Gabriel Fahrenheit used mercury in 1714 for his invention. What was it?
8. What useful and accurate timepiece did John Harrison invent in 1735?
9. What is myxomatosis?
10. An advancement in making textiles was announced in 1883 by Sir Joseph Swan. What was it?
11. What did Charles Goodyear invent in 1839?
12. The science of directing a craft or a vehicle from place to place is called what?
13. What is geodesy?
14. What does Moh's Scale measure?
15. What laboratory aid was named after its inventor, Robert Bunsen?

ANSWERS

1. Psychiatry 2. Radiochemistry. 3. Fibrositis. 4. Fishes. 5. The strength of earthquakes. 6. The brightest star in the sky. 7. The mercury thermometer. 8. The ship's chronometer. 9. A disease of rabbits. 10. The first synthetic fibre. 11. Vulcanised rubber. 12. Navigation. 13. The study and measurement of the earth on a large scale. 14. Different levels of hardness in minerals. 15. The Bunsen burner.

SESSION 20
QUIZ 4

• •

1. The caribou is an American variety of what sort of deer?
2. What is another name for belladonna?
3. Which is the smallest mammal in the world?
4. What sort of animal is a Pomeranian?
5. What is the name of the tiny rodent with long hind legs, which hops like a kangaroo?
6. What is a chive?
7. Is it true that marsupials are only found in and around Australia?
8. What does a koala bear feed on?
9. Which is the most dangerous fish in the world?
10. What sort of animal is a husky?
11. What is a medlar?
12. Hessian, or sacking, is made from which plant?
13. Which reptile is able to change its colour?
14. What is orris-root?
15. What sort of animal is a boxer?

ANSWERS

1. The reindeer. 2. The deadly nightshade. 3. The bumblebee bat, found in Thailand, averages 30 mm. 4. A breed of dog. 5. The jerboa. 6. A herb like the leek or onion. 7. No. The opossum is a marsupial found in America. 8. Eucalyptus leaves. 9. The piranha, which attacks in masses, stripping flesh from victims. 10. A breed of dog. 11. A small tree with fruit similar to an apple. 12. Jute. 13. The chameleon. 14. The root of the iris, which smells of violets, and is used in perfumery. 15. A breed of dog.

203

SESSION 20
QUIZ 5

• •

1. What does 'Mediterranean' mean?
2. Kilauea and Mauna Loa are volcanoes in what country?
3. Where would you find 'Spaghetti Junction'?
4. Where are the Royal Botanic Gardens, and how are they better known?
5. Whereabouts would you find the River Yarrow?
6. On which island is the State of Brunei?
7. Yucatan is a region of which country?
8. Where is Lake Katrine?
9. 'Frisco' is a nickname for which city?
10. Where and what is Mount Erebus?
11. What city in Northern Ireland stands on the River Lagan?
12. What is the name of the London Underground line which is colour-coded yellow on maps?
13. Which is the most populous city in Canada?
14. What is the longest river in the world?
15. Which British territory is famous for its apes?

ANSWERS

1. The middle of the land or earth. 2. Hawaii. 3. On the motorway near Birmingham. 4. Kew Gardens. 5. In the border region between England and Scotland. 6. Borneo. 7. Mexico. 8. In central Scotland. 9. San Francisco. 10. An active volcano in Antarctica. 11. Belfast. 12. Circle Line. 13. Toronto. 14. The Amazon. 15. Gibraltar.

204

· ·

1. What does an American mean by 'notions'?
2. What happens when you 'buttonhole' someone?
3. What does 'mens sana in corpore sano' mean?
4. What were once referred to as 'Hatches, Matches and Despatches'?
5. An emir is (a) an extinct bird (b) a University student (c) a Muslim chieftain
6. What does 'N.B.' stand for?
7. If someone is 'tarred with the same brush' as yourself, what does it mean?
8. What's wrong with this: We voted for a new chairman, and the bulk of the votes went to Joe Harris.
9. What would have happened, in earlier times, if you were 'shanghaied'?
10. Which is the correct spelling; (a) hiccough (b) hiccup (c) hickup?
11. How do we get the word 'posh'?
12. Finish the proverb: 'Accidents will happen in...'
13. When an American keeps to the sidewalk, what would he be doing?
14. Jean Nicot, French diplomat, gave his name to what drug?
15. What does 'obsequious' mean?

ANSWERS

1. Haberdashery; miscellaneous small items, like pins, needles, cotton. 2. You detain that person in conversation. 3. 'A sound mind in a sound body'. 4. Births, Marriages and Deaths: the personal column announcements in *The Times*. 5. (c) a. 6. 'Nota bene': note well. 7. He would have the same faults and qualities as you. 8. It should be: We voted for a new chairman, and the majority of the votes went to Joe Harris. 9. You were kidnapped, often to serve aboard a ship. 10. (b) hiccup. 11. From the old P & O shipping line, which used the initials to denote the preferred cabins Port side Out, Starboard Home. 12. '...the best regulated families'. 13. Staying on the pavement. 14. Nicotine. 15. Dutiful, to the point of fawning.

SESSION 20
QUIZ 7

1. Which three football teams were promoted to the Premiership in 1997 only to be relegated the following year?
2. What is the technical term for making a sail smaller, whilst it's still attached to the mast?
3. On what course is golf's U.S. Masters played?
4. Name Cincinnati's American football team?
5. Which sport do the London Towers play?
6. In cricket, what is the maximum length of a Test Match?
7. Which sport was played at the Olympic Games in 1900, where the French collected all six Gold medals, but was never again an Olympic sport?
8. Jill Hammersley and Carl Prean are known for playing which sport?
9. What two skills are combined in the sport of Orienteering?
10. Name three events in a heptathlon?
11. In Netball, what do the initials WA stand for?
12. Which Football team plays at Craven Cottage?
13. Over which course is the Irish Derby run?
14. Where is Golf's 'Royal and Ancient Club' based?
15. How long is a cricket bail; 8cm, 7cm, 10cm or 11cm?

SESSION 20
QUIZ 8

• •

1. Who was Valentina Vladimirovna Tereshkova?
2. Who was Michael Collins?
3. London's first railway terminus opened on 20th July, 1837. What was it called?
4. In which year did Papua New Guinea become independent of Australia?
5. Who was David Ben Gurion?
6. What was a 'clippie'?
7. Who was Llewelyn ap Gruffydd, or Llewelyn the Great?
8. Which British national newspaper went on sale for the first time on 7th October, 1986?
9. When did the first election for the European Parliament take place?
10. The population of Malta is reputed to be descended from which ancient people?
11. In the Vietnam War, what was the name of the North Vietnam communist forces?
12. In France, on 7th April, 1795, what measuring unit was made official?
13. Mother Theresa received the Order of Merit from whose hands in 1983?
14. In 1886, the longest railway tunnel in Britain to date, opened. What was its name?
15. Who was the Supreme Commander of the Allies at the end of World War 1?

ANSWERS

1. A Soviet cosmonaut, the first woman to go into space. 2. Irish politician and leader of Sinn Fein, killed in 1922. 3. Euston. 4. 1975. 5. Zionist leader. 6. A female bus conductor during WW2. 7. The last Welsh Prince of Wales. 8. *The Independent*. 9. 7th June, 1979. 10. The Carthaginians. 11. The Vietcong. 12. The metre. 13. The Queen. 14. The Severn. 15. Marshal Ferdinand Foch.

207

SESSION 20
QUIZ 9

• •

1. Who played the part of Clark Gable in *Gable and Lombard?*
2. Who starred in the film *Rebel Without a Cause?*
3. Name the 'Road' films starring Crosby, Hope and Lamour.
4. In *Terms Of Endearment,* what was Jack Nicholson's character's previous occupation?
5. What wheelchair-bound actor was once Superman?
6. Who starred in many roles in the film *Kind Hearts and Coronets?*
7. Who played the part of Al Jolson in *The Jolson Story?*
8. Who starred in the 1933 film *King Kong?*
9. Which movie star was 'The Iron Butterfly'?
10. Which actor retired from acting in the movies at the age of four?
11. Who directed the film *Bridge on the River Kwai?*
12. Who wrote, produced, directed and starred in the film *Yentl?*
13. Who starred in the film *Who Framed Roger Rabbit?*
14. On which author's book was the film *Get Shorty* based?
15. Which British child actor is now an advertising executive?

ANSWERS

1. James Brolin. 2. James Dean. 3. ...to Hong Kong, ...to Morocco, ...to Rio, ...Singapore, ...Utopia. 4. An astronaut. 5. Christopher Reeve. 6. Dennis Price, Alec Guinness, Valerie Hobson. 7. Larry Parks. 8. King Kong himself, and Robert Armstrong, Fay Wray and Bruce Cabot. 9. Jeanette MacDonald. 10. Baby Le Roy (LeRoy Winebrenner), after about a dozen films, in 1936. 11. Sir David Lean. 12. Barbara Streisand. 13. Bob Hoskins. 14. Elmore Leonard. 15. Freddie Bartholomew, who became a vice-president of Benton & Bowles.

208

SESSION 20

QUIZ 10

• •

1. Frankie goes to Hollywood's first 3 hits reached number 1, the first being, 'Relax' and the second, 'Two Tribes'. What was the third?
2. Name the Four Tops' only UK number 1?
3. What was unusual about the music of The Flying Pickets?
4. Which TV series was Joe Fagin's, 'That's Living Alright' the theme to?
5. Which musician and songwriter is the link between Depeche Mode, Yazoo and The Assembly?
6. Which new wave band's only top 10 hit was, 'Do Anything You Want To Do'?
7. Which area of London do the band East 17 come from?
8. Who recorded top ten hits with, 'Boogie Wonderland', 'After The Love Has Gone' and 'September'?
9. Thereze Bazar and David Van Day, who made up duo, 'Dollar', were originally part of which group?
10. Max Bygraves has never had a UK number 1. True or false?
11. In 1990, Donovan scored a minor hit with a re-recording of, 'Jennifer Juniper' billed as, Singing Corner meets Donovan. Who were, Singing Corner?
12. Boyzone's first UK top 10 hit was, 'Love Me For A Reason'. Who recorded the original?
13. In May 1986 who reached number 1 with, 'The Chicken Song'?
14. In 1980, 'Splodgenessabounds', recorded which drinkers' lament?
15. What nationality was Plastic Bertrand?

ANSWERS

1. The Power of Love. 2. Reach Out (I'll Be There). 3. It was sung a capella (totally unaccompanied). 4. Auf Wiedersehen Pet. 5. Vince Clark. 6. Eddie and the Hotrods. 7. Walthamstow (London, E17). 8. Earth Wind and Fire. 9. Guys and Dolls. 10. True. 11. Trevor and Simon from BBC TV's Going Live. 12. The Osmonds. 13. Spitting Image. 14. Two Pints Of Lager And A Packet Of Crisps Please'. 15. Belgian

209

SESSION 21
QUIZ 1

1. What, in Switzerland, are rappen?
2. What is baba au rhum?
3. The name of which naval hero is concealed by the anagram Honor est a Nilo?
4. St Raphael is the patron saint of whom?
5. What is an eclair?
6. Which anniversary does a bronze or electrical appliance wedding celebrate?
7. The Fishes represent which sign of the Zodiac?
8. What is a Mormon?
9. How did damask come to be named?
10. What does a Tarot pack of 78 cards comprise?
11. Jews who in early times settled in Spain and Portugal are called what?
12. If you suffered from ombrophobia, what would you fear?
13. What is gazpacho?
14. Who was Jean-Baptiste Corot?
15. Of what group does one find a sheaf?

Doctor, I have this fear of having a phobia...

ANSWERS

1. The lowest value coins, also known as centimes. 2. A small cake, leavened with yeast, and soaked in a rum syrup. 3. Horatio Nelson. 4. Physicians. 5. A long, light pastry, covered with chocolate and filled with cream. 6. The eighth. 7. Pisces. 8. A religion founded in the United States by Joseph Smith in 1830. 9. It originated in Damascus. 10. Four suits each of 14, 21 permanent trumps and the Fool card. 11. Sephardim. 12. Rainstorms. 13. A spicy Spanish vegetable soup, served cold. 14. French landscape painter. 15. Arrows, papers, corn.

210

SESSION 21
QUIZ 2

. . . .

1. What is the lightest metal?
2. The letters EPNS on cutlery stand for what?
3. What sort of cloud is a nimbus?
4. What is an alternator?
5. What is an icosahedron?
6. What, in WW2, was a Hurricane?
7. Archaeology is the study of what?
8. Which transparent wrapping material was invented by Jacques Brandenburger in 1908?
9. What is the name given to the calendar at present used internationally?
10. The longest side of a right-angled triangle is called what?
11. Factories for the manufacture of what were opened for the first time in Manchester in 1641?
12. What was a Luger?
13. What is dermatology?
14. Who was responsible for the special theory of relativity?
15. Who, in 1888, invented the Kodak camera?

ANSWERS

1. Lithium. 2. Electro-plated nickel silver. 3. A rain cloud. 4. A kind of electric generator which produces alternating current. 5. A solid figure with twenty faces. 6. A British fighter aircraft. 7. Human history and prehistory through human remains and antiquities. 8. Cellophane. 9. The Gregorian. 10. The hypotenuse. 11. Cotton. 12. A pistol. 13. The science of the treatment of the skin. 14. Albert Einstein. 15. George Eastman.

SESSION 21
QUIZ 3

• •

1. What is the name give to an animal defined as a small type of llama and whose wool is prized?
2. The parsley plant is a plant relative of hemlock. True or false?
3. How many different kinds of snakes are there:
   (a) hundreds (b) thousands (c) dozens?
4. What is a beagle?
5. What is a marmoset?
6. Garlic is a plant relative of the lily. True or false?
7. What sort of animals are known as 'anthropoids'?
8. Is there, or was there, ever a white elephant?
9. What sort of animal is a serval?
10. A small mouse-sized creature with a slightly bushy tail is called what?
11. The radish is a member of the cabbage family. Yes or no?
12. What is a vixen?
13. The shaddock was an early form of which fruit?
14. What is the offspring of a male horse and female donkey called?
15. What, in early times, was a turnspit?

ANSWERS

1. Alpaca. 2. True. 3. About 2,400 species. 4. A breed of dog. 5. A small South American monkey. 6. True. 7. Man-like apes. 8. No. The closest colouring is a kind of darkish pink! 9. A long-legged, short-tailed African wild cat. 10. A dormouse. 11. Yes. 12. A female fox. 13. The grapefruit. 14. A hinny. 15. A small dog placed in a revolving wire cage to turn the meat on a roasting spit.

SESSION 21
QUIZ 4

. . . .

1. Which country was awarded the George Cross in 1942?
2. Which is the largest salt-water lake or inland sea?
3. In which county would you find the Cotswold Hills?
4. The 'Palace of Westminster' is the official title of which famous building?
5. Where in the world is Saab airport?
6. In 1935, a US aviator named James Angel crash-landed in Venezuela, discovering what?
7. The Hanging Gardens of Babylon, in Iraq were regarded as what?
8. What is familiarly known as the 'V and A'?
9. For what, historically, is Pitcairn Island famed?
10. Which is Britain's smallest colony?
11. Where in the world do they speak Letzeburgesh?
12. Which major river flows through Brazil?
13. The American capital, Washington, is in 'D.C.' What does that stand for?
14. What is the highest mountain in the continent of Africa?
15. The Andaman Islands, in the Indian Ocean are part of which country?

ANSWERS

1. Malta. 2. The Caspian, in Russia. 3. Gloucestershire. 4. The Houses of Parliament. 5. Linköping, Sweden. 6. A waterfall in the jungle, now called the Angel Falls. 7. One of the Seven Ancient Wonders of the World. 8. The Victoria and Albert Museum, London. 9. It was settled by the mutineers from the Bounty in 1790. 10. Gibraltar. 11. Luxembourg. 12. The Amazon. 13. District of Columbia. 14. Mount Kilimanjaro. 15. India.

SESSION 21
QUIZ 5

1. What was 'To wot' an old way of saying?
2. Which word means 'similar to' and 'to think well of'.
3. Can you name two words, sounding alike, which mean the same as this pair: work to a dough/want?
4. What does 'queasy' mean?
5. What is molasses, as understood by Americans?
6. What would you ask for in the United States, if you wanted a pair of knickers?
7. To what do the slang terms, 'wonga' and 'wedge' refer?
8. What does an American call rubbish?
9. What is the female version of 'hart'?
10. Which word, beginning with A, is another word for aspect or look?
11. If you have a secret idea held in reserve, what would you have up your sleeve?
12. In cockney rhyming slang, what does 'Barnet Fair' mean?
13. What is the Ship of the Desert?
14. What would you mean if you said to someone 'mea culpa'?
15. How do we get the word nark, meaning a 'police informer'?

ANSWERS

1. To know. 2. Like. 3. Knead/need. 4. Sick, inclined to vomit. 5. Treacle. 6. Panties. 7. Money. 8. Trash. 9. Hind. 10. Appearance. 11. An ace. 12 Hair. 13. A camel. 14. You would mean 'it's my fault'. 15. It comes from the Romany (Gipsy) word nak, meaning 'nose'.

SESSION 21
QUIZ 6

• •

1. In American football, which player scores, 'the point after'?
2. Which Italian footballer missed the deciding penalty to give Brazil victory in the 1994 World Cup Finals?
3. Which game is faster, Rugby Fives or Eton Fives?
4. In Tennis, name the four Grand Slam events?
5. In Squash, which ball is slowest, a red dot, a blue dot or a yellow dot?
6. Name the famous snooker and billiards playing brothers who dominated the games in the middle of this century?
7. In which sport would you use, a Do, a Shinai, a Kote and a Hakama?
8. How old was Mike Tyson when he won his first World Heavyweight title?
9. Which football team plays it home matches at, 'The Hawthorns'?
10. Which form of skiing was the first to be organised competitively?
11. Between 1920 and 1928, this great swimmer won five Olympic swimming golds and set 67 World Records. He later became more famous as Tarzan. Who was he?
12. When was the Oxford and Cambridge boat race first contested; 1815, 1821, 1829 or 1840?
13. In the Tour de France, what is signified by a red polka dot jersey?
14. Over which course is 'The Oaks' run?
15. Who won the first Rugby Union World cup in 1987?

ANSWERS

1. The Kicker. 2. Roberto Baggio. 3. Rugby Fives. 4. Wimbledon and the Australian, French and US Opens. 5. Yellow dot. 6. Joe and Fred Davis. 7. Kendo. 8. Twenty. 9. West Bromwich Albion. 10. Ski Jumping. 11. Johnny Weissmuller. 12. 1829. 13. King of the Mountains. 14. Epsom. 15. New Zealand.

215

• •

1. What was the Stern Gang in Palestine?
2. Who was the last king of Scotland?
3. Sir Oswald Mosley was expelled from which political party in 1931?
4. On 10th February, 1840, at the Chapel Royal, St James's, London, a marriage took place between whom?
5. Which king of England acknowledged that he had at least 20 illegitimate children?
6. The death of Ruth Ellis in 1955 marked what?
7. What did the Soviet Union do between 1979 and 1989?
8. What happened to Rufus, son of William I, while hunting in the New Forest?
9. What disaster struck Lynmouth, Devon, in August, 1952?
10. Which former British monarch became Governor of the Bahamas in 1940?
11. What was Irgun Zvai Leumi, and what did it do in July, 1946?
12. What was the *General Belgrano*, and what happened to it in May, 1982?
13. In King Arthur, a place called Caerleon is mentioned. What is this place known as today?
14. Where and what was Bernicia?
15. Who was John Cabot?

ANSWERS

1. A Zionist terrorist group. 2. James VI (James I of England). 3. The Labour Party. 4. Queen Victoria and Prince Albert. 5. King Henry I. 6. She was the last woman to be executed in Britain. 7. Invaded and occupied Afghanistan. 8. He was shot. 9. A flash flood destroyed the town, killing 34 people. 10. The Duke of Windsor. 11. It was a Jewish terrorist gang which blew up the King David Hotel, the British GHQ in Jerusalem. 12. An Argentinian battle cruiser, and was sunk when torpedoed by HM submarine *Conqueror*. 13. It's the modern city of Chester. 14. One of the old kingdoms of England before A.D.808. Bernicia was Northern England. 15. An explorer from Genoa who discovered Newfoundland.

SESSION 21
QUIZ 8

1. Who starred in the film *Anna Karenina?*
2. Who starred in the film *Pygmalion?*
3. Which actress and singer married a French film director, and now lives near Paris?
4. Who starred in the film *Dr Strangelove?*
5. Which film, starring Jack Hawkins, dealt with the problems of a deaf child?
6. Which American child star became a leading diplomat?
7. Who starred in the film *Destry Rides Again?*
8. Which clay characters found themselves with *The Wrong Trousers* and had *A Grand Day Out?*
9. Who starred in the 1931 film *Dracula?*
10. What was the name of the actor who played a Vulcan who was Captain Kirk's second-in-command?
11. In *Roxanne,* what unusual physical feature did Steve Martin's character possess?
12. Who starred in the film *The Manchurian Candidate?*
13. Which actor gives a brilliant performance in the film *A Place in the Sun?*
14. Who starred in the film *The Grapes of Wrath?*
15. Who starred in the film *Raging Bull?*

ANSWERS

1. Greta Garbo and Fredric March. 2. Leslie Howard, Wendy Hiller.
3. Deanna Durbin. 4. Peter Sellers, George C. Scott, Keenan Wynn.
5. Mandy. 6. Shirley Temple. 7. James Stewart, Marlene Dietrich.
8. Wallace and Gromit. 9. Bela Lugosi. 10. Leonard Nimoy (played Captain Spock). 11. An enormous nose. 12. Frank Sinatra, Laurence Harvey.
13. Montgomery Clift. 14. Henry Fonda. 15. Robert De Niro, Cathy Moriarty.

217

SESSION 21
QUIZ 9

• •

1. Which Pink Floyd album featured a prism and refracted light on the cover?
2. With whom did Robert Palmer record, 'I'll Be Your Baby Tonight'?
3. Who reached number 6 in 1981 with, 'Reward'?
4. What nationality are the Isley Brothers?
5. Which film did Cliff Richard star with Una Stubbs and Melvyn Hayes?
6. Which film featured Go West's, 'King Of Wishful Thinking' on the soundtrack?
7. Brian Adams' '(Everything I Do), I Do It For You' featured in which film?
8. What nationality are Ace of Bass?
9. In 1982, which alphabetical group had top ten hits with, 'The Look Of Love', 'Poison Arrow' and 'All Of My Heart'?
10. Adam and the Ants had three number one hits, 'Goody Two Shoes', 'Stand And Deliver' being two. What was the third?
11. Who is the lead singer with Bad Manners?
12. Which Australian clocked up the most weeks in the UK chart for the year 1988?
13. With which group did Diana Ross record a large number of her hits?
14. In 1974/75 The Wombles were achieving great chart success. Who was the, vocalist, arranger, producer and inspiration behind the act?
15. Who was the lead singer with 'The Who'?

ANSWERS

1. 'Dark Side Of The Moon. 2. UB40. 3. Teardrop Explodes. 4. American.
5. Summer Holiday. 6. Pretty Woman. 7. Robin Hood, Prince Of Thieves.
8. Swedish. 9. ABC. 10. 'Prince Charming'. 11. Buster Bloodvessel.
12. Kylie Minogue. 13. The Supremes. 14. Mike Batt. 15. Roger Daltrey.

SESSION 21
QUIZ 10

• •

1. Complete the proverb: 'Curses, like chickens...'
2. Who is the current Poet Laureate?
3. Under what name was Eric Arthur Blair better known?
4. Who wrote *The Information?*
5. Who said, 'There's a sucker born every minute'?
6. Who wrote *Lucky Jim?*
7. Who wrote *Anna Karenina?*
8. Which well-known comedian has written a number of novels including *Stark* and *Gridlock?*
9. In which play by Shakespeare does 'Desdemona' appear?
10. Which juvenile magazine was started in 1879 to counter the 'blood and thunder' novelettes?
11. Complete the proverb: 'Desperate diseases...'
12. Who wrote *The Constant Nymph?*
13. The Bible says, 'Life for life, eye for eye, tooth for tooth...' What follows?
14. Who wrote *The Go-Between?*
15. Complete the proverb: 'Don't make a mountain...'

ANSWERS

1. '...come home to roost'. 2. Ted Hughes. 3. George Orwell. 4. Martin Amis. 5. Phineas T. Barnum. 6. Kingsley Amis. 7. Leo Tolstoy. 8. Ben Elton. 9. *Othello.* 10. *The Boy's Own Paper.* 11. '...must have desperate remedies'. 12. Margaret Kennedy. 13. Hand for hand, foot for foot. 14. L.P. Hartley. 15. '...out of a molehill.

SESSION 22
Quiz 1

• •

1. What are hailstones?
2. Who was Alfred Adler?
3. To whom was Sir Max Mallowan the archaeologist married?
4. What does 'aerofoil' mean?
5. What unit of measure is equivalent to 1.76 pints?
6. What pioneer of photography was born in Evershot in 1800?
7. What is anthomania?
8. Scaly debris under the skin on the hair is called what?
9. Who was Sigmund Freud?
10. In computer language, what is a byte?
11. The science of building massive structures is called?
12. What handy cooking device was invented by Frenchmen, Denis Papin, as long ago as 1675?
13. William Lee invented the stocking frame in 1589, the first example of what machine?
14. What did Sir Alexander Fleming discover?
15. Argent is another name for what?

ANSWERS

1. Hard balls of ice which fall during thunderstorms. 2. An Austrian psychiatrist. 3. Agatha Christie. 4. A body so shaped that it receives lift when it travels through the air. 5. A litre. 6. William Fox Talbot. 7. An overpowering desire for and love of flowers. 8. Dandruff. 9. Psychiatrist, founder of psychoanalysis. 10. Eight bits. 11. Civil engineering. 12. The pressure cooker. 13. Knitting machine. 14. Penicillin. 15. Silver.

SESSION 22
Quiz 2

• •

1. What is the most that an elephant can weigh; (a) 3 tonnes (b) 5 tonnes (c) 7 tonnes?
2. What is a group of lions called?
3. What is another name for honeysuckle?
4. What is a leech?
5. A galago is a small large-eyed animal like a small monkey. What is it also called?
6. What sort of animal is a retriever?
7. What is a cicada?
8. A basilisk is a type of lizard. True or false?
9. A group of turtles is called; (a) a bale (b) a turn (c) a shell?
10. What is woad?
11. The cauliflower is a plant relative of the cabbage. True or false?
12. What is a gecko, and what is peculiar about it?
13. A gecko in the West Indies is the smallest what of its kind?
14. What is a citron?
15. What is a buzzard?

ANSWERS

1. 7 tonnes. 2. A pride or a troop. 3. Woodbine. 4. A blood-sucking worm, once used by doctors to take blood from patients. 5. A bush baby. 6. A dog. 7. A small insect which makes a very loud buzzing sound. 8. True. 9. A bale. 10. It's a plant from which a blue dye is obtained. 11. True. 12. It's a lizard with suction pads on its feet. 13. The smallest reptile, measuring just over one cm. 14. A fruit resembling a lemon, from which the lime and lemon evolved. 15. A bird of prey, also known as a buteo.

221

SESSION 22
Quiz 3

• •

1. Which British cities have underground railways?
2. Whereabouts is Nova Scotia?
3. Rhodesia is the old name for where?
4. Which is the hottest place in the world?
5. Which fictional character is said to have lived at 221b Baker Street, London?
6. Which is the deepest lake in the world?
7. Where is Beachy Head?
8. What first occurred in London on 18th December, 1890?
9. What is the capital city of Finland?
10. Which island group includes Fuerteventura and Lanzarote?
11. What is the capital of China?
12. Who lives at Lambeth Palace, London?
13. Which express American train ran between Cincinnati and New Orleans?
14. The cities of Kyoto and Nara are in which country?
15. What is the Gota opened in Sweden in 1832?

ANSWERS

1. London, Liverpool, Tyne and Wear, and Glasgow. 2. Canada. 3. Zimbabwe. 4. Death Valley, California, 120°F. 5. Sherlock Holmes. 6. Baikal, Siberia, is 5,371 feet deep. 7. A headland on the south coast near Eastbourne. 8. The opening of the first underground electric railway in the world. 9. Helsinki. 10. The Canary Islands. 11. Beijing. 12. Archbishop of Canterbury. 13. The Chattanooga Choo-Choo. 14. Japan. 15. A canal.

SESSION 22
Quiz 4

• •

1. What's the plural of 'chateau'?
2. What does R.S.V.P. stand for?
3. Which single word means someone who expects the best will happen?
4. What does the German word 'Kaiser' mean?
5. What, in the 1920s, was a 'bootlegger' in the United States?
6. What does 'at a loose end' mean?
7. If you want to play draughts with an American, what would he call the game?
8. What happens if you 'send someone to Coventry'?
9. Which word, beginning with A, means forbear or refrain?
10. Which word, beginning with R, means abominable or disgusting?
11. What are 'darbies'?
12. Which word, beginning with M, means meek or unpretentious?
13. There are nine possessive pronouns. Name three.
14. Which word, beginning with E, can mean elongate or stretch?
15. What was 'To ween' an old way of saying?

ANSWERS

1. Chateaux. 2. 'Répondez, s'il vous plaît': Reply, if you please. 3. Optimist. 4. Emperor. 5. A trafficker in illegal liquor. 6. Temporarily have nothing to do. 7. Checkers. 8. You completely ignore him (or her). 9. Abstain. 10. Repulsive. 11. Handcuffs. 12. Modest. 13. Mine, yours, his, hers, its, ours, theirs, whose, one's. 14. Extend. 15. To think.

223

SESSION 22
Quiz 5

• •

1. The 'Yankees' baseball team comes from which city?
2. In Rugby Union who competes for the Calcutta Cup?
3. The Hennessy Gold Cup is run over which race course?
4. From where does the sport of Pelota originate?
5. What other sport is regularly played at Lord's Cricket Ground?
6. Who was the number two driver for Ferrari's Formula One team in the 1997 & 1998 seasons?
7. What calibre rifles are used in the Biathlon, Nordic Skiing event?
8. In a four man Bobsleigh, where does the, 'brakeman' sit?
9. In championship darts from what score do competitors start each leg?
10. In Judo if the Referee says, 'Hajime!', what should you do?
11. In cycling who wears the yellow jersey?
12. In which year did Rhythmic Gymnastics first appear in the Olympic Games?
13. In an Olympic Discus competition, how many throws is each contestant allowed?
14. For which Formula 1 team was Ayrton Senna driving, when he was killed?
15. Which 1970s Chelsea player reputedly became the object of Raquel Welch's desire, after she watched him play at Stamford Bridge?

ANSWERS

1 New York. 2. Scotland and England. 3. Newbury. 4. The Basque region of Spain. 5. Real Tennis. 6. Eddie Irvine. 7. .22. 8. At the rear. 9. 501. 10. Start fighting. 11. The Race Leader. 12. 1984. 13. Six. 14. Williams. 15. Peter Osgood.

• •

1. Where would you look for the site of ancient Carthage?
2. What post did Gaelic scholar, Dr Douglas Hyde take in June, 1938?
3. Who was the last Viceroy of India?
4. John George Diefenbaker was prime minister of which country?
5. What was the League of Nations?
6. Who was 'Bloody Mary'?
7. Who was the famed American John Brown?
8. Which Royal person in Britain died of typhoid fever on 14th December, 1861?
9. Who met whom in Ujiji, Africa, on 10 November, 1871?
10. The first meeting of which international peace body was held in Paris in 1920?
11. Which French ruler was reported to be afraid of cats?
12. Which American senator was fatally wounded in Los Angeles on 5th June, 1968?
13. What became the name of the territory administered by the British South Africa Company?
14. Which notorious Australian bushranger was hanged at Melbourne in 1880?
15. What historical event took place in England from 1642 to 1646?

ANSWERS

1. Near the modern city of Tunis, in North Africa. 2. First president of the Irish Republic. 3. Rear-Admiral Lord Louis Mountbatten in 1947. 4. Canada. 5. An international peace-making body, superseded by the United Nations. 6. Mary I, queen of England in 1553. 7. He helped to free the slaves. 8. Albert, Prince Consort. 9. Henry Stanley met Dr Livingstone. 10. The League of Nations. 11. Napoleon. 12. Robert Kennedy. 13. Rhodesia (now Zimbabwe). 14. Ned Kelly. 15. The Civil War.

SESSION 22

Quiz 7

• •

1. The Italian star Rossano Brazzi was a sports champion. In what field?
2. The US character actress Marie Blake was sister of which famous singing star of Hollywood?
3. Who, in the movies, was the 'It Girl'?
4. Who starred in the film *Sunset Boulevard?*
5. Which radio show featured the characters Eccles and Bluebottle?
6. Who played the part of George Raft in *The George Raft Story?*
7. *Bananas, Sleeper* and *Love and Death* were films made by which New York-based director?
8. From which film and stage show did the song 'Summertime' come?
9. Which film starred Johnny Depp as an eccentric B-movie director?
10. Who starred in the film *Road to Morocco?*
11. In the *Dixon of Dock Green* TV series, who needed to be raised from the dead?
12. Which movie actor started out named Malden Sekulovich?
13. What was the name of the sequel to the film *Jurassic Park?*
14. Who starred in the film *Ghostbusters?*
15. From which film and stage show did the song 'There's No Business Like Show Business' come?

ANSWERS

1. He was featherweight boxing champion of Italy. 2. Jeanette MacDonald. 3. Clara Bow. 4. William Holden, Gloria Swanson. 5. The Goon Show. 6. Ray Danton. 7. Woody Allen. 8. *Porgy and Bess.* 9. Ed Wood. 10. Bing Crosby, Bob Hope, Dorothy Lamour. 11. P.C. Dixon. In the film *The Blue Lamp,* he was shot dead. 12. Karl Malden. 13. *The Lost World.* 14. Bill Murray, Dan Aykroyd. 15. *Annie Get Your Gun.*

SESSION 22
Quiz 8

• •

1. Which Kenyan vocalist enjoyed chart success in the 1970s and 1980s with, 'The Last Farewell' and 'The Skye Boat Song'?
2. T'Pau enjoyed chart success in the late 1980's with, 'Heart And Soul' and 'China In Your Hand'. Which TV series gave the band its name?
3. With whom did the Beachboys, re-release, 'Fun Fun Fun', in March 1996?
4. In the early 1960's, who had UK number 1's with, 'You Don't Know', and 'Walking Back To Happiness'?
5. Which hard rock band released the album, 'Break Like The Wind' featuring collaborations with Cher and Jeff Beck?
6. What sporting event helped Luciano Pavarotti reach number 1 with 'Nessun Dorma'?
7. With whom did Van Morrison record, 'When God Shines His Light', in 1989?
8. Who recorded the best-selling album, 'Jagged Little Pill'?
9. With whom did Craig McLachlan re-record the Grease song, 'You're The One That I Want', in 1993?
10. Louise was formerly with which all-girl band?
11. Which band's first full vocal song 'Firestarter', reached number one in 1996?
12. Which actor/singer has had considerable chart success, as well as playing Oz in 'Auf Wiedersehen Pet', and writing and starring in the TV drama, Crocodile Shoes?
13. Which band was Alison Moyet half of in 1983?
14. Who had top ten hits in the early 1970's with 'All The Young Dudes', 'All The Way From Memphis' and 'Roll Away The Stone'?
15. What was the charge when singer, Mark Morrison was arrested?

ANSWERS

1. Roger Whittaker. 2. Star Trek. 3. Status Quo. 4. Helen Shapiro. 5. Spinal Tap. 6. Italia 90 World Cup. 7. Cliff Richard. 8. Alanis Morisette. 9. Debbie Gibson 10. Eternal. 11. Prodigy. 12. Jimmy Nail. 13. Yazoo. 14. Mott the Hoople. 15. Possession of Stun Gun.

SESSION 22

Quiz 9

• •

1. What happened to the character 'Jack Griffin' in a novel by H.G. Wells?
2. Who was Honoré de Balzac?
3. Complete the proverb: 'As well be hanged for a sheep...'
4. Complete the proverb: 'Conscience does make...'
5. According to Voltaire, 'God is always on the side' of what?
6. 'Daisy Buchanan' appears in which novel by F. Scott Fitzgerald?
7. Who wrote *The Time Machine*?
8. What 'desert island' story was written by R.M. Ballantyne?
9. Who wrote *A Passage to India*?
10. John Milton wrote: 'And did those feet in ancient time...?' how did he continue?
11. A.E.W. Mason wrote a book about courage and cowardice. Can you name it?
12. Complete the proverb: 'Blessed is he who expects nothing...'
13. Rupert Brooke wrote, 'Stands the Church clock at ten to three?' How did he continue?
14. Who wrote *Tristram Shandy*?
15. The Wesley brothers, Charles and John wrote hymns. How many? (a) 1,100 (b) 550 (c) 5,500

ANSWERS

1. He became invisible. 2. French novelist. 3. '...as a lamb'. 4. '...cowards of us all'. 5. 'the heaviest battalions'. 6. *The Great Gatsby*. 7. H.G. Wells. 8. *The Coral Island*. 9. E.M. Forster. 10. 'Walk upon England's mountains green?' 11. *The Four Feathers*. 12. '...for he shall never be disappointed'. 13. 'And is there honey still for tea?' 14. Lawrence Sterne. 15. (c) 5,500.

• •

1. The Lion represents which sign of the Zodiac?
2. St Vitus is the patron saint of whom?
3. Is it true that Mormons are allowed several wives?
4. If your surname is 'Miller', what might your nickname be?
5. Of whom was Noël Coward speaking when he referred to 'Aunt Edna'?
6. The fava, or Windsor bean is better known as what?
7. Which word, beginning with post- means 'in the afternoon'?
8. What kind of food item comes from Yorkshire?
9. Name the first three who went to Widecombe Fair!
10. Name the second three who went to Widecombe Fair!
11. How was 'mayonnaise' named?
12. To the ancient Romans, who was Mars?
13. What is a paella?
14. What kind of food is a custard-cream?
15. Which musical play featured the song 'Climb Ev'ry Mountain'?

ANSWERS

1. Leo. 2. Comedians. 3. It was true, but the practice is no longer allowed. 4. Dusty. 5. A fictional audience character, typical of those attending matinees. 6. The broad bean. 7. Post-meridian (usually shortened to p.m.). 8. Pudding. 9. Bill Brewer, Jan Stewer, Peter Gurney. 10. Peter Davy, Dan'l Whidden, Harry Hawk. 11. It was first used at the port of Mahón, Minorca, and named after it. 12. The god of war. 13. A dish of meat with rice and seafood. 14. A kind of sandwich biscuit with a centre layer of cream. 15. *The Sound of Music*.

SESSION 23
QUIZ 1

● ●

1. What are the two kinds of rats found in Britain?
2. What sort of animal is a Kerry Blue?
3. Which fish is faster - the sailfin or the guppy?
4. The fig is a member of the mulberry family. Yes or no?
5. What famous flightless bird lives in New Zealand?
6. What kind of animal could be described as a Landrace?
7. Which is the world's fastest mammal?
8. What is a crowberry?
9. What is a bustard?
10. Which mammals have the shortest life?
11. What is a tuna?
12. Which is the only bird in the world which can hover?
13. Which plant is called 'queen-of-the-meadows'?
14. Why is a rattlesnake able to rattle?
15. A group of goldfinches is called (a) a charm (b) a guild.

ANSWERS

1. The brown rat and the black rat. 2. A breed of dog. 3. Sailfish. 4. Yes. 5. The kiwi. 6. A breed of pig. 7. The cheetah, which can run at speeds of up to 60 m.p.h. 8. A creeping shrub found on moorlands, with small black berries. 9. A large game bird, similar to the cranes and rails. 10. The tree shrews, which live less than two years. 11. A very large fish of the mackerel family. 12. The humming-bird. 13. The meadow-sweet. 14. It has horny rings on its tail, which it shakes. 15. A charm.

SESSION 23
QUIZ 2

• •

1. Which continent contains more than 50% of the world's population?
2. Constantinople is the old name for where?
3. Where is the River Tamar?
4. What island was knwon as Van Diemen's Land?
5. The 7th Earl of Shaftesbury is commemorated by which central London statue?
6. Where is the driest place on Earth?
7. What are the Ellice Islands called now?
8. Which town is geographically nearest the centre of England?
9. Where in the world is Richmond airport?
10. Which town traverses two major rivers in Berkshire?
11. What is the capital of Brazil?
12. What, in ancient times, stood at the harbour of Alexandria, Egypt?
13. What are the names of the four main Channel Islands?
14. Why was the character 'Paddington Bear' so called?
15. What is the currency used in India?

ANSWERS

1. Asia. 2. Istanbul. 3. It flows through Devon and Cornwall. 4. Tasmania. 5. The Statue of Eros in Piccadilly Circus. 6. Atacama Desert, Chile. 7. Tuvalu. 8. Meriden. 9. Virginia, USA. 10. Reading. 11. Brasilia. 12. The Pharos, or lighthouse, 135 metres high, one of the Seven Wonders of the World. 13. Jersey, Guernsey, Alderney and Sark. 14. Because he was originally found at Paddington Station, London. 15. The rupee.

• •

1. To an American, what is the difference between a jalopy and a junker?
2. To what drink did the city of Geneva give its name?
3. A scattermouch is (a) a native of Asia Minor (b) a buffoon (c) a large four-wheeled wagon.
4. Which word, beginning in E, means raise or uplift?
5. How did the expression 'to eat humble pie' originate?
6. Can you name two words, sounding alike, which mean: 'male child' and 'floating anchor'?
7. What do the letters 'ad lib.' stand for?
8. What is the female version of 'stag'?
9. What does 'eldritch' mean?
10. What is a 'gringo'?
11. What is a 'poncho'?
12. What is meant by 'Strine'?
13. Which word, beginning with P, means toxin or venom?
14. What did people do when they were 'streaking'?
15. Would you be prosecuted if you 'went off in a high dudgeon'?

ANSWERS

1. A jalopy is an old and battered car: a junker is fit only for scrap. 2. Gin. 3. (a) a native of Asia Minor. 4. Elevate. 5. Poor people ate pie made from umbles, the cheap entrails of animals. 6. Boy/buoy. 7. 'Ad libitum': at pleasure. 8. Hind. 9. Weird or uncanny. 10. To a Mexican, it meant a foreigner. 11. A kind of blanket with a hole for the head. 12. Australian English. 13. Poison. 14. Running naked (often at a sports event). 15. Probably not, but you would be very angry and annoyed.

• •

1. In Golf, what is the term used for two under par at a hole?
2. Where did the 1992 summer Olympics take place?
3. After retiring from international competition, which British shot putter made his name by winning international, 'Strong Man', competitions?
4. Which Scottish footballer is the only player to have scored 100 goals in both the English and Scottish football leagues?
5. How many players are there in a Baseball team?
6. With which sport do you associate Carl Fogarty?
7. What six-a-side sport starts with a 'face-off'?
8. In which sport would you compete for the Davis Cup?
9. Which sport was ruled by the Hambledon Club, from Halfpenny Down in the 1700s?
10. Which country do the, 'Socceroos', represent?
11. Who won the 1986 World Cup?
12. In 1998 what colour was a McLaren Formula 1 Car?
13. With which sport do you associate Laura Davies?
14. What nationality is tennis star Mark Philippoussis?
15. By what score did the England Rugby Union team lose the first test against Australia, on their 1998 tour, (their heaviest defeat in 150 years)?

ANSWERS

1. Eagle. 2. Barcelona. 3. Geoff Capes. 4. Kenny Dalglish. 5. Nine. 6. Motor Cycling. 7. Ice Hockey. 8. Tennis. 9. Cricket. 10. Australia. 11. Argentina. 12. Silver. 13. Golf. 14. Australian. 15. 76-0.

SESSION 23
QUIZ 5

• •

1. Who, in WW2, was Bomber Harris?
2. In 1867, Quebec, Ontario, New Brunswick and Nova Scotia united to form what?
3. Approximately how old was Henry VI when he came to the throne?
4. Where in Czechoslovakia, and what was Lidice?
5. Which English monarch was excommunicated by the Pope in 1570?
6. Which British monarch spoke no English?
7. Who was the first British monarch to live in Buckingham Palace?
8. Who was imprisoned on Devil's Island on 22nd December, 1894?
9. Which historic document was published by Marx and Engels in February, 1848?
10. When did decimal coinage replace the old pounds, shillings and pence?
11. Who said, "A modest little man, with much to be modest about", and who was he referring to?
12. Who was Richard Milhous Nixon?
13. What was first dropped on 6th August, 1945?
14. What was the name of the tax paid by the Britons to keep out Danish invaders?
15. Which governor-general in India was impeached for alleged corruption?

ANSWERS

1. Sir Arthur Harris, Marshal of the RAF. 2. The Dominion of Canada. 3. Ten months. 4. A mining village, totally destroyed by the Nazis as a punishment. 5. Queen Elizabeth I. 6. King George I. 7. Queen Victoria. 8. Alfred Dreyfus. 9. The Communist Manifesto. 10. On 15th February, 1971. 11. Winston Churchill said this about Clement Attlee. 12. He was the 37th American president. 13. The atom bomb over Hiroshima. 14. Danegeld. 15. Warren Hastings. He was acquitted.

SESSION 23

QUIZ 6

• •

1. Which movie star was the 'Man You Love to Hate'?
2. How many times has *Doctor Jekyll and Mr Hyde* been filmed: (a) 24 (b) 43 (c) 46?
3. About whom was this remark made: 'Most of the time he sounds like he has a mouth full of wet toilet paper'?
4. Who starred in the film *Vertigo?*
5. What event was the film *Dog Day Afternoon* about?
6. Who starred in the film *Zulu Dawn?*
7. Who devised the T.V. series *Grange Hill* and *Brookside?*
8. From which stage show did the song 'Wand'rin' Star' come?
9. Who, in movies and television, was the 'Meanest Man in the World'?
10. Exactly what was *The Titfield Thunderbolt* in the 1952 film?
11. Which spoof picture of a terrible heavy metal band featured their albums, 'Smell The Glove' and 'Shark Sandwich'?
12. Who starred in the film *The Railway Children?*
13. Which veteran chat show host was savaged by Rod Hull and Emu?
14. Which oriental actor played alongside Peter Sellers in the Pink Panther films?
15. Who starred in the 1989 film *Henry V?*

ANSWERS

1. Erich von Stroheim. 2. (c) 46. 3. Marlon Brando. 4. James Stewart. 5. A failed bank robbery. 6. Burt Lancaster, Peter O'Toole. 7. Alec Guinness, Joan Greenwood. 8. *Paint Your Wagon.* 9. Jack Benny. 10. A train. 11. *This Is Spinal Tap.* 12. Dinah Sheridan, Bernard Cribbins, Jenny Agutter. 13. Michael Parkinson. 14. Burt Kwok. 15. Kenneth Branagh, Derek Jacobi, Brian Blessed.

235

SESSION 23
QUIZ 7

1. Name Kylie's younger sister who's also had chart hits?
2. Who was the bass player with The Rolling Stones?
3. Which actor and singer reached number one in 1956 with 'Memories Are Made Of This'?
4. In 1976 Laurie Lee and the Dipsticks' reached number four with 'Convoy GB'. Name the hairy Disc Jockey who made up half the act?
5. In which year was Elvis Presley number 1 in the UK chart with, 'All Shook Up'; 1951, 1957, 1959 or 1962?
6. Who released the album, 'All Mod Cons'?
7. Which singer, who's real name was Jerry Dorsey, reached number one in 1967 with 'Release Me' and 'The Last Waltz'?
8. Which singer married Whitney Houston?
9. What nationality are the group, Hothouse Flowers?
10. With which band was Buddy Holly the lead singer?
11. 'I'm Into Something Good' was a debut hit for which British band?
12. What was the name of Jimi Hendrix's best-known band?
13. Which band were originally called Composition Of Sound?
14. Pete Best was the original drummer with which group?
15. With whom did Gabrielle record 'If You Ever' in 1996?

ANSWERS

1. Dannii Minogue. 2. Bill Wyman. 3. Dean Martin. 4. Dave Lee Travis. 5. 1957. 6. Billy Joel. 7. Englebert Humperdink. 8. Bobby Brown. 9. Irish. 10. The Crickets. 11. Herman's Hermits. 12. The Jimi Hendrix Experience. 13. Depeche Mode. 14. The Beatles. 15. East 17.

SESSION 23

QUIZ 8

. . . .

1. Who, in *Treasure Island,* was Captain Flint?
2. Which famous children's book did L.M. Montgomery write?
3. Complete Oliver Cromwell's line: 'Put your trust in God and...'
4. Complete the proverb: 'As you make your bed...'
5. Who wrote *Lolita?*
6. The character Topsy appears in which famous book?
7. Who wrote the play *The Second Mrs Tanqueray?*
8. Robert Browning wrote: 'Oh, to be in England...' How did he continue?
9. The character Emma Roualt appears in which famous French book?
10. 'Age cannot wither her, nor custom stale her infinite variety'. Who is the line about?
11. In which Shakespeare play do three witches appear?
12. Who wrote *Babbitt?*
13. The character Sergeant Troy appears in which famous book?
14. How does the following limerick continue: There was a young lady named Bright / Whose speed was faster than light?
15. Which Durrell had a brother called Gerald?

ANSWERS

1. The parrot. 2. *Anne of Green Gables.* 3. keep your powder dry'. 4. '...so you must lie in it'. 5. Vladimir Nabokov. 6. *Uncle Tom's Cabin.* 7. Sir Arthur Pinero. 8. Now that April's there. 9. *Madame Bovary.* 10. Cleopatra, according to Shakespeare. 11. *Macbeth.* 12. Sinclair Lewis. 13. *Far From the Madding Crowd.* 14. She set out one day / In a relative way / And returned home the previous night. 15. Lawrence Durrell.

237

SESSION 23
QUIZ 9

• •

1. Who was the Yorkshire Ripper?
2. Who invented the lawnmower?
3. What is a 'romany rye'?
4. What kind of food item comes from Bakewell?
5. A legume with flat, dishlike seeds is called what?
6. Who was Honoré de Balzac?
7. St Lawrence is the patron saint of whom?
8. What kind of food was known as a 'wally'?
9. Which Sunday newspaper was first issued on 28th January, 1990
10. What did Mrs Mary Baker Eddy found?
11. What are gnocchi?
12. Who is the reigning prince of Luxembourg?
13. St Fiacre is the patron saint of whom?
14. According to the 'language of flowers', what does the peony signify?
15. What suits are found in a traditional pack of Tarot cards?

ANSWERS

1. Peter Sutcliffe. 2. James Edward Ransome in 1902. 3. It is gypsy language, and means an outsider who joins them, learning their ways and language. 4. A tart. 5. Lentil. 6. French novelist. 7. Cooks. 8. A pickled gherkin. 9. *The Independent on Sunday*. 10. Christian Science. 11. Italian savoury dumplings. 12. Jean. 13. Cab-drivers. 14. Shame or bashfulness. 15. The Italian suits of Batons, Swords, Coins and Cups.

238

SESSION 23
QUIZ 10

• •

1. Linus Yale invented what device in 1865?
2. What sort of vehicle was a Sherman?
3. Who invented milk chocolate?
4. What kind of animals would an entomologist study?
5. What is toxiphobia?
6. What are an A340 and a 767?
7. In 1901 Alva J. Fisher invented and developed the first domestic machine of this kind, electrically powered. It was what?
8. What is mycology?
9. What is bone china?
10. Who invented the fountain pen?
11. Oil of vitriol is an old name for which chemical?
12. The study of the atmosphere and the weather is called what?
13. What does a sextant measure?
14. What did Christopher Cockerell invent?
15. What is Jacques-Yves Cousteau famed for?

ANSWERS

1. The cylinder lock. 2. A military tank. 3. Daniel Peter, Switzerland, 1875. 4. Insects. 5. A fear of being poisoned. 6. Modern jet airliners. 7. The washing machine. 8. The study of fungi. 9. An imitation porcelain containing bone ash. 10. Lewis Waterman in 1884. 11. Sulphuric acid. 12. Meteorology. 13. Latitude. 14. Hovercraft. 15. Underwater exploration.

SESSION 24
QUIZ 1

. . . .

1. Where in London is 'Poets' Corner'?
2. What kind of people would go sailing in a dhow?
3. What are the Gilbert Islands in the Pacific now called?
4. There are four Ben Lomonds: two in Australia, one in the US and one in Scotland which is the tallest of the four. True or false?
5. Which cathedral in the United Kingdom has the tallest spire?
6. What country is the Pacific island of Luzon part of?
7. The term 'Kypros' or 'Kibris' refers to which country?
8. Which is the world's longest railway tunnel?
9. Where are the Atlas Mountains?
10. What is meant by 'Asia Minor'?
11. Where would you find Derwent Water?
12. Where is the River Dove?
13. What is the deepest part of the Atlantic Ocean called?
14. The term 'Österreich' refers to which country?
15. How long is the Eurotunnel?

ANSWERS

1. In Westminster Abbey. 2. The Arabs. 3. Kiribati. 4. False. The Scottish mountain is the lowest. 5. Salisbury Cathedral. 6. The Philippines. 7. Cyprus. 8. The Simplon. 9. Algeria, North Africa. 10. The part of Turkey in Asia. 11. It's a lake in the Lake District, Cumbria. 12. In Staffordshire and Derbyshire. 13. Puerto Rico Trench. 14. Austria. 15. 31 miles.

SESSION 24
QUIZ 2

• •

1. An ayah is: (a) an Indian nurse (b) a Mediterranean boat (c) a Malayan knife?
2 When an American refers to the 'hood' of his car, what does it mean?
3. What is a sombrero?
4. What would a fanlight in your hall be called by an American?
5. What happens if you, 'go off the deep end'?
6. What is wrong with this phrase: 'The freshly cleaned ladies' toilet'?
7. Which is the only possessive pronoun which takes an apostrophe?
8. What's the difference between emigrate and immigrate?
9. What is another word for motto or saying?
10. What is the meaning of the acronym DPP?
11. What is the name for someone who studies the sound of words?
12. What is the female version of 'gander'?
13. What does an American mean by a 'derby' hat?
14. 'King Arthur telephoned his wife every day'. This is patently untrue, but what is the name for this sort of phrase?
15. What happens if you 'chance your arm'?

ANSWERS

1. (a) an Indian nurse. 2. The bonnet. 3. A wide-brimmed hat. 4. A transom. 5. You get very angry. 6. It should read 'The ladies' freshly cleaned toilet'. 7. One's. 8. Emigrate means to leave a country to live in another, and immigrate means to come into a country to stay. 9. Proverb. 10. Department of Public Prosecution. 11. Phonetician. 12. Goose. 13. A bowler. 14. An anachronism. 15. You take a risk.

241

SESSION 24
QUIZ 3

1. Edgbaston is the home ground of which County cricket team?
2. Name Sheffield Wednesday's football ground?
3. Which former striker and Gladiators host was accused of match fixing?
4. What happened to Colombian defender Andres Escobar when he returned home after scoring an own goal to put his team out of the 1994 World Cup?
5. How long is a squash racket's handle: 27ins, 29ins, 30ins or 32ins?
6. With which sport do you associate Canadians, Gasper & Benoit?
7. True or false in the 1900 Olympic Games, live birds were used in the pigeon shooting contest?
8. From which country does Muki boxing come?
9. If you were a Juryo entering a Basho, which sport would you be taking part in?
10. In total how many players are permitted in an Ice Hockey team?
11. How many points are awarded for a Drop Goal in Rugby League?
12. Which saloon car racing team did Nigel Mansell drive for as a guest in 1998?
13. Which British football team play their home games at Carrow Road?
14. Who won the 1997 US Masters golf tournament?
15. In which sport do you have a square wicket and a bat shaped like a frying pan?

ANSWERS

1. Warwickshire. 2. Hillsborough. 3. John Fashanu. 4. He was shot. 5. 27ins. 6. Luge Tobogganing. 7. True. 8. India. 9. Sumo Wrestling. 10. 20. 11. One. 12. Mondeo. 13. Norwich City. 14. Tiger Woods. 15. Stool Ball.

SESSION 24

QUIZ 4

1. By what name is Siddhartha Gautama better-known?
2. What was the surname of King Edward VII?
3. Who was George Lansbury, and what publication did he start in 1919?
4. Who was the last of the Plantagenet kings?
5. What in the 1930s, was the Anschluss?
6. What international document was signed on 11th November, 1918?
7. Who conquered Mexico for Spain?
8. In 1922, Benito Mussolini led a march on Rome. What was the result?
9. Who is James Earle Carter?
10. Who was Muhammed Ali Jinnah?
11. Who was Calvin Coolidge?
12. In 1945, the 15th August was celebrated as VJ Day. What was that?
13. What or was Vidkun Quisling?
14. When did Queen Victoria die?
15. What was Buchenwald, Germany, notorious for during the Secound World War?

ANSWERS

1. Buddha ('the Enlightened'). 2. Members of the Royal Family have no surname. 3. A leader of the Labour Party and founder of the *Daily Herald* newspaper. 4. King Richard II (1377-1399). 5. The union between Germany and Austria. 6. The Armistice between the Allies and Germany 7. Hernando Cortés. 8. He took over running the country and formed the Fascist government. 9. The 39th American president. 10. The founding father of the republic of Pakistan. 11. The 30th American president. 12. Victory over Japan day. 13. A Norwegian traitor, who betrayed his own country to the Germans. 14. 1901. 15. A terrible concentration camp.

SESSION 24
QUIZ 5

1. What silent movie great starred in *The Freshman?*
2. What T.V. series did David Hasselhof star in before *Baywatch?*
3. Name four films whose title starts with the word Top?
4. Who starred in the film *Saturday Night and Sunday Morning?*
5. Who were Fleago, Bingo, Drooper and Snorky?
6. What T.V. police drama starred Jack Lord and was set on a beautiful set of islands?
7. Who starred in the film *To Kill a Mockingbird?*
8. What was the name of the cowboy toy in the film *Toy Story?*
9. Who directed the film *The Searchers?*
10. Which famous soul singer took a starring role in one of the Mad Max films?
11. Who starred in the film *The Fallen Idol?*
12. Name the two films for which Tom Hanks won best actor Oscars?
13. Who directed the films *The Lost Weekend* and *The Apartment?*
14. Who starred in the 1927 film *The Jazz Singer?*
15. Which French actor and singer was the following remark made about, 'A great artiste, but a small human being'?

ANSWERS

1. Harold Lloyd. 2. Night Rider. 3. *Top Banana, Top Gun, Top Hat, Top Man, Top o' the Morning, Top of the Town, Top Secret, Top Secret Affair.* 4. Albert Finney. 5. The Banana Splits. 6. *Hawaii Five-O.* 7. Gregory Peck. 8. Woody. 9. John Ford. 10. Tina Turner. 11. Ralph Richardson. 12. *Philadelphia* and *Forrest Gump.* 13. Billy Wilder. 14. Al Jolson. 15. Maurice Chevalier.

SESSION 24
QUIZ 6

. . . .

1. In 1995, who recorded the album 'Different Class'?
2. Which 1991 Alan Parker film depicted the forming of a fictitious Dublin Soul band, and featuring reworked versions of classic Soul songs?
3. What band was lead by Steve Marriot?
4. Which group is associated with Australian, Nick Cave?
5. Name Blue Oyster Cult's only hit single released in 1978?
6. In August 1995, the media whipped up competition between Blur's 'Country House' and Oasis' 'Roll With It'. Which Single sold the most copies?
7. In 1992 who recorded the album '0898'?
8. What was the Beatles' first single to hit the Charts in 1962?
9. Who recorded her only number one hit with Nielson's 'Without You'?
10. Who had top ten hits with 'Heaven Is A Place On Earth', 'I Get Weak' and 'Leave A Light On'?
11. In 1995 who recorded the album 'Paranoid and Sunburnt'?
12. In the early 1970's which family was David Cassidy a member of?
13. Who's first solo album release was called 'Faith'?
14. Which female singer recorded 'Unforgettable' with her dead father in 1991?
15. Which cartoon characters dueted with Cher, singing 'I Got You Babe' in 1994?

ANSWERS

1. Pulp. 2. The Commitments. 3. The Small Faces. 4. The Bad Seeds. 5. '(Don't Fear) The Reaper'. 6. Blur's 'Country House'. 7. Beautiful South. 8. 'Love Me Do'. 9. Mariah Carey. 10. Belinda Carlisle. 11. Skunk Anansie. 12. The Partridge Family. 13. George Michael. 14. Natalie Cole. 15. Beavis and Butt-head.

245

SESSION 24

QUIZ 7

• •

1. Dikrán Kuyumjian is better known as whom?
2. Complete the proverb: 'The quality of mercy is not...'
3. Complete the proverb: 'A cat may...'
4. Who wrote *Whisky Galore?*
5. According to the old recitation, to the north of which city is the Chinese idol?
6. Who wrote *Death on the Nile?*
7. Complete the Shakespearean line: 'A rose by any other name would...'
8. According to Edward Lear, in what did the Jumblies go to sea?
9. Which newspaper would you buy if you were an actor?
10. Who was François-Eugène Vidocq?
11. Who wrote *Far From the Madding Crowd?*
12. Dashiell Hammett created a husband-and-wife team named 'Nick and Nora Charles' What was the name of the book?
13. Agatha Christie created 'Hercule Poirot'. What was the name of her other major detective?
14. In which work by Dylan Thomas does the character 'Captain Cat' appear?
15. 'Fagin' is a character in which book by Dickens?

ANSWERS

1. Michael Arlen. 2. '...strained'. 3. '...look at a king'. 4. Compton Mackenzie. 5. Kathmandu. 6. Agatha Christie. 7. '...smell as sweet'. 8. A sieve. 9. *The Stage.* 10. A real-life French policeman and former convict. 11. Thomas Hardy. 12. *The Thin Man.* 13. 'Miss Marple'. 14. *Under Milk Wood.* 15. *Oliver Twist.*

SESSION 24
QUIZ 8

• •

1. Which anniversary does a china wedding celebrate?
2. What is a sorbet?
3. What is an atheist?
4. Which 19th-century event is concealed by the anagram :
    I require love in a subject?
5. St Valentine is the patron saint of whom?
6. Which European princess had children named Albert,
    Caroline and Stephanie?
7. How many deadly sins are there?
8. Which anniversary does a coral wedding celebrate?
9. Who is the patron saint of wine-growers?
10. The river Medway runs through Kent. What is a man
    born east of it called?
11. Who would be taking the advice 'vamp till ready'?
12. Who is Ken Dodd?
13. Which architect designed Waterloo Bridge and the present
    Anglican Cathedral in Liverpool?
14. St Augustine is the patron saint of whom?
15. What is doner kebab?

ANSWERS

1. The twentieth. 2. A water-ice. 3. Someone who does not believe in a
God. 4. Queen Victoria's Jubilee. 5. Lovers. 6. Princess Grace of Monaco.
7. Seven. 8. The thirty-fifth. 9. St Vincent. 10. A man of Kent. 11. A
piano accompanist. 12. A Lancashire comedian. 13. Sir Giles Gilbert Scott.
14. Brewers. 15. Thin slices of seasoned lamb grilled on a spit.

247

SESSION 24
QUIZ 9

1. What is meant by the 'occult sciences'?
2. How many sides has a heptagon?
3. A land region devoid of water is called what?
4. What does an altimeter measure?
5. What are cantilever, beam and cable-stayed types of?
6. Saturn is the only planet that has rings around it. True or false?
7. What was the R101?
8. What is the familiar name for sodium bicarbonate?
9. What is a dodecahedron?
10. What is alabaster?
11. What is phobophobia?
12. Who invented the centigrade thermometer?
13. What is a rectangle?
14. Pollenosis is a name for a common complaint, usually called what?
15. What is a billion?

ANSWERS

1. Alchemy, astrology, palmistry, fortune-telling, etc. 2. Seven. 3. A desert. 4. Altitude. 5. Bridges. 6. False (Uranus and Neptune also have rings). 7. An airship which crashed in France in 1930. 8. Baking powder. 9. A solid figure having twelve faces. 10. A soft translucent gypsum rock, used for carving. 11. A fear of being afraid. 12. Anders Celsius. 13. A four-sided plane figure with right angles. 14. Hay fever. 15. A British billion is one million million; an American billion is a thousand million.

SESSION 24
QUIZ 10

1. The avens plant is also called what?
2. What is a ratel?
3. What sort of animal is called a Shorthorn?
4. The ancestors of horses and rhinoceroses were very alike. What does this prove?
5. Which is the largest British butterfly?
6. A booby is a kind of sea-bird. True or false?
7. What is another name for the sycamore?
8. A gavial is a water reptile - a long slender version of what?
9. Chives are members of the lily family. Yes or no?
10. How many legs has a spider?
11. What kind of animal could be described as a Berkshire?
12. Do sea birds drink salt sea-water?
13. Is an ant-lion a large ant?
14. What is jute?
15. The ladybird is a kind of beetle. True or false?

ANSWERS

1. Herb bennet. 2. A badger-like animal found in India and Africa. 3. A breed of cattle. 4. That they were closely related. 5. The monarch. 6. True. 7. The great maple. 8. Crocodile. 9. Yes. 10. eight. It's a kind of gannet. 7. The great maple. 8. Crocodile. 9. Yes. 10. eight. 11. A breed of black pig. 12. Yes. There is no alternative! 13. No. It's the larva of another insect which preys on ants and small insects. 14. A plant which grows in India, whose fibre is used for making sacks and mats. 15. True.

SESSION 25
QUIZ 1

· ·

1. Can you give another word, beginning with S, for hygienic or antiseptic?
2. Complete this simile: 'To turn up like a bad...'
3. What is the name for someone who studies the origin of words?
4. Which of these three spellings is correct: (a) desicated, (b) desiccated or (c) dessicated?

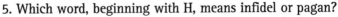

5. Which word, beginning with H, means infidel or pagan?
6. What is the difference between 'yolk' and 'yoke'?
7. If someone says 'the ball is in your court', what does it mean?
8. What's the male version of a 'maidservant'?
9. Which of the following words is misspelled: Sythe, paralel, conquerer?
10. What's the male version of an 'usherette'?
11. Which word, starting with N, can mean armada or fleet?
12. Which word, starting with A, means detached or reserved?
13. What was 'Thenceforth' an old way of saying?
14. What is meant by a persona non grata?
15. What is the female version of 'boar'?

ANSWERS

1. Sanitary or sterile. 2. '...penny'. 3. Etymologist. 4. (b) desiccated.
5. Heathen. 6. The first means 'the yellow part of an egg', and the second is a kind of wooden collar for oxen. 7. You are responsible. 8. Manservant.
9. All of them. They should be scythe, parallel, conqueror. 10. Usher.
11. Navy. 12. Aloof. 13. From that time onwards. 14. Someone who is not in favour or not welcome. 15. Sow.

250

SESSION 25
QUIZ 2

• •

1. Which British swimmer won a breaststroke gold medal in the 1980 Olympics?
2. With which sport do you associate Mary Peters?
3. What do, Chris Waddle, Stuart Pearce and Paul Ince have in common?
4. Name Washington's American football team?
5. Which Scottish defender suffered the indignity of Paul Gascoigne lobbing the ball over his head to then chip it into the goal, during Euro 96?
6. With which sport do you associate David Bryant?
7. Which British sports personality of the year gained notoriety for swearing while collecting the trophy from the Princess Royal?
8. With which athletic event do you associate Sergei Bubka?
9. Which England football manager was controversially portrayed as a turnip by the tabloid press?
10. Great Britain have won the Olympic Hockey gold medal three times. True or false?
11. Which British entrepreneur owns the London Broncos Rugby League team?
12. Who captained England's Grand Slam, winning team in 1980?
13. With which sport do you associate the, 'Cresta Run'?
14. In which country is the Paul Ricard racing circuit?
15. Name Miami's American football team?

ANSWERS

1. Duncan Goodhew. 2. Heptathlon. 3. They have all missed penalties in World Cup penalty shootouts where England have been eliminated. 4. Redskins. 5. Colin Hendry. 6. Bowls. 7. Daley Thompson. 8. Pole Vault. 9. Graham Taylor. 10. False. 11. Richard Branson. 12. Bill Beaumont. 13. Bobsleigh (tobogganing). 14. France. 15. Dolphins.

251

SESSION 25
QUIZ 3

• •

1. Which driverless, computer-run railway began operating on 30th July, 1987?
2. What was the occupation of Adolf Hitler's father?
3. What is the Orange Order?
4. 11 Victoria Crosses were awarded as a result of an action which took place against Zulus in 1879. What was it?
5. Which king of England is believed to have had 23 children?
6. Who was James Garfield?
7. Which head of state visited China on a 7-day visit in October, 1986?
8. What was the Lusitania?
9. Which future British monarch was born on 9th November, 1841?
10. What was the Spanish Inquisition?
11. What was the Comintern?
12. Who were the Bolsheviks?
13. In 1933 in Germany, all political parties except one were banned. Which one?
14. Who was the fattest of all British monarchs?
15. Who was 'the Lady with the Lamp'?

ANSWERS

1. The Docklands Light Railway in east London. 2. He was an Austrian customs official. 3. An anti-Catholic society, originally secret, supported by some Protestants in Ireland. 4. The Battle of Rorke's Drift. 5. King Henry I. 6. The 20th American president 7. H.M. the Queen. 8. A British liner sunk by a German submarine in 1915. 9. King Edward VII. 10. Ar religious court directed against suspected 'converts'. 11. An agreement between the Communist parties of the world. 12. Revolutionary socialists in Russia. 13. The National Socialist party, or Nazis. 14. King George IV, who died from obesity. 15. Florence Nightingale.

SESSION 25
QUIZ 4

• •

1. Prince Charles is credited with having described someone as, 'Terribly nice one minute, and well, not so nice the next.' Who was he talking about?
2. What comic-book character did Buster Crabbe play?
3. What animal follows the landlord Jack Lemmon in *Under the Yum Yum Tree?*
4. Which film featured Kevin Costner and Whitney Houston in lead roles?
5. In the film *Turner and Hooch,* who was Hooch?
6. Who starred in the film *Caesar and Cleopatra?*
7. Who starred in the film *My Darling Clementine?*
8. In the film *Pulp Fiction,* what was a Quarterpounder with cheese in France called?
9. Which movie star's real name was Ruth Elizabeth Davis?
10. Which movie star's real name was Ruby Stevens?
11. Who has been married to Frank Sinatra and Woody Allen?
12. Who starred in the film *Home Alone?*
13. Who played the ambitious, smalltown T.V. star in the film *To Die For?*
14. Who played the name part in the film *Alfie?*
15. Which cartoon show featured Thelma and Shaggy amongst others?

ANSWERS

1. Frank Sinatra. 2. Flash Gordon. 3. A cat. 4. *The Bodyguard.* 5. A big dog. 6. Claude Rains and Vivien Leigh. 7. Henry Fonda, Linda Darnell. 8. A Royale. 9. Bette Davis. 10. Barbara Stanwyck. 11. Mia Farrow. 12. Macaulay Culkin, Joe Pesci, Daniel Stern. 13. Nicole Kidman. 14. Michael Caine. 15. *Scooby Do.*

SESSION 25

QUIZ 5

• •

1. Which group, 'Lost That Lovin' Feeling'?
2. Who recorded the album 'Stanley Road' in 1995?
3. Who sang 'I Feel Good' and 'Sex Machine' and was known as 'the hardest working man in showbusiness'?
4. Which guitarist recorded a version of the US National Anthem in the late 60's, on his left-handed 'Strat'?
5. What links the bands Genesis and Mike And The Mechanics
6. 'One Day In Your Life' was the first number one for which US mega star?
7. Which actress and singer featured Neil Kinnock in her pop video during his General Election Campaign?
8. Who walked 'On The Bright Side Of The Road' looking for his 'Brown-eyed Girl', saying 'Baby Please Don't Go'?
9. What was the title of Bjork's second album?
10. Who recorded the album 'Wild Wood' in 1993?
11. Elvis Costello And The Attractions had their first top ten hit in 1979. What was the song?
12. Who was the lead singer with Thin Lizzy?
13. Which blues singer has a cherished guitar called 'Lucille'?
14. Who recorded the albums, 'No Need To Argue' and 'Everybody Else Is Doing It, So Why Can't We?'?
15. Michael Crawford has only entered the Chart twice. On both occasions with different versions of the same song. Can you name the song?

ANSWERS

1. The Righteous Brothers. 2. Paul Weller. 3. James Brown. 4. Jimi Hendrix. 5. Mike Rutherford (he's a member of both bands). 6. Michael Jackson. 7. Tracey Ullman. 8. Van Morrison. 9. 'Post'. 10. Paul Weller. 11. 'Oliver's Army'. 12. Phil Lynott. 13. B.B. King. 14. The Cranberries. 15. The Music Of The Night.

254

SESSION 25
QUIZ 6

• •

1. According to Keats, what is the, 'Season of mists and mellow fruitfulness?'
2. Robert Burns wrote, 'Wee, sleekit, cow'rin', tim'rous beastie...' How did he continue?
3. 'Captain Dobbin' appears in which book by Thackeray?
4. Genius, according to Thomas Edison, is, 'One percent inspiration and...'
5. Who wrote *The World According To Garp*?
6. 'Sir Toby Belch' appears in which play by Shakespeare?
7. The character 'Clara Peggoty' appears in which book by Charles Dickens?
8. In which Shakespeare play does 'Shylock' appear?
9. Who wrote *The Sportswriter*?
10. 'Full fathom five thy father lies;' is the beginning of a poem by whom?
11. Which American author wrote *The Scarlet Letter*?
12. In which books will you find the characters Zaphod Beeblebrox and Ford Prefect?
13. Complete the proverb: 'Children should be seen...'
14. Complete the line: 'Some are born great, some achieve greatness, and some...'
15. Complete the proverb: 'Burn not your house...'

ANSWERS

1. Autumn. 2. O what a panic's in thy breastie! 3. *Vanity Fair*. 4. '99 per cent perspiration'. 5. John Irving. 6. *Twelfth Night*. 7. *David Copperfield*. 8. *The Merchant of Venice*. 9. Richard Ford. 10. William Shakespeare. 11. Nathaniel Hawthorne. 12. *The Hitch-Hiker's Guide* series by Douglas Adams. 13. '...and not heard'. 14. '...have greatness thrust upon them'. 15. '...to fright the mouse away'.

• •

1. Which anniversary does a copper or pottery wedding celebrate?
2. The Ram represents which sign of the Zodiac?
3. What were, or are, the Gnomes of Zurich?
4. Which word, beginning with post- means 'published after the death of the composer or author'?
5. Indian ink didn't come from India. Where does it come from?
6. Who is the patron saint of sailors?
7. Dutch clocks didn't come from Holland. Where do they come from?
8. What is lobscouse?
9. Who, on stage in 1937, did the Lambeth Walk?
10. What does the abbreviation NATO stand for?
11. St Hubert is the patron saint of whom?
12. Which kind of bridge is largely played nowadays: Auction or Contract?
13. Which spacecraft was the first to land on Mars?
14. Tuesday is named after Tiw, or Tyr, the German god of the rules of war. True or false?
15. Who invented jeans?

ANSWERS

1. The ninth. 2. Aries. 3. Swiss bankers and financiers. 4. Posthumous. 5. China. 6. St Cuthbert. 7. Germany. 8. An old seaman's dish of vegetables and sea-biscuit. 9. Lupino Lane. 10. North Atlantic Treaty Organisation. 11. Hunters. 12. Contract. 13. Viking. 14. True. 15. The firm of Levi-Strauss in 1872.

SESSION 25
QUIZ 8

• •

1. An important medical preventive system was invented in 1796 by Edward Jenner. What was it?
2. What aerial device was invented in André-Jacques Garnerin in 1802?
3. What is varicella another name for?
4. Which medical procedure involves the use of many needles all over the body?
5. What is a bathyscape?
6. What is acoustics?
7. What is a chiropodist?
8. What is measured by the gallon?
9. What is humidity?
10. Stainless steel is an alloy of which metals?
11. What is measured by a watt?
12. Who was Isambard Kingdom Brunel?
13. What is an ammonite?
14. What does the prefix 'kilo-' mean?
15. The femur is another name for which bone?

ANSWERS

1. Vaccination. 2. The parachute. 3. Chicken-pox. 4. Acupuncture 5. A diving vessel for underwater exploration. 6. The science of sound. 7. One who practises in, and deals with, ailments of the feet. 8. Liquid. 9. The amount of moisture in the atmosphere. 10. Iron, chromium and nickel. 11. Power. 12. Inventor and engineer. 13. An extinct mollusc with a coiled shell. 14. A thousand. 15. The thigh bone.

SESSION 25
QUIZ 9

· ·

1. What is cassava?
2. What is an iguana?
3. What sort of animal is a Saint Bernard?
4. The lory is a member of which very noisy family of birds?
5. What is the name for the large South American cat with leopard-like spots?
6. What sort of animal is a chihuahua?
7. What is a caterpillar the larva of?
8. Is the horn on a rhinoceros similar to a tusk on an elephant?
9. What is a more familiar name for the cavy?
10. A group of ants is called an angle or a colony?
11. What is the name for the large, spotted wild cat, smaller than a tiger?
12. What sort of animal is a Doberman pinscher?
13. What is a young kangaroo called?
14. A mammal with heavy armour plates on its body is called what?
15. What kind of animal is said to gobble?

ANSWERS

1. A plant whose roots produce a pleasant-tasting starch. 2. A large, tree-dwelling lizard. 3. A breed of dog. 4. The parrots. 5. The jaguar. 6. A breed of dog. 7. A moth or butterfly. 8. No. A rhinoceros horn is made of compacted hair. 9. The guinea-pig. 10. A colony. 11. The leopard. 12. A breed of dog. 13. A joey. 14. An armadillo. 15. A turkey.

SESSION 25
QUIZ 10

•••••••••••••••••••••••••••••••

1. The old country of Babylonia is now called?
2. Which major American city stands on the Hudson river?
3. Camulodunum was the ancient name for which Essex city?
4. What is the capital of India?
5. Where is Bermuda?
6. Provençal is a language spoken in which part of the world?
7. How many people live on the Scilly Isles: 25, 250 or 2,500?
8. In which city would you find Waverley railway station?
9. In which country does the Mekong river end?
10. Where and what is Sandringham?
11. What language is spoken in the Channel Isles?
12. What was Sri Lanka previously known as?
13. What is Abyssinia now called?
14. In which country is the town of Rotarua?
15. Persia is the old name for which country?

ANSWERS

1. Iraq. 2. New York City. 3. Colchester. 4. New Delhi. 5. In the West Indies. 6. Southern France. 7. About 2,500. 8. Edinburgh. 9. Vietnam. 10. It's a royal residence in Norfolk. 11. English, and a dialect of French called Jerseyaise. 12. Ceylon. 13. Ethiopia. 14. New Zealand. 15. Iran.

SESSION 26
QUIZ 1

• •

1. What was Nigel Benn's fighting nickname?
2. What music usually accompanies Chris Eubank as he enters the boxing arena?
3. Name Green Bay's American football team?
4. With which sport do you associate Peekaboo Street?
5. Which England goalkeeper had a premature end to his career when he injured an eye in a car accident?
6. In the 1997/98 season who did Mohammed Al Fayed appoint as Director of Football at Fulham?
7. Which Formula One driver also owned an airline?
8. Which former Tottenham player captained Germany during the 1998 World Cup?
9. Which horse is buried at the Aintree winning post?
10. Who won the 1998 European Cup Winners Cup?
11. In 1998 which County Cricket team did Robin Smith captain?
12. With which county is the family name Cowdrey synonymous?
13. In which year did Virginia Wade win the Wimbledon singles title?
14. Who captained the England Rugby Union team during their 1998 tour of the southern hemisphere?
15. What nationality is the athlete Haile Gebresilassie?

ANSWERS

SESSION 26
QUIZ 2

• •

1. Who was the Black Prince?
2. Who were the Aztecs?
3. After the collapse of the French government, who became head of state of France in July, 1940?
4. What did the 1763 Peace of Paris end?
5. What was the Louisiana Purchase?
6. What was the name of the famous son of Philip II of Macedonia?
7. Who was Aristotle?
8. During the American Civil War what happened in Appomattox, Virginia on 9th April, 1865?
9. On 13th January, 1898, Émile Zola used a newspaper to publish his famous open letter *J'accuse.* What cause provoked the writing of the letter?
10. What were the Nuremberg Trials held in 1945-1946?
11. The first screw-propelled iron transatlantic steamship made her maiden voyage in 1845. What was she called?
12. Who was the first King of Scots?
13. Which well-known New York bridge was designed by the father but built by the son of the Roebling family?
14. The National Viewers and Listeners Association against 'bad taste' was founded in 1965 by whom?
15. 10,000 people died of what 1854 epidemic in London?

ANSWERS

1. Edward, Prince of Wales, (1330-1376). 2. One of the original and native peoples of Mexico. 3. Marshal Pétain. 4. The Seven Years War. 5. The acquisition by the USA in 1803 of the huge French territory of Louisiana. 6. Alexander the Great. 7. A Greek philosopher of enormous knowledge. 8. The Confederate Army surrendered. 9. The innocence of Alfred Dreyfus. 10. International trials of war criminals. 11. The Great Britain. 12. King Malcolm II, in 1005. 13. The Brooklyn Bridge. 14. Mrs Mary Whitehouse. 15. Cholera.

SESSION 26
QUIZ 3

• •

1. Which movie star was the 'Mexican Spitfire'?
2. Who, in show business, was 'Ol' Blue Eyes'?
3. Which film featured Mr Black and Mr Pink?
4. Who directed the film in question three?
5. Who starred in the film *Midnight Cowboy*?
6. How many Marx Brothers spent *A Night at the Opera*?
7. The film *The Gold Rush* shows Charlie Chaplin eating his boots. Was this a fake?
8. Who starred in the film *Back to the Future*?
9. Which movie star's real name was Byron Elsworth Barr?
10. Who starred in the film *Letter from an Unknown Woman*?
11. Which fictional character has been used most in films?
12. Which American president appeared in the movie *Bedtime for Bonzo*?
13. Which British TV star has held a 'Swap Shop' a 'House Party' and is a bit of a 'Telly Addict'?
14. From which film did the song 'Nice Work If You Can Get It' come?
15. From which film did the song 'Be a Clown' come?

ANSWERS

1. Lupe Velez. 2. Frank Sinatra. 3. *Reservoir Dogs*. 4. Quentin Tarantino. 5. Dustin Hoffman, Jon Voight. 6. Four. 7. In a sense: the boots were made of liquorice. 8. Michael J. Fox and Christopher Lloyd. 9. Gig Young. 10. Joan Fontaine, Louis Jourdan. 11. Sherlock Holmes, in about 200 films. 12. Ronald Reagan. 13. Noel Edmonds. 14. *A Damsel in Distress*, 1937. 15. *The Pirate*, 1948.

SESSION 26
QUIZ 4

• •

1. Who reached number one in 1976 with 'Don't Cry For Me Argentina'?
2. Who performed the title song to Dudley Moore's film Arthur?
3. Which combined Australian and New Zealand band reached number 7 in 1992 with 'Weather With You'?
4. Which actor did Madonna marry on a cliff top?
5. Which US band had top ten hits in 1982 with 'I'm A Wonderful Thing Baby', 'Stool Pigeon' and 'Annie I'm Not Your Daddy'?
6. Which female American singer won two Grammies with 'All I Wanna Do' in 1995?
7. Who had top ten hits with 'Joe Le Taxi' and 'Be My Baby' as well as appearing in Chanel perfume adverts?
8. The Heartbreakers' recording career has spanned nearly twenty years, with great success in the United States. Yet they have never made the UK top ten. Name their lead vocalist?
9. In 1960 Johnny Preston reached number one with a song about a Red Indian love story. Can you name the song?
10. Who was The Who's original drummer who died from a drugs overdose.
11. Who recorded the album 'Kissing Gate' in 1993?
12. Who went straight in at number one in June 1998 with their debut single 'C'est La Vie'?
13. Which band had albums, 'New World Record', 'Eldorado' and 'Out Of The Blue'?
14. Who re-recorded his 1974 number one single 'Kung Fu Fighting' in 1998 with Bus Stop?
15. 'The Whole Of The Moon' and 'The Return Of Pan' were hits for which Irish band led by Mike Scott?

ANSWERS

SESSION 26
QUIZ 5

· ·

1. What sort of fictional character was 'Jules Maigret'?
2. Who wrote Moby Dick?
3. Complete the proverb: 'Catch your bear...'
4. From which Shakespeare play does the quotation, 'All the world's a stage' come?
5. 'Up the airy mountain,/Down the rushy glen' is the beginning of a poem by whom?
6. Who is the main character in Arthur Conan Doyle's The Lost World?
7. Who, in , wrote The Castle of Otranto?
8. Who was the great adversary of Robin Hood?
9. Who wrote Fahrenheit 451?
10. The character 'Augustus Snodgrass' appears in which famous book?
11. Who wrote Call of the Wild?
12. 'John Gilpin was a citizen/Of credit and renown' is the beginning of a poem by whom?
13. Complete the proverb: Advice when most needed...
14. 'Reggie Fortune' is a fictional detective created by whom?
15. The character 'Bill Sikes' appears in which book by Charles Dickens?

ANSWERS

SESSION 26
QUIZ 6

• •

1. What is the name given to the beam placed above a window or door?
2. In what place do Hindu people worship?
3. What did George Cruikshank do?
4. Turkish baths weren't started in Turkey. Where were they started?
5. In the Army who is more senior, a Major or a Colonel?
6. Which day is the Jewish Sabbath?
7. Who was Aubrey Beardsley?
8. Who was Karl Benz?
9. To the ancient Romans who was Venus?
10. What are *marrons glacés*?
11. Who in the world would be called 'Taffy'?
12. What is an 'idiot board'?
13. Who is the patron saint of sculptors?
14. What anniversary does a leather wedding celebrate?
15. In ancient times what was King Midas's big problem?

ANSWERS

1. Lintel. 2. A temple. 3. He was a caricaturist and illustrator of books. 4. The Near East. 5. Colonel. 6. Saturday. 7. A black and white artist. 8. German maker of an early car. 9. The goddess of love. 10. Chestnuts coated with sugar. 11. A Welshman. 12. A card used in a television studio to prompt an actor. 13. St Claude. 14. The third. 15. Everything he touched turned to gold.

SESSION 26
QUIZ 7

1. Hepatitis is inflammation of what?
2. Which weather-measuring instrument was invented in 1643 by Torricelli?
3. What object in the sky is called Triton, and is about 1,680 miles in diameter?
4. The study of the minute structure of tissues and organs is called what?
5. What is enteritis?
6. Which planet is the Morning Star?
7. Who invented saccharine?
8. What is dipsomania?
9. André-Marie Ampère gave his name to what?
10. What is pyrophobia?
11. In Roman numerals, what is M?
12. Mothers could not survive without Walter Hunt's invention in 1849. What was it?
13. What is a rhomb?
14. What is the familiar name for sodium carbonate?
15. The Silver Ghost, introduced in 1906, was the first example of what by a famous company?

ANSWERS

1. The liver. 2. The barometer. 3. It is Neptune's largest moon. 4. Histology. 5. Inflammation of the intestines. 6. Venus. 7. C.H. Fahlberg, who discovered it by accident when working on something else. 8. An almost overpowering desire for alcoholic drink. 9. The ampere, a unit of electric current. 10. Fear of fire. 11. 1,000. 12. The safety-pin. 13. An equilateral parallelogram. 14. Washing soda. 15. The first car by Rolls-Royce.

SESSION 26
QUIZ 8

• •

1. Jasmin is a plant relative of the olive. True or false?
2. The Caffer cat, found originally in Egypt, was the ancestor of what?
3. What is a cygnet?
4. In Britain what is unusual about the stag beetle?
5. What is saffron?
6. What colour is a lobster when it's alive in the water?
7. What sort of animal is a Samoyed?
8. What domestic animal could be described as a Manx?
9. In the movies, what was Blondie and Dagwood's dog called?
10. What kind of animal is said to howl?
11. What is a leveret?
12. What is an auk?
13. What is gorse?
14. How many legs can a centipede have; (a) more than 300 (b) more than 200 (c) more than 100?
15. What is a basenji?

ANSWERS

1. True. 2. The domestic cat. 3. A young swan. 4. It's our heaviest beetle.
5. A yellow-coloured pigment obtained from the saffron crocus. 6. A bluish-grey. It only turns red when it's cooked. 7. A breed of dog. 8. A cat.
9. Daisy. 10. A wolf. 11. A young hare. 12. A diving bird of the northern seas, usually black and white. 13. A wild shrub with yellow flowers and very sharp spines. 14. More than 300. 15. A breed of dog.

SESSION 26

QUIZ 9

• •

1. We call this place Leghorn; what do the Italians call it?
2. Where is the Forest of Dean?
3. Eboracum was the name given by the Romans to which city?
4. The Mont Blanc vehicular tunnel is between which two countries?
5. Where in the world do they speak Frisian?
6. To which country does Madeira belong?
7. What is the capital of Poland?
8. Where is the Sphinx?
9. Where is the Caledonian Canal?
10. What was remarkable about the Temple of Artemis at Ephesus?
11. Where is the Kariba Dam?
12. The official language of Andorra is Spanish. True or false?
13. The Battle of Hastings wasn't fought in Hastings at all. Where was it fought?
14. Where does the Rhine river rise?
15. What is the capital of Romania?

ANSWERS

1. Livorno. 2. Gloucestershire. 3. York. 4. France and Italy. 5. In northern Holland. 6. Portugal. 7. Warsaw. 8. Giza, Egypt. 9. In northern Scotland. 10. It was one of the Seven Wonders of the World, 110 by 55 metres in size. 11. On the Zambesi river, on the Zimbabwe/Zambia border. 12. False. It's Catalan. 13. At Battle, about six miles inland. 14. In Switzerland. 15. Bucharest.

SESSION 26
QUIZ 10

● ●

1. What was an 'albert'?
2. What word, beginning with E, means costly or dear?
3. What does the old word 'Caitiff' mean?
4. Can you name two words, sounding alike, which mean the same as this pair: male offspring/heavenly body?
5. What two words, sounding alike, mean 'entire' and 'hole-making tool'?
6. 'Don't buy a pig in a poke', goes the advice. What was a 'poke'?
7. A tiro is; (a) a South American fish (b) a novice (c) a circular building in a park?
8. What is a *magnum opus*?
9. What is the meaning of the abreviation, ATC?
10. Which women, in earlier times, were known as 'The Fishing Fleet'?
11. What was meant by the phrase, 'to ken'?
12. What does an American mean by 'dry goods'?
13. Who or what was a 'nippy'?
14. What is the name for someone who studies the history of words?
15. What is the female version of 'buck'?

ANSWERS

1. A short watch-chain fastened to a waist-coat pocket. 2. Expensive. 3. Coward. 4. Son/Sun. 5. All/awl. 6. A poke was a sack or bag, in which animals were sold in the market-place. 7. (b) a novice. 8. A great work of literature. 9. Air Traffic Control. 10. Young women who went out to India in search of husbands. 11. To know. 12. Drapery and linen products. 13. A waitress in Lyons's tea shop during the 1920s and 1930s. 14. Lexicologist. 15. Doe.

269

SESSION 27
QUIZ 1

1. Who in 1895 set sail from Boston on the first solo round-the-world voyage?
2. What experiment took place in Monte Bello islands, off northwest Australia, in 1952?
3. In which war were the Boers in South Africa victorious at Magersfontein, on 11 December 1899?
4. A purpose-built supermarket was opened in Croydon in August, 1950, by which company?
5. When were Life Peerages introduced?
6. What did the heroine Grace Darling do in 1838?
7. Which Soviet president visited the Queen at Windsor in 1989?
8. To which president was Eleanor Roosevelt married?
9. What was the name given to Oliver Cromwell's soldiers?
10. Who landed on Pitcairn Island in 1790?
11. Who defeated whom at the Battle of Flodden Field in 1513?
12. Egbert was the first English king to be converted to what?
13. Who was Nikita Sergeyevich Khrushchev?
14. What happened to the MP Spencer Perceval in 1812?
15. In which London underground station did fire break out in 1987?

ANSWERS

SESSION 27
QUIZ 2

• •

1. Who starred in the film *Mr Smith Goes to Washington*?
2. The film *The Women* in 1939 had an all-women cast. How many women were involved; (a) 64 (b) 97 (c) 5?
3. Which movie star's real name was Dawn Evelyeen Davis?
4. Who played Seymour in the film *Little Shop Of Horrors*?
5. Which film, made in 1963, used an all-boy cast?
6. What was unusual about the original version of the 1924 silent film *Greed*?
7. Who wrote the book on which the film *2001: A Space Odyssey* was based?
8. What is the connection between *Austin Powers: International Man Of Mystery* and *Wayne's World*?
9. Who starred in the film *Psycho*?
10. Who starred in the film *The Best Years of Our Lives*?
11. Which movie star was the 'Oomph Girl'?
12. Who starred in the film *Great Expectations*?
13. Which movie star is the 'Professional Virgin'?
14. Who starred in the film *Taxi Driver*?
15. Who starred in the film *The Constant Husband*?

ANSWERS

1. Jean Arthur, James Stewart. 2. (c) Five. 3. Anne Shirley. 4. Rick Moranis. 5. Lord of the Flies. 6. Its length. The film was well over six hours long. 7. Arthur C. Clarke. 8. Mike Myers devised and starred in both. 9. Anthony Perkins, Janet Leigh. 10. Fredric March, Myrna Loy. 11. Ann Sheridan. 12. John Mills, Bernard Miles, Finlay Currie, Jean Simmons. 13. Doris Day. 14. Robert De Niro. 15. Rex Harrison.

SESSION 27
QUIZ 3

1. Who recorded the 1987 album 'Now That's What I Call Quite Good'?
2. Who is Led Zeppelin's lead singer?
3. What was the title of 'Take That's' first album?
4. Which Quentin Tarantino film sound track featured 'Jungle Boogie' by Kool and the Gang?
5. Which band will be best remembered for 'Love Shack' and 'Rock Lobster'?
6. Which super model featured on Bon Jovi's 'Please Come Home For Christmas' video in 1994?
7. Name Madonna's 1998 album?
8. Name Natalie Imbruglia's debut album.
9. What nationality is Enya?
10. On which Beatles album would you find 'Helter Skelter', 'Dear Prudence' and 'Back In The USSR'?
11. Name Radiohead's third album featuring the tracks, 'Paranoid Android' and 'Karma Police'?
12. Name Rod Stewart's 1998 'Covers' album?
13. Which 1998 movie sound track features Puff Daddy singing Led Zeppelin and The Wallflowers performing David Bowie's 'Heroes'?
14. Which musical legend reached number three in the US album chart in June 1998 (soon after his death) with 'In The Wee Small Hours'?
15. Who released the album 'Pilgrim' in 1998?

ANSWERS

1. The Housemartins. 2. Robert Plant. 3. 'Take That and Party'. 4. Pulp Fiction. 5. B52's. 6. Cindy Crawford. 7. 'Ray Of Light'. 8. 'Left Of The Middle'. 9. Irish. 10. The White Album'. 11. 'OK Computer'. 12. 'When We Were New Boys.13. Godzilla. 14. Frank Sinatra. 15. Eric Clapton.

272

SESSION 27
QUIZ 4

. . . .

1. The character 'Captain Rawdon' appears in which book by Charles Dickens?
2. Who wrote *Barchester Towers*?
3. What author became most famous for his nonsense verse and limericks?
4. In which book by Thomas Hardy does 'Angel Clare' appear?
5. Complete the proverb: 'The devil finds work...'
6. 'Though I've belted you and flayed you, By the livin' Gawd that made you,' wrote Kipling. What was the next line?
7. Complete Kipling's line: 'God of our fathers, known of old...'
8. Who wrote *Les Misérables*?
9. Who wrote *The Third Man*?
10. Who wrote *A Farewell to Arms*?
11. Who often accompanied, and was usually baffled by, Hercule Poirot on his investigations?
12. Who wrote *The Ginger Man*?
13. Complete the proverb: 'Don't count your chickens...'
14. James Dixon, a lecturer in history, appears as a character in which book by Kingsley Amis?
15. How old was the title character in the book *Lolita*?

ANSWERS

1. *Bleak House*. 2. Anthony Trollope. 3. Edward Lear. 4. *Tess of the D'Urbervilles*. 5. '...for idle hands to do'. 6. 'You're a better man than I am, Gunga Din!' 7. '...Lord of our far-flung battle-line'. 8. Victor Hugo. 9. Graham Greene. 10. Ernest Hemingway. 11. Captain Hastings. 12. J.P. Donleavy. 13. '...before they are hatched'. 14. *Lucky Jim*. 15. 12.

273

SESSION 27
QUIZ 5

● ●

1. What kind of food item is associated with Bombay?
2. Who was Jean Renoir's father?
3. How many is a baker's dozen?
4. Who was Jesus?
5. What is the Trinity?
6. In a pack of cards, which way does the Jack of Spades look, to his left, or to his right?
7. According to the 'language of flowers', what does the jasmine signify?
8. Which daily newspaper was first published on 7th October, 1986?
9. What anniversary does a tin wedding celebrate?
10. Why is a bowler hat so called?
11, What is a pizza?
12. A clutch is composed of what items?
13. In British movies and on stage, which actress was famed for her portrayal of eccentric elderly ladies?
14. What is *paté de fois gras*?
15. Who is the patron saint of secretaries?

ANSWERS

1. Duck. It's not a duck at all, but a kind of fish. 2. Auguste Renoir. 3. Thirteen. 4. Christians believe he was the Son of God, and part of the Trinity. 5. The belief that God, Jesus and The Holy Spirit are all one. 6. To his left. 7. Amiability. 8. The Independent. 9. The tenth. 10. It was first sold by the hatters, Thomas and William Bowler. 11. An open pie of bread dough, with various toppings. 12. Eggs. 13. Margaret Rutherford. 14. Goose liver pâté. 15. St Cassian.

SESSION 27
QUIZ 6

• •

1. In 1769 Nicholas-Joseph Cugnot built a tractor driven by what sort of power?
2. What's the medical term for loss of memory?
3. What is ailurophobia?
4. What is chlorine?
5. What is ophthalmology?
6. The art of making motion pictures is called what?
7. Whitcomb Judson, in 1892, invented something that avoided the use of buttons. What was it?
8. What did King C. Gillette invent in 1895?
9. What is craniology?
10. Which man and wife discovered radium in 1898?
11. What is pomology?
12. The study of the properties of substances and their interaction is called what?
13. The square of the hypotenuse is equal to the sum of the squares on the other two sides. What is this?
14. The science of the mind is called what?
15. What was a V1?

ANSWERS

1. Steam. 2. Amnesia. 3. A fear of cats. 4. A gas. 5. The science of the eye; its study, and its diseases. 6. Cinematography. 7. The zip fastener. 8. The safety-razor. 9. The study of skulls. 10. Pierre and Marie Curie. 11. The study of fruit-growing. 12. Chemistry. 13. The famous theorem of Pythagorus, Greek philosopher. 14. Psychology. 15. A flying bomb in the form of a pilotless aircraft.

275

SESSION 27
QUIZ 7

• •

1. What is a boa?
2. Gorillas, chimpanzees, and orang-utans are all what?
3. The hyacinth is a plant relative of the lily. True or false?
4. What is the difference between a frog and a toad?
5. Are there any mammals able to fly?
6. Is an ant-lion an insect or a mammal?
7. What is a cowrie?
8. Which insect makes a loud chirping sound?
9. Which common, everyday creature has eight eyes?
10. The kestrel is also known as a what?
11. How many legs does a lobster have?
12. A mastodon was an early example of a what?
13. What domestic animal could be described as a tabby?
14. What sort of animal is called an Ayrshire?
15. The hamster is a small animal native to which areas?

ANSWERS

1. A snake that kills by squeezing its prey to death. 2. Apes. 3. True.
4. A frog hops or leaps along and a toad walks. 5. Yes, bats. 6. An insect.
7. The shell of a mollusc, used by some early peoples as money. 8. The
cricket. 9. The spider. 10. A windhover. 11. Eight. 12. An elephant. 13. A
cat. 14. A breed of cattle. 15. Asia and eastern Europe.

276

SESSION 27

QUIZ 8

• •

1. What is Formosa now called?
2. What was remarkable about the Temple of Zeus at Olympia?
3. What is Etna, and where is it?
4. Which two countries form the island of Hispaniola?
5. What is the name of the stretch of water that lies between Australia and Papua New Guinea?
6. Which is the world's oldest republic?
7. The official name 'Misr' refers to which country?
8. What is the capital of Japan?
9. Where in the world do they speak Coptic?
10. Where in Spain is the Alhambra Palace?
11. What is the capital of the Sudan?
12. Which is the largest lake in the United Kingdom?
13. Where and what is Wookey Hole?
14. Which is Britain's longest river?
15. How many bridges are there across the River Thames?

ANSWERS

1. Taiwan. 2. It was one of the Seven Wonders of the World, 12 metres high and plated with gold and ivory. 3. An active volcano in Sicily. 4. Haiti and the Dominican Republic. 5. Torres Strait. 6. San Marino. 7. Egypt. 8. Tokyo. 9. Egypt. 10. Granada. 11. Khartoum. 12. Lough Neagh, Northern Ireland. 13. It's a cave near Wells in Somerset. 14. The Severn. 15. 27.

SESSION 27
QUIZ 9

• •

1. How did we acquire the word 'pram'?
2. What word, beginning with B, means bold or courageous?
3. A snob is (a) a shoemaker (b) a kind of linen cap (c) a kind of door-handle.
4. What is a 'malapropism'?
5. Can you name two words, sounding alike, which mean the same as this pair: take by theft/metal?
6. What is, or was, 'cheesecake'?
7. What does 'buckshee' mean?
8. What do the Americans mean by a 'freeway'?
9. What was a 'flapper'?
10. Which group were known as 'The Few'?
11. What is the difference between 'balmy' and 'barmy'?
12. Can you name two words, sounding alike, which mean the same as this pair: a market/price for rail ticket?
13. How did the 'doily' get its name?
14. What does 'e.g.' stand for?
15. Can you suggest a palindrome for 'Eve'?

ANSWERS

1. It's a shortened form of 'perambulator'. Perambulate means to walk or travel. 2. Brave. 3. (a) a shoemaker. 4. A failed attempt to sound 'educated', as in 'The threat of nuclear war was a real detergent' (instead of deterrent). 5. Steal/steel. 6. A pin-up picture of a film star or other semi-clad female. 7. Something which turns up, free of charge. 8. A motorway. 9. A voguish, somewhat high-spirited young woman of the 1920s. 10. Allied fighter pilots during the Battle of Britain in 1940. 11. The first means 'mild and pleasant' and the second 'silly or foolish'. 12. Fair/fare. 13. It was first made by a famous haberdasher named Doyley or d'Oyley. 14. Exempli gratia: 'for example'. 15. Madam I'm Adam.

278

SESSION 27

QUIZ 10

• •

1. With which sport do you associate Michael Doohan?
2. In American football how many yards do you have to gain, in order to achieve a 'First down'?
3. With which sport do you associate the Searle brothers?
4. Who scored for England in the 1966 World Cup final, apart from Geoff Hurst?
5. Judo, in Japanese, means, 'the Gentle way'. True or False?
6. With which sport do you associate Jesper Parnevik?
7. Name Warrington's Rugby League team?
8. What nationality is three-day eventer, Mark Todd?
9. With which sport do you associate Armand de la Cuevas?
10. Which sport is famous for being played at the 'Guards Club'?
11. Name Utah's NBA Basketball team?
12. Which of the following is not a coarse fish, Chub, Dace, Grayling, Carp?
13. With which sport do you associate David Campese?
14. Who scored England's opening goal in the 1998 World Cup?
15. Who sponsored Rugby League's Super League in 1998

ANSWERS

1. Motor Cycling. 2. Ten. 3. Rowing. 4. Martin Peters. 5. True. 6. Golf.
7. Wolves. 8. New Zealand. 9. Cycling. 10. Polo. 11. The Jazz.
12. Grayling. 13. Rugby Union. 14. Alan Shearer. 15. JJB.

SESSION 28

QUIZ 1

• •

1. Was Joyce Grenfell English or American?
2. Which English film actor was born Laruska Mischa Skikne?
3. Which gentlemanly English actor was brought up speaking only German?
4. Who starred in the film Carve Her Name with Pride?
5. What was unique about the Nestor Film Studio on Sunset Boulevard?
6. Who starred in the film Wonder Man?
7. What was unique about the film The World, the Flesh and the Devil?
8. Which was the first full-length talking film?
9. Who starred in the film The Citadel?
10. Which movie star's real name was Spangler Arlington Brugh?
11. Which movie star's real name was Robert Taylor?
12. Who is Larry Hagman's mother?
13. Who starred in the film Force of Evil?
14. Who starred in the film Home at Seven?
15. How are the film actors Dana Andrews and Steve Forrest connected?

ANSWERS

1. American. 2. Laurence Harvey. 3. Leslie Howard. 4. Virginia McKenna, Paul Scofield. 5. It was Hollywood's first, established 1911. 6. Danny Kaye. 7. It was the world's first movie in natural colour, made in the UK in 1914. 8. The Jazz Singer, 1927. 9. Robert Donat. 10. Robert Taylor. 11. Rod Taylor (from Australia). 12. Mary Martin. 13. John Garfield. 14. Ralph Richardson, Margaret Leighton. 15. They are brothers.

SESSION 28
QUIZ 2

• •

1. Who took the title role in the film Buster?
2. Which super model is married to Rod Stewart?
3. Who was the lead singer of the Pretenders?
4. Who's only Christmas hit was 'Last Christmas'?
5. Who's daughter recorded 'These Boots Were Made For Walking'?
6. Who was the lead singer of the Undertones?
7. Which Canadian guitarist's backing bands have included The International Harvesters, The Blue Notes and Crazy Horse
8. Who said 'You're Unbelievable' in 1990?
9. Who had top ten hits with 'War', 'Contact' and 'H.A.P.P.Y. Radio'?
10. Who recorded the album 'Listen without Prejudice'?
11. Who was labelled the 'New Dylan' and went on to write and sing rock anthems like 'Born To Run' and 'Born In The USA?
12. 'Sheena Is A Punk Rocker' was the first UK hit for which US Punk band?
13. After which 1982 advertising campaign did John Lee Hooker chart with 'Boom Boom'?
14. Which singer starred in the film The Young Ones?
15. Who reached number one in 1996 with 'Killing Me Softly' and 'Ready Or Not'?

ANSWERS

281

SESSION 28

QUIZ 3

• •

1. What was the fate of the author Erskine Childers, who wrote *The Riddle of the Sands*?
2. Complete the proverb: 'Constant dripping...'
3. Complete this line by Charles Kingsley: 'For men must work...'
4. Who was the author of *King Solomon's Mines, She* and *Allan Quatermain*?
5. Who said: 'I am on the side of the angels'?
6. In which play does Captain Hook appear?
7. Which author introduced the character Dr Fu Manchu?
8. Complete the line of Richard Lovelace, 'Stone walls do not a prison make...'
9. What, according to Phineas T. Barnum, is born every minute?
10. 'Fear no more the heat of the sun/Nor the furious winter's rages;' is the beginning of a poem by whom?
11. In which book are Becky Sharp and Amelia Sedley friends?
12. Who wrote *The Tenant of Wildfell Hall*?
13. Complete the proverb: 'Better be a fool...'
14. 'Not a drum was heard, not funeral note' begins a poem by whom?
15. 'In Xanadu did Kubla Khan/A stately pleasure-dome decree;' is the beginning of a poem by whom?

ANSWERS

1. He was executed by a firing squad. 2. '...wears away the stone.' 3. '...and women must weep'. 4. Henry Rider Haggard. 5. Benjamin Disraeli. 6. *Peter Pan*. 7. Sax Rohmer. 8. '...Nor iron bars a cage'. 9. A sucker. 10. William Shakespeare. 11. *Vanity Fair*. 12. Anne Brontë. 13. '...than a knave'. 14. Charles Wolfe. 15. Samuel Taylor Coleridge.

• •

1. What is a prairie oyster?
2. Which American President was the last to be impeached?
3. What is a facade?
4. If you are a red-headed Australian, what might your nickname be?
5. What is gingerbread?
6. What is a 'blockbuster'?
7. What is abalone?
8. Which vitamin helps bone formation and keeps teeth healthy?
9. Which sign of the Zodiac represents the Virgin ?
10. What is 'bubble and squeak'?
11. Who is the patron saint of workers?
12. What creature is sometimes known as 'Devil's Fingers'?
13. What are blinis or blintzis?
14. What word, beginning with ante-, means 'a small room leading to another'?
15. What is cribbage?

ANSWERS

1. A raw egg with vinegar and other condiments. 2. Richard Nixon. 3. The front of a building. 4. Bluey. 5. A cake flavoured with ginger and treacle. 6. A great success, as of a book, film or stage show. 7. A mollusc, like the sea snail, with a flat, oval shell. 8. Vitamin D. 9. Virgo. 10. A mashed, fried mixture of cabbage and potato. 11. St Joseph. 12. The starfish. 13. Russian thin, stuffed pancakes. 14. Anteroom. 15. A card game for a varying number of players.

SESSION 28

QUIZ 5

1. Violet, indigo, blue, green, yellow, orange and red are the colours of what?
2. What is Gallophobia?
3. Barthelemy Thimonnier invented the 'girls' best friend' in 1830. What was it?
4. Quicksilver is an ancient name for what substance?
5. What did the underwater robot Jason help discover?
6. Who invented the waterproof macintosh?
7. What is an adhesive?
8. What's another name for an Air-Cushioned Vehicle?
9. What did Samuel Christian Friedrich Hahnemann found?
10. How many sides has a tetragon?
11. What is measured in decibels?
12. The sugar in milk is called what?
13. What long-distance signalling system was introduced in 1794?
14. What is *The Lancet*?
15. What does a barometer measure?

ANSWERS

SESSION 28

QUIZ 6

● ●

1. The world's largest reptile, a crocodile of the Far East, is how long; (a) 12 feet (b) 14 feet (c) 16 feet?
2. What is a group of dolphins called?
3. What is cinnamon?
4. When is a snake not a snake?
5. What is arrowroot?
6. Give an example of a mammal which lives in the sea.
7. What kind of animal could be called a hackney?
8. Which sea creature has eyes at the ends of its 'arms'?
9. What is variously known as a dace, dare or dart?
10. What is the difference between a panther and a leopard?
11. What is a cranberry?
12. What is a wryneck?
13. What is krill?
14. A bongo is a type of antelope or a small tropical lizard?
15. Barley is really a special kind of grass. True or false?

ANSWERS

1. 16 feet long. 2. A school. 3. The spicy bark of a tree found in Sri Lanka. 4. When it's a blind snake, which is actually a legless lizard. 5. A kind of starchy substance made from a plant of the same name. 6. Whale, porpoise, seal, sealion. 7. A breed of horse. 8. The starfish. 9. A small river fish. 10. There isn't any! 11. A red acid berry growing on an evergreen shrub. 12. A small bird like a woodpecker with a habit of twisting its neck. 13. Small crustaceans such as shrimps, forming the main diet of whales. 14. It's an antelope. It's also called a bushbuck. 15. True.

SESSION 28
QUIZ 7

● ●

1. The thistle is the national symbol of which country?
2. Which city is on the River Manzanares?
3. What are the Trossachs?
4. Which island's capital is Nuuk?
5. If you bought a pack of cards, and found the suitmarks to be hearts, leaves, bells and acorns, where might you be?
6. Where is Lundy Island?
7. What is the largest city in New Zealand?
8. The diameter of each dial on the Big Ben clock tower is; (a) 10 feet (b) 31 feet (c) 23 feet?
9. Where and what is Mauritius?
10. Which is the 'Land of the Rising Sun?'
11. Where and what is Maxim's?
12. What is the capital of the Russian Federation?
13. What stands on the rocks off Plymouth in Devon?
14. What is the capital of Greece?
15. Which is the world's smallest sovereign state?

ANSWERS

• •

1. What might you be nicknamed if your surname was Murphy?
2. What single word means 'a prophet of doom'?
3. What is the term for a man who has two wives at the same time?
4. What one word can mean 'a place where money is kept' and 'sloping ground'?
5. What does 'hindermost' mean?
6. What would a 'light-fingered' person have a tendency to do?
7. What is the female version of the equine term, 'sire'?
8. What is a female 'fox' called?
9. What is a 'bastion'?
10. What are words like 'Hooray!, Hey!, Gosh!' called?
11. What is a Canuck?
12. What is, or was, an Anzac?
13. What is the difference in meaning between continuous and continual?
14. What kind of confection is called 'cotton candy' in America?
15. What word means beast or brute?

ANSWERS

1. Spud. 2. Pessimist. 3. A bigamist. 4. Bank. 5. Hindmost. 6. Steal. 7. Dam. 8. Vixen. 9. A fortified position. 10. Interjections. 11. Originally, a French-Canadian, but later extended to all Canadians. 12. A member of the Australian and New Zealand Army Corps. 13. Continuous means 'proceeding without a break' and continual means 'frequent'. 14. Candy floss. 15. Animal.

SESSION 28
QUIZ 9

1. What nationality the is golfer Tom Lehman?
2. In which sport would you compete for the Curtis Cup?
3. What is the term used to describe a female horse less than four years old?
4. At which weight did boxer Chris Eubank make a comeback in 1998?
5. Who captained Glamorgan County Cricket team during their championship winning season, 1997?
6. With which sport do you associate John Francome?
7. Name San Diego's American football team?
8. What number did Paul Gascoigne usually wear for England?
9. How many points is a free throw in basketball worth if scored?
10. In Judo, apart from throwing your partner or pinning him to the ground, how do you score points?
11. In the 1970s which brand of cigarettes became synonymous with the Lotus Formula One team.
12. Which County Cricket team plays the majority of their home games at the Oval?
13. With which sport do you associate Robert Fox?
14. Which football club plays its home games at the Riverside?
15. Who provided the engines for William's F1 team, during their triumphant 1996 season?

ANSWERS

1. American. 2. Golf (Women's). 3. Filly. 4. Cruiserweight. 5. Matthew Maynard. 6. Horse Racing. 7. Chargers. 8. Eight. 9. One. 10. By gaining a submission. 11. JPS. 12. Surrey. 13. Modern Pentathlon. 14. Middlesborough. 15. Renault.

SESSION 28

QUIZ 10

• •

1. What, in Nazi Germany, was the SS?
2. Who succeeded James Callaghan as leader of the Labour Party in November, 1980?
3. Six experimental objects were installed in London by the Post Office in 1855. What were they?
4. Which American general was relieved of his command during the Korean War?
5. Who was British Prime Minister for a total of over 20 years?
6. Where and what was Deira?
7. Who was Bonnie Prince Charlie?
8. Who was proclaimed Empress of India on 1st January, 1877?
9. Korea was annexed by which country in 1910?
10. Who was Herbert Hoover?
11. In what year were identity cards abolished in Britain?
12. Which was the last monarch of the House of Tudor?
13. Since he spoke no English, how did George I communicate with Sir Robert Walpole?
14. In London, 1946, the first assembly of which international body took place?
15. What happened in September, 1939, that started World War II?

ANSWERS

1. An elite Nazi force set to seek out and destroy enemies of Nazism. The letters stand for Schutz Staffeln. 2. Michael Foot. 3. Pillar boxes. 4. General Douglas MacArthur. 5. Sir Robert Walpole. 6. One of the old kingdoms of England before A.D.808. Deira roughly covered what is now Yorkshire. 7. Charles Edward Stuart. 8. Queen Victoria. 9. Japan. 10. He was the 31st American president. 11. 1952. 12. Elizabeth I. 13. They conversed in Latin. 14. The United Nations. 15. Germany invaded Poland.

SESSION 29
QUIZ 1

1. 'You Were Made For Me', 'I'm Telling You Now' and 'I Understand' were all top ten hits for which UK group?
2. Which car company used Brian May to sing 'Everything we do, is driven by you'?
3. Apart from Oasis, who was in the top ten in December 1995 with 'Wonderwall'?
4. Who was the front man with Rock band, Rainbow?
5. Who developed the trade mark of crying on stage whilst singing 'Just Walking In The Rain' in the 1950's?
6. With which group was Lionel Richie the lead singer?
7. Which instrument did Jazz musician Buddy Rich play?
8. Who, in the 60's had hits with 'Twenty Four Hours From Tulsa' and 'Something's Gotten Hold Of My Heart'?
9. With whom did Iggy Pop record 'Well Did You Evah' in 1991?
10. Who had a UK top ten hit with Kenny Rogers, singing, 'Islands In The Stream' in 1983?
11. Which car company told us to, 'Search For The Hero Inside Yourself' courtesy of M People?
12. In 1981, with whom did Lionel Richie record 'Endless Love'?
13. Which was Cliff Richard's first UK number one hit?
14. Which instrument did Benny Green play?
15. What nationality were Men At Work?

ANSWERS

1. Freddie and the Dreamers. 2. Ford. 3. Mike Flowers' Pops. 4. Richie Blackmoore. 5. Johnnie Ray. 6. The Commodores. 7. Drums. 8. Gene Pitney. 9. Debbie Harry. 10. Dolly Parton. 11. Peugeot. 12. Diana Ross. 13. 'Living Doll'. 14. Saxophone. 15. Australian.

SESSION 29
QUIZ 2

. . . .

1. The character 'Passepartout' appears in which famous book by Jules Verne?
2. Who wrote *The Jungle Book*?
3. In which book by Anthony Trollope does 'Obadiah Slope' appear?
4. Who wrote the play *Under Milk Wood*?
5. Complete the proverb: 'Charity covers a...'
6. Complete the proverb: 'Birds of a feather...'
7. 'Sam Spade' was a fictional private detective conceived by whom?
8. Which famous children's book did E. Nesbit write?
9. Louisa May Alcott wrote which book in three weeks?
10. In which book by Daphne du Maurier does the character 'Mrs Danvers' appear?
11. 'This is the way the world ends,' wrote T.S. Eliot, 'not with a bang, but...'
12. Which of the following children's books was not written by Roald Dahl; *Mathilda, Charlie and the Chocolate Factory, Junk*?
13. What line follows, 'It was a lover and his lass,'
14. Who wrote *Lord Peter Views the Body*?
15. Who wrote *Zorba the Greek*?

ANSWERS

1. Around the World in Eighty Days. 2. Rudyard Kipling. 3. Barchester Towers. 4. Dylan Thomas. 5. '...multitude of sins'. 6. '...flock together'. 7. Dashiell Hammett. 8. The Railway Children. 9. Little Men. 10. Rebecca. 11. '...a whimper'. 12. Junk. 13. 'With a hey, and a ho, and a hey nonino.' 14. Dorothy L. Sayers. 15. Nikos Kazantzakis.

• •

1. What anniversary does a flower or fruit wedding celebrate?
2. What is galantine?
3. To the ancient Greeks who was Pluto?
4. If you suffered from theophobia, what would you fear?
5. Which popular French drink contains wormwood oil?
6. What is a fondue?
7. Rule by a privileged class is called what?
8. Who invented the crossword puzzle?
9. St John of God is the patron saint of whom?
10. In which religion is the god Brahma found?
11. What is the name given to a lake of sea water bounded by a coral reef?
12. What anniversary does a ruby wedding celebrate?
13. What is a kipper?
14. What food comes from Eccles in Lancashire?
15. St Augustine of Hippo is the patron saint of whom?

ANSWERS

1. The fourth. 2. A dish of poultry, veal, game, etc. served cold in a jelly. 3. The god of the dead. 4. God. 5. Absinthe. 6. A sauce made with cheese and wine, eaten by dipping pieces of bread or meat into it. 7. Aristocracy. 8. Arthur Wynne published the first one in the New York World in 1913. 9. Booksellers and publishers. 10. Hinduism. 11. Lagoon. 12. The fortieth. 13. A smoked herring. 14. A cake. 15. Printers.

SESSION 29

QUIZ 4

• •

1. Who invented the Diesel engine in 1892?
2. What is solder made of?
3. Which is the most abundant metal on earth?
4. Which metal has the chemical symbol, Sn?
5. What is kleptomania?
6. If a car is described as a coupé, what is it like?
7. Ants use an acid to sting. What's it called?
8. Hydrogen, combined with oxygen, makes what?
9. Botany is the study of what?
10. What is gutta-percha?
11. What does a telescope do?
12. What did the Montgolfier Brothers achieve in 1783?
13. What is the more common name for sodium chloride?
14. What kind of weapon is a Gatling?
15. What is the exosphere?

ANSWERS

1. Rudolf Diesel. 2. It's an alloy of tin and lead. 3. Aluminium. 4. Tin. 5. A morbid desire to steal and hide things. 6. It has two doors and a sloping roof. 7. Formic acid. 8. Water. 9. Plants. 10. A material like rubber made from the latex of trees in Malaysia. 11. Magnifies distant objects. 12. The first successful balloon flight. 13. Salt. 14. A machine-gun. 15. The outermost part of the Earth's atmosphere.

SESSION 29
QUIZ 5

• •

1. What is a potto?
2. Which wild small rodent with long ears once was native only to Spain and North Africa?
3. What are cashews?
4. What is the name of the South American fruit shaped like a pine-cone?
5. What is the difference between a tortoise and a turtle?
6. A female rat can give birth to how many young at a time; (a) 8 (b) 12 (c) 20?
7. The scarab, or dung-beetle, was sacred to which people?
8. What is another name for the mountain ash?
9. Does an elephant drink through its trunk?
10. A cross between a she-ass and a stallion is called what?
11. What sort of creature is a bunting?
12. What is a snail?
13. A genet is cat-like creature which purrs like a kettle boiling. True or false?
14. Celery is a plant relative of the carrot. Yes or no?
15. What is the world's largest mammal?

ANSWERS

1. A lemur found in West Africa. 2. The rabbit. 3. Kidney-shaped nuts from an American tree. 4. A pineapple. 5. A tortoise lives on land; a turtle lives in water. 6. 20. 7. The ancient Egyptians. 8. The rowan. 9. No. It sucks up water with its trunk and squirts it into the mouth. 10. A hinny. 11. A small, seed-eating finch-like bird which can be quite tame. 12. A gastropod, like a slug, but with a shell. 13. True. 14. Yes. 15. The blue whale.

SESSION 29
QUIZ 6

• •

1. What is the national language of Brazil?
2. What are the Dolomites and where are they?
3. What is the capital of the Isle of Man?
4. Amsterdam is the capital of which country?
5. Where in Europe is the 'Blue Grotto?'
6. Who lives at the Mansion House, London?
7. Where would you find 'The Shambles'?
8. Nyasaland is the old name for where?
9. Britain is unusually warm considering its latitude. Why?
10. Where is the Forest of Arden?
11. What contains about 70% of the entire planet's fresh water?
12. Which major port stands on the Douro river?
13. Is there really such a place as 'Lambeth Walk?'
14. Where are the Goodwin Sands?
15. Where and what is the 'Old Bailey'?

ANSWERS

1. Portuguese. 2. They are part of the Alps, and are in Italy. 3. Douglas. 4. The Netherlands. 5. Capri, in Italy. 6. The Lord Mayor of London. 7. York. 8. Malawi. 9. Because the islands are warmed by the currents from the Gulf Stream. 10. Warwickshire. 11. Antarctica (frozen in its ice). 12. Oporto. 13. Yes, it's a street in Lambeth, London. 14. At the Straits of Dover. 15. The Central Criminal Court, London.

295

SESSION 29
QUIZ 7

• •

1. What does 'doughty' mean?
2. How did the word galvanise originate?
3. What, in earlier times, was an object called a 'churchwarden'?
4. If you were clever enough to translate the name of the composer Giuseppe Verdi into English, what could it be?
5. Can you name two words, sounding alike, which mean the same as this pair of phrases: giving a security/bundle of soft goods?
6. What word, beginning with P, means trade or vocation?
7. What would you be doing in cockney rhyming slang if you were having a 'butcher's'?
8. If you believe 'that's the way the cookie crumbles', what are you in effect doing?
9. Finish the proverb: 'He who excuses himself...'
10. What is 'gasoline'?
11. Why do prisoners say 'in stir' for prison?
12. What is an acronym?
13. What does the acronym NATO mean?
14. Which is the correct spelling: 'license; licence'.
15. In French, what is *le magasin*?

ANSWERS

1. Brave. 2. It was named after the inventor Luigi Galvani. 3. A long, clay pipe. 4. Joe Green or Greens. 5. Bail/bale. 6. Profession. 7. A look. From 'butcher's hook'. 8. Accepting things the way they are. 9. '...accuses himself'. 10. The American word for 'petrol'. 11. It is a gypsy word, shortened from stirpen, meaning prison. 12. A word formed from the initials of a phrase. 13. (North Atlantic Treaty Organisation). 14. Both are correct. The first is the verb, the second is the noun. 15. A shop.

SESSION 29
QUIZ 8

● ●

1. True or false, the Tour de France always takes place exclusively within France?
2. What always goes to the FA Cup final but never appears?
3. In the mid 1980's F1 team, Zakspeed were sponsored by cigarette manufacturer, West. What did the team paint on the side of the cars to beat tobacco advertising bans?
4. Which football team's official nickname is, 'The Lillywhites'?
5. Which day of the week is 'Ladies day' at Royal Ascot?
6. In which sport might you use the controversial 'Great Big Bertha', or 'Ti Bubble 2'?
7. What nationality is the tennis star Martina Hingis?
8. If I was throwing my ball with a 'chistera', against the wall of the 'cancha', what sport would I be playing?
9. What sport do the Washington Bullets play?
10. In which year was the America's Cup won for the first time by a boat not from the United States?
11. With which sport do you associate John Parrott?
12. Who won the 1997 FA Cup?
13. How many American footballers per team are allowed on the field at any one time?
14. What material are boules made from?
15.. In athletics what is the maximum permitted amount of wind assistance that can be received for a record to stand?

ANSWERS

1. False. 2. The losing team's ribbons. 3. East. 4. Tottenham Hotspur. 5. Thursday. 6. Golf. 7. Swiss. 8. Pelota. 9. Basketball. 10. 1983. 11. Snooker. 12. Chelsea. 13. 11. 14. Steel. 15. 2m per second.

SESSION 29
QUIZ 9

• •

1. Which well-known Irish political party was founded in Dublin in 1905?
2. When was the first Labour government formed?
3. Which future king and queen of the United Kingdom were married on 10th March, 1863?
4. Above whose head did a sword, suspended by a hair, hang?
5. Who opened his first shelter for abandoned children in Stepney, London, in 1867?
6. Ambassadors accredited to the Court of St James go to which country?
7. In March, 1837, which new Australian city was named after the then Prime Minister?
8. When did Britain change to decimal currency?
9. Who was the last Emperor of Austria?
10. Henry V of England defeated the French in 1415. What was the battle?
11. Which general, in early times, used elephants to cross the Alps?
12. What happened in at Scapa Flow, Scotland, in June, 1919?
13. Who was the first English monarch to be addressed as 'Your Majesty'?
14. Who was Kemal Atatürk?
15. Debate in the House of Lords was televised for the first time in what year?

ANSWERS

1. Sinn Féin. 2. 1924. 3. Edward, Prince of Wales, and Princess Alexandra of Denmark. 4. Damocles. 5. Dr Thomas Barnardo. 6. The United Kingdom. 7. Melbourne, after William Lamb, 2nd Viscount Melbourne. 8. 15th February, 1971. 9. Karl, who reigned until 1918, when he abdicated. 10. Agincourt. 11. Hannibal of Carthage. 12. The remaining German Battle Fleet was scuttled. 13. King Henry VIII. 14. The founder and builder of modern Turkey. 15. 1985.

SESSION 29
QUIZ 10

• •

1. Which African president played an African chief in the film *Sanders of the River*?
2. Which double act starred in the 1929 silent film *Big Business*?
3. Which two film stars starred in the TV show *The Persuaders*?
4. From which film did the song 'Jeepers Creepers' come?
5. Exactly what, or who, was 'Jeepers Creepers'?
6. Who starred in the film *Nashville*?
7. What did James Cagney do to Mae Clarke's face in the film *The Public Enemy*?
8. Which movie star's real name was Bernard Schwartz?
9. Who starred in the film *City Lights*?
10. Who provided the voices in the cartoon film *Animal Farm*?
11. What memorable part did Sessue Hayakawa play in a David Lean film of 1957?
12. Who starred in the film *Meet Me In St Louis*?
13. Who starred in the film *Batman* in 1966?
14. Who starred in the 1973 film *American Graffiti*?
15. Which film featured a mermaid played by Darryl Hannah?

ANSWERS

1. Jomo Kenyatta. 2. Laurel and Hardy. 3. Roger Moore and Tony Curtis. 4. *Going Places*, 1938, sung by Louis Armstrong. 5. It was a racehorse. 6. Ned Beatty, Karen Black. 7. Pushed a grapefruit into it. 8. Tony Curtis. 9. Charlie Chaplin, Virginia Cherrill. 10. Maurice Denham. 11. Colonel Saito in *Bridge on the River Kwai*. 12. Judy Garland, Margaret O'Brien. 13. Adam West, Cesar Romero, Burgess Meredith. 14. Richard Dreyfuss and Ron Howard. 15. *Splash*.

299

SESSION 30
QUIZ 1

• •

1. Who wrote *Fear Of Flying*?
2. In which story does 'Sam Weller' appear?
3. Complete the proverb: 'Do not halloo till you're...'
4. Who wrote *The Great Gatsby*?
5. Who wrote *Cold Comfort Farm*?
6. 'Tom Canty' is a character in which story by Mark Twain?
7. 'I hear a sudden cry of pain!/There is a rabbit in a snare' is the beginning of a poem by whom?
8. Complete the proverb: 'A bird in hand...'
9. Who wrote *Ross Poldark*?
10. Who or what was 'Excalibur'?
11. 'Superintendent Roderick Alleyn' was created by whom?
12. The Compleat Angler, or the Contemplative Man's Recreation, was written by whom?
13. Who invented the comic-strip super-sleuth 'Dick Tracy'?
14. In which Shakespeare play does Caliban appear?
15. Who wrote the fairy stories *The Cuckoo Clock, The Tapestry Room* and *Four Winds Farm*?

ANSWERS

1. Erica Jong. 2. *Pickwick Papers*. 3. '...out of the wood'. 4. F. Scott Fitzgerald. 5. Stella Gibbons. 6. *The Prince and the Pauper*. 7. James Stephens. 8. '...is worth two in the bush'. 9. Winston Graham. 10. King Arthur's sword. 11. Ngaio Marsh. 12. Izaak Walton. 13. Chester Gould. 14. *The Tempest*. 15. Mary Louisa Molesworth.

SESSION 30
QUIZ 2

• •

1. What is sauerkraut?
2. What is the Army equivalent of an Air Chief Marshal?
3. What is Cumberland sauce?
4. What was the occupation of Sir Jacob Epstein?
5. What anniversary does a woollen wedding celebrate?
6. What is stroganoff?
7. Who was Sheridan Morley's father?
8. Who was Thomas Arnold?
9. What was loo, as a game?
10. What word, beginning with post-, means 'a part added to a letter after the signature'?
11. St Nicholas is the patron saint of whom?
12. In cricket who is the Twelfth Man?
13. Who was Boofy Gore?
14. To the ancient Romans who was Saturn?
15. What is meant by 'Dutch comfort'?

ANSWERS

1. Cabbage fermented with salt. 2. General. 3. A redcurrant sauce with lemons, oranges, and port wine. 4. Sculptor. 5. The seventh. 6. Thinly-cut meat, onions and mushrooms in a sour cream sauce. 7. Robert Morley. 8. Famous headmaster of Rugby school. 9. A card game with many variants. 10. Postscript. 11. Bakers. 12. The substitute. 13. 8th Earl of Arran, politician and journalist. 14. The god of agriculture. 15. Cold comfort.

SESSION 30
QUIZ 3

● ●

1. Etymology is the study of what?
2. In what year was the first American space probe successfully launched?
3. What is hydrophobia?
4. The chemical formula CO means what?
5. The first microphone was invented by Edward Hughes in (a) 1878 (b) 1898 (c) 1908?
6. Michael Faraday invented an electrical generating machine in 1831. What was it?
7. Who invented the electric razor?
8. What object in the sky is called Callisto, and is 3,000 miles in diameter?
9. What historic event involved Orville and Wilbur Wright in 1903?
10. What is ornithology?
11. What is amber?
12. What is anthracite?
13. Cobalt takes its name from the German word *Kobold*, meaning a goblin. True or false?
14. Word-blindness, and a deep-rooted difficulty in learning to read, is called what?
15. What are Saturn's rings made of?

ANSWERS

1. Words and their history. 2. 1958. 3. A fear of water, especially of drinking it. 4. Carbon Monoxide. 5. (a) 1878. 6. The dynamo. 7. Joseph Schick. 8. It is Jupiter's second-largest moon. 9. The first flight by a powered heavier-than-air aircraft. 10. The study of birds. 11. A yellow fossil resin, regarded by many as a gem. 12. A hard coal which burns with very little smoke. 13. True. 14. Dyslexia. 15. Lumps of ice-covered rocks.

SESSION 30
QUIZ 4

• •

1. Including its tusks, how many teeth does an elephant have?
2. What is a pomegranate?
3. What sort of animal is a dalmatian?
4. Which is North America's largest meat-eating animal?
5. What is an aardvark?
6. What is another name for allspice?
7. A litter of piglets is called a farrow. True or false?
8. Mustard is a member of the cabbage family. Yes or no?
9. The banded ant-eater is a marsupial from where?
10. What's remarkable about the King's holly plant of Tasmania?
11. What kind of animal is said to cackle?
12. Brussels sprouts are plant relatives of the cabbage. Yes or no?
13. Are there foxes which can fly?
14. What is a beech?
15. What is a scorpion?

ANSWERS

1. Four. 2. A fruit with thick, leathery skin and filled with seeds (which are not edible). 3. A breed of dog. 4. The grizzly bear. 5. A nocturnal mammal, which feeds on ants and is found in Africa. 6. Pimento. 7. True. 8. Yes. 9. Australia. 10. It's thought to be about 40,000 years old. 11. A hen. 12. Yes. 13. No. The animal called a flying-fox is a bat. 14. A common forest tree, of much value as timber. 15. A creature related to the spider with four pairs of legs.

303

SESSION 30
QUIZ 5

• •

1. The Balearic Islands are part of which country?
2. On which island would you have been if you had were at the original Raffles Hotel?
3. In which country would you find the town of Cuzco?
4. What large former church, now a mosque, stands in Istanbul?
5. What Palace, built by Cardinal Wolsey, stands by the Thames in Surrey?
6. Where in the world do the people speak Urdu?
7. Where in the world would you find a Walloon or Wallon?
8. Which county is known as the 'Garden of England'?
9. In which English town would you find 'The Lanes'?
10. Where and what is Alcatraz?
11. Where are the Brecon Beacons?
12. Where and what is Stromboli?
13. The River Danube flows through how many countries?
14. Where and what is Roedean?
15. What is the highest peak in the Alps?

ANSWERS

1. Spain. 2. Singapore. 3. Peru. 4. St Sophia. 5. Hampton Court. 6. Pakistan. 7. Belgium. 8. Kent. 9. Brighton. 10. It's a former prison built on an island in San Francisco Bay. 11. South Wales. 12. It's an Italian volcano. 13. Six. 14. A famous girls' school near Brighton. 15. Mont Blanc.

304

SESSION 30
QUIZ 6

• •

1. We all know what an asterisk is, but what does the word actually mean?
2. Do Panama hats come from Panama?
3. What word, beginning with S, means beckon or call?
4. How many sides does a pentagon have?
5. What is the female version of 'drake'?
6. What does the acronym SNAFU mean?
7. If someone lacks the sense of '*meum et tuum*', he is likely to be a what?
8. What are (or were) 'backroom boys'?
9. Kerosene to an American, is the same thing as what to a Briton?
10. To what did Captain Charles Lynch, of Virginia, give his name?
11. What are moccasins?
12. What does this cockney expression mean: 'He has half-inched a whole lot of tomfoolery'.
13. If you 'needle' someone, what are you really doing?
14. What was a 'billycock'?
15. The windscreen of a car is called what in America?

ANSWERS

1. A small star. 2. No, and never did. The 'palmata' hat comes from South America, made from the leaves of a plant like a palm. 3. Summon. 4. Five. 5. Duck. 6. Situation Normal, All Fouled Up. 7. A thief. The words mean 'mine and thine'. 8. Scientists or boffins. 9. Paraffin. 10. Lynching. 11. Soft shoes or slippers made of deerskin. 12. He has stolen a whole lot of jewellery. 13. Annoying them. 14. A soft felt hat with a wide brim. 15. The windshield.

305

SESSION 30

QUIZ 7

• •

1. During cycling time trials how many cyclists are on the track at any one time?
2. How many times has Tom Watson won the US Masters Championship?
3. Which country will become the 10th Cricketing Test Nation?
4. Which football team plays their home matches at the Stadium of Light?
5. Robin Cousins and John Curry are the only British men to have won Olympic Men's Figure Skating gold medals. True or False?
6. In Ten Pin Bowling what term describes knocking ten pins down with two balls?
7. Who was the last Briton to win a singles title at Wimbledon?
8. What nationality is former Newcastle striker Faustino Asprilla?
9. Which cricketer had the nickname 'Beefy'?
10. Who is Great Britain's delegate on the International Olympic Committee?
11. Whom did Tony Blair appoint as Sports Minister in 1997?
12. In Polo, how long does a 'Chuka' last?
13. Which sport do the West Coast Eagles play?
14. How many men form a line out in Rugby League?
15. In Euro 96 how many teams did England beat without the use of a penalty shoot-out?

ANSWERS

1. One. 2. Twice. 3. Bangladesh. 4. Sunderland. 5. True. 6. Spare.
7. Virginia Wade. 8. Colombian. 9. Ian Botham. 10. The Princess Royal.
11. Tony Banks. 12. Seven minutes. 13. Australian Rules Football.
14. None (you don't have line outs in Rugby League). 15. Two.

SESSION 30
QUIZ 8

• •

1. What was the name of the wife of King Louis XVI of France?
2. What happened in the year 971 when the body of St Swithin was moved to a cathedral?
3. Who is Gerald Ford?
4. What opened between Stockton and Darlington in September, 1825?
5. In what year was the Great Exhibition held in Hyde Park, London?
6. On 27 January, 1859, Queen Victoria became a grandmother. Who was her grandson?
7. Who was Rutherford Hayes?
8. Which Mongol conqueror succeeded his father at the age of 13?
9. Who was Bertha Krupp, and what was named after her?
10. Which area in Southern Africa became a British colony in 1813?
11. Which group of buildings, costing a million pounds, opened in Birmingham in 1964?
12. In which country is the Republican Party a major political unit?
13. Who was Field Marshal Paul von Beneckendorf und von Hindenburg?
14. In A.D. 301, Edward, son of King Edward I, was invested as what?
15. Who was the first English king to be divorced?

ANSWERS

1. Marie Antoinette. 2. It rained for 40 days continuously. 3. He was the 38th American president. 4. The first steam-locomotive railway. 5. 1851. 6. The future Kaiser Wilhelm II of Germany. 7. The 19th American president. 8. Genghis Khan. 9. A German woman who inherited the Krupp armaments firm. A large gun was named 'Big Bertha'. 10. The Cape of Good Hope. 11. The Bull Ring. 12. The United States. 13. A pre-war German general and President. 14. The first English Prince of Wales. 15. King Henry VIII.

307

SESSION 30

QUIZ 9

- -

1. Who starred in the film *Lucky Jim*?
2. What makes *Snow White and the Seven Dwarfs* of historic significance?
3. Who's real name was Archibald Leach?
4. The lead role in this film was turned down by John Wayne, Paul Newman and Frank Sinatra before being taken by Clint Eastwood. Name this film?
5. Which film star became Miss Hungary in 1936, but was disqualified for being under age?
6. Who starred in the films *The Conversation* and *The French Connection*?
7. Which movie star was the 'Sweater Girl'?
8. Which film actor was born Herbert Charles Angelo Kuchacevich ze Schluderpacheru?
9. Who wore the vest and was the hero in *Die Hard*?
10. Who is the oldest winner of the best actress Oscar?
11. Who starred in the film *Stagecoach*?
12. From which film did the song 'A Fine Romance' come?
13. Who starred in the 1941 film *The Maltese Falcon*?
14. Which of these film stars began as extras; Michael Caine, Gary Cooper, Marlene Dietrich?
15. Which film star wrote the novel *Diamond Lil*?

ANSWERS

1. Ian Carmichael, Terry-Thomas. 2. It was Disney's first feature film. 3. Cary Grant. 4. Dirty Harry. 5. Zsa Zsa Gabor. 6. Gene Hackman. 7. Lana Turner. 8. Herbert Lom. 9. Bruce Willis. 10. Jessica Tandy. 11. John Wayne. 12. *Swing Time*, 1936. 13. Humphrey Bogart, Mary Astor. 14. All of them. 15. Mae West.

SESSION 30
QUIZ 10

1. Which Leicester band had nine top ten singles between 1975 & 1978, all cover versions of classic rock & roll songs?
2. In 1996, PJ & Duncan, changed their names to what?
3. With whom did the Pet Shop Boys record 'What Have I Done To Deserve This', the theme to the film, 'Scandal',?
4. Which pop quiz programme, is hosted by Mark Lamarr?
5. Kylie Minogue reached number one with 'Especially For You' in collaboration with whom?
6. Ska band Madness only had one UK number one, name the song?
7. What was Madonna's first UK hit single?
8. Which rock group had eight number 1 albums between 1969 and 1979?
9. By what name is Reg Dwight better known?
10. Which long-running band replaced their famous drummer and lead singer with the singer from Stiltskin?
11. By what name is Harry Webb better known?
12. Who recorded the theme song 'Love Song For A Vampire', for the 1993 film, Dracula starring Gary Oldman and Keanu Reeves?
13. Level 42 never had a UK number 1. True or false?
14. Which Welshman has had 15 UK top ten hits, between 1965 and 1988?
15. Which comic indie band have written songs including, 'Rod Hull Is Still Alive - Why?' 'The Trumpton Riots' and 'Paintball's Coming Home'?

ANSWERS

1. Showaddywaddy 2. Ant & Dec 3.Dusty Springfield 4. Never Mind The Buzzcocks 5. Jason Donovan 6. 'House Of Fun' 7. 'Holiday' 8. Led Zeppelin 9. Elton John 10.Genesis 11. Cliff Richard 12. Annie Lennox 13. True 14. Tom Jones 15. Half Man Half Biscuit

● ●

1. Monday is named after the Moon. True or false?
2. Where in Britain would you find our oldest surviving clock?
3. What word, beginning with ante-, means 'before dinner'?
4. What is a Wiener schnitzel?
5. Who or what was Chad?
6. Who was Britain's answer to Louis Armstrong?
7. What was, or is, a billycock hat?
8. What is a Latter-Day Saint?
9. In a pack of cards, which way does the Queen of Diamonds look: to her left or to her right?
10. What anniversary does a wooden wedding celebrate?
11. What did Albert Schweitzer set up in Lambaréné?
12. What is the Army equivalent of a Lieutenant Commander in the Navy?
13. How did 'knickers' get their name?
14. A methuselah is a measure of wine equivalent to how many bottles?
15. What article of clothing is a mantilla?

ANSWERS

1. True. 2. Salisbury Cathedral, whose clock dates from 1386. 3. Anteprandial. 4. Veal cutlet covered in egg and breadcrumbs. 5. A little cartoon character who asked "Wot, no ......?" 6. Nat Gonella, who died in 1998 aged 90. 7. A bowler hat if you're British, a derby hat if you're American. 8. Another name for a Mormon. 9. To her left. 10. The fifth. 11. A hospital to combat leprosy. 12. Major. 13. From Knickerbocker, a character in a Washington Irving book, who wore knee-length breeches. 14. Eight. 15. A kind of lace cap worn in Spain.

310

SESSION 31

QUIZ 2

• •

1. What is the Red Planet?
2. What does one measure with an anemometer?
3. What is a chinook?
4. What does 'opaque' mean?
5. What is the difference between 'inflammable' and 'flammable'?
6. The study of microscopic organisms is called what?
7. What is a Polaris?
8. Haematite is a metal ore. Which metal?
9. Which of these metals is the lightest: gold, lead or platinum?
10. What, during WW1, were Camels and Pups?
11. Graphology is the study of what?
12. What is vulcanology?
13. What very light metal was discovered in 1827 by Hans Christian Oersted?
14. What is Kevlar?
15. With which weapon is the physicist Robert Oppenheimer connected?

ANSWERS

SESSION 31
QUIZ 3

• •

1. What is a group of kangaroos called?
2. What is a group of chickens called?
3. What kind of animal is said to chatter?
4. Can a porcupine shoot its quills?
5. How fast can a racehorse run in miles per hour; (a) 50 (b) 60 (c) 70?
6. What are animals without backbones called?
7. A male horse aged four or under is called a what?
8. What is unusual about the wings of a baby hoatzin bird?
9. What kind of animal could be described as a Tamworth?
10. The smell of skunk's fluid can be detected half a mile away. True or false?
11. What does the word 'hippopotamus' mean?
12. What is a gillyfllower?
13. What is a katydid?
14. What is another name for the pumpkin?
15. The gooseberry is a plant relative of the saxifrage. True or false?

ANSWERS

1. A mob. 2. A brood. 3. A jay. 4. No. 5. (a) About 50 miles per hour. 6. Invertebrates. 7. A colt. 8. They have three clawed fingers on each. 9. A breed of pig. 10. True. 11. River-horse. 12. A flower which smells like cloves. 13. An American insect like a grasshopper which makes a sound like its name. 14. Squash. 15. True.

SESSION 31
QUIZ 4

• •

1. Where would you find Bow Bells?
2. Where is the Bull Ring in England?
3. It is extremely difficult to see Big Ben in London. Why?
4. 'Erin' was a poetic name for which country?
5. To which country do the Faroe Islands belong?
6. Which city is on the River Elbe?
7. Which cities are on the River Arno?
8. How many hills was Rome believed to be built on?
9. Where did liquorice originate?
10. What is the village of Hambledon, in Hampshire, famed for?
11. In which English city would you find Parkway railway station?
12. Which is the world's smallest republic?
13. On which stretch of water does Toronto stand?
14. In which city would you find King's Cross railway station?
15. Where is the Cathedral of Notre Dame?

ANSWERS

1. In the City of London, at St Mary-le-Bow Church. Not the East London district of Bow. 2. Birmingham. It's a shopping centre. 3. Because 'Big Ben' is the bell inside the clock tower. 4. Ireland. 5. Denmark. 6. Hamburg. 7. Florence and Pisa. 8. Seven. 9. Egypt. 10. Being the birthplace of cricket. 11. Bristol. 12. Nauru (5,261 acres). 13. Lake Ontario. 14. London. 15. In Paris. Its full title is 'Notre-Dame de Paris' (Our Lady of Paris).

SESSION 31
QUIZ 5

• •

1. What is an 'agony aunt'?
2. What do the initials UFO stand for?
3. What is the wife of an earl called?
4. What is the meaning of 'defunct'?
5. What, in an American bank, is a 'teller'?
6. What does the word 'Mart' mean?
7. Can you name a word, beginning with Q, that can mean extract or excerpt?
8. In cockney rhyming slang what does 'tit-for-tat' mean?
9. What is your derrière?
10. What's the difference between eminent and imminent?
11. What one word means both, 'a type of crop' and 'a horny, sore place on the foot'?
12. What politician's name is an anagram of 'that great charmer'?
13. What was a 'Dolly Varden'?
14. What does 'prolix' mean?
15. What is, or was, a 'bimbo'?

ANSWERS

1. A newspaper columnist who specialises in personal advice. 2. Unidentified Flying Object. 3. Countess. 4. Dead, finished or no longer working. 5. A cashier. 6. Market. 7. Quotation. 8. Hat. 9. Your behind or posterior. 10. Eminent means 'outstanding or distinguished' and imminent means 'soon to take place or occur'. 11. Corn. 12. Margaret Thatcher. 13. A style of flowered print dress as worn by the Dickens character of the same name. 14. Unduly long and verbose. 15. A sexually attractive, but dim, young woman.

314

SESSION 31
QUIZ 6

• •

1. Which football team plays their home games at 'The New Den'?
2. What is the accepted length of a field hockey pitch?
3. What do the initials TCCB stand for?
4. Which sporting archive was established at Cooperstown, New York State, in 1934?
5. With which sport do you associate Michael Whitaker?
6. Which sport is descended from Byerly Turk, Darley Arabian and Godolphin Arabian?
7. What did Belgian Joseph Merlin invent in 1760, which was improved on 100 years later by American Everett Plimpton, which today is the basis for several leisure sports?
8. How many disciplines are there in a Women's international gymnastics event?
9. In Olympic athletics, how long is a steeplechase?
10. This sport first became popular in the 13th Century. Its first purpose-built playing area was opened in Southampton in 1299. Its rules were unified in the 19th century, although different variations still prevail in the North of England. What is it?
11. Which football team play their home games at Ewood Park?
12. Which Brazilian won the Formula One World Drivers Championships in 1981, 1983 and 1987?
13. How high is a table tennis net; 4ins, 5ins, 6ins, or 7ins?
14. What sport do the Sacramento Kings play?
15. How long is a quarter in Water Polo?

ANSWERS

• •

1. Who was Georges Pompidou?
2. Where, in London, is the Queen forbidden entry?
3. What drastic measure against illegal parking was introduced in May, 1983?
4. When was the royal fortress of Bastille stormed by French workers?
5. What was called 'Dad's Army'?
6. In which century did the Vikings start their raids on Britain?
7. On which mountain climb did eight men lose their lives in May, 1996?
8. Who came to power in Japan in 1926?
9. Who was William Howard Taft?
10. What event was televised in June, 1953?
11. What is meant by the Third Reich?
12. Whose last words were: "Let not poor Nelly starve"?
13. Who dismissed 5,000 employees in East London in February, 1986?
14. Which important building connected with the law was opened on 27th February, 1907?
15. In Chicago, the St Valentine's Day Massacre took place. Who was involved?

ANSWERS

1. President of France, (1969-1973). 2. The House of Commons. 3. The wheel clamp. 4. 14th July, 1789. 5. The Home Guard during WW2. 6. The 8th century A.D. 7. Everest. 8. Emperor Hirohito. 9. He was the 27th American president. 10. The Coronation of Queen Elizabeth II. 11. That period of German history during which the Nazis ruled. 12. King Charles II. 13. Rupert Murdoch. 14. The Central Criminal Court, Old Bailey, London. 15. Rival groups of gangsters

SESSION 31
QUIZ 8

1. Who starred in the film *The Cruel Sea*?
2. Who were Petra and Goldie?
3. Who starred in the spoof film *Dracula: Dead And Loving It*?
4. Who was originally considered to star in *The Wizard of Oz*?
5. Which Disney film was re-made as a live action film starring Glenn Close as the villain?
6. Which well-known actor played himself in *The Love Lottery*?
7. Which well-known actor played himself in *Starlift*?
8. Who starred in the film *Shane*?
9. Which black actor starred in *Jackie Brown* and *Eve's Bayou*?
10. Who starred in the film *The Quatermass Experiment*?
11. 'In space, no one can hear you scream' was the slogan for which series of sci-fi horror films?
12. Which disaster movie starred Steve McQueen, Paul Newman, Fred Astaire, O.J. Simpson, Robert Wagner and Richard Chamberlain?
13. Who starred in the film *I'm All Right Jack*?
14. What sitcom did Wilfred Bramble and Harry H. Corbett star in?
15. Which US comic played Ace Ventura in several films?

ANSWERS

1. Jack Hawkins. 2. Pet dogs in Blue Peter. 3. Leslie Nielsen. 4. Shirley Temple. 5. *101 Dalmatians*. 6. Humphrey Bogart. 7. Gary Cooper. 8. Alan Ladd. 9. Samuel L. Jackson. 10. Brian Donlevy. 11. *Alien*. 12. *Towering Inferno*. 13. Ian Carmichael, Peter Sellers, Irene Handl. 14. *Steptoe And Son*. 15. Jim Carrey.

SESSION 31
QUIZ 9

• •

1. Which Mel & Kim reached number one at Christmas 1987?
2. In 1981, Starsound, had hits with 'Stars on 45' volume 1 and 2. What nationality were Starsound?
3. Who recorded the album Architecture and Morality?
4. Which US/German act had number ones with 'The Power' and 'Rhythm is a dancer'?
5. Who is the lead singer of Eurythmics?
6. Which former Radio one DJ had top ten hits including 'Everyone's Gone To The Moon', 'Loop di Love' and 'Una Paloma Blanca'?
7. With which movie and TV theme did Irene Cara, reach number one in 1982?
8. What is the link between, Mark Lamarr, BBC2 and 'What Do I Get'?
9. In 1993, with whom did Frank Sinatra record 'I've Got You Under My Skin'?
10. Which movie theme song did Boy George record in 1992?
11. With which US female singer did BoyZ II Men record 'One Sweet Day ' in 1995?
12. Which group of recording artists, designed to appeal to young Labour voters during the 1992 Election Campaign, featured Billy Bragg?
13. Boy George recorded which cover version to register his only solo number one to date?
14. Celine Dion has never had a UK number one hit. True or false?
15. Who is the lead singer/guitarist with Dire Straits?

ANSWERS

SESSION 31

QUIZ 10

● ●

1. What have Marple, Mason and Morse in common?
2. The character 'King Rudolf' appears in which famous book?
3. Who wrote *The Book of Nonsense*?
4. 'You are old, Father William,' the young man said': begins a poem by whom?
5. Complete the proverb: 'Don't empty the baby out...'
6. Which English author was regarded as the most popular 'thriller' writer of all time?
7. Who wrote *Cider With Rosie*?
8. Who was 'Biggles'?
9. Who created the fictional detective, 'John Appleby'?
10. Which of the following is not a play; *The Laughing Cavalier, The Faerie Queene, Vanity Fair*?
11. Who wrote *A Town Like Alice*?
12. Who created the first blind fictional detective 'Max Carrados'?
13. Who was Algernon Blackwood?
14. On being told that her people had no bread, Marie-Antoinette replied: Qu'ils mangent de la brioche. What does this mean?
15. Who wrote *The Vicar of Wakefield*?

ANSWERS

SESSION 32
Quiz 1

• •

1. Photophobia is (a) fear of light or (b) fear of being photographed?
2. What device for long-distance speech was invented in 1876?
3. What is a stethoscope used for?
4. From which plant do we obtain linseed oil?
5. How many pounds are there in a hundredweight?
6. What is porcelain?
7. Who discovered the circulation of the blood?
8. Desdemona is a satellite of which planet?
9. Spectacles were first reported in use in which century?
10. A day on Mars lasts only 40 minutes longer than on Earth. True or false?
11. What communications system was laid between England and France in 1891?
12. The wreck of which famous liner was found in 1985?
13. What was scientist Theodore Maimam famous for building?
14. The clavicle is another name for which bone?
15. What is a pantograph?

ANSWERS

1. Fear of light. 2. The telephone. 3. To hear sounds in the body, such as the heartbeat. 4. Flax. 5. 112. 6. A fine, white, thin, translucent earthenware. 7. William Harvey. 8. Uranus. 9. 13th century AD. 10. True. 11. The telephone cable. 12. The Titanic. 13. The first working laser. 14. The collar-bone. 15. A drawing instrument for tracing, by which means to enlarge or reduce a drawing.

SESSION 32
Quiz 2

. . . .

1. An ant-eating mammal in South Africa has a name meaning 'earth-pig'. Can you name it?
2. What is a kumquat?
3. How fast can an ostrich run? (a) 40 mph. (b) 50 mph. (c) 60 mph.
4. What sort of animal is a Pekingese?
5. What are the names for a male and a female goat?
6. A camel can go without water for up to ten days. True or false?
7. What kind of animal could be described as a Dorset Horn?
8. The okapi is the closest relative to which tall mammal?
9. Are bats really blind?
10. What is cowslip?
11. What is a cockle?
12. What is an elver?
13. What sort of animal is a Friesian?
14. The woolly mammoth was a kind of hairy, prehistoric example of what modern-day creature?
15. What kind of animal could be described as a Merino?

ANSWERS

1. The aardvark or ant-bear. 2. A small kind of orange. 3. 50 m.p.h. 4. A breed of dog. 5. A billy-goat and a nanny-goat. 6. True. 7. A breed of sheep. 8. The giraffe. 9. Some have very poor vision, but none is known to be totally blind. 10. A species of wild primrose with yellow, densely-tufted flowers. 11. A shell-fish, highly-prized by Londoners not so long ago. 12. A young eel. 13. A breed of cattle. 14. Elephant. 15. A breed of sheep.

SESSION 32
Quiz 3

• •

1. What record does Mount Whitney hold?
2. Where, and what, is the 'Windy City'?
3. Between which two cities did the original Orient Express train run?
4. 'Pompey' is the nickname for which English city?
5. What is the capital of Ghana?
6. In which county in the New Forest?
7. Where is Lizard Point?
8. What is the capital of Malta?
9. What is the capital of New Zealand?
10. Where in the World is the highest waterfall found?
11. To which country does the Pacific island of Guam belong?
12. 'The Big Apple' is a colloquial name for where?
13. What is the Sargasso Sea?
14. Vectis was the name given by the Romans to what?
15. Whereabouts in the world would you find New England?

ANSWERS

322

• •

1. Can you name two words, sounding alike, which mean the same as this pair: flesh for food/to encounter?
2. What is 'hyperbole'?
3. What were 'bluestockings'?
4. What is a rhetorical question?
5. What does the phrase, 'In days of yore' mean?
6. What word, beginning with A, means false or synthetic?
7. What is the name for someone who studies insects?
8. If you had a white elephant (figuratively!) what in fact would you have?
9. Gypsies were so called because of what?
10. What do the initials, DOA stand for?
11. Which one word can mean both, 'a large furry animal' and 'to carry'?
12. If your surname is Martin, you might be nicknamed what?
13. What is the British equivalent of the American 'drug store'?
14. What is the female version of 'abbot'?
15. What word, beginning with C, means chat or talk?

ANSWERS

1. Meat/meet. 2. A figure of speech: exaggeration for emphasis, such as 'tons of money'. 3. Literary or studious women. 4. One that does not require an answer. 5. In ancient times, in times past. 6. Artificial. 7. Entomologist. 8. Something which was more of a nuisance than of value. 9. Because it was thought that they came from Egypt. 10. Dead On Arrival. 11. Bear. 12. Pincher. 13. A chemist's. 14. Abbess. 15. Conversation.

SESSION 32
Quiz 5

• •

1. What makes Sculls different to conventional rowing?
2. In 1990 Hale Irwin won the US Open Golf Championship. What record did he set in doing this?
3. What nationality is Tennis star Anna Kournikova?
4. With which sport do you associate Dennis Rodman?
5. Who set the world 100m record of 9.84 seconds at the 1996 Olympics?
6. Which World Cup hero was knighted in the 1998 Queens Birthday honours list?
7. Name New York's AFC American Football team?
8. In Martial Arts such as Judo and Karate, what name is given to the ritual exercises that develop technique, and physical and mental strength?
9. In horse racing, by what name is a male horse less than four years old referred to?
10. Where did the sport of Polo originate?
11. How long is the Service Court in Tennis; 19ft, 20ft, 21ft, or 22ft?
12. Who succeeded Sean Fitzpatrick in 1998 as captain of the All Blacks?
13. What offence was supposed to have meant an automatic sending off during the 1998 World Cup?
14. In Polo, with what do you hit the ball?
15. In a Motorcycle Grand Prix, how many points are awarded for first place?

ANSWERS

1. In Sculls, each oarsman has two oars, in Rowing they have one. 2. Oldest player to win the tournament. 3. Russian. 4. Basketball. 5. Donovan Bailey. 6. Sir Geoff Hurst. 7. The Jets. 8. Kata. 9. A Colt. 10. Persia (Iran). 11. 21ft. 12. Taine Randell. 13. A tackle from behind. 14. A mallet. 15. Twenty.

324

SESSION 32
Quiz 6

• •

1. What flag was first adopted in Britian in 1606?
2. The Witan was the name for a parliament held by which early people in Britain?
3. Who was the first of the Plantagenet kings?
4. In which year did Japan invaded Manchuria?
5. Where did Italy invade in 1935?
6. Who became Empress of Russia in succession to Peter the Great in 1725?
7. Who were the Incas?
8. On the 11th April, 1689, which two people were crowned together?
9. In Whitechapel, East London, in 1888, many prostitues were murdered. Who was held responsible?
10. In the House of Lords, on what does the Lord Chancellor sit?
11. In religious terms, what was the Great Schism?
12. What did Russia sell to the United States in 1867?
13. Before the reign of King Henry VIII, how were monarchs addressed?
14. After seven months of resistance, the South African town of Mafeking was relieved by troops under the command of which military figure?
15. Who and what were the Spartacists?

ANSWERS

SESSION 32
Quiz 7

• •

1. What was the name of the toy astronaut in the film Toy Story?
2. From which film did the song 'My Kind of Town' come?
3. Who starred in the film The Magnificent Ambersons?
4. Who played the country vicar in the film The Holly and the Ivy in 1952?
5. With which war was the film The Deerhunter concerned?
6. Which spoof sci-fi film was directed by Tim Burton and included Tom Jones in its cast?
7. Which actor was a former member of the IRA?
8. In which film did Dudley Moore play a 'chief elf' in Santa Claus's workshop?
9. What was Michael Caine's occupation before acting?
10. Who starred in the 1927 silent film The General?
11. What was the name of the sequel to The Blues Brothers?
12. In the film Peter's Friends, who played Peter?
13. Who starred in the film Gone With the Wind?
14. Who starred in the film Mrs Doubtfire?
15. What was the name of Blackadder's loyal but dopey servant?

ANSWERS

SESSION 32
Quiz 8

1. In which year did Elvis Presley die?
2. Which singer started her career as lead singer with The GoGo's?
3. True or false, Bananarama had five UK number 1's?
4. Canadian singer Terry Jacks reached number one in 1974 with which song?
5. Which football team do the Gallagher brothers support?
6. Who recorded the album 'The Lodger'?
7. Which group included Levon Helm, Rick Danko and Robbie Robertson?
8. Who fronts the group Radiohead?
9. Which band included the dancer and 'vibes manager' Bez?
10. In 1956 who reached number three with 'I'm Walking Backwards For Christmas/Bluebottle Blues'?
11. Who had hits in 1982/83 with 'I Don't Wanna Dance' and 'Electric Avenue'?
12. Which musician, the inspiration behind the band, Nine Inch Nails, also wrote the acclaimed sountrack to Oliver Stone's film, Natural Born Killers.
13. Singer Michelle Gayle was better known to BBC viewers as which character?
14. In 1990 Lindisfarne recorded 'Fog On The Tyne (revisited)'. Which footballer was credited on the record?
15. Warren G and Nate Dogg had a top ten hit with 'What's Love Got To Do With It'. Who had previously had a top ten hit with this song?

ANSWERS

1. 1977. 2. Belinda Carlisle. 3. False. 4. 'Seasons In The Sun'. 5. Manchester City. 6. David Bowie. 7. The Band. 8. Thom Yorke. 9. Happy Mondays. 10. The Goons. 11. Eddie Grant. 12. Trent Reznor. 13. Hattie from Eastenders. 14. Paul Gascoigne (Gazza). 15. Tina Turner.

SESSION 32
Quiz 9

• •

1. What 10,000 word tale of a seagull, first published in 1970, sold 7 million copies within five years?
2. 'Sir Andrew Aguecheek' appears in which play by Shakespeare?
3. What, according to Karl Marx, was the 'opium of the people'?
4. Which author wrote under the name 'James Bridie'?
5. Who wrote The Satanic Verses?
6. Who wrote Brave New World?
7. In which play does 'Jack Worthing' appear?
8. Complete Wellington's sentence: 'I don't know what effect they will have on the enemy...'
9. Who wrote Crime and Punishment?
10. Who wrote the children's books Jackanapes and The Brownies, and Other Tales?
11. Who is the leading character in Thomas Hardy's Far From the Madding Crowd?
12. Complete the proverb: 'Don't cross a bridge...'
13. Who wrote Adam Bede?
14. 'I come from haunts of coot and hern' is the beginning of a poem by whom?
15. Complete this line by Thomas Gray: 'For many a flower is born...'

ANSWERS

1. Jonathan Livingston Seagull. 2. Twelfth Night. 3. Religion. 4. Osborne Henry Mavor. 5. Salman Rushdie. 6. Aldous Huxley. 7. The Importance of Being Earnest. 8. 'But by God, they frighten me'. 9. Dostoevsky. 10. Julia Horatia Ewing. 11. Bathsheba Everdene'. 12. '...until you come to it'. 13. George Eliot. 14. Lord Tennyson. 15. '...to blush unseen'.

SESSION 32
Quiz 10

● ●

1. If you asked for a 'biscuit' in the United States, what would you get?
2. What did American Express introduce in 1891?
3. What has been estimated at 50 million farenheit?
4. Who was the first 'Supermac'?
5. And which tennis player was the second 'Supermac'?
6. Who is Old Nick?
7. According to the 'language of flowers', what does the nasturtium signify?
8. What animal is grouped in packs?
9. If your surname is 'Martin', what might your nickname be?
10. In a pack of cards, which way does the King of Diamonds look, to his left, or to his right?
11. What is stingo?
12. What is smörgåsbord?
13. What is a ragout?
14. Whalebone isn't the bone of a whale. What is it?
15. In card-playing, how did the word 'trump' come into being?

ANSWERS

1. A kind of scone. 2. Travellers' cheques. 3. The temperature at the centre of the sun. 4. Harold Macmillan. 5. John McEnroe. 6. Satan, or the Devil. 7. Patriotism. 8. Wolves. 9. Pincher. 10. To his right. 11. Strong malt liquor. 12. A Swedish hors d'œuvres dish. 13. A highly-seasoned stew of meat and vegetables. 14. A horny substance from the whale's jaw. 15. It was taken from the word 'triumph'.

329

• •

1. What is edelweiss?
2. A dolphin is a mammal related to the whale. True or false?
3. What is a death-watch beetle?
4. What kind of animal could be described as a Black Suffolk?
5. Which bird lays the largest eggs?
6. Which bird lays the smallest eggs?
7. What kind of bird is said to boom?
8. Are there lizards which can fly?
9. Broccoli is plant relative of the cabbage. Yes or no?
10. The tomato is a member of the nightshade family. Yes or no?
11. Another name for the sea cow is what?
12. White ants are not ants at all. What are they?
13. What is a group of beavers called?
14. What kind of animal could be called a shire?
15. Which animal lives in a 'lodge'?

ANSWERS

1. A plant which grows in alpine areas; having small yellow flowers, woolly white bracts and downy grey-green leaves. 2. True. 3. An insect which makes a ticking sound. It is also called the anobid. 4. A breed of black pig. 5. The ostrich. 6. The humming-bird, whose eggs can measure less than 6mm in length. 7. The bittern. 8. Yes. In Malaysia there are some, also called flying-dragons. 9. Yes. 10. Yes. 11. Dugong. 12. Termites. 13. A colony. 14. A breed of horse. 15. A beaver.

SESSION 33
QUIZ 2

● ●

1. What was the Boulder Dam, on the Colorado River, renamed?
2. Which is the world's largest active volcano?
3. Albany is the capital city of which American state?
4. What is the capital of Egypt?
5. Where, not far from Paris, would you find the Hall of Mirrors?
6. Which famous church clock in London has only one hand?
7. What is the main city of Transvaal, South Africa?
8. The Friendly Islands is another name for which country?
9. What is the capital of Tunisia?
10. To which country does Puerto Rico belong?
11. What country's capital city is Quito?
12. Which is the world's largest freshwater lake?
13. Madrid is the capital of which country?
14. Which important Polish city stands on the Vistula river?
15. If you were standing in Ueno Park, which city would you be visiting?

ANSWERS

1. The Hoover Dam. 2. Mauna Loa, Hawaii, 13,680 feet high. 3. New York State. 4. Cairo. 5. At the Palace of Versailles. 6. The clock of Westminster Abbey. 7. Johannesburg. 8. Tonga. 9. Tunis. 10. The United States. 11. Ecuador. 12. Lake Superior, North America, 31,800 sq.m. 13. Spain. 14. Warsaw. 15. Tokyo.

331

1. What is an 'archaism'?
2. If you were a cockney, where would you wear your 'almond rocks'?
3. What would you find at a carnival in the United States?
4. Which of these words has the same vowel sound as 'show': cough, nought, furlough?
5. What's wrong with this sentence: 'Mum was angry with the mess in the kitchen.'?
6. Can you name two words, sounding alike, which mean the same as this pair: market for goods/wind-catcher?
7. What word, beginning with A, means assign or designate?
8. What is the meaning of the word 'omniscient'?
9. If you wanted the equivalent of a solicitor in the US, you would go to whom?
10. Who were the 'blackshirts'?
11. What does 'à la mode' mean?
12. What does 'à la mode' mean in the United States?
13. What is a 'quango'?
14. What is the meaning of 'omnipotent'?
15. What substance used to be known as 'Coal oil'?

ANSWERS

1. The use of out-of-date words like peradventure, albeit, quoth. 2. On your feet. It means 'socks'. 3. It would be the equivalent of a fair in Britain, with roundabouts, swings, etc. 4. Furlough. 5. It should read: Mum was angry at the mess in the kitchen. 6. Sale/sail. 7. Appoint. 8. All-knowing. 9. An attorney. 10. Followers of Oswald Mosley in the Fascist party. 11. It simply means 'in fashion'. 12. Something served with ice-cream. 13. A Quasi Autonomous Non-Governmental Organisation. 14. All-powerful. 15. Kerosene or paraffin.

SESSION 33
QUIZ 4

• •

1. What is the premier UK Rally event?
2. Which British Racing driver came second in the Monte Carlo Rally in 1952, second at Le Mans in 1956, as well as winning 36 Grand Prix?
3. Which sport was invented by American William G. Morgan, a physical training instructor from Holyoke, Massachusetts, involves 2 teams of 6 players, held its first world championship in 1949, and has accepted as an Olympic sport in 1964?
4. In which sport would you compete for the Federation Cup?
5. What sport do the Denver Nuggets play?
6. In m.p.h., how fast is a Knot?
7. In which 1982 event did Mark Thatcher get lost?
8. Which British Formula One driver was nicknamed 'The Shunt'?
9. Which sports does the FINA organisation preside over?
10. In which sport do you aim to get a ringer but sometimes get a leaner whilst standing in the pitching box?
11. For which sport is Bo Jackson famous?
12. Who was born in Hong Kong in 1943, named Lee Yuen Kan, became a master of Wing Chun, before developing his own, Jeet Kune Do, style of fighting, before dying in mysterious circumstances in 1973.
13. What is the first event in a Heptathlon?
14. With which sport do you associate Lanfranco 'Frankie' Dettori?
15. In show jumping, how many faults are given for, 'a foot in the water', at the water jump?

ANSWERS

SESSION 33
QUIZ 5

1. Whose last words were "Et tu, Brute"?
2. Who was the last monarch of France?
3. Albania was invaded by which country in 1939?
4. What was a suffragette?
5. Joseph Paxton completed what 600-yard-long building in Hyde Park in 1851?
6. Who entered Havana in triumph in January, 1959?
7. What were Bevin Boys?
8. In 1900, in China, what was the Boxer Rebellion?
9. The Charge of the Light Brigade took place during which war?
10. Which British novelist and statesman was a friend of Queen Victoria?
11. What were the supporters of the royal House of Stuart called?
12. What was destroyed by fire in Hong Kong harbour on 9th January, 1972?
13. What has Cleopatra's Needle to do with Cleopatra?
14. Who was Edward Longshanks?
15. Which national leaders took part in the Yalta Conference in 1945?

ANSWERS

1. Julius Caesar's. 2. Louis-Philippe (1830-1848). 3. Italy. 4. A woman campaigner for women's right to vote. 5. The Crystal Palace. 6. Fidel Castro. 7. Young men who were called up to work in the mines. 8. An uprising of peasants. 9. The Crimean. 10. Benjamin Disraeli, Earl of Beaconsfield. 11. Jacobites. 12. The liner, Queen Elizabeth. 13. Nothing at all. It is dedicated to the pharaoh Thothmes III. 14. King Edward I. 15. Churchill, Roosevelt and Stalin.

SESSION 33
QUIZ 6

• •

1. Name four regulars who starred in the Carry On films.
2. Which actor starred in both *Trainspotting* and *The Full Monty*?
3. Whose life was the basis of the film *Funny Girl*?
4. Who is Tula Ellice Funklea?
5. What were the real names of the Marx Brothers?
6. Who's haunting music was adopted for the film *The Exorcist*?
7. Who plays Frasier in the TV show of the same name?
8. Who starred in the 1995 film *Jumanji*?
9. Morgan Freeman plays the President in which recent disaster movie?
10. Name the film which became a TV series centred on the New York School Of Performing Arts?
11. Which film starred Martin Clunes as a bridegroom left stranded on a remote island?
12. Which film used the slogan 'Size Does Matter' and starred Matthew Broderick and Jean Reno?
13. Rex Harrison and Eddie Murphy have both starred in what role?
14. Which film starred Wynona Ryder and Christian Slater as two murderous teenagers?
15. Whose last words were, 'I should never have switched from Scotch to Martinis'?

ANSWERS

1. Kenneth Williams, Charles Hawtrey, Kenneth Connor, Sid James, Bernard Bresslaw, Hattie Jacques, Jim Dale, Peter Butterworth, Jack Douglas. 2. Robery Carlysle. 3. Fanny Brice's. 4. The actress Cyd Charisse. 5. Chico=Leonard, Harpo=Adolph, Groucho=Julius, Gummo=Milton, Zeppo=Herbert. 6. Mike Oldfield. 7. Kelsey Grammer. 8. Robin Williams. 9. *Deep Impact*. 10. *Fame*. 11. *Staggered*. 12. *Godzilla*. 13. *Dr Dolittle*. 14. *Heathers*. 15. Humphrey Bogart.

335

SESSION 33
QUIZ 7

. . . .

1. With which female singer did the Pogues record, 'Fairy Tale Of New York'?
2. Who reached number 1 in January 1959 with, 'Smoke Gets In Your Eyes'?
3. What was Donny Osmonds' first UK number 1?
4. Who recorded the album, 'Diamonds and Pearls'?
5. Complete the trio, Keith Emerson, Greg Lake and ....?
6. What comic band have radio DJ, Mark Radcliffe and ex-Fall musician, Marc 'Lard' Riley formed?
7. With which Prince song did Sinead O'Connor reach number 1 in January 1990?
8. Marvin Gaye had his only UK number 1, 'I Heard It Through The Grapevine' in 1969. Who previously recorded the song in 1967?
9. Which Beatles album cover featured the band walking across a zebra crossing?
10. Who recorded the albums, 'Leisure' and 'Parklife'?
11. Boris Gardner hit number 1 in 1986 with, 'I Want To Wake Up With You'. What nationality is he?
12. Who recorded the album, 'For Those Who Are About To Rock'?
13. Which instrument does Kenny G play?
14. With whom did Peter Gabriel record his top ten hit, 'Don't give up'?
15. Which blues guitarist was described by Eric Clapton as the 'greatest guitarist alive'?

ANSWERS

1. Kirsty McColl. 2. Platters. 3. 'Puppy Love'. 4. Prince and the New Power Generation. 5. Carl Palmer. 6. The Shite Horses. 7. 'Nothing Compares 2 You'. 8. Gladys Knight and the Pips. 9. Abbey Road. 10. Blur. 11. Jamaican. 12. AC/DC. 13. Saxophone. 14. Kate Bush. 15. Buddy Guy.

336

SESSION 33

QUIZ 8

• •

1. 'The splendour falls on castle walls/And snowy summits old in story' is the beginning of a poem by whom?
2. Who wrote *The Picture of Dorian Gray*?
3. Complete the proverb: 'Better be an old man's darling...'
4. 'I remember, I remember,/The house where I was born,' is the beginning of a poem by whom?
5. 'Carter Dickson' and 'Carr Dickson' were pseudonyms of which American writer?
6. In which book does the character 'Tinker Bell' appear?
7. The character 'Scrooge' appears in which story by Charles Dickens?
8. A.A. Milne wrote: 'Hush! Hush! Whisper who dares!' How did he continue?
9. The character 'Rikki Tikki Tavi' appears in which famous book?
10. In which Shakespeare play does 'Cordelia' appear?
11. 'Tread softly,' says WB Yeats, because......
12. Who wrote *A Connecticut Yankee in King Arthur's Court*?
13. The *Fortunes of Philippa* was the first book by the most prolific of girls' story writers. Who?
14. Complete the proverb: 'The devil is not so black...'
15. Which American author and journalist wrote *The Old Man And The Sea* and was famous for doing much of his writing standing up?

ANSWERS

1. Lord Tennyson. 2. Oscar Wilde. 3. '...than a young man's slave'. 4. Thomas Hood. 5. John Dickson Carr. 6. *Peter Pan.* 7. *A Christmas Carol.* 8. 'Christopher Robin is saying his prayers.' 9. *The Jungle Book.* 10. *King Lear.* 11. 'Because you tread on my dreams'. 12. Mark Twain. 13. Angela Brazil. 14. '...as he is painted'. 15. Ernest Hemingway.

SESSION 33
QUIZ 9

• •

1. What is 'Murphy's Law'?
2. What are duchesse potatoes?
3. What is laverbread?
4. What is a rissole?
5. What is a group of chickens called?
6. What is biltong?
7. Who was the 'Bouncing Czech'?
8. What did the S. stand for in the name of Harry S. Truman?
9. What is the Naval equivalent of a Field Marshal?
10. What is the London Palladium?
11. What word, beginning with ante- means 'before midday'?
12. What was Dr. Who's time machine called?
13. What is charlotte russe?
14. According to the 'language of flowers', what does the foxglove signify?
15. What is halva?

ANSWERS

1. Briefly, it says that what can go wrong, will go wrong. 2. Mashed potato, baked with butter, milk and egg-yolk. 3. Fronds of the porphyra seaweed, dipped in oatmeal and fried. 4. A fried meat ball or cake. 5. A brood. 6. Strips of dried lean meat from South Africa. 7. Robert Maxwell. 8. Nothing at all! 9. Admiral of the Fleet. 10. A famous theatre where top performers have appeared. 11. Ante meridian. 12. The TARDIS. 13. A sponge-cake containing cream, biscuit and flavourings. 14. Insincerity. 15. A sweet made with sesame seeds and honey.

SESSION 33
QUIZ 10

1. What is zoophobia?
2. What colour is the peridot stone?
3. The cotton gin, for separating the seeds from the fibres, was invented in the US in 1793 by whom?
4. Perspex is a trade name for what?
5. If something is 'extraterrestrial', where would it be found?
6. Hero of Alexandria invented the aeolipile in AD 100. What was it?
7. Apart from being a young horse, what else is called a colt?
8. Who was Jean-François Champollion?
9. What's the record for someone being struck by lightning (and surviving)? (a) 4 times (b) 10 times (c) 7 times
10. What is odontology?
11. KLM is what?
12. What is a triangle with three different sides called?
13. A machine for altering the voltage of alternating current is called what?
14. What colour is an emerald?
15. Alexander Parkes invented a well-known early plastic (very inflammable) in 1855. Name?

ANSWERS

1. A fear of animals. 2. Green. 3. Eli Whitney. 4. Transparent plastic, used instead of glass. 5. Outside, or beyond the Earth. 6. A primitive kind of steam turbine. 7. A revolver. 8. French decipherer of the Rosetta Stone. 9. (c) 7 times: Roy Sullivan, USA. 10. The science and study of the teeth. 11. The Dutch national airline. 12. Scalene. 13. A transformer. 14. Green. 15. Celluloid.

• •

1. Siam is the old name for where?
2. In what country would you find the Temple of the Sun and the Temple of the Moon?
3. Where is the Giant's Causeway?
4. Where and what is Chesil Bank?
5. If you landed at Orly Airport, where would you be?
6. Sumatra is an island, part of which country?
7. The official name 'Nippon' refers to which country?
8. In which city would you find Lime Street railway station?
9. The official term 'Hrvatska' refers to which country?
10. In what country would you be if your currency was in Drachma?
11. The Topkapi Palace and museum is in what city?
12. What should one do at the Trevi Fountain in Rome?
13. What countries does 'Scandinavia' include?
14. Where in the world would you find a Fleming?
15. 'Salop' is another name for which county?

ANSWERS

1. Thailand. 2. Mexico. 3. Northern Ireland. 4. A long ridge of shingle off the Dorset coast. 5. Just outside Paris. 6. Indonesia. 7. Japan. 8. Liverpool. 9. Croatia. 10. Greece. 11. Istanbul. 12. Throw in coins and wish. 13. Norway, Sweden, Denmark, Finland and Iceland. 14. Belgium. 15. Shropshire.

• •

1. What is the meaning of 'garrulous'?
2. Complete the following phrase: 'ready, willing and....'
3. What word, beginning with R, means agent or delegate?
4. What do Britons call an American 'closet'?
5. A quean is; (a) a fallen woman (b) a wooden quoit (c) a rare kind of African deer?
6. What is another word for deluge or engulf?
7. What is the female equivalent of 'marquis'?
8. What were 'beatniks'?
9. What is the name for someone who studies poisons?
10. What is a lady's handbag called in the United States?
11. What is meant by the *crème de la crème*?
12. What do the initials, GPO stand for?
13. What is meant by The Fourth Estate?
14. What does it mean if a meeting is held 'in camera'?
15. If an American were to spank his child, what would he call it?

ANSWERS

1. Talkative. 2. Able. 3. Representative. 4. Cupboard. 5. (a) a fallen woman. 6. Flood. 7. Marchioness. 8. Nonconforming young people in the 1950 and 1960s. 9. Toxicologist. 10. A purse. 11. The very, very best. 12. General Post Office. 13. The Press. 14. It's held in secret. 15. Paddling.

SESSION 34
QUIZ 3

• •

1. In Baseball which player wears the most protective clothing?
2. What did Frenchman, Baron Pierre de Courbetin, do in the late 19th Century that would provide a whole new focus for the sporting world?
3. Which Rugby Union club plays its home games at Welford Road?
4. With which sport, other than football, do you associate Jack Charlton?
5. What is the term used in Golf to describe two over par at a hole?
6. Which sport holds its main British events at Santa Pod?
7. Which American event, first run in 1911, requires competitors to cover 200 laps of a 2.5 mile circuit?
8. Which sport does the ITTF govern?
9. True or false. In Netball, only 2 players on each team are allowed to score goals?
10. Which sport did the All England Croquet Club take responsibility for in 1874, asking the Marylebone Cricket Club to write the rules?
11. For major Water Polo matches, what is the minimum depth of the pool; 1.8m, 2.0m, 2.1m or 2.3m?
12. For which Premiership club did Colin Hendry play before joining Glasgow Rangers?
13. Which country has more Polo Clubs than any other?
14. In which country is Lacrosse said to have originated?
15. In which year was the FA Cup first held; 1862, 1870, 1871 or 1872?

ANSWERS

1. The Catcher. 2. Resurrected the Olympic Games. 3. Leicester. 4. Fishing. 5. Double Bogey. 6. Drag Racing. 7. Indianapolis 500. 8. Table Tennis. 9. True. 10. Lawn Tennis. 11. 1.8m. 12. Blackburn Rovers. 13. Argentina. 14. Canada. 15. 1872.

SESSION 34
QUIZ 4

1. Which king of England was crowned on the battlefield?
2. Two men were hanged at Newgate, London, in 1868. What was notable about this?
3. The pedal cycle was perfected in 1839 by whom?
4. To whom was Princess Mary of Teck married?
5. The 'five-and-ten-cent-store' which opened in Utica, New York in 1879 was so successful that it spread throughout the United States and into Britain. Can you name the famous store?
6. Which Bohemian prince commanded the Royalist cavalry during the English Civil War?
7. Where in England was the first Roman colony?
8. To which English king did the Pope award the title 'Defender of the Faith'?
9. Following the deaths of Kaisers Frederick III and Wilhelm I, who became the German Kaiser on 15th June, 1888?
10. Which great institution celebrated its 900th anniversary in December, 1965?
11. What happened in Krakatoa island in August, 1883?
12. Which wars took place in England starting in 1455 and ending in 1471?
13. On which day does the Orthodox Church celebrate Christmas?
14. Which famous British aircraft-carrier was sunk off Gibraltar on 12th November, 1941?
15. What is the purpose of this: Willy, Willy, Harry, Steve Harry, Dicky, John, Harry Three?

ANSWERS

1. King Henry VII in 1485. 2. It was the last public hanging in Britain. 3. Kirkpatrick Macmillan. 4. King George V. 5. Woolworths. 6. Prince Rupert. 7. Colchester. 8. King Henry VIII. 9. Wilhelm II. 10. Westminster Abbey. 11. The island exploded via an enormous volcanic eruption, killing 36,380 people. 12. The Wars of the Roses. 13. 7th January. 14. HMS Ark Royal. 15. A device for remembering the first eight English kings after the Norman Conquest.

343

SESSION 34
QUIZ 5

• •

1. Which playwright has had his works filmed more than any other?
2. Which composer often provides the music for Steven Spielberg films?
3. Who plays Scully in *The X-Files*?
4. Who co-wrote *Fawlty Towers* with her husband, John Cleese?
5. Which director made the films *Taxi Driver* and *Raging Bull*?
6. What was the first film in Cinemascope?
7. Who starred in the film *Love Story*?
8. Who played the female lead in *Personal Services* and *Educating Rita*?
9. Which British film, scripted by Colin Welland, won the 1981 Best Picture Oscar?
10. What does a key grip do on a film set?
11. Which TV soap is based around the lives of the people on Ramsey Street?
Who directed the film *Midnight Cowboy*?
13. Who claimed to go nearly mad making a film alongside a cartoon rabbit?
14. Who directed the 1935 film *The Informer*?
15. Yogi Bear's partner was Boo Boo, but who was his girlfriend?

ANSWERS

1. William Shakespeare. 2. John Williams II. 3. Gillian Anderson. 4. Connie Booth. 5. Martin Scorsese. 6. *The Robe*, 1953. 7. Ryan O'Neal and Ali McGraw. 8. Julie Walters. 9. *Chariots Of Fire*. 10. He's in charge of the grips who look after construction and production equipment. 11. Neighbours. 12. John Schlesinger. 13. Bob Hoskins during the making of *Who Framed Roger Rabbit*. 14. John Ford. 15. Cindy.

SESSION 34
QUIZ 6

• •

1. In which TV show did Ant and Dec start their show business careers?
2. In which James Bond film did singer Grace Jones play a villain?
3. TV presenter Cheryl Baker was formerly with which chart-topping group?
4. Who won the 1976 Eurovision Song Contest with 'Save All Your Kisses For Me'?
5. Which group became synonymous with flying pigs over Battersea Power Station?
6. Name Little Jimmy Osmond's debut single which reached number one In 1972?
7. What was Oasis' first single release?
8. In which year did Mark Morrison reach number one with 'Return of the Mack'; 1993, 1995, 1996 or 1997?
9. In 1981 Ennio Morricone reached number 2 in the UK chart with, Chi Mai', the theme from which TV series?
10. Who reached number 3 in 1988 with, 'I Don't Want To Talk About It'?
11. Who was the lead singer with the Electric Light Orchestra?
12. With whom did Olivia Newton John record Xanadu in 1980?
13. What instrument did Duane Eddy play?
14. Which TV show's theme tune was the Ian Dury and the Blockheads' song, 'Profoundly in love with Pandora?
15. Who had top ten hits with, 'Straight Up', 'Rush Rush' and 'Opposites Attract'?

ANSWERS

1. Byker Grove. 2. View To A Kill. 3. Bucks Fizz. 4. Brotherhood Of Man. 5. Pink Floyd. 6. Long-haired Lover From Liverpool. 7. Supersonic. 8. 1996. 9. The Life and Times of Lloyd George. 10. Everything But The Girl. 11. Jeff Lynne. 12. ELO. 13. Guitar. 14. The Diary of Adrian Mole aged 13 and ¾. 15. Paula Abdul.

345

SESSION 34
QUIZ 7

• •

1. What line follows 'The curfew tolls the knell of parting day'?
2. Who was Robert Bridges?
3. Which famous children's book did Hugh Lofting write?
4. 'Mrs Bardell' appears in which book by Charles Dickens?
5. Who created the fictional Chinese detective 'Charlie Chan'?
6. Who wrote *The Story of an African Farm*?
7. In which book does 'Raffles' appear?
8. In which children's comic did 'Desperate Dan' appear?
9. Who wrote the original *Jaws* novel?
10. What fictional character did Francis Durbridge create?
11. Complete the proverb: 'A constant guest...'
12. Who wrote *Five Children – and It*, and *The Phoenix and the Carpet*?
13. Who wrote *Cranford*?
14. Complete the proverb: 'Absence makes...'
15. Which was Shakespeare's first play?

ANSWERS

1. 'The lowing herd wind slowly o'er the lea'. 2. Poet Laureate and phonetiscist. 3. *The Story of Doctor Dolittle*. 4. *Pickwick Papers*. 5. Earl Derr Biggers. 6. Olive Schreiner. 7. Several stories by E.W. Hornung. 'Raffles' was a gentleman burglar. 8. *The Dandy*. 9. Peter Benchley. 10. Paul Temple. 11. ... is never welcome. 12. E. Nesbit. 13. Mrs Elizabeth Gaskell. 14. '...the heart grow fonder'. 15. *The Two Gentlemen of Verona*.

346

• •

1. Jews who in early times settled in Poland and Germany are called what?
2. The Archer represents which sign of the Zodiac?
3. Who's catchphrases included 'Nay, nay and thrice, nay'?
4. Who is the patron saint of tailors?
5. What was a 'penny gaff'?
6. The Isle of Portland, Dorset is not an island. What is it?
7. St Barbara is the patron saint of whom?
8. St Andrew is the patron saint of where?
9. What is perry?
10. What is a Bath bun?
11. Saturday is named after Saturn, the Roman god of culture and vegetation. True or false?
12. Which artist was renowned for his paintings of horses?
13. Which Dutch liqueur is sometimes called 'egg brandy'?
14. St Christopher is the patron saint of whom?
15. What word, beginning with ante-, means 'before birth'?

ANSWERS

1. Ashkenazim. 2. Sagittarius. 3. English comedian, Frankie Howerd. 4. St Homobonus. 5. In Victorian times, a cheap, low-class music hall. 6. A peninsula. 7. Miners. 8. Scotland. 9. A drink made from fermented pear juice. 10. A rich, rather sweet, bun. 11. True. 12. George Stubbs. 13. Advocaat. 14. Travellers. 15. Antenatal.

SESSION 34
QUIZ 9

• •

1. Who invented the vacuum flask?
2. What is limnology?
3. Two Germans, Wilhelm Maybach and Gottlieb Daimler, invented what vehicle?
4. What can be seen through something translucent?
5. At what temperature does water boil?
6. Aluminium is so called because it takes its name from the chemical alum. True or false?
7. What is acrophobia?
8. What is the hardest of all natural substances?
9. What is the name of the planet Pluto's satellite?
10. Nitric acid is also known as what?
11. What is beri-beri?
12. Who invented the gramophone?
13. What object in the sky is called Titan, and is 3,200 miles in diameter?
14. Blaise Pascal made a calculator in 1642, which was the ancestor of what?
15. What are Phobos and Deimos?

ANSWERS

1. James Dewar in 1885. 2. The scientific study of lakes and freshwater sites. 3. The motor-cycle, in 1885. 4. Light. 5. 100 degrees centigrade. 6. True. 7. Fear of heights. 8. Diamond. 9. Charon. 10. Aqua fortis, or 'strong water'. 11. A disease caused by a lack of vitamin B. 12. Thomas Edison (actually, he called it the 'phonograph'). 13. It is Saturn's largest moon. 14. The modern calculating machine. 15. The moons of Mars.

348

SESSION 34

QUIZ 10

• •

1. If a racehorse and a greyhound raced, which would win?
2. The marsupial wolf is not a wolf at all, but is believed extinct in its home country of...?
3. What sort of animal is a whippet?
4. What was the name of Tarzan's chimpanzee?
5. What sort of animal is a liger?
6. What is a canary?
7. Maize is really a special kind of grass. True or false?
8. What ox-like creature, found now only in zoos, once roamed wild in Europe?
9. Asparagus comes from the lily family of plants. Yes or no?
10. A duiker is an antelope found in South America. True or false?
11. What is a terrapin?
12. What is goldenrod?
13. The gibbon is the smallest of which group of animals?
14. The goliath beetle is found in the tropics, and holds what record?
15. What sort of animal is a ridgeback?

ANSWERS

1. The racehorse. 2. Tasmania. It's also called the Tasmanian wolf. 3. A breed of dog like a small greyhound. 4. Cheta. 5. A cross between a lion and female tiger. 6. A yellow cage-bird with a wonderful song, its home being the Canary Islands. 7. True. 8. The bison. 9. Yes. 10. False. It's found in South Africa. 11. A water-tortoise. 12. A perennial herb of the aster family with a woody stem and with yellow spray-shaped flowers. 13. The apes. 14. At over four inches, it's the world's largest insect. 15. A breed of dog.

● ●

1. What word is both a pain and a type of newspaper column?
2. Complete this simile: 'Look like a dying duck in a...'
3. A spanner in the USA is a what?
4. What is a 'bobby'?
5. What slang word has been used to describe teeth, billiard balls and piano keys?
6. What's the difference between illegible and eligible?
7. What is 'Betwixt' an old way of saying?
8. If you 'hid your light under a bushel' what would it mean?
9. How did the word 'mob' arise?
10. Can you quote a famous proverb, meaning the opposite of 'More haste, less speed'.
11. What's wrong with this: Offered a choice between beef and lamb, Fred chose the first?
12. What is an 'anecdote'?
13. What is a 'busby'?
14. What is the American term for the corridor in a train?
15. Which word, beginning with C means infantile or juvenile?

ANSWERS

15. Childish.
14. The aisle.
1. Agony. 2. '...thunderstorm'. 3. A wrench. 4. A policeman. 5. Ivories. 6. Illegible means 'unreadable' and eligible means 'fit to be chosen'. 7. Between. 8. That you were being very modest about your true talents. 9. It comes from the Latin, 'mobile vulgus', 'the fickle crowd'. 10. 'He who hesitates is lost'. 11. It should read: Offered a choice between beef, pork and lamb, Fred chose the former. 12. A brief, entertaining account of some incident. 13. A tall fur hat worn by guardsmen.

SESSION 35

QUIZ 2

1. Which sport do the Hawthorn Hawks play?
2. In Rugby Union, how far must the ball travel from the kick off?
3. In 1921 the Fédération Equestre Internationale laid down the rules for which sport?
4. In which year was the first 'Modern' Olympic Games held in Athens?
5. How long is the wire on a hammer in Athletics; 0.9m, 1.2m, 1.5m or 1.9m?
6. What was introduced into America in 1644 by Colonel Richard Nicholls, Commander of the English Forces?
7. What nationality is sprinter Frankie Fredericks?
8. Who took over as Chairman of Newcastle United after his son resigned amid controversy?
9. What does the word 'Karate' mean in Japanese?
10. With which sport do you associate Jonah Barrington and Susan Devoy?
11. Name Houston's NBA Basketball team?
12. What first took place in 1829, is 4 miles and 74 yards long, involves 18 competitors in 2 teams and is held once a year in London?
13. Which football team plays its home games at Portman Road?
14. With which sport do you associate Greg Louganis?
15. In which sport would you stand on the Hack Stay behind the Hogline, aiming for the tee at the centre of the house?

ANSWERS

1. Australian Rules Football. 2. 10 yards. 3. Dressage. 4. 1896. 5. 1.2m. 6. Horse Racing (Flat Racing). 7. Namibian. 8. Sir John Hall. 9. Empty Hand. 10. Squash. 11. Rockets. 12. The University Boat Race 13. Ipswich Town. 14. Diving. 15. Curling.

351

SESSION 35
QUIZ 3

1. Which Chinese dynasty ruled between 1368 and 1644??
2. What would a country be called if it was ruled entirely by its wealthy class?
3. What was the Marshall Plan?
4. Who were the Anzacs?
5. Where and what was Byzantium?
6. Which Chinese leader died on 9th September, 1976?
7. Which religion was officially re-established in Britain in September, 1850?
8. Who set sail aboard HMS *Beagle* to South America in December, 1831?
9. Who was the first monarch to be crowned in Westminster Abbey?
10. Who was George Blake, who escaped from Wormwood Scrubs in 1966?
11. Who were the Janissaries?
12. What was Sir Francis Drake doing when the Spanish Armada was sighted?
13. Who is George Herbert Walker Bush?
14. In what year did clothes rationing end?
15. Who attended schools in Cheam, Surrey, Gordonstoun, Scotland, and Timbertop, Australia?

ANSWERS

1. The Ming Dynasty. 2. A plutocracy. 3. A US economic aid programme to help nations recover from WWII. 4. The Australian and New Zealand soldiers in World War I. 5. It was an early name for Constantinople, which later became Istanbul. 6. Mao Tse-tung. 7. Roman Catholicism. 8. Charles Darwin. 9. William the Conqueror. 10. A traitor and spy. 11. The army of the Ottoman Empire. 12. Playing bowls. 13. He was the 41st American president. 14. 1949. 15. Prince Charles.

SESSION 35
QUIZ 4

• •

1. Which famous Disney film used spare scenes and footage from *Pinocchio* and was released in 1942?
2. Which film used a Boeing 707 to generate some of the high winds necessary for the plot?
3. Who played David McCallum's agent partner in the TV programme The Men From U.N.C.L.E.?
4. Who directed the Beatles' film *A Hard Day's Night*?
5. Which actress starred along Richard Gere in *Pretty Woman*?
6. Which film actress's name was given to a lifejacket?
7. Hawkeye, Hotlips and Klinger were characters in which popular TV show?
8. Who won a Best Actor Oscar for his role in the film *My Left Foot*?
9. In which film did Goldie Hawn join the army?
10. In which film did Jack Nicholson and Meryl Streep star as tramps?
11. Who were the husband and wife team who created the programmes *Stingray* and *Thunderbirds*?
12. Who was the 'Peekaboo Girl'?
13. Who was the 'Last of the Red Hot Mamas'?
14. Who directed the film *Reds*?
15. What's the gaffer in charge of on a film set?

ANSWERS

1. *Bambi*. 2. *Twister*. 3. Robert Vaughn. 4. Richard Lester. 5. Julia Roberts. 6. Mae West. 7. *M.A.S.H.* 8. Daniel Day-Lewis. 9. *Private Benjamin*. 10. *Ironweed*. 11. Gerry and Sylvia Anderson. 12. Veronica Lake. 13. Sophie Tucker. 14. Warren Beatty. 15. All the electrical equipment.

SESSION 35
QUIZ 5

• •

1. With whom did the Smurfs record their first hit, 'The Smurf Song'?
2. Who recorded the album, 'The Wall'?
3. Who had top ten hits with, 'So Macho', 'Toy Boy' and 'Cross My Broken Heart'?
4. In which year did Sister Sledge reach number 1 with, 'Frankie'; 1983, 1984 or 1982?
5. The Shamen had a string of hits in the early 1990's. What is a Shamen?
6. Who's 1998 album was titled, 'Hello Nasty'?
7. Who recorded the, 'Free Wheelin', album in 1963?
8. What is Boy George's real name?
9. Who did singer Barbara Streisand marry in 1998?
10. Who is the lead singer with Blur?
11. Rock and roll suicide was the final show for which of David Bowie's creations?
12. Which actors were the original Blues Brothers?
13. Which 1980 film starred singer, Hazel O'Connor?
14. Who recorded the album, 'First Of A Million Kisses'?
15. Who sang the theme song to, 'The Spy Who Loved Me'?

ANSWERS

1. Father Abraham. 2. Pink Floyd 3. Sinitta. 4. 1984. 5. A mystic/faith healer. 6. The Beastie Boys. 7. Bob Dylan. 8. George O'Dowd 9. James Brolin 10. Damon Albarn 11. Ziggy Stardust. 12. John Belushi and Dan Aykroyd. 13. Breaking Glass. 14. Fairground Attraction. 15. Carly Simon.

SESSION 35
QUIZ 6

• •

1. Who published the first issue of the magazine *Answers* in 1888?
2. What was the fictional creation of the Rev. W.V. Awdry?
3. Who wrote the original 'James Bond' novels?
4. Complete the proverb: 'All cats are...'
5. Complete Dorothy Parker's line: 'Men seldom make passes...'
6. Who wrote *Uncle Tom's Cabin*?
7. Which Australian poet was nicknamed 'Banjo'?
8. Whose children were named Hamnet, Judith and Sussanah?
9. What was Paddington Bear's favourite food?
10. Which famous children's book did Mary Norton write?
11. What was Oscar Wilde describing when he said 'The unspeakable in pursuit of the uneatable'?
12. Who wrote *A Clockwork Orange*?
13. Who wrote *The Cruel Sea*?
14. In which book does the villainous 'Simon Legree' appear?
15. Who wrote *The Prime of Miss Jean Brodie*?

ANSWERS

1. Alfred Charles Harmsworth, later Lord Northcliffe. 2. Thomas the Tank Engine. 3. Ian Fleming. 4. '...grey in the dark'. 5. '...At girls who wear glasses'. 6. Harriet Beecher Stowe. 7. Andrew Barton Paterson. 8. Shakespeare's. 9. Marmalade. 10. *The Borrowers*. 11. Foxhunting. 12. Anthony Burgess. 13. Nicholas Monsarrat. 14. *Uncle Tom's Cabin*. 15. Muriel Spark.

• •

1. What is béchamel?
2. What is fascism?
3. What, to a soldier, is a redcap?
4. Who was known as, 'the fifth Beatle'?
5. Turkeys didn't come from Turkey. Where did they originally come from?
6. The 'Abominable Snowman' is also known as?
7. What word, beginning with ante-, means 'before the existence of the world'?
8. Who is Allah?
9. Where did the orange originate?
10. What is gumbo?
11. St Joseph is the patron saint of whom?
12. What were Lyons' Corner Houses?
13. Heracles is another name for Hercules. True or false?
14. What word, beginning with ante- means 'before, in time or place'?
15. What had Queen Victoria and Harpo Marx in common?

ANSWERS

1. A white sauce flavoured with onion and herbs. 2. A system of government which has only one political party headed by a dictator. 3. A military policeman. 4. Producer, George Martin. 5. North America. 6. The Yeti. 7. Antemundane. 8. According to the Muslims, the Supreme Being, or God. 9. China. 10. A soup made with the okra plant. 11. Carpenters. 12. Large restaurants in London where the cost of entertainment was within reach of ordinary people. 13. True. 14. Anterior. 15. They were both left-handed.

SESSION 35
QUIZ 8

• •

1. What is measured by the quire?
2. What is an asteroid?
3. Aeroflot is what?
4. What kind of military vehicle is an APC?
5. What is an anaesthetic?
6. What is an ingot?
7. Sir Isaac Newton built the first of a kind of optical instrument in 1668. What was it?
8. A pump using what kind of power was invented in 1698 by Thomas Savery?
9. The branch of science which deals with the study and application of electron devices is called?
10. What is the term for a mixture of solid particles floating in a liquid or gas?
11. How many sides has a hexagon?
12. What makes up 21% of air?
13. What metric weight is equal to 0.04 ounces?
14. What is German silver?
15. The cranium is another name for what?

ANSWERS

1. Paper. 2. A minor planet, often no more than a chunk of rock. 3. The Russian national airline. 4. An armoured personnel carrier. 5. A drug or gas used in medicine to produce loss of feeling. 6. A convenient shape for a piece of cast metal. 7. The reflecting telescope. 8. Steam. 9. Electronics. 10. A suspension. 11. Six. 12. Oxygen. 13. A gram. 14. An alloy of copper, zinc and nickel. 15. The skull.

357

SESSION 35
QUIZ 9

. . . .

1. What is wrong with this statement, 'Crowds of wombats flew up as we passed'?
2. What is a group of oysters called?
3. A group of gorillas is called a gang, a tree or a band?
4. What is a group of caterpillars called?
5. What is flax?
6. A peccary is; (a) a kind of wild horse (b) a kind of wild pig (c) a kind of wild cat?
7. Eland is; (a) a small island off Scilly Isles (b) a kind of antelope (c) a kind of frog?
8. The banana is a member of the same plant family as ginger. True or false?
9. What is a group of apes called?
10. The lilac is a member of the olive family. Yes or no?
11. Which British wild mammal digs a home called a 'set'?
12. How many different kinds of beetle are there; (a) 50,000 (b) 100,000 (c) 250,000?
13. What is henna?
14. How long is Britain's longest centipede?
15. The average house-fly lives; (a) about 20 days (b) about one day (c) about a week?

ANSWERS

1. A wombat is a non-flying marsupial. 2. A bed. 3. A band. 4. An army. 5. The fibres of the Linum plant, from which linen is made. 6. (b) A kind of wild pig. 7. (b) A kind of antelope. 8. True. 9. A shrewdness. 10. Yes. 11. A badger. 12. (c) 250,000. 13. A reddish-orange pigment made from a shrub of the same name. 14. About three inches. 15. (a) About 20 days.

SESSION 35

QUIZ 10

• •

1. What is the capital of Chile?
2. Which five counties were included in the ancient Wessex?
3. In which country does 23% of the World's population live?
4. Where and what is Snowdon?
5. What is the capital of the Republic of Ireland?
6. What country's capital city is La Paz?
7. Who (or what) is the Old Lady of Threadneedle Street?
8. If a foreign car displayed the letters JA, what would its country of origin be?
9. Where and what is Liechtenstein?
10. Where in England is The Lake District?
11. By what name were these five towns known in medieval times: Hastings, Sandwich, Dover, Romney and Hythe?
12. The Little St Bernard Pass runs between which two countries?
13. The republic, Slovenia was formerly part of which country?
14. In which country do they speak Shona?
15. How many Channel Isles are there?

ANSWERS

1. Santiago. 2. Berkshire, Dorset, Hampshire, Somerset and Wiltshire. 3. China. 4. A mountain, the highest in Wales. 5. Dublin. 6. Bolivia. 7. The Bank of England, in the City of London. 8. Jamaica. 9. It's an independent principality between Austria and Switzerland. 10. Cumbria. 11. The Cinque Ports. 12. France and Italy. 13. Yugoslavia. 14. Zimbabwe. 15. Four, and a number of small islets.

SESSION 36
QUIZ 1

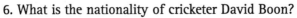

1. In Snooker, how many points is the blue ball worth?
2. Name Tampa Bay's American football team?
3. Which County Cricket team does Andrew Flintoff play for?
4. Which football club has the nickname the 'Eagles'?
5. With which sport do you associate Kirk Stevens?
6. What is the nationality of cricketer David Boon?
7. Who are the only father and son ever to both win the Formula One Drivers World Championship?
8. Which sport competes for the Bledisloe Cup?
9. What nationality is racing driver, Thierry Boutson?
10. With which sport do you associate David Broom?
11. Which sport celebrates Cowes Week?
12. Who won the 1998 US Masters golf title?
13. Which football club plays its home games at Elland Road?
14. Which county captain of Middlesex became an England selector in the 1990s?
15. Which football team started at the Goldstone Ground, played away, and are now at home at the Withdean Stadium?

ANSWERS

1. Five. 2. Buccaneers 3. Lancashire. 4. Crystal Palace. 5. Snooker. 6. Australian. 7. Graham and Damon Hill. 8. Rugby Union. 9. Belgian. 10. Show Jumping. 11. Sailing. 12. Mark O'Meara. 13. Leeds United. 14. Mike Gatting. 15. Brighton and Hove Albion

SESSION 36

QUIZ 2

● ●

1. What was the R101 and what happened to it?
2. Wroclaw, Poland, was the former German city of what?
3. How many King James have there been in Scotland?
4. By winning the Battle of Plassey in India, 1757, what did the British commander, Robert Clive achieve?
5. Who made the first telephone call on 11th March, 1876?
6. Which British monarch reigned longest?
7. What political activity were Roman Catholics in Britain first allowed to do in 1829?
8. Who was Ernesto 'Che' Guevara?
9. The first 'Peelers' appeared on the streets of London in 1829. What were they?
10. Which famous British motor-car company was founded in 1904?
11. How does a Member of Parliament resign?
12. Who was Ulysses S. Grant?
13. Which former British King died in Paris in 1972?
14. The Prussian city of Danzig is now called what?
15. In what year was the intoduction of the Penny Post in Britain?

ANSWERS

1. A British airship which crashed on her maiden voyage, killing 48 passengers and crew in 1930. 2. Breslau. 3. Six. 4. The beginning of the British Empire in India. 5. Alexander Graham Bell. 6. Queen Victoria. 7. Stand for parliament. 8. A Latin American revolutionary. 9. Policemen. 10. Rolls-Royce. 11. He applies for a post in the Chiltern Hundreds or the Manor of Northstead. 12. He was the 18th American president. 13. The Duke of Windsor, formerly King Edward VIII. 14. Gdansk. 15. 1840

SESSION 36
QUIZ 3

. . . .

1. Where and when did the first commercial radio station in Britain open?
2. What TV show featured a band whose first names were Mickey, Peter, Mike and Davey?
3. Which famous film director's first film was *The Pleasure Garden* in 1925?
4. In the film *Bugsy Malone*, which star's singing was dubbed?
5. Ian Fleming wanted his cousin to play the role of *Dr No* in the Bond film of the same name. Who was the actor?
6. For which role were a staggering 1400 actresses auditioned?
7. Who was Dominic Felix Amici?
8. How many extras were used in the film, Ghandi; (a) 3000 (b) 30,000 (c) 300,000?
9. From which musical play comes the song 'Big Spender'?
10. Who starred as a butler in the film *The Remains Of The Day*?
11. Which film actor's real name is Allen Stewart Konigsberg?
12. Who was the Jersey Lily?
13. Which Carradine had a brother called Keith?
14. Who was Satchmo?
15. Was the horse's head featured in *The Godfather* real or fake?

ANSWERS

1. 1964, on the Isle of Man. 2. The Monkees. 3. Alfred Hitchcock. 4. Jodie Foster. 5. Christopher Lee. 6. Scarlet O'Hara in Gone With the Wind. 7. The film actor Don Ameche. 8. (c) 300,000. 9. Sweet Charity. 10. Anthony Hopkins. 11. Woody Allen. 12. Lily Langtry, actress. 13. David Carradine. 14. Louis Armstrong. 15. Real.

SESSION 36
QUIZ 4

....

1. Who sang Britain's 1991 Eurovision song contest entry, 'A Message To Your Heart'?

2. What ended Jan and Dean's, recording career?

3 With which song did Jazzy Jeff and the Fresh Prince reach number 1 in 1993?

4. Godley and Crème reached number 3 in 1981 with, 'Under Your Thumb'. Which band were the duo previously part of?

5. Which artist has recorded more weeks on the UK chart than any other?

6. Which artist has recorded duets with, Dionne Warwick, Cliff Richard, Luciano Pavarotti and Kiki Dee?

7. Who was George Michael's partner in Wham?

8. In 1979, who sang, ' The silicon chip inside her head is switched to overload'?

9. Who went straight in at number 1 in 1991 with, 'The Fly'?

10. What do Al Martino, Whigfield, Robson & Jerome and Babylon Zoo, have in common?

11. What do the songs, 'Can't Help Falling In Love', 'Dizzy', 'I Believe' and 'Living Doll', have in common?

12. With which 1970s glam band was Les Gray the lead singer?

13. What do A-ha, Shirley Bassey, Nancy Sinatra and Sheena Easton, have in common?

14. Roger Taylor was the drummer with which group?

15. Who had hits in the 1970's with, 'Don't Take Away The Music', 'Whodunnit' and 'More Than A Woman'?

ANSWERS

1. Samantha Janus. 2. A car crash. 3. Boom! Shake the room. 4. 10cc. 5. Elvis Presley. 6. Elton John. 7. Andrew Ridgley. 8. The Boomtown Rats (Bob Geldof). 9. U2. 10. Their debut singles have gone straight in at number one. 11. All have been number 1 in 2 separate versions. 12. Mud. 13. All have recorded Bond Themes. 14. Queen. 15. Tavares.

SESSION 36

QUIZ 5

• •

1. Who wrote the story *The Murders in the Rue Morgue*?
2. In which book is 'Toad' a leading character?
3. Who is reputed to have said, 'A verbal contract is not worth the paper it's written on'?
4. Who wrote *Sanders of the River* and its sequels?
5. The magazine *Punch* carried this line in 1845: 'Advice to persons about to marry.' How did it continue?
6. Who wrote *Of Human Bondage*?
7. Who wrote *The History of the World* while imprisoned in the Tower of London?
8. What is the actual name of the Count in *The Count of Monte Cristo*?
9. Complete Benjamin Franklin's advice: 'We must all hang together or...'
10. Who were Frank Richards, Martin Clifford and Charles Hamilton?
11. Hazel, Fiver and Bigwig appear in which book?
12. In which Shakespeare play does 'Polixenes' appear?
13. Who wrote *Ulysses*?
14. 'The world is so full of a number of things......' How did R.L. Stevenson continue?
15. Who wrote *Pride and Prejudice*?

ANSWERS

1. Edgar Allan Poe. 2. *The Wind in the Willows*. 3. Sam Goldwyn, Hollywood movie mogul. 4. Edgar Wallace. 5. 'Don't'. 6. W. Somerset Maugham. 7. Sir Walter Raleigh. 8. Edmond Dantes. 9. '...Most assuredly we shall all hang separately.' (he was signing the Declaration of Independence). 10. Names used by Charles Hamilton who wrote school stories of Greyfriars and St Jim's. 11. *Watership Down*, by Richard Adams. 12. *A Winter's Tale*. 13. James Joyce. 14. 'I'm sure we should all be as happy as kings'. 15. Jane Austen.

SESSION 36
QUIZ 6

1. What word, beginning with post-, means 'to put off until a future time?'
2. Who in the world would be called a Canuck?
3. According to the 'language of flowers', what does the bluebell signify?
4. What is cock-a-leekie?
5. Who was Sir Malcolm Campbell?
6. How long have playing-cards been known in England; (a) 400 years (b) 500 years (c) 200 years?
7. In what place do Muslim people worship?
8. What group of people are referred to as a troupe?
9. Which English Admiral saw off the Spanish Armada?
10. Scorpions are immune to their own poison. True or false?
11. In a pack of cards, which way does the Queen of Hearts look, to her left, or to her right?
12. What is chop suey?
13. What is pumpernickel?
14. What are *crêpes suzettes*?
15. In Britain, we had the game ninepins. The Americans have tenpins. Why?

ANSWERS

1. Postpone. 2. A Canadian. 3. Constancy. 4. A soup made from a fowl and leeks. 5. Land-speed and water-speed record holder. 6. (a) 400 years. 7. A mosque. 8. Actors, acrobats, dancers, minstrels. 9. Sir Francis Drake. 10. False. 11. To her right. 12. A US-invented Chinese dish usually containing beansprouts. 13. A coarse, malted rye bread. 14. Thin, hot pancakes with lemons or oranges. 15. Ninepins was banned in America. Using the extra pin got around the law.

SESSION 36
QUIZ 7

• •

1. Helium takes its name from the Greek word helios, meaning the Sun. True or false?
2. New York would be quite different without William Le Baron Jenney's idea. What was it?
3. How many pints in an imperial gallon?
4. What food-processing system was invented in 1812 by Brian Donkin?
5. Ernest Swinton, in 1914, invented which monstrous engine of war?
6. Chester Carlson's idea was copied many times. What was it?
7. What object in the sky is called Europa, and is 1,950 miles in diameter?
8. What aerial event did Henri Giffard undertake in 1852?
9. What is oology?
10. What is the diameter of Saturn's widest ring? (a) 200,000 miles (b) 170,000 miles.
11. The French chemist Charles Gerhardt made acetylsalicylic acid in 1853. What is it now widely used as?
12. What is air?
13. Nitrous oxide is better known as what?
14. In Roman numerals, what is C?
15. Osmium is (a) a rare metal (b) a tropical plant (c) an Asian country.

ANSWERS

1. True. 2. The skyscraper. 3. Eight. 4. The canning of food. 5. The tank. 6. Xerography, or the copying machine. 7. It is Jupiter's fourth-largest moon. 8. The first balloon flight with powered propulsion. 9. The science or study of birds' eggs. 10. (b) 170,000 miles. 11. Aspirin. 12. A mixture of 78% nitrogen, 21% oxygen and traces of argon and carbon dioxide. 13. Laughing gas. 14. 100. 15. (a) A rare metal.

SESSION 36
QUIZ 8

. . . .

1. How old is the oldest living tree; (a) 1,500 years (b) 25,000 years (c) 12,000 years?
2. The glass snake is not a snake. What is it?
3. The aubergine is a member of the nightshade family. Yes or no?
4. Which land animal is the heaviest of all?
5. What is a silver birch?
6. A shoat is a young pig. True or false?
7. Which is the only bird in the world that can fly backwards?
8. What is ambergris?
9. The carrot is a plant relative of the poisonous plant, hemlock. True or false?
10. What is a group of bees called?
11. A marsupial which lives in trees and is similar to a bat is called what?
12. What is a chow chow?
13. The plum is a member of the rose family. Yes or no?
14. What kind of animal is said to screech?
15. What sort of animal is an Airedale?

ANSWERS

1. (c) 12,000 years. 2. A legless lizard. 3. Yes. 4. The African elephant. 5. A graceful tree with silvery bark. 6. True. 7. The humming-bird. 8. It's something used in perfumery, which comes from a whale's intestines. 9. True. 10. A swarm. 11. A phalanger. 12. A breed of dog. 13. Yes. 14. An owl. 15. A breed of dog.

367

SESSION 36
QUIZ 9

• •

1. In what country do some of the people speak Romansch?
2. Which ancient city was on the River Euphrates?
3. What did Sir Stamford Raffles found in 1819?
4. What was once called 'the Dark Continent'?
5. Tasmania is named after the discoverer of New Zealand. What was his name?
6. Mesopotamia is the old name for where?
7. The Collegiate Church of St Peter is the correct name for which famous building in London?
8. In which county would you find the River Medway?
9. Where is Patagonia?
10. In what country would you find the cities of Amoy and Foochow?
11. Persia is a country now called what?
12. Which is the largest sea?
13. On which river does Vienna stand?
14. Where is Sherwood Forest?
15. Where and what is Pearl Harbor?

ANSWERS

1. Switzerland. 2. Babylon. 3. The settlement of Singapore. 4. Africa. 5. Abel Tasman. 6. Iraq. 7. Westminster Abbey. 8. Kent. 9. It's at the southern end of South America. 10. China. 11. Iran. 12. The South China Sea, 1,148,500 sq.m. 13. The Danube. 14. Mainly in Nottinghamshire. 15. The US naval base at Hawaii.

SESSION 36
QUIZ 10

· ·

1. What is the difference between a homonym and a homophone?
2. What, in earlier times, was a 'hackney'?
3. What was a 'clippie'?
4. Some languages use a cedilla. What exactly is that?
5. What is the name for someone who studies the meaning of words?
6. What is a 'quack'?
7. What is an 'aigrette'?
8. Can you give a word starting with M, meaning 'numskull' or 'simpleton'?
9. What is the name for words derived from someone's name, like 'braille', 'sandwich', 'wellingtons'?
10. What do the initials CPU stand for in computing?
11. What does 'incandescent' mean?
12. What does an American mean by 'banana-oil'?
13. What is the name for someone who studies and makes maps?
14. Which armed service is sometimes referred to as 'the Andrew'?
15. What is, or was, a Sloane Ranger?

ANSWERS

1. Homonyms are words which are spelt alike but mean different things. Homophones are words which sound alike but are spelt differently. 2. A horse for general use. 3. A female bus-conductor during and just after WW2. 4. A mark beneath letter, usually 'c', as in the French word 'garçon'. 5. Semanticist. 6. It strictly means a fake doctor, but is often used generally in a derogatory manner. 7. A diamond head ornament. 8. Moron. 9. They are called eponyms. 10. Central Processing Unit. 11. White-hot. 12. Flattery. 13. Cartographer. 14. The Royal Navy. 15. A well-off girl from the country who lives around Sloane Square, London.

SESSION 37
QUIZ 1

• •

1. Who was 'Lord Haw Haw'?
2. Who succeeded to the British throne in 1837?
3. Britain's first prime minister was appointed in 1721. Who was he?
4. Who was killed by a terrorist bomb in a boat off Ireland in 1979?
5. Howard Carter and Earl of Carvarvon were first to see what in 1922?
6. The Queen opened which major London exhibition centre in 1982?
7. What, on the River Thames, London, was raised for the first time in 1982?
8. Which group of men first arrived in Botany Bay, Australia in 1788?
9. Which area in the British Isles received its independence in 1921?
10. Which major German battleship was sunk in December, 1943?
11. Which television channel was launched in Britain on 2nd November, 1982?
12. George Pullman died on 19th October 1897. What did he do?
13. Which patriotic song was sung for the first time on 28th September, 1745?
14. Which world-famous discoverer died in poverty in 1506?
15. Which war between Britain and the US ended on 24th December, 1814?

ANSWERS

1. William Joyce, a traitor who broadcast propaganda from Germany in WW2. 2. Queen Victoria. 3. Sir Robert Walpole. 4. Lord Louis Mountbatten. 5. The inside of the tomb of Tutenkhamun. 6. The Barbican Centre. 7. The Thames Barrier. 8. The first transported convicts. 9. The Irish Free State. 10. The Scharnhorst. 11. Channel 4. 12. Designed the first Pullman railway coaches. 13. God Save The King. 14. Christopher Columbus. 15. The War of 1812.

SESSION 37
QUIZ 2

• •

1. Were any real pigs used in the filming of *Babe*?
2. What film festival awards Golden Palms to winning films?
3. Which writer has the TV shows *The Liver Birds*, *Butterflies* and *Bread* to her credits?
4. What type of film has Hollywood made more often than any other?
5. What famous actor and director first became known for his role in the TV series *Rawhide*?
6. Who starred as the straw man in *The Wiz*, the updated version of *The Wizard Of Oz*?
7. Who played Captain Hook in the 1991 film, *Hook*?
8. What T.V. show featured the butler Hudson and the cook, Mrs Bridges?
9. With which director is the Dreamworks film studio associated?
10. Which film dealt with a plot to assassinate Winston Churchill?
11. Which film actors have played the part of Ben Hur?
12. Which film dealt with the life of Douglas Bader?
13. From which musical play comes the song, 'Hopelessly Devoted to You'?
14. On what stage play is the film *My Fair Lady* based?
15. What was Gary Cooper's job before he was discovered by film director, Henry King?

ANSWERS

1. Yes, 48 of them. 2. The Cannes film festival. 3. Carla Lane. 4. Comedy. 5. Clint Eastwood. 6. Michael Jackson. 7. Dustin Hoffman. 8. *Upstairs Downstairs*. 9. Steven Spielberg. 10. *The Eagle Has Landed*, 1977. 11. Ramon Navarro and Charlton Heston. 12. *Reach for the Sky*, 1956. 13. Grease. 14. Pygmalion. 15. Stunt man.

SESSION 37
QUIZ 3

1. Rod Stewart once recorded a song for the England football team? True or false?
2. Who were on a, 'Road To Nowhere' in 1985?
3. Who were number one in the UK chart at the end of June 1998?
4. Which Las Vagas star had minor hits in the UK during the 1950's, with, 'Unchained Melody' and 'I Don't Care'?
5. Who had top ten hits with, 'Oops Up Side Your Head' and 'Big Fun'?
6. Why did Gabrielle have a two year gap from recording between 1994 and 1996?
7. 'Rage Hard' and 'Warriors (of the wasteland)', were minor hits for which chart topping band?
8. Who did Shane Fenton become in 1973, having a number one hit with, 'Jealous Mind', in 1974?
9. Who had number one hits with, 'Nights on Broadway' and 'Young Hearts Run Free', in 1976/77?
10. Who sang, 'Let Me Entertain You', in 1998?
11. Mick Hucknall is the lead singer with which group?
12. Victoria Adams is better known by what name?
13. Under what name did Jefferson Starship, reach number one with, 'Nothing's Gonna Stop Us Now'?
14. What was Elvis Presley's last UK number one?
15. How many number ones did Elton John have in the 1980s?

ANSWERS

1 False. 2 Talking heads. 3. Baddiel and Skinner with the Lightning Seeds. 4. Liberace. 5. The Gap band. 6. To have a baby. 7. Frankie Goes To Hollywood. 8. Alvin Stardust. 9. Candi Staton. 10. Robbie Williams. 11. Simply Red. 12. Posh Spice. 13. Starship. 14. 'Way Down'. 15. None.

- -

1. Who was the author of *Stalky and Co.*?
2. Who wrote the play *A Doll's House*?
3. Who wrote *Testament of Youth*?
4. Who was the translator of the *Rubaiyát of Omar Khayyam*?
5. In which Shakespeare play does 'Orlando' appear?
6. Who wrote *The Turn of the Screw*?
7. Who wrote the play *Waiting For Godot*?
8. Who wrote *Brideshead Revisited*?
9. Who created the detective character 'Father Brown'?
10. Complete the proverb: 'Don't cut off your nose...'
11. Complete the proverb: 'Discretion is...'
12. Who was Bertold Brecht?
13. Which famous children's book did Louisa May Alcott write?
14. What line follows 'I remember, I remember' ?
15. The writer H.H. Munro, known as 'Saki', wrote: 'The cook was a good cook, as cooks go,'   How did he continue?

ANSWERS

1. Rudyard Kipling. 2. Henrik Ibsen. 3. Vera Brittain. 4. Edward Fitzgerald. 5. *As You Like It.* 6. Henry James. 7. Samuel Beckett. 8. Evelyn Waugh. 9. G.K. Chesterton. 10. '...to spite your face'. 11. '...the better part of valour'. 12. A German poet and playwright. 13. *Little Women.* 14. 'The house where I was born'. 15. 'and as cooks go, she went'.

SESSION 37
QUIZ 5

1. What is blutwurst?
2. Wednesday is named after Woden, the German god of war. True or false?
3. What is a Chelsea bun?
4. What is quiche?
5. What was 'ragtime'?
6. What is chilli con carne?
7. In a pack of cards, which way does the King of Clubs look, to his left, or to his right?
8. Who was Albrecht Dürer?
9. What are 'Grape Nuts' and who invented them?
10. What does LBW stand for?
11. R. Harmenzoon van Rijn was one of the most famous of all painters. What does the R stand for?
12. St Patrick is the patron saint of what?
13. What is the Fabian Society?
14. St Amand is the patron saint of whom?
15. What type of entertainment is a 'Charleston'?

ANSWERS

1. The German version of black pudding. 2. True. 3. A rolled bun filled with currants and raisins. 4. A shell of unsweetened pastry which can hold a savoury filling. 5. A type of very popular music which preceded jazz. 6. Minced meat, beans and chillis. 7. To his right. 8. A German painter and engraver. 9. A breakfast cereal invented by Charles Post in 1898. 10. Leg Before Wicket in cricket. 11. Rembrandt. 12. Ireland. 13. A socialist group founded in 1884. 14. Innkeepers and wine-merchants. 15. A type of dance.

SESSION 37
QUIZ 6

• •

1. Gravity on the moon is a third, a quarter or a sixth of what it is on Earth?
2. What is osteology?
3. What is a monorail?
4. What is oneirology?
5. What does DC stand for?
6. What is alum?
7. How many moons does Neptune have (a) 2 (b) 3 (c) 4.
8. What optical instrument was invented in 1608 by Hans Lippershey?
9. What is 'latex'?
10. What's it used for?
11. What metal has the chemical symbol Fe?
12. Who was Tycho Brahe?
13. What is a megalomaniac?
14. What did Mariner 10 do in 1973?
15. Radium is so called because it comes from the Latin word radius, meaning a ray. True or false?

ANSWERS

1. A sixth. 2. The study of bones. 3. A railway which uses only a single rail, rather than the twin rails on normal lines. 4. The study of dreams. 5. Direct current. 6. A chemical. It's a double sulphate of aluminium and potassium. 7. (a) 2. 8. The telescope. 9. The milky fluid given off by trees in South America and elsewhere. 10. Making rubber. 11. Iron. 12. A Danish astronomer. 13. Someone who thinks he is all-powerful and all-important. 14. It flew by Mercury and took photographs of the planet. 15. True.

375

SESSION 37

QUIZ 7

1. Which is the longest snake?
2. The pear is a member of the rose family. Yes or no?
3. The bobcat is a kind of wild lynx found in North America. True or false?
4. If an American found a flicker in his garden, what should he or she be looking out for?
5. The bluebell is a member of the lily family. Yes or no?
6. How much water does a koala bear drink in a day?
7. The Borzoi is; (a) a breed of dog (b) a breed of cat or (c) a breed of horse?
8. Which animal is the most flea-ridden?
9. The raspberry is a member of the rose family. Yes or no?
10. What is a dromedary?
11. What is a bullfinch?
12. What is unique about the Komodo dragon lizard?
13. Cotton is a member of the Rubia family. Yes or no?
14. What is a chrysanthemum?
15. If you were a herpetologist, what would you be expert on?

ANSWERS

1. The python. 2. Yes. 3. True. 4. Holes in his trees. It's a woodpecker. 5. Yes. 6. None. It relies on the moisture in eucalyptus leaves. 7. (a) A breed of dog. 8. Red Squirrel. 9. Yes. 10. A camel with one hump. 11. An attractive songbird, black and white with pink underparts. 12. It's the world's heaviest lizard, weighing over 360 pounds. 13. Yes. 14. A flower related to the corn marigold and ox-eye daisy. The national flower of Japan. 15. Reptiles.

SESSION 37
QUIZ 8

• •

1. To which country do the Galapagos Islands belong?
2. Where and what is the Solway Firth?
3. Walmer Castle, near Deal, was the home of which famous military leader?
4. What is the capital of Portugal?
5. The population of the world is approximately (a) 5,300 million (b) 7,400 million (c) 4,900 million?
6. How many people live in Monaco? (a) 30,500 (b) 45,100 (c) 75,300
7. Which country's capital city is Seoul?
8. On which islands in the South Atlantic are there approximately 370 sheep for every person?
9. In which country would you find the Apennnine mountain range?
10. What was meant by the North West Passage?
11. Where and what is the Old Man of Hoy?
12. How many islands comprise Tristan da Cunha?
13. Which is the largest lake in England?
14. In which city would you find 'The Royal Mile?'
15. Where and what are 'The Needles'?

ANSWERS

1. Ecuador. 2. An inlet from the Irish Sea, forming part of the border between England and Scotland. 3. The Duke of Wellington. 4. Lisbon. 5. (a) 5,300 million. 6. (a) 30,500. 7. South Korea. 8. The Falklands. 9. Italy. 10. A supposed seaway through the north-west of America. 11. It's a rock off the Orkney Islands. 12. Five. 13. Windermere. 14. Edinburgh. 15. Three sharp chalk pillars off the Isle of Wight.

• •

1. An 'angel of mercy' could be described as....?
2. What's wrong with this sentence: 'The visit to Canterbury was a great treat for my sisters and I'?
3. What was formerly meant by the slang 'a pony'?
4. What is the female version of 'ram'?
5. What was a fletcher?
6. What word, beginning with I, means advise or notify?
7. Can you quote a proverb meaning the opposite of 'Many hands make light work'?
8. What is the difference in meaning between 'biennial' and 'biannual'?
9. What we call 'maize' in Britain is called what in the United States?
10. A wallet for keeping money is called what in America?
11. What do the initials MoD stand for?
12. 'Eftsoons' was an old way of saying what?
13. What is an 'autocrat'?
14. If you 'put all your eggs in one basket', what would that mean?
15. What does '*bona fide*' mean?

ANSWERS

1. Someone who helps out in a desperate situation. 2. It should read: The visit to Canterbury was a great treat for my sisters and me. 3. £25. 4. Ewe. 5. A maker of arrows. 6. Inform. 7. 'Too many cooks spoil the broth'. 8. The first means 'occurring every two years', and the second 'twice a year'. 9. Corn. 10. A billfold. 11. Ministry of Defence. 12. Forthwith or often. 13. One who rules by his own power. 14. That you were risking all on one venture. 15. 'Good faith'; genuineness.

SESSION 37

QUIZ 10

• •

1. Where were the 1968 Olympics held?
2. With which club side did Will Carling finish his playing career?
3. In which sport would you use a 'Trace, a 'Beaked Barb' and a 'Waggler'?
4. Who was Italy's manager/coach during France '98?
5. With which sport do you associate Kieran Fallon?
6. Up to 1998, Will Carling was the last England Captain to win a Grand Slam. True or False?
7. In Offshore Power Boat racing, the task of piloting the boat is usually shared between two people. If one steers what does the other do?
8. Who manufactured England's 1998 World Cup strip?
9. With which sport do you associate Nancy Kerrigan?
10. In Italia '90, which England player scored the winner that knocked out Belgium?
11. With which sport do you associate Serge Blanco?
12. Who resigned as Vice Chairman of the RFU in April 1998 over a dispute with the top English clubs?
13. Which racehorse owner was the inspiration behind the Godolphin Racing operation?
14. Who won the 1997 Britannic Assurance County Championship?
15. For which country does Colin Jackson run in the Commonwealth Games?

ANSWERS

1. Mexico. 2. Harlequins. 3. Fishing. 4. Cesare Maldini. 5. Horse Racing. 6. True. 7. Controls the throttles. 8. UMBRO. 9. Ice Skating. 10. David Platt 11. Rugby Union 12. Fran Cotton. 13. Sheikh Mohammed. 14. Glamorgan. 15. Wales.

SESSION 38
QUIZ 1

1. What was special about the 1906 Australian film The Story of the Kelly Gang?
2. Dylan, Brian and Dougal were some of the stars of which animated show?
3. Who starred in the 1933 film She Done Him Wrong?
4. Which movie star's real name was Doris von Kappelhoff?
5. Who starred in the film Sweet Smell of Success?
6. Who directed the film Titanic?
7. What is the basic theme of the film The Exorcist?
8. Yves Montand the French singer and actor wasn't French at all. Where was he born?
9. Who directed the 1929 film Blackmail?
10. Which famous actor has a tattoo reading, 'Scotland Forever'?
11. Elizabeth Taylor is English by birth and parentage. True or false?
12. Who starred in the film The Browning Version?
13. William Friese-Greene, movie pioneer, had a grandson famed as an actor. Who?
14. Who won the best actor Oscar for his role in the film Shine?
15. Who starred in the film Cabaret?

ANSWERS

1. It was the first full-length feature film, lasting an hour. 2. The Magic Roundabout. 3. Mae West. 4. Doris Day. 5. Burt Lancaster, Tony Curtis. 6. James Cameron. 7. A small girl is possessed by the devil and turned into a monster. 8. He was born Ivo Livi in Italy. 9. Alfred Hitchcock. 10. Sean Connery. 11. She is English by birth, but of American parents. 12. Michael Redgrave. 13. Richard Greene. 14. Geoffrey Rush. 15. Liza Minelli and Joel Grey.

SESSION 38
QUIZ 2

• •

1. Holly Johnson was the lead singer with which group?
2. What links Nirvana with Garbage?
3. With which band was Morrissey the lead singer?
4. With which song did MN8 reach number Two in 1995?
5. In 1991 the Justified Ancients of Mu Mu reached number 10 with, 'It's Grim Up North'. By what other name are the group better known?
6. From which album did Michael Jackson's single, 'Rock With You', come?
7. In 1989, Curiosity Killed The Cat, changed their name to what?
8. 3T are the nephews of which mega star?
9. Who first released, 'Leader Of The Pack'?
10. What was Billy Joel's first UK top ten hit?
11. Under which name did Julian Clary release, 'Leader Of The Pack', in 1988?
12. Who had a top ten hit in 1978 with, 'Airport'?
13. With whom did En Vogue have a top ten hit in 1994 with, 'Whatta Man'?
14. Who were George Michael's female backing singers, who later released singles in their own right?
15. Peaches & Herb reached number 4 in 1979 with which song?

ANSWERS

1. Frankie Goes To Hollywood. 2. Butch Vig who produced Nirvana and is part of the band, Garbage. 3. The Smiths. 4. I've Got A Little Something For You. 5. KLF. 6. Off The Wall. 7. Curiosity. 8. Michael Jackson. 9. Shang-ri-la's. 10. Uptown Girl. 11. Joan Collins Fan Club. 12. The Motors. 13. Salt-N-Pepa. 14. Pepsi & Shirley. 15. 'Reunited'.

SESSION 38
QUIZ 3

• •

1. Complete the proverb: 'Better the devil you know...'
2. Who wrote *The Catcher in the Rye*?
3. Who was 'Lawrence of Arabia'?
4. In which story does 'The White Rabbit' appear?
5. Who wrote *The Last of the Mohicans*?
6. Henry Ford, speaking of his cars and their colour, originally said what?
7. The fictional detective 'Albert Campion' was created by whom?
8. Who wrote *The Day of the Jackal*?
9. Complete the proverb: 'All work and no play...'
10. What D.H. Lawrence book was the subject of a famous court case in the 1960s?
11. Name a play by Shakespeare in which a ghost appears.
12. 'O, what can ail thee, knight at arms,/Alone and palely loitering;' is the beginning of a poem by whom?
13. What did Blind Pew give to Billy Bones in *Treasure Island*?
14. Complete the proverb: 'Cowards die many times...'
15. On which play was the musical *My Fair Lady* based?

ANSWERS

1. '...than the devil you don't'. 2. J.D. Salinger. 3. T.E. Lawrence, soldier and writer. 4. *Alice in Wonderland*. 5. James Fenimore Cooper. 6. 'You can have it any colour you want as long as it's black'. 7. Margery Allingham. 8. Frederick Forsyth. 9. '...makes Jack a dull boy'. 10. *Lady Chatterley's Lover*. 11. *Hamlet, Julius Caesar, Macbeth*. 12. John Keats. 13. The Black Spot. 14. '...before their deaths'. 15. *Pygmalion*, by George Bernard Shaw.

SESSION 38
QUIZ 4

1. St Anne is the patron saint of whom?
2. Who is the patron saint of shoemakers?
3. Where does the word 'patter', meaning stage 'chat', come from?
4. In a pack of cards, which way does the King of Spades look, to his left, or to his right?
5. What word, beginning with ante-, means 'in the time before the war'?
6. From an edible point of view, what are bullseyes?
7. What does ROM stand for in computing?
8. What items are called by names such as Plantin, Baskerville and Garamond?
9. What is a *tortilla*?
10. Who was Tommy Atkins?
11. St John Bosco is the patron saint of whom?
12. What year was the Battle of Britain?
13. If you were rudely called a coot, what is it likely you'll be?
14. The first public restaurant was opened in 1765 in what city?
15. Name two well-known plays by Terence Rattigan.

ANSWERS

1. Housewives. 2. St Crispin. 3. From the name of the Our Father prayer in Latin, Paternoster. 4. To his left. 5. Antebellum. 6. Round, hard, black-and-white striped peppermint-flavoured sweets. 7. Read Only Memory. 8. Printers' typefaces. 9. A Spanish omelette of potato and egg; also a Mexican maize pancake. 10. A typical British soldier. 11. Editors. 12. 1940. 13. Bald. 14. Paris. 15. *Flare Path, French Without Tears, While the Sun Shines, The Winslow Boy.*

SESSION 38
QUIZ 5

• •

1. How many bones does an adult human being have?
2. What is 'jet' as used in jewellery or other decorations?
3. The Jumbo Jet is a name given to which aircraft?
4. What is epistemology?
5. Who invented margarine?
6. How did we invent the word 'radar'?
7. What is trichology?
8. What are OR, NAND and NOT examples of?
9. Which anaesthetic was used for the first time in 1847?
10. What is an insulator?
11. What does AC stand for?
12. A special kind of flour was invented by Henry Jones of Bristol in 1845. What was special about it?
13. What device for making geometric patterns was invented in 1817 by Sir David Brewster?
14. If something is ferrous, what does it contain?
15. Who is widely regarded as the inventor of the bicycle?

ANSWERS

1. 206. 2. Very hard coal, called lignite. 3. The Boeing 747. 4. The scientific study of knowledge and its acquisition. 5. Mège-Mouriès, in France, 1868. 6. From the words of its full name, radio detection and ranging. 7. The scientific study of the hair and its disorders. 8. Logic gates used in electronics. 9. Chloroform. 10. A substance which prevents the flow of electricity or heat. 11. Alternating current. 12. It was self-raising. 13. The kaleidoscope. 14. Iron. 15. Kirkpatrick MacMillan, in 1839.

SESSION 38
QUIZ 6

• •

1. A gila monster is venomous lizard. Is this unusual?
2. Cloves are a members of the carnation family. Yes or no?
3. A cross between a male ass and a mare is called what?
4. What is a spider?
5. What is a crayfish?
6. What is the favourite food of the aardvark?
7. What sort of animal is a harrier?
8. What is an endive?
9. The cottontail is another name for the American rabbit. True or false?
10. What are glow worms?
11. What is a 'bug'?
12. What kind of animal is said to hiss?
13. Which distant relative of the camel lives in South America?
14. Caviar is obtained from a fish. Which one?
15. The turnip is a member of the cabbage family. Yes or no?

ANSWERS

1. Yes. There is only one other venomous lizard, the related bearded lizard. 2. Yes. 3. A mule. 4. A small creature with four pairs of legs, which spins a web to catch its prey. 5. A kind of edible freshwater lobster, also called a crawfish. 6. Ants and termites. It eats nothing else! 7. A breed of dog. 8. A salad plant of the chicory family. 9. True. 10. The larvae of insects, which are able to emit light or flashes. 11. An insect which infests bedding. In the USA the word means 'any insect'. 12. A goose, or a snake. 13. The llama. 14. The sturgeon. 15. Yes.

SESSION 38
QUIZ 7

• •

1. To which country do the Azores belong?
2. Where is the Blue Mosque?
3. In which city would you find the Eiffel Tower?
4. Which city is on the River Clyde?
5. Which family lived at Haworth Parsonage?
6. For what is the village of Camberley, Surrey, famed?
7. Which country's currency has 100 kobo worth one naira?
8. Which city is on the Tagus river?
9. If it's 6 pm in London, what time is it in Norway?
10. What did early travellers mean by the New World?
11. In which English city would you find New Street railway station?
12. Which is the most populous of Canada's provinces?
13. Name three other Canadian provinces.
14. What is the city of Batavia now called?
15. There are more canals in Birmingham than in Venice. True or False?

ANSWERS

1. Portugal. 2. In Istanbul, Turkey. 3. Paris. 4. Glasgow. 5. The Brontës.
6. It is the home of the Royal Military Academy for training Army officers.
7. Nigeria. 8. Lisbon. 9. 7 p.m. 10. America. 11. Birmingham. 12.
Ontario. 13. British Columbia, Alberta, Quebec, Manitoba, Nova Scotia,
Saskatchewan, Prince Edward Island, Newfoundland, New Brunswick.
14. Djakarta. 15. True.

● ●

1. What does the phrase, 'Apple-pie order' mean?
2. What's wrong with this sentence: Our cat always licks it's paws after a meal?
3. If you were playing checkers in America, what would you be doing?
4. What is the name for someone who studies mankind?
5. What is the name for someone who studies or collects postage-stamps?
6. What is the difference between adventitious and adventurous?
7. A peon is (a) a flower (b) a labourer in Spain (c) a comedian.
8. What does 'carry a torch' mean?
9. What would it mean if you 'cast pearls before swine'?
10. A 'shambles' is a real mess, but what was it originally?
11. What modern term replaces the word, 'Methinks'?
12. What does compos mentis mean?
13. What is a 'ham', theatrically-speaking?
14. What does 'Twain' mean?
15. What is a 'chipolata'?

ANSWERS

1. Everything neat and in its place. 2. It should read: Our cat always licks its paws after a meal. 3. You'd be playing draughts. 4. Anthropologist. 5. Philatelist. 6. The first means 'accidental' and the second means 'venturesome'. 7. (b) a labourer in Spain. 8. To be in love with someone. 9. That you offered something of value to someone who could not understand its value. 10. A butcher's slaughterhouse. 11. I think. 12. Sane, in one's right mind. 13. An actor who overacts, and lacks real ability. 14. Two. 15. A small sausage.

SESSION 38
QUIZ 9

1. Which female British Athlete won the New York marathon in 1991?
2. Which county does Sally Gunnell come from?
3. After completing his studies, what career did Will Carling, embark on?
4. Which British athlete was cleared of drugs charges on appeal in March 1996?
5. What's the nationality of racing driver Nelson Piquet?
6. Which snooker ball is worth six points?
7. Which sport do the Worthing Bears play?
8. For what county did BBC cricket commentator, Jonathon Agnew, play most of his cricket?
9. In racing, what does the abbreviation SP stand for?
10. The Bulls versus the Rhinos is a local derby in which county?
11. Who does Ryan Giggs play for at International level?
12. Over which race course is the Whitbread Gold Cup run?
13. Which Formula 1 racing driver, known as, 'The Professor', won the 1989 World Driver's Championship?
14. If I were wearing a, Shooting Glove, an Arm Brace, preparing to shoot an end, always aiming for Gold, what sport would I be taking part in?
15. Who managed Chelsea during the first half of the 1997/98 season?

ANSWERS

1. Liz McColgan. 2. Essex. 3. An Army Officer. 4. Diane Modahl. 5. Brazil. 6. Pink. 7. Basketball. 8. Leicestershire. 9. Starting Price. 10. Yorkshire (Rugby League). 11. Wales. 12. Sandown Park. 13. Alain Prost. 14. Archery. 15. Ruud Gullit.

• •

1. £1 and 10 shilling notes were issued for the first time in Britain in what year?
2. Which islands in the Indian Ocean became a republic in 1953?
3. Which South African prime minister was assassinated in September, 1966?
4. What did The Times newspaper publish for the first time in 1966?
5. Who succeeded General Perón of Argentina as president on his death in July, 1974?
6. Which princess died in a car crash in September, 1982?
7. How was York Minster badly damaged in 1984?
8. The baby of which famous US airman was kidnapped in March, 1932?
9. By what new country name was Persia known after 1935?
10. In 1958, Imre Nagy of Hungary was executed. Who was he?
11. Which two London newspapers merged in 1960?
12. Which group of people were first allowed on to the floor of the London Stock Exchange in 1973?
13. Which Pope died in 1978 after reigning for only 33 days?
14. Who assumed the throne of Denmark in 1972?
15. What happened at Eniwetok Atoll on 6th November, 1952?

ANSWERS

1. 1914. 2. The Maldives. 3. Dr Verwoerd. 4. News on its front page. 5. His wife, Maria Estella Perón. 6. Princess Grace of Monaco. 7. By lightning. 8. Charles Lindbergh's. 9. Iran. 10. Former president. 11. The Evening News and the Star. 12. Women. 13. Pope John Paul I. 14. Queen Margrethe. 15. The US exploded the first hydrogen bomb.

SESSION 39
QUIZ 1

• •

1. Who had hits with 'Hooked on Can Can' and 'Hooked on Classics' in 1982?
2. On Meatloaf's, 'Dead Ringer For Love', who features, but is not credited on the label?
3. Who recorded the song, 'Sound Of The Suburbs' in 1979?
4. Mark Owen was formerly a member with which band?
5. What was Sting's first UK hit?
6. Who released the album 'Like a Prayer'?
7. Who's first hit single was 'I Only Want To Be With You' in 1963?
8. What do the initials OMD stand for?
9. Which Irish, all-girl band, had top ten hits with, 'I'm In The Mood For Dancing' and 'Attention To Me'?
10. In 1984, Foreigner reached number one in the UK and number two in the US, with which ballad?
11. What was the Glitter Band's first hit without Gary?
12. Who was the entrepreneurial master-mind who managed the Sex Pistols?
13. Which Goon reached number fourteen in 1965 with a re-working of the Beatles' 'Hard Days Night'?
14. How many were in the band Showaddywaddy?
15. Who recorded the album 'Diamond Life'?

ANSWERS

SESSION 39

QUIZ 2

• •

1. Who's dead business partner, Jacob Marley, returns to haunt him and teach him to be charitable and kind?
2. Charles Wesley had an older brother called?
3. Who wrote the play, *Blithe Spirit*?
4. Reputedly, what did the Austrian governor Gessler instruct William Tell to do?
5. In which pantomime would you find the character 'Buttons'?
6. Which British author wrote *The Magus*?
7. In what novel do the characters, 'Professor Van Helsing', 'Jonathan Harker' and 'Lucy Westernra' appear?
8. Exactly what was 'Chitty-Chitty Bang-Bang'?
9. Who wrote the story Dr Jekyll and Mr Hyde?
10. Who wrote the words for a *Policeman's Lot is Not a Happy One*?
11. What or who, is *She*?
12. What is the Boston Globe? Is it (a) a theatre (b) a sports stadium (c) a newspaper?
13. What is Gill Sans Extra Bold?
14. Who was 'Old Nick'?
15. Who was Geoffrey of Monmouth?

ANSWERS

SESSION 39
QUIZ 3

• •

1. Which British exponent of jazz on radio died very recently?
2. What is chowder?
3. A magnum is a measure of wine equivalent to how many bottles?
4. What does 'kosher' mean?
5. What is the second most expensive property on a Monopoly board?
6. Why 'dead as a doornail'?
7. Who is Viscount Linley's mother?
8. St Thomas is the patron saint of whom?
9. What is a hot dog?
10. What is a fricassee?
11. What is the maximum break in snooker?
12. What is *borsht*?
13. Who is the Pope?
14. What word, beginning with ante,- means 'existing before the Great Flood'?
15. Where is the Golden Gate?

ANSWERS

1. Benny Green. 2. A thick soup made from meat or fish. 3. Two. 4. Fit to be eaten according to Jewish law. 5. Park Lane. 6. A door nail is the bit which is whacked by the knocker. 7. Princess Margaret. 8. Architects. 9. A frankfurter inside a long soft bun. 10. A dish of cut pieces of fowl or meat, cooked in a sauce. 11. 147. 12. Russian beetroot soup. 13. The head of the Roman Catholic Church. 14. Antediluvian. 15. The entrance to the bay of San Francisco.

SESSION 39
QUIZ 4

• •

1. Acetic acid is more familiarly known as what?
2. How many days does Mercury take to orbit the sun; 88, 205, 335 or 428?
3. A triangle with all sides equal is what?
4. What is a parallelogram?
5. The mineral bauxite produces which metal?
6. Who invented the carpet-sweeper?
7. What is a propeller?
8. What are fossils?
9. What is an accumulator?
10. How long is a furlong?
11. What is kaolin?
12. Francis Crick and James Watson are linked with the discovery of what?
13. What is sodium chloride more commonly known as?
14. What is a chronometer?
15. In Roman numerals, what is L?

ANSWERS

1. Vinegar. 2. 88. 3. Equilateral. 4. A four-sided figure whose opposite sides are parallel. 5. Aluminium. 6. Melville Bissell, in 1876. 7. A kind of screw used to propel a ship or an aircraft. 8. Remains of plants and animals found in ancient rocks. 9. A rechargeable lead-acid battery. 10. 220 yards. 11. Another name for china-clay. 12. The structure of DNA. 13. Table salt. 14. A machine for the accurate measurement of time. 15. 50.

SESSION 39
QUIZ 5

• •

1. Which animal lives in a lair?
2. What is meant by 'horsefeathers'?
3. The Jerusalem artichoke is a plant relative of the sunflower. True or false?
4. Which member of the lemur family is only 10 inches long, looks like a monkey, and lives in Madagascar?
5. How many bones does a shark have?
6. What kind of animal could be called a Clydesdale?
7. What is a fig?
8. Are there bats that suck human blood?
9. What is the name for a large rodent covered with sharp spines?
10. What sort of animal is a schipperke?
11. What is another name for the wildebeest?
12. What is a sidewinder?
13. What kind of animal is said to roar?
14. What is a titmouse?
15. What is a palomino?

ANSWERS

1. A wolf. 2. It's an American term meaning 'nonsense'. 3. True. 4. The mouse lemur. 5. None. Its skeleton is made of cartilage. 6. A breed of horse. 7. A fruit of the mulberry family which grows in warm climates. 8. Yes. The vampire bat of Central America. 9. The porcupine. 10. A breed of dog. 11. Gnu. 12. A kind of rattlesnake. 13. A lion. 14. A small bird related to the nuthatches. 15. A horse, golden-haired with a pale mane.

SESSION 39
QUIZ 6

● ●

1. What happens at Oberammergau, Bavaria, every ten years?
2. Queen Street railway stations can be found in two British cities. Which?
3. Where in London is Nelson's Column?
4. Of which country is the pomegranate the national symbol?
5. What is the coldest place on record in the UK?
6. Where in the world do they speak Amharic?
7. What, exactly, was the Flying Scotsman?
8. Where are the Menai Straits?
9. Where and what is the Solent?
10. Which place in the world is often called just 'The Rock'?
11. Which country has the most land boundaries with other countries?
12. New Amsterdam was the original name for which American city?
13. What country's currency comes in bututs and dalasi?
14. Which country has the longest life expectancy for both men and women?
15. Where is the Land of the Midnight Sun?

ANSWERS

1. A Passion Play is performed. 2. Cardiff and Glasgow. 3. Trafalgar Square. 4. Spain. 5. Braemar, Aberdeenshire, −17°F. 6. This is the language of Ethiopia. 7. An express train that ran between London and Edinburgh. 8. The channel between Anglesey and the Welsh mainland. 9. The channel between the Isle of Wight and the mainland. 10. Gibraltar. 11. China, with 15 boundaries. 12. New York. 13. Gambia. 14. Iceland. 15. The Arctic circle, where the Sun never sets during the summer.

SESSION 39
QUIZ 7

1. What is the female version of 'stallion'?
2. Can you name two words, sounding alike, which mean the same as this pair: part of a sentence/brawls?
3. What does 'emeritus' mean, after someone's job title?
4. What is wrong with this sentence: 'Her words had a good affect upon me'?
5. What does infra dig. mean?
6. What is 'a wet blanket'?
7. Whose motto is 'Per Ardua ad Astra', and what does it mean?
8. Name the adjectives derived from the following: Denmark, Slav, Isle of Man.
9. What word for a kind of pottery means 'cooked earth'?
10. What's the difference between artist and artiste?
11. How many is a 'score'?
12. If you drank some rye in the United States, what would it be?
13. What does 'up the creek without a paddle' mean?
14. What is the female version of 'Indian brave'?
15. How did the word flak, meaning anti-aircraft fire, originate?

ANSWERS

1. Mare. 2. Phrase/frays. 3. It means he or she has retired from their job. 4. The word 'affect' should read 'effect'. 5. 'Infra dignitatem': beneath one's dignity. 6. Someone whose lack of spirit spoils a party or gathering. 7. That of the RAF, meaning 'By struggle to the stars'. 8. Danish, Slavonic, Manx. 9. Terracotta. 10. The first means someone who draws or paints; the second, someone who performs. 11. 20. 12. Whisky. 13. In real trouble. 14. Squaw. 15. It's the abbreviation for the German *Flugzeugabwehrkanone*.

396

SESSION 39
QUIZ 8

1. Name New England's American Football Team?
2. How many players are there on a 'Bandy' team?
3. How long is a 'Period' in an NBA basketball match?
4. The husband of Princess Caroline of Monaco, Stefano Cariraghi, died in 1990 taking part in which sport?
5. What nationality is footballer Davor Suker?
6. Which four-man event was accepted into the Olympic Games when it was held at Chamonix, France, in 1924?
7. Which sport, governed by the ICF, was introduced into the Calgary Olympics as a demonstration sport in 1988?
8. If you were playing 14:1 continuous play rules, what game would you be taking part in?
9. In '3 Position' target shooting events, what are the 3 positions?
10. Which sport held its first professional world championships in 1978, now held annually, at the Lakeside Club in Camberley?
11. Which sport was included in the 1900 Olympic games, was dropped after 1920, then re-introduced in 1972?
12. Actor Brian Glover was formerly a professional sportsman at which sport?
13. Vladimir Smirnov died in a tragic accident whilst defending his Olympic Gold Medal in which sport?
14. With which sport do you associate Clive Woodward?
15. What nationality is footballer Torre Andre Flo?

ANSWERS

1. Patriots. 2. Eleven. 3. Twelve minutes. 4. Power Boat Racing. 5. Croatian. 6. Bobsleigh. 7. Curling. 8. Pool. 9. Prone, kneeling and standing. 10. Darts. 11. Archery. 12. Wrestling. 13. Fencing. 14. Rugby Union. 15. Norwegian.

SESSION 39
QUIZ 9

• •

1. Which well-known priest was excommunicated by the Roman Catholic Church in 1521?
2. The German National Socialist Party was formed in 1919 in Munich. Who became its leader?
3. What did Frank Hornby patent in 1901?
4. Which English monarch died at Richmond Palace in 1603?
5. What nation-wide service came into operation on 10th January, 1840?
6. The first London telephone directory appeared with 250 names. True or false?
7. In which year did the 1p (decimal) coin first appear?
8. Who became the first Kaiser of a newly united Germany in 1871?
9. Who was stabbed to death in the Senate House in Rome in 44BC?
10. Rationing of what commodity ended on 15 March 1949?
11. Which famous Australian bridge opened on 19th March, 1932?
12. Which famous sporting trophy was stolen in 1966?
13. The Italian Fascist party was founded by whom in 1919?
14. The US Navy was formed in 1794. True or false?
15. Which notorious American outlaw was shot by his own gang in 1882?

ANSWERS

SESSION 39
QUIZ 10

. . . .

1. What film featured Richard Dreyfuss sculpting a mountain out of mash potato?
2. What nationality was the film star Greta Garbo?
3. Who was Olivia de Havilland's film-star sister?
4. Which film featured a group of transvestites travelling through the Australian outback on a dilapidated bus?
5. Which Monty Python star now travels the world?
6. *The Big Lebowski* was largely set around what sort of entertainment?
7. Who or what is 'Auntie'?
8. Kevin Costner's scenes were completely cut out of what famous film?
9. What type of animal was a star in both *A Private Function* and *Babe*?
10. In what film did the number 'Springtime for Hitler' occur?
11. Who wrote the song *There's No Business Like Show Business*?
12. The many films of Frankenstein were based on a book by which author?
13. Joan Collins starred in which TV soap?
14. Name the actress in the famous shower scene in *Psycho*?
15. The film *Yankee Doodle Dandy* was based on whose life?

ANSWERS

SESSION 40
QUIZ 1

1. Who was Christopher Plantin?
2. What was the *City Press*, which first appeared in 1857?
3. Who wrote 'Was this the face which launch'd a thousand ships?'
4. Who wrote the book *Eyeless in Gaza* in 1936?
5. Whose stock phrase was 'Now here's a funny thing...'?
6. What does 'kick the bucket' mean?
7. Who, or what, were Pip, Squeak and Wilfred?
8. What D.H. Lawrence novel was originally entitled Paul Morel?
9. The American poet Ezra Pound was the nephew of which very famous poet?
10. What have W.H. Auden, Dylan Thomas and Edith Sitwell in common?
11. What is alliteration?
12. Who wrote Watership Down?
13. What is a 'malapropism'?
14. Who were the 'Famous Five'?
15. Who were 'Janet and John'?

ANSWERS

1. A French printer who worked in 16th-century Antwerp. 2. The first local newspaper for the City of London. 3. Christopher Marlowe. 4. Aldous Huxley. 5. Max Miller. 6. To die. 7. Children's cartoon characters which appeared in the *Daily Mirror* from 1920. 8. *Sons and Lovers*. 9. Longfellow. 10. They were all poets. 11. Two or more words in a sentence, each starting with the same letter. 12. Richard Adams. 13. A word or phrase used wrongly due to ignorance or carelessness. 14. There were two lots! The Greyfriars Famous Five (Wharton, Nugent, Cherry, Bull and Hurree Singh), and Enid Blyton's: Julian, Dick, Anne and Georgina. 15. Characters from reading-books for children issued from 1949.

SESSION 40
QUIZ 2

• •

1. On which radio programme would you find CMJ, Blowers and Fred?
2. St Vincent Ferrer is the patron saint of whom?
3. What is housed at Hertford House in London?
4. What is risotto?
5. Which musician was known as 'Flash Harry'?
6. Rule by an hereditary monarch in his or her own right is called what?
7. St George is the patron saint of where?
8. How does the Archbishop of Canterbury sign himself?
9. What kind of food item comes from Kendal?
10. What's the connection between baloney and polony?
11. What did athlete Darren Campbell win in the 1998 European Championships?
12. What are a Manhattan and a Screwdriver?
13. The titmouse isn't a mouse. What is it?
14. Who is the patron saint of scientists?
15. What are 'petits fours'?

ANSWERS

1. Test Match Special. 2. Builders. 3. The Wallace Collection. 4. Rice cooked in stock, with meat, saffron, vegetables and cheese. 5. Sir Malcolm Sargent. 6. A monarchy. 7. England. 8. His name, followed by Cantuar. 9. A mint cake. 10. From the Bologna sausage: the first means 'rubbish, nonsense', and the second is the sausage (US version). 11. A Gold Medal in the 100m. 12. Cocktails. 13. A small bird. 14. St Albert. 15. Small, very fancy, biscuits or cakes.

SESSION 40
QUIZ 3

• •

1. What colour is an amethyst?
2. Which is lighter - helium or hydrogen?
3. What is chronology?
4. Captain Albert Berry, in 1912, did what from an aircraft for the first time?
5. What is a magneto?
6. The mandible is another name for which bone?
7. What did Clarence Birdseye invent in 1925?
8. What vehicle was first launched in 1981?
9. Iron pyrites has a golden colour, and is sometimes called what?
10. What is arboriculture?
11. Does a concave mirror or lens bend inwards or outwards?
12. What kind of engine did Richard Trevithick invent in 1804?
13. What's the record for snowfall in Britain? (a) 60 inches (b) 40 inches (c) 84 inches.
14. What is egomania?
15. Carbon takes its name from the Latin word carbo, meaning charcoal. True or false?

ANSWERS

1. Violet or purple. 2. Hydrogen. 3. The science of computing time. 4. Made a parachute jump. 5. A simple electrical generator. 6. The lower jawbone. 7. The frozen food process. 8. The Space Shuttle. 9. Fool's gold. 10. Forestry and the study of trees. 11. Inwards. 12. The steam locomotive. 13. (a) 60 inches, in Yorkshire and Wales, 1947. 14. The belief that one is of enormous importance. 15. True.

SESSION 40
QUIZ 4

• •

1. What is a dingo?
2. Who or what was the Yeti?
3. The strawberry is a member of the rose family. Yes or no?
4. An animal with a bill like a duck, four webbed feet and covered in soft fur is called what?
5. Britain's largest dragonfly is about (a) 2 inches long (b) 3 inches long (c) 4 inches long.
6. Where are an earthworm's eyes?
7. What kind of animal is said to mew?
8. What is ebony?
9. What kind of animal is said to twitter?
10. What is clover?
11. Which dinosaur had a series of heavy plates along its back?
12. What sort of animal is called a Hereford?
13. What is a mallow?
14. Which animal lives in a 'set'?
15. What is salsify?

ANSWERS

1. An Australian wild dog. 2. The Abominable Snowman. 3. Yes. 4. A platypus. 5. 3 inches long. 6. Nowhere, it hasn't any. 7. A kitten. 8. The very dark wood of a tree grown in India and Sri Lanka. 9. A swallow. 10. A plant with small flowers and leaves, prized as pasturage. 11. Stegosaur. 12. A breed of cattle. 13. A plant with soft, downy leaves. 14. A badger. 15. A green vegetable of which the root is eaten.

403

SESSION 40
QUIZ 5

. . . .

1. Pomona is the main island of which group?
2. Which is the most southerly point in England?
3. Which town in Belgium is famed for its lace-making?
4. The official name Côte d'Ivoire refers to which country?
5. In which country is Europe's highest waterfall?
6. What is the name of the London Underground line usually shown by the colour green?
7. In which country would you find Montevideo?
8. What are a people or tribe if they are said to be nomadic?
9. Where is the EPCOT centre?
10. Which city is known as The Granite City?
11. Bechuanaland is the old name for which country?
12. Malaga is a popular holiday destination in which country?
13. The U-Bahn in Berlin is what, exactly?
14. Where would you find Copacabana beach?
15. To which country does Guadeloupe belong?

ANSWERS

1. The Orkneys. 2. The Lizard, Cornwall. 3. Brugges. 4. The Ivory Coast. 5. Norway. 6. The District Line. 7. Uruguay. 8. They have no fixed home but wander around a region. 9. Orlando, Florida, USA. 10. Aberdeen. 11. Botswana. 12. Spain. 13. An underground railway. 14. Brazil. 15. France.

404

SESSION 40
QUIZ 6

• •

1. What word can mean attorney or barrister?
2. What one word means both 'a large, flat dish' and 'an officer's horse'?
3. Can you name two words, sounding alike, which mean the same as this pair: layer of gold/sinfulness?
4. What's wrong with this sentence: 'Dad was able to get a large amount of people into his car'?
5. What's the difference between 'ferment' and 'foment'?
6. A dragoman was: (a) an Eastern guide (b) a slave-driver (c) a fanciful bogeyman?
7. What do the initials, TUC stand for?
8. What is 'parsimony'?
9. To what type of conveyance did Lord Brougham gave his name?
10. What did 'Burgess' mean in earlier times?
11. What would you be, if you were a *goy*?
12. What is it called when sentences or phrases have words all starting with the same letter?
13. What does 'ersatz' mean?
14. What is a 'troglodyte'?
15. Can you give a word starting with D, meaning 'loathe' or 'scorn'?

ANSWERS

1. Lawyer. 2. Charger. 3. Gilt/guilt. 4. It should read: Dad was able to get a large number of people into his car. 5. 'Ferment' means 'to boil up something'; 'foment' means 'to stir up trouble. 6. (a) an Eastern guide. 7. Trades Union Congress. 8. Stinginess. 9. A kind of horse-drawn carriage. 10. Citizen. 11. Not Jewish. It's a Hebrew term for a gentile. 12. Alliteration. As in Sister Susie's sewing shirts for soldiers. 13. Substitute, usually an imitation. 14. A cave-dweller. 15. Despise.

SESSION 40
QUIZ 7

1. Name Baltimore's Major League baseball team?
2. At which football club's ground would you find the Stretford End?
3. Which sport do the Barcelona Dragons play?
4. Who or what are Goldie and Isis?
5. Which Rugby Union club does British Lion and Army officer, Tim Rodber, play for?
6. What is the total width of a Badminton court. 18ft, 20ft, 22ft or 26ft?
7. Who won an incredible six World Snooker Championships in the 1980s?
8. How many players are there on a Basketball court at any one time?
9. Name the three Olympic athletic field events that are still men-only?
10. What is the minimum weight of a tennis ball; 55g, 55.9g, 56.3g or 56.7g?
11. In which year was women's Shooting introduced to the Olympic Games?
12. Which Motor Sport did Barry Sheene take up, after he retired from Motor Cycling?
13. Which football team plays its home games at St James' Park?
14. In America, what do the initials NCAA, stand for?
15. In Cricket, how do you commonly describe 'out first ball'?

ANSWERS

1. Orioles. 2. Manchester United. 3. American Football. 4. Oxford and Cambridge Number Two Crews. 5. Northampton. 6. 20 ft. 7. Steve Davis. 8. Ten. 9. Triple Jump, Hammer and Pole Vault. 10. 56.7g. 11. 1984. 12. Truck Racing 13. Newcastle United. 14. National Collegiate Athletic Association 15. A Golden Duck.

SESSION 40
QUIZ 8

• •

1. Who was knighted aboard his ship, the Golden Hind, in 1581?
2. In April, 1909, a US Naval officer was the first to reach the North Pole. Who was he?
3. What did Dr Samuel Johnston publish in 1755?
4. What was permitted in the Serpentine for the first time in 1930?
5. What did Charles Macintosh patent in 1823?
6. What did John Cabot discover in 1497?
7. Joseph Smith and his brother were killed in a US jail in 1844. For what were they famed?
8. In what year did the 999 telephone emergency service begin?
9. A rally held by William Booth in Whitechapel founded what in 1865?
10. Which Russian socialist died in 1883, and was buried in Highgate Cemetery, London?
11. What happened to Sir Thomas More in 1535 when he refused to swear allegiance to Henry VIII as Head of the Church of England?
12. The first underground trains in Paris started in 1900, 1905 or 1910?
13. Who did Henry VIII marry on 12th July, 1543?
14. In 1865, Edward Whymper made the first ascent of what?
15. Europe's first banknotes were issued in 1661 in which country; (a) England (b) Scotland (c) Sweden?

ANSWERS

1. Francis Drake. 2. Robert Perry. 3. His English dictionary. 4. Mixed bathing. 5. Waterproof cloth. 6. Newfoundland. 7. Founding the Mormon Church. 8. 1937. 9. The Salvation Army. 10. Karl Marx. 11. He was beheaded. 12. 1900. 13. Catherine Parr. 14. The Matterhorn. 15. Sweden.

SESSION 40
QUIZ 9

. . . .

1. The Noël Coward play *Still Life* was made into a film under what title?
2. What film featured dozens of skydiving Elvis Presley impersonators?
3. What film featured a famous soundtrack from the Australian group The Bee Gees?
4. Ambridge is the fictional setting for which long-running radio drama?
5. From which musical play comes the song 'Anything You Can Do'?
6. Who won an Oscar for directing *Forrest Gump*?
7. The Christopher Isherwood play *I Am a Camera* was made into a film under what title?
8. Who created the cartoon character 'Bugs Bunny'?
9. 'I Wanna Be Like You' and 'Bear Necessities' are songs from which film?
10. 'Be Careful Out There' was a catchphrase of which American TV cop show?
11. Who was the female lead in the Alan Parker film, Evita?
12. What is Equity?
13. Who was married to Humphrey Bogart and Jason Robards?
14. Who was the first Director-General of the BBC?
15. Which Disney cartoon tells the story of a princess in America in the 17th Century?

ANSWERS

1. *Brief Encounter.* 2. *Honeymoon In Las Vegas.* 3. *Saturday Night Fever.* 4. *The Archers.* 5. *Annie Get Your Gun.* 6. Robert Zemeckis. 7. *Cabaret.* 8. Chuck Jones. 9. *Jungle Book.* 10. *Hill Street Blues.* 11. Madonna. 12. The actors' trade union. 13. Lauren Bacall. 14. John Reith. 15. *Pocahontas.*

• •

1. Which 1979 film starred the Sex Pistols?
2. Name Prince's 1984 semi-autobiographical film?
3. With which children's TV theme did Mike Oldfield reach number 19 in 1979?
4. Ocean Colour Scene's guitarist Steve Craddock played keyboards on Paul Weller's first solo album. True or false?
5. 'Use It Up And Wear It Out' was number one in 1980 for which US group?
6. Which singer starred in the film, Blue Hawaii?
7. Who reached number one in 1979 with 'Brass In Pocket'?
8. Name Supergrass's debut album?
9. Which artist along with The Luvvers, reached number seven in 1964 with 'Shout'?
10. Name David Bowie's band who had minor hits between 1989 and 1991 including 'You Belong In Rock and Roll?
11. Who was the lead singer with Tenpole Tudor?
12. Which band joined Vic Reeves to have a number one with the song, 'Dizzy'?
13. Who was the lead singer of punk band X-Ray Spex?
14. With whom did Stevie Wonder record 'Ebony And Ivory'?
15. Which bearded band gave us the songs, 'Gimme All Your Lovin' in 1983 and 'Viva Las Vegas' in 1992?

ANSWERS

1. The Great Rock And Roll Swindle. 2. Purple Rain. 3. Blue Peter. 4. False. 5. Odyssey. 6. Elvis Presley. 7. Pretenders. 8. 'I Should Coco". 9. Lulu. 10. Tin Machine. 11. Eddie Tenpole. 12. The Wonder Stuff. 13. Poly Styrene. 14. Paul McCartney. 15. ZZ Top.

SESSION 41
QUIZ 1

1. What is cassata?
2. What is poker?
3. What anniversary does a diamond wedding celebrate?
4. What word, beginning with ante- means 'going before, in time'?
5. What is *bratwurst*?
6. The Water Carrier represents which sign of the Zodiac?
7. What is a *Bar Mitzvah*?
8. St Michael is the patron saint of whom?
9. Whose motto is: '*E Pluribus Unum*'?
10. Chips with Everything was a successful play by which author?
11. What is *Yom Kippur*?
12. What were Pioneer, Galileo and Magellan?
13. A stitch in time will save how many?
14. St Boniface is the patron saint of what?
15. The impresario Lewis Winogradsky is better known as whom?

SESSION 41
QUIZ 2

• •

1. What is the chemical symbol for sodium?
2. What colour is a turquoise?
3. What does a Geiger counter measure?
4. Sulphuric, hydrochloric and nitric are the three what?
5. The study of the action of forces on bodies is called what?
6. What is guano?
7. What is the object in space called Saturn?
8. What was a Sten?
9. After 1865, what needed to precede any 'horseless carriage' in the streets of Britain?
10. What kind of unusual car engine was introduced by Felix Wankel in 1957?
11. What is horology?
12. Reginald Booth, in 1901, invented which now-essential household device?
13. Ebb and flow is the regular movement of what?
14. In Roman numerals, what is XV?
15. The pelvis is another name for which bone?

ANSWERS

1. Na. 2. Blue. 3. Radiation. 4. Main mineral acids. 5. Mechanics. 6. A natural fertiliser, formed from bird droppings on the Peruvian islands. 7. One of the nine planets. 8. A sub-machine gun. 9. A man with a red flag. 10. The rotary petrol engine. 11. The science of measuring time. 12. The vacuum cleaner. 13. The sea. 14. Fifteen. 15. The hip-bone.

411

SESSION 41

QUIZ 3

1. What part of the vegetable okra is eaten?
2. What is a colugo?
3. What is a gerenuk?
4. What is fenugreek?
5. From which area does the chameleon come?
6. Where do blueberries come from?
7. What is an ibex?
8. What are caraway seeds used for?
9. What is a macaque?
10. What endangered animal rarely mates, eats largely only bamboo shoots, and estimates state that there are only 500 of them in the wild?
11. The watercress is from the Nasturtium family. True or false?
12. What is the difference between a marten and a martin?
13. What part of a soya is eaten?
14. What is a narwhal?
15. Where did the kiwi fruit originate?

ANSWERS

1. The pods and seeds. 2. A monkey-like animal, also called the flying lemur. 3. A kind of African antelope. 4. A spice whose seeds are used in cooking. 5. Asia, Africa, part of Europe. 6. North America. 7. A large-horned mountain goat. 8. As a spice and ingredient. 9. A kind of monkey. 10. Giant Panda. 11. True. 12. A marten is an animal like a weasel and the martin is a bird. 13. The beans. 14. A kind of whale with a large, projecting tusk. 15. China.

SESSION 41
QUIZ 4

. . . .

1. Where would you find the republic of San Marino?
2. In which county would you find the Mendip Hills?
3. Where is the language Romany spoken?
4. Where would you expect to find 'Number Ten'?
5. What is the national language of Mexico?
6. The length of the River Thames is; (a) about 160 miles (b) about 200 miles (c) about 90 miles?
7. Where in the world is there a giant statue of Christ on a high mountain?
8. If you were changing your money into ore and krona, where would you be going?
9. King Jigme Singye Wangchuk is the ruler of which country?
10. In which English town would you find 'The Pantiles'?
11. Cambridge is on the River Cam. What is the river also called?
12. In which country is the Yellow River?
13. Stalagtites and Stalagmites: which go up?
14. Excluding Alaska, which is the largest state in the USA?
15. In which city would you find The Gorbals?

ANSWERS

1. In Northern Italy. 2. Somerset. 3. Wherever there are true Gypsies. 4. In Downing Street, London. 5. Spanish. 6. (a) about 160 miles. 7. Above Rio de Janeiro, Brazil. 8. Sweden. 9. Bhutan. 10. Tunbridge Wells. 11. The Granta. 12. China. 13. Stalagmites. 14. Texas. 15. Glasgow.

413

• •

1. What do the initials, RAAF stand for?
2. Can you name two words, sounding alike, which mean the same as this pair: revenge or punish/smoke or smell?
3. A moonraker was: (a) a cheesemonger (b) a man from Wiltshire (c) a kind of male witch?
4. A kulak is: (a) a rich Russian peasant (b) a two-wheeled pony-cart (c) a wild ass?
5. What do Americans mean by the game called 'tic tac toe'?
6. What does the phrase 'volte-face' mean?
7. Re-arrange these three single-word anagrams: Angle, pirates, telegraph.
8. What does 'above-board' mean?
9. What is a 'Yippie'?
10. 'Trusty' was an old way of saying what?
11. A bodger is (a) a travelling artisan or salesperson (b) a small dagger (c) an implement for making holes.
12. What is a ménage a trois?
13. What, in earlier times, did 'varlet' mean?
14. If you 'washed up' in the United States, what would it mean?
15. What is a 'daguerreotype'?

ANSWERS

1. Royal Australian Air Force. 2. Wreak/reek. 3. A man from Wiltshire. 4. (a) a rich Russian peasant. 5. Noughts and crosses. 6. To turn around. Usually meant in relation to one's views or politics. 7. They can be arranged to read: glean, sea trip, great help. 8. Honest, frank and unconcealed. 9. A politically-active 'hippie'. 10. Trustworthy. 11. (a) a travelling artisan or salesperson. 12. A household or situation including a couple and the lover of one of the couple. 13. Villain. 14. That you had washed yourself (not the dishes!) 15. An early photographic process.

414

SESSION 41 Sport

QUIZ 6

• •

1. In American football, how many points are awarded for a field goal?
2. In which sport are you not allowed to refer to females as women, but always as ladies?
3. What are a jockey's Silks?
4. Whilst Cardiff Arms Park was being renovated, where did the Welsh Rugby Union team play their home games?
5. Where is the British Grand Prix currently held?
6. Which football club did Brian Robson manage in the 1997/98 football season?
7. True or false. Tim Henman and Greg Rusedski have the same birthday?
8. Name Britain's top woman Boxer who became the first woman to be granted a Licence by the British Boxing Board of Control?
9. Who were the main sponsors of the Jordan Formula One team during the 1998 season?
10. Which professional sport does the WPBSA preside over?
11. Where does the National Rifle Association of Great Britain hold its prestigious annual Championships?
12. In Archery, what are the feathers on an arrow called?
13. Who scored England's last goal in open play during the 1990 World Cup?
14. In American football, what is the name of the line between the two teams on which the ball is placed?
15. In which year did Board Sailing become an Olympic sport?

ANSWERS

1. Three. 2. Show Jumping. 3. His coloured shirt. 4. Wembley. 5. Silverstone. 6. Middlesborough. 7. True. 8. Jane Couch. 9. Benson and Hedges. 10. Billiards and Snooker. 11. Bisley. 12. Fletching. 13. Alan Shearer. 14. The Line of Scrimmage. 15. 1984.

SESSION 41
QUIZ 7

1. The foundation stone of which London Cathedral was laid in 1675?
2. What did New Hampshire elect to become in 1788?
3. In 1900, the Wallace Collection was opened. Where is it based?
4. Burgess and Maclean were two diplomats. What did they do in 1951?
5. In 1812, Napoleon's armies began the invasion of which country?
6. What took place aboard the Russian battleship Potemkin in 1905?
7. Which theatre in London burned down in 1613?
8. In what year was the pillory abolished; 1820, 1837 or 1890?
9. What happened to James Garfield, US President, in 1881?
10. Over whom was Saladin victorious in 1187?
11. What notorious legal institution was abolished in 1641?
12. What coin was issued for the first time in 1817?
13. What racing circuit was opened in 1907?
14. Which Glasgow exhibition hall was destroyed by fire in 1925?
15. What was the verdict in the famous case of Madeleine Smith in Edinburgh, 1857?

ANSWERS

1. St Paul's. 2. The 9th state of the United States. 3. In London. 4. Fled to the USSR. 5. Russia. 6. A mutiny. 7. Shakespeare's Globe. 8. 1837. 9. He was shot, and later, died from those wounds. 10. The Crusaders. 11. The Star Chamber. 12. The gold sovereign. 13. Brooklands. 14. Kelvin Hall. 15. 'Not proven'.

QUIZ 8

• •

1. What connects Ishtar, *The Adventures Of Baron Munchausen* and *Heaven's Gate*?
2. Which long-running TV show was hosted for many years by presenters, William Woollard and Raymond Baxter?
3. In what film did Bruce Willis provide the voice of a baby?
4. Who wrote the music 'The Entertainer'?
5. From which musical play comes the song 'It Ain't Necesarily So'?
6. In what film did Dennis Hopper, Jack Nicholson and Peter Fonda star?
7. Who provided the voices for the animated films starring Wallace and Gromit?
8. What film featured Rick Moranis reducing the size of his family?
9. What Disney film mixed cartoon and live action and featured a magical bed?
10. Percy Thrower and Alan Titchmarsh have both hosted TV programmes on what subject?
11. Who directed the films *The Big Chill* and *Grand Canyon*?
12. Where does the expression: 'May the force be with you' come from?
13. What role did David Niven play just once and Timothy Dalton twice?
14. Who play the hit men in the film *Pulp Fiction*?
15. Who played the character 'Virgil Tibbs'?

ANSWERS

1. They're amongst the biggest loss-making movies, ever. 2. *Tomorrow's World*. 3. *Look Who's Talking*. 4. Scott Joplin. 5. *Porgy and Bess*. 6. *Easy Rider*. 7. Peter Sallis. 8. *Honey, I Shrunk The Kids*. 9. *Bedknobs And Broomsticks*. 10. Gardening. 11. Lawrence Kasden. 12. From the film *Star Wars*. 13. James Bond. 14. John Travolta and Samuel L. Jackson. 15. Sidney Poitier.

SESSION 41

QUIZ 9

• •

1. By what name were the band 'The Who' originally known?
2. Which band backed Cliff Richard in the 1960s?
3. On the Specials single 'A Message To You Rudi' who played the trombone?
4. Who was the lead singer with the Communards?
5. Who reached number one in 1978 with 'Three Times A Lady'?
6. Who released the 'Velvet Rope' album in 1998?
7. Who had top ten hits with, 'System Addict', 'Find The Time' and 'The Slightest Touch'?
8. What was Brian Ferry's first solo top ten hit?
9. Which TV Series's theme tune was the song, 'Suicide Is Painless'?
10. Which TV characters reached number 5 in 1994, with 'Them Girls, Them Girls'?
11. Rita Coolidge performed this Tim Rice-composed song as the theme to the Bond film Octopussy. Can you name it?
12. Who reached number 5 in May 1981 with, 'Ossie's Dream'?
13. Who was the lead singer with The Style Council?
14. Who had top ten hits with 'Simon Smith And His Amazing Dancing Bear' and 'Jarrow Song'?
15. Who was 'Leavin' On A Jet Plane' in 1970?

ANSWERS

1. High Numbers. 2. The Shadows. 3. Rico. 4. Jimmy Sommerville. 5. Commodores. 6. Janet Jackson. 7. Five Star. 8. 'A Hard Rain's Gonna Fall'. 9. M.A.S.H. 10. Zig and Zag. 11. 'All Time High' (Octopussy). 12. Tottenham Hotspur F.A. Cup final squad. 13. Paul Weller. 14. Alan Price. 15. Peter, Paul and Mary.

SESSION 41
QUIZ 10

• •

1. What H.G. Wells novel was originally called *The Chronic Argonauts*?
2. Who was Rumpelstiltskin?
3. In Kipling's story, what was Kim's real name?
4. Who wrote *A Connecticut Yankee at King Arthur's Court*?
5. Who was the author of *The Cloister and the Hearth*?
6. How many lines are there in Chaucer's Canterbury Tales; 2,000, 8,000 or 17,000?
7. What famous book did Walter Pater write in 1885?
8. Who wrote the play *Street Scene* in 1929?
9. Who wrote *The Decameron*, in 1351?
10. 'Mr Bumble' appears in which Dickens novel?
11. The clown 'Touchstone' appears in which Shakespeare play?
12. *The Daisy Chain* was a novel for young people written in 1856 by whom?
13. What kind of novels did Bret Harte write?
14. Who is the narrator of the story in *Treasure Island*?
15. Who wrote the novel *Phineas Finn*?

ANSWERS

1. The Time Machine. 2. A character in fairy stories by the brothers, Grimm. 3. Kimball O'Hara. 4. Mark Twain. 5. Charles Reade. 6. 17,000. 7. *Marius the Epicurean*. 8. Elmer Rice. 9. Giovanni Boccaccio. 10. *Oliver Twist*. 11. *As You Like It*. 12. Charlotte M. Yonge. 13. Westerns. 14. Jim Hawkins. 15. Anthony Trollope.

419

SESSION 42
Quiz 1

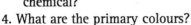

1. What is carbon dioxide?
2. What is a Sea-King?
3. Brimstone is an old name for which chemical?
4. What are the primary colours?
5. What was a Thompson?
6. Who invented the concertina?
7. How much salt is there in seawater? (a) 3% (b) 6% (c) 10%.
8. What is theomania?
9. What are the pointed arms on an anchor called?
10. What is an antenna?
11. Who built the Rocket railway locomotive?
12. What is the difference between wolfram and tungsten?
13. Epsom salts is another name for what?
14. What is bibliomania?
15. A lump or swelling on the big toe is called a what?

ANSWERS

1. A gas formed when carbon burns. 2. A type of helicopter. 3. Sulphur. 4. For pigments, they are red, yellow and blue, but for light, they are red, green and blue. 5. A sub-machine-gun, usually abbreviated to tommy-gun. 6. Charles Wheatstone in 1844. 7. It varies, but the average seawater will contain about 3% salts. 8. Religious madness. 9. Flukes. 10. An aerial rod, wire or display used for receiving radio, TV or radar signals. 11. George Stephenson. 12. None. The first is an old name for the second. 13. Magnesium sulphate. 14. An enormous desire to acquire, collect or own books. 15. Bunion.

SESSION 42
Quiz 2

• •

1. What are Manx cats missing?
2. What unusual feature does the tuatara have?
3. What is a deciduous tree?
4. What is a clementine?
5. A condor is a bird of prey. True or false?
6. What is the common stinkhorn?
7. A phalarope is a shore-bird. Yes or no?
8. Where did the lychee originate?
9. What is a skink?
10. What is the most common vegetable grown in British gardens?
11. A drongo is; (a) a foolish fellow (b) a songbird (c) a fish?
12. What is a tinamou?
13. Where did bamboo originate?
14. What is a wolverine?
15. What speedy bird has been timed at over 105mph?

ANSWERS

1. Their tails. 2. It's a reptile with a third eye in its forehead. 3. One which sheds its leaves periodically. 4. A small orange from the Mediterranean region. 5. True. 6. An edible mushroom. 7. Yes. 8. China. 9. A tree-dwelling reptile. 10. Beetroot. 11. (b) a songbird. 12. A South American flightless bird. 13. America. 14. A kind of mountain cat of North America. 15. Spinetail Swift.

SESSION 42

Quiz 3

. . . .

1. Which is the most densely populated country; Macao, Monaco or Hong Kong?
2. What is the main town on Easter Island called?
3. Which country has three capital cities, depending on the function?
4. Which city contains the world's oldest zoo?
5. What is the population of Pitcairn Island; (a) 104 (b) 55 (c) 277?
6. If you looked down from the air and observed the Royal Albert Hall, London, what shape would you see?
7. Where was the North West Frontier?
8. Where, in London, is the original 'Oranges and Lemons' church?
9. Where and what is the '*Moulin Rouge*'?
10. What is the capital of Australia?
11. What part of the United States is nicknamed The Lone Star State?
12. Which country has the longest total coastline?
13. In which country is the Ganges river?
14. Which major Russian city stands on the Neva river?
15. Which is the world's largest land gorge?

ANSWERS

1. Macao with over 68,000 people per sq. mile. 2. Hanga Roa. 3. South Africa; Pretoria, Cape Town or Bloemfontein. 4. Vienna. 5. (b) 55. 6. An oval, or ellipse. 7. Between Afghanistan and India. 8. St Clement Danes, in the Strand. 9. A theatre night-club in Paris. 10. Canberra. 11. Texas. 12. Canada. 13. India. 14. St Petersburg. 15. The Grand Canyon, Arizona, 277 miles long.

• •

1. What does an American mean by a 'nickel'?
2. What is the name for someone who studies living things?
3. In cockney rhyming slang, what does 'Rosie Lee' mean?
4. In America, you take an elevator to the upper floors. In Britain, what would we take?
5. What does the Latin 'ad nauseam' mean?
6. What does q.v. stand for?
7. What does 'acme' mean?
8. What does an American housewife mean by 'drapes'?
9. What does the A.D. stand for in '1998 A.D.'?
10. What object would you have, 'to grind', if you had something on your mind?
11. What did 'Ere' mean?
12. What word, beginning with S, means caustic or sardonic?
13. What is the female version of 'bachelor'
14. What one word means, 'The covering of tree trunks' and 'the cry of a dog'?
15. What is the meaning of 'itinerant'?

ANSWERS

1. Five cents. 2. Biologist. 3. Tea. 4. A lift. 5. Boring 'to the point of sickness'. 6. *Quod vide*; which see. 7. The highest point. 8. Curtains. 9. *Anno Domini*; the Year of Our Lord. 10. An axe. 11. Before. 12. Sarcastic. 13. Spinster. 14. Bark. 15. Making journeys from place to place.

SESSION 42

Quiz 5

● ●

1. Which winter sport does ex-England Cricket Captain David Gower regularly take part in at St Moritz?
2. Which football team plays its home games at Goodison Park?
3. With which sport do you associate Brian Johnston?
4. Name the American football team based in Dallas?
5. In Formula One, what change in the rules led to the running of two separate Grand Prix Championships in the mid 1980's?
6. In Water Polo, what happens to a player who commits three personal faults in one match?
7. In which year was Canoeing introduced into the Olympic Games; 1920, 1924, 1932 or 1936?
8. Footballer Ian Rush was granted a Soccer scholarship, by a US university. True or false?
9. What did swimmer Captain Matthew Webb achieve in 1875?
10. How many balls are there on a Billiards Table?
11. Which English football team has the nickname the Magpies?
12. Why in Tennis does the scoring follow the pattern - 15, 30, 40 and Game?
13. In which city is the San Siro Stadium?
14. Name Philadelphia's American football team?
15. With which Formula One team did Michael Schumacher win his first World Driver's Championship?

ANSWERS

1. Tobogganing (Skeleton). 2. Everton 3. Cricket. 4. The Cowboys 5. The banning of Turbo Chargers. 6. Banned for the rest of the game. 7. 1936. 8. False. 9. First person to swim the English Channel. 10. Three 11. Newcastle United. 12. Quarters of the clock (40 was originally 45, and Game was 60). 13. Milan. 14. Eagles. 15. Benetton

SESSION 42
Quiz 6

• •

1. What set sail from Spain to England in 1588?
2. Who did Charlotte Corday murder in 1793?
3. The Crusaders were successful in capturing what in 1099?
4. What was adopted by the French as their national anthem in 1795?
5. Jacques Cartier landed in North America, in 1534 and claimed it for France. What area of North America?
6. Whom did Philip of Spain marry in 1554?
7. What status did New York assume in 1788?
8. What city in South Australia was founded in 1836?
9. Parliament granted a 12-year charter to which bank in 1694?
10. Peru declared its independence from which country in 1821?
11. Which great liner was launched at Birkenhead in 1938?
12. Kurt von Schuschnigg became Chancellor of which country in 1934?
13. Le Morte D'Arthur, by Thomas Mallory, was published by whom in 1485?
14. What kind of tax duties were first introduced and imposed in 1894?
15. Which opera house in Milan was opened in 1778?

ANSWERS

SESSION 42
Quiz 7

• •

1. Who starred in the 1994 movie *Bullets Over Broadway*?
2. Who played the leading role in *The Madness of King George*?
3. How many Oscars did the film *The English Patient* receive in 1996?
4. Judy Garland played 'Dorothy Gale' in which film?
5. 'Andy Hardy' was played by whom?
6. Dustin Hoffman and Tom Cruise are together in this story of an autistic brother. Title?
7. Gene Hackman stars with whom in the 1995 film *Get Shorty*?
8. Who starred in *Blue Sky*, made in 1995?
9. In *Yankee Doodle Dandy*, what part does James Cagney play?
10. A car salesman gets his wife kidnapped in order to swindle her father. Title of the 1996 movie?
11. Kevin Costner, a US Civil War soldier, communes with the Indians and becomes one of them. Title?
12. What character was played in the movies by Sean Connery, David Niven, George Lazenby, Roger Moore, Timothy Dalton and Pierce Brosnan?
13. This 1996 Australian movie is about a young dysfunctional piano prodigy. Lynn Redgrave and John Gielgud appear. What is the name of the film?
14. Which character was played by both Peter Sellers and Alan Arkin?
15. Who played opposite Henry Fonda in *On Golden Pond*?

ANSWERS

1. Woody Allen. 2. Nigel Hawthorne. 3. Eight. 4. *The Wizard of Oz*. 5. Mickey Rooney. 6. *Rain Man*. 7. John Travolta. 8. Jessica Lange and Tommy Lee Jones. 9. George M. Cohan. 10. *Fargo*. 11. *Dances with Wolves*. 12. James Bond. 13. *Shine*. 14. Inspector Clouseau. 15. Katharine Hepburn.

SESSION 42
Quiz 8

• •

1. Which singer married footballer Jamie Redknapp in 1998?
2. Which former Eastender had hits with 'Someone To Love' and, 'Good Day'?
3. Name one of the two bands Trevor Horn has been a member of?
4. Who is the lead singer of The Fall?
5. Up until 1998, which act has had the most UK hits without ever entering the top ten?
6. Who recorded 'Matchstalk Men And Matchstalk Cats And Dogs?
7. In which film did Art Garfunkel's, 'Bright Eyes' appear?
8. Which, Bond theme was recorded by Matt Munroe in 1963?
9. Who sang the theme to the first Ghostbusters movie?
10. Who was 'Forever In Blue Jeans', in 1979?
11. Who had hits in the 1960s and 1970s with 'Wouldn't It Be Nice', 'Sloop John B' and 'Good Vibrations'?
12. Which tartan-clad lads, kept on dancing, gave a little love and said, bye bye baby?
13. Who recorded the theme to the Bond film, Goldfinger?
14. Which group was Lynsey De Paul a quarter of?
15. Name Abba's, semi auto-biographical film?

ANSWERS

1. Louise. 2. Sean Maguire. 3. Yes, The Buggles. 4. Mark E. Smith. 5. AC/DC. 6. Brian And Michael. 7. Watership Down. 8. From Russia With Love. 9. Ray Parker Jnr. 10. Neil Diamond. 11. The Beach Boys. 12. The Bay City Rollers. 13. Shirley Bassey. 14. The New Seekers. 15. ABBA The Movie.

SESSION 42
Quiz 9

• •

1. What was the *Book of the Dead*?
2. What are dead languages?
3. What was the magical land portrayed in *The Lion, The Witch And The Wardrobe*?
4. Complete the line: 'Now is the time for all good men...'
5. Solomon Grundy was born on Monday. What happened to him on Friday?
6. According to the *Communist Manifesto*, what are workers of the world expected to do?
7. Lucy Locket lost her pocket. How much was in it?
8. According to the BBC motto, what should nations do?
9. Who wrote *The Shining*, *Carrie* and *Bag Of Bones*?
10. Which Jane was concerned with aspects of human pride and prejudice?
11. Which William was famous for his odes to the lakes?
12. Which William was renowned for his *Vanity Fair*?
13. Which James probably never wanted to grow up?
14. Which sci-fi author wrote *Rendezvous With Rama*?
15. Who wrote the influential ecology book, *Small Is Beautiful*?

ANSWERS

1. A collection of Ancient Egyptian texts. 2. Languages, like Latin, which are no longer spoken regularly. 3. Narnia. 4. '...to come to the aid of the party.' 5. He died. 6. Unite! 7. Not a penny. 8. Speak peace unto nations. 9. Stephen King. 10. Austen. 11. Wordsworth. 12. Thackeray. 13. Barrie. 14. Arthur C. Clarke. 15. E.F. Schumacher.

SESSION 42
Quiz 10

1. What does 'to bellyache' mean?
2. Where did the Flintstones live?
3. What does 'beef up' mean?
4. What is an ampersand?
5. What does the expression 'in the can' mean?
6. What were 'Teddy Boys'?
7. What is a 'Hooray Henry'?
8. What does 'in the buff' mean?
9. What is a 'sleuth'?
10. What is a 'shemozzle'?
11. If you went by Shanks's pony, how would you be travelling?
12. What is 'plonk'?
13. What is an 'Oscar'?
14. If someone asked you to be QUEBEC UNIFORM INDIA ECHO TANGO what would you have to do?
15. What does 'above board' mean?

ANSWERS

1. To complain. 2. Bedrock. 3. To strengthen or reinforce. 4. The symbol & meaning 'and'. 5. Something has been successfully accomplished. 6. Gangs of young lads who wore long jackets and narrow trousers. 7. An upper-class twit with an affected accent. 8. Naked. 9. A detective. 10. A mess, row or rumpus. 11. On foot. 12. Cheap wine; a term originating in Australia. 13. An Academy Award in the film business. 14. Be quiet! 15. Honest, genuine.

1. What is a rhea?
2. What is a black widow?
3. Exactly what is a 'ship of the desert'?
4. What sort of creature is a Portuguese man of war?
5. What sort of an animal would be feline?
6. In which countries does the bowerbird live?
7. How far can a flying-fish fly: hundreds of feet, hundreds of yards, or even miles?
8. A flamingo is a water-bird. Yes or no?
9. What sort of animal is a carnivore?
10. What sort of animal is a teal?
11. Which bird was originally called the apteryx?
12. A group of eggs, all laid at one time, is called what?
13. What animal has the heaviest brain?
14. What kind of tree grows dates?
15. Crabs, lobsters and shrimps all have the same number of legs. How many?

ANSWERS

1. A flightless bird found on the plains of South America. 2. A poisonous spider. 3. A camel. 4. A jellyfish. 5. A cat. 6. Australia and New Guinea. 7. Several hundred yards. 8. Yes. 9. One that eats meat. 10. A freshwater duck. 11. The kiwi. 12. A clutch. 13. The sperm whale. 14. A date palm. 15. Ten.

SESSION 43
QUIZ 2

• •

1. What is the capital of Malaysia?
2. What, in Australia, is a billabong?
3. What is the Troposphere?
4. Middlesex Street in London is a street market, better known as?
5. Hibernia was the name given by the Romans to where?
6. The official name 'Helvetica' refers to which country?
7. What is a native of the county of Shropshire called?
8. What body of water does the American city Tampa border?
9. Where are the Tivoli Gardens?
10. Albion was the name given by the Romans to where?
11. Which city is on the Garonne river?
12. Which is the world's loneliest inhabited island?
13. Anglesey is an island, part of which country?
14. Where in the world is Swaziland?
15. British Honduras is the old name for where?

ANSWERS

1. Kuala Lumpur. 2. A waterhole. 3. The lowest region of the atmosphere. 4. Petticoat Lane. 5. Ireland. 6. Switzerland. 7. A Salopian. 8. Gulf of Mexico. 9. Copenhagen. 10. Britain. 11. Bordeaux. 12. Tristan da Cunha. 13. Wales. 14. Southern Africa. 15. Belize.

431

SESSION 43
QUIZ 3

• •

1. What is the meaning of 'acquiesce'?
2. What does 'R.I.P.' stand for?
3. Can you name two words, sounding alike, which mean the same as this pair: plaited binding/cried like an ass?
4. A Wend is: (a) A German of Slav descent (b) a letter in the Runic alphabet (c) an ear infection?
5. What is wrong with this sentence: It is over a year ago since we met?
6. What, in the US is a 'victrola'?
7. What do 'toothbrush' and 'walrus' have in common?
8. 'Beaver' was old slang for what male appendage?
9. What is a 'flying buttress'?
10. What is a rasp?
11. What is a spiritual?
12. What, in US showbiz talk, is a 'boffo'?
13. What kind of amphibian is not an animal at all?
14. What does 'larceny' mean?
15. A cataract is (a) a waterfall (b) a malfunction of the eye?

ANSWERS

1. To rest satisfied, to agree. 2. 'Requiescat in pace': Rest In Peace. 3. Braid/brayed. 4. (a) A German of Slav descent. 5. The use of both 'ago' and 'since' is wrong. Omit 'since' or say It is over a year ago that we met. 6. A record-player. 7. They are both kinds of moustache. 8. A beard. 9. A bar of masonry from a pier or arch. 10. A kind of heavy file. 11. A kind of religious song. 12. A box-office hit. 13. A vehicle which can travel on land or in water. 14. Stealing. 15. It's both!

432

SESSION 43
QUIZ 4

• •

1. What is the diameter of a Basketball hoop; 30cm, 40cm, 45cm or 50cm?
2. How long is an Olympic-sized swimming pool?
3. Which ski's are narrower - Cross Country (Nordic) or Downhill?
4. What material is the tip of a Snooker Cue made from?
5. Who won the Men's Singles at Wimbledon in 1997?
6. With which sport do you associate Iwan Thomas?
7. In international swimming events, how warm must the water be; 20°C, 22°C, 24°C or 26°C?
8. Which team scored in injury time in all three of its group matches in France '98?
9. With which sport do you associate James Wattana?
10. Which football team play their home games at the Nou Camp Stadium?
11. Name Los Angeles' NFC American football team?
12. Name Britain's Ladies tennis number 1 who reached the 4th round of Wimbledon in 1998?
13. In Australian Rules Football, how many points are scored by putting the ball between the opposition's goal posts?
14. In Rugby Union, which player is at the back of the scrum?
15. In which sport do men compete for the King George V Gold Cup at the Birmingham NEC?

_____

ANSWERS

1. 45cm. 2. 50m. 3. Downhill. 4. Leather. 5. Pete Sampras. 6. Athletics (400m). 7. 24°C. 8. Austria. 9. Snooker. 10. Barcelona. 11. Rams. 12. Sam Smith. 13. Six. 14. Number Eight. 15. Show Jumping.

SESSION 43

QUIZ 5

● ●

1. What social practice was abolished in Turkey in 1924?
2. Which famous London hotel opened in 1889?
3. By what name was Bytown known when it became capital of Canada in 1858?
4. Why is Adelaide, Australia, sometimes called the, 'City of Light'?
5. What was founded in 1864 by Jean-Henri Dunant, and granted international immunity?
6. What Atlantic communication was completed in 1858 by Cyrus Field?
7. The Austrians and English defeated whom at Blenheim in 1704?
8. Which island in the Atlantic was annexed to Britain in 1816?
9. Which cathedral, started in 1248, was completed in 1880?
10. Which Zulu chief was received by Queen Victoria in 1882?
11. Which religious group was founded in 1534 by Ignatius de Loyola?
12. What took place at St Peter's Field, Manchester, 1819?
13. What was the Peterloo Massacre?
14. Which London art gallery was opened in 1897?
15. Which Mediterranean island became an independent republic in 1960?

ANSWERS

1. Polygamy. 2. The Savoy. 3. Ottawa. 4. Because its founding was partially due to the work of Lieutenant William Light. 5. The Red Cross League. 6. The Atlantic cable. 7. The French. 8. Tristan da Cunha. 9. Cologne. 10. Cetewayo. 11. The Jesuits. 12. The Peterloo Massacre. 13. The violent dispersal by cavalry of some radical campaigners. 14. The Tate. 15. Cyprus.

SESSION 43
QUIZ 6

• •

1. Name two English stars in this 1995 remake of *Sense and Sensibility*?
2. What was the title of the film which featured a group of young New Yorkers going on a cattle drive led by Jack Palance?
3. *Nobody's Fool* (1994) stars which seasoned film actor?
4. What is the name of Superman's girl-friend?
5. Who played the lead role in the film *Barbarella*?
6. Which of these three British sitcoms was NOT made into a feature film; *Porridge, Are You Being Served, Birds Of A Feather*?
7. Who starred in the 1992 movie *Scent of a Woman*?
8. Meryl Streep and Robert Redford stared in this epic true story about Africa. What was the title of this film?
9. What TV sitcom starred Neil Morrissey and Martin Clunes?
10. The 1993 film *The Piano* tells of a woman arriving in New Zealand, to do what?
11. Who is Popeye's great enemy?
12. Who starred with Patrick Swayze and Demi Moore in *Ghost* (1990)?
13. What was the Disney cartoon which told the story of a lion cub in the jungle?
14. *Leaving Las Vegas* tells the story of which two kinds of lonely people?
15. In which film did the character 'Harry Lime' appear?

ANSWERS

1. Emma Thompson, Alan Rickman, Hugh Grant, Robert Hardy. 2. City Slickers. 3. Paul Newman. 4. Lois Lane. 5. Jane Fonda. 6. *Birds Of A Feather*. 7. Al Pacino. 8. *Out of Africa*. 9. *Men Behaving Badly*. 10. Get married to an local man. 11. Bluto. 12. Whoopi Goldberg. 13. *The Lion King*. 14. An alcoholic and a hooker. 15. *The Third Man*.

SESSION 43
QUIZ 7

• •

1. Whose albums include 'Siamese Dream' and 'Gish'?
2. Who recorded the album, 'Raintown' in 1988?
3. Who reached number 1 in 1969 with, 'The Israelites'?
4. Who recorded the album, 'Hello I Must Be Going' in 1982?
5. Whose music is used througout the 1968 film, 'The Graduate'?
6. Which Australian band recorded the, 'Business As Usual' album in 1982?
7. Who recorded the album, 'Running in the family' in 1987?
8. Who had top ten hits with, '2-4-6-8 Motorway' and 'War Baby'?
9. Who recorded the 'Invisible touch' album in 1986?
10. Which John Lennon and Yoko Ono album featured 'Woman' and 'Beautiful Boy'?
11. Celine Dion, although Canadian at birth, won the Eurovision song contest for which country?
12. Whose song, 'Come on Eileen' won best single at the 1983, 'Brits'?
13. Who is the lead singer of The Divine Comedy?
14. With whom did The Fat Boys reach number 2 in 1987, with, 'Wipeout'?
15. Who reached number one in 1991 with, 'The Stonk'?

ANSWERS

1. Smashing Pumpkins. 2. Deacon Blue. 3. Desmond Dekker and the Aces.
4. Phil Collins. 5. Simon & Garfunkel. 6. Men at Work. 7. Level 42. 8.
Tom Robinson (Band). 9. Genesis. 10. Double Fantasy. 11. Switzerland.
12. Dexy's Midnight Runners. 13. Neil Hannon. 14. The Beach Boys. 15.
Hale & Pace (and the Stonkers).

SESSION 43
QUIZ 8

1. How much did Charley Barley sell his wife for?
2. Who wrote a series of humorous books featuring the butler, Jeeves?
3. Who wrote *Three Men In A Boat*?
4. Complete this proverb: 'If you were born to be hanged, you'll never be...'
5. Which science fiction writer was the author of the Foundation trilogy?
6. Which author's books include *The Coup, Rabbit Run* and *Couples*?
7. Complete this proverb: 'There's no so blind as...'
8. Which author whose works include Idoru and Neuromancer is known as the, 'father of Cyberpunk'?
9. Complete the proverb: 'Blessed is he who expect nothing...'
10. Who wrote the novel, *100 Years of Solitude*?
11. Complete the proverb: 'Those whom the Gods love...'
12. Who wrote *The Water-Babies*?
13. Which Booker prize-winning novel by Kazuo Ishiguro was made into a feature film starring Anthony Hopkins as the butler, 'Stevens'?
14. Which satirical magazine has been edited by Richard Ingrams and Ian Hislop?
15. The First Baron Tweedsmuir was a novelist better known as?

ANSWERS

1. Three duck eggs. 2. P.G. Wodehouse. 3. Jerome K. Jerome.
4. '...Drowned'. 5. Issac Asimov. 6. John Updike. 7. '...Those who won't see'. 8. William Gibson. 9. '...For he shall never be disappointed'.
10. Gabriel Garcia Marquez. 11. '...Die young'. 12. Chalres Kingsley.
13. *The Remains of the Day*. 14. *Private Eye*. 15. John Buchan.

SESSION 43
QUIZ 9

• •

1. What, according to the old schoolboys' joke, is the meaning of *coup de grâce*?
2. What, to a British soldier, was 'Blighty'?
3. If you were 'in the altogether', what would you be?
4. If you asked the price, and were told 'gratis', what would you pay?
5. Who made the phrase, 'Clunk, Click - Every Trip' famous?
6. Which comic featured the characters, Biffa Bacon, Billy The Fish and Black Bag?
7. In American English, what is a 'rubberneck'?
8. What is, or was, a spoonerism?
9. What is a busker?
10. If you were in the Army, and 'got a rocket', what would have happened?
11. What is 'Adam's ale'?
12. What does the symbol © mean?
13. What is an 'oik'?
14. If, in the Navy, the captain gave the order 'splice the mainbrace', what would happen?
15. What's a 'Walter Mitty'?

ANSWERS

1. A lawn-mower. 2. Home. 3. Naked. 4. Nothing! 5. Jimmy Savile. 6. Viz. 7. Someone who stares and gawps. 8. A habit of transposing initial letters of words, as 'shoving leopard' for 'loving shepherd'. 9. A street singer or performer. 10. You would have received a severe telling-off. 11. Water. 12. Copyright. 13. An ignorant lout. 14. All sailors received an extra tot of rum. 15. A day-dreaming fantasist.

438

SESSION 43
QUIZ 10

• •

1. The maxilla is another name for which bone?
2. The scientific study of drugs is called what?
3. What is the name given to a structure built to check the flow of water?
4. The study of heredity and mutation is called?
5. What is the name given to a solid figure with six square sides?
6. What is constantan?
7. Photogravure, lithography and letterpress are different methods of what?
8. We'd have a bumpy time in a vehicle without John Boyd Dunlop's invention of 1888. What was it?
9. What is caffeine?
10. Which of the planets is farthest from the Sun?
11. You taste lactic acid when you drink what?
12. A Bessemer converter used to make what?
13. A human being has how many chromosomes?
14. 'Yin' and 'yang' are expressions used in what kind of treatment?
15. The Sea of Tranquility is near the South Pole. True or false?

ANSWERS

1. The upper jawbone. 2. Pharmacology. 3. A dam. 4. Genetics. 5. A cube. 6. An alloy of 40% nickel and 60% copper. 7. Printing. 8. The pneumatic tyre. 9. A stimulant drug found in tea and coffee. 10. Pluto. 11. Sour milk. 12. Steel. 13. 46. 14. Acupuncture. 15. False. It's an area on the Moon.

SESSION 44
QUIZ 1

• •

1. What, exactly, was the Golden Arrow?
2. Whereabouts is Holy Island, or Lindisfarne?
3. On which sea is British Honduras situated?
4. What is the capital of Bulgaria?
5. What is the present name of what was called South-West Africa?
6. Where in the world do they speak Latin?
7. A native of Sardinia is not called a Sardine. What is he or she called?
8. Where is known as the 'Eternal City'?
9. In which London park is 'Speakers' Corner'?
10. In which countries is Mont Blanc situated?
11. Brussels is the capital of which country?
12. What is the Savoy, London?
13. Which is the most populous city in Africa?
14. Edinburgh is the capital of which country?.
15. In St Paul's Cathedral the following inscription is above a tomb: *Lector, sic momumentum requiris, circumspice* (Reader, if thou seekest his monument, look around). Who is buried beneath?

ANSWERS

1. An express train that ran between London and Paris. 2. Off the Northumberland coast. 3. The Caribbean. 4. Sofia. 5. Namibia. 6. It is still used to some extent in the Vatican City. 7. A Sard. 8. Rome. 9. Hyde Park. 10. France, Italy and Switzerland. 11. Belgium. 12. A famous hotel, built on the the site of the Savoy Palace. 13. Cairo. 14. Scotland. 15. Sir Christopher Wren.

• •

1. What part of the body is the maxilla?
2. The tower and spire of a church is called what?
3. In films, what is the 'best boy'?
4. What is a Klieg light?
5. If someone out of hospital told you he'd had a shunt, what would it mean?
6. What in WW1 army slang, was an 'army banjo'?
7. What is a duffel coat?
8. In 'cat' terminology, what is a queen?
9. What is a quagmire?
10. What is a copse?
11. What is a young whale called?
12. What is a campanella?
13. What do the initials WHO stand for?
14. 'Digital', in human terms, refers to what?
15. What does 'English bond' refer to?

ANSWERS

1. The upper jawbone. 2. The steeple. 3. Assistant to the chief electrician. 4. A powerful light used in film studios. 5. He'd had a bypass operation. 6. A shovel. 7. A short coat closed with toggles rather than buttons. 8. A female cat used for breeding. 9. Marshy or boggy ground. 10. A thicket of small trees or bushes. 11. A calf. 12. A small bell. 13. World Health Organisation. 14. Fingers and toes. 15. A style of bricklaying.

SESSION 44
QUIZ 3

1. In Athletics, how high is a Steeplechase Hurdle; 2ft 6ins, 2ft 9ins, 3ft 0ins or 3ft 6ins?
2. In Rugby Union, which players form part of the back row on each side of the scrum?
3. Which County Cricket team plays the majority of their home matches at Chester-le-Street?
4. Who kept goal for Scotland in the 1998 World Cup finals, after Andy Goram returned home amid allegations concerning his personal life?
5. Which wood is a cricket bat traditionally made from?
6. Which sport do the Richmond Tigers play?
7. Which football team play their home games at Craven Cottage?
8. How many players are there in a Lacrosse team?
9. For which British Touring Car Championship Team did TV presenter Mike Smith drive?
10. With which team did Nigel Mansell win the Formula One World Driver's Championships?
11. Who won the 1998 Women's French Open Tennis Championships?
12. Which County Cricket Team play some home games at Ilford?
13. Which cricketer holds the record for the highest individual test score?
14. Which football team play their home games at Filbert Street?
15. Name the Rugby Union player in the middle of the front row of the scrum?

ANSWERS

1. 3ft 0ins. 2. Flanker (Wing Forward). 3. Durham 4. Jim Leighton 5. Willow. 6. Australian Rules Football. 7. Fulham. 8. Ten. 9. BMW. 10. Williams. 11. Arantxa Sanchez Vicario. 12. Essex. 13. Brian Lara. 14. Leicester City. 15. Hooker.

442

SESSION 44
QUIZ 4

1. What important social registry was begun in 1836?
2. What was discovered in Klondyke, Canada, in 1896?
3. What did the town of Long Beach, California, buy from Britain in 1967?
4. What wartime position did General Montgomery assume in 1942?
5. What began operating at Calder Hall in 1956?
6. What famous painting was stolen from the Louvre in Paris in 1911?
7. What status did Hawaii assume in 1959?
8. What nation-wide event took place in England, starting in 1642?
9. Hong Kong was taken by the British in which year?
10. In which year did the Blitz on London start?
11. What happened to the cities of Pompeii and Herculaneum in AD79?
12. What did Matthew Webb, the swimmer, achieve in 1875?
13. A raid on London resulted in eight deaths in 1916. What caused them?
14. In 1940, the RAF made the first raid on which city?
15. Which Roman landed in Britain in 55 BC?

ANSWERS

1. Registration of births, marriages and deaths. 2. Gold. 3. The liner Queen Mary. 4. Commander-in-Chief, Middle East. 5. A nuclear power station. 6. The Mona Lisa. 7. It became the 50th state of the United States. 8. The Civil War. 9. 1839. 10. 1940. 11. They were buried under volcanic ash following the eruption of Vesuvius. 12. He became the first man to swim the Channel. 13. An aerial bombardment by Zeppelins. 14. Berlin. 15. Julius Caesar.

SESSION 44
QUIZ 5

1. What were the better-known names of Arthur Stanley Jefferson and Norvell Hardy?
2. Who starred in the film *Breakfast at Tiffany's*?
3. In which film featured an epic chariot race?
4. Name the 1994 film starring Brad Pitt as a wild son being raised in Montana?
5. Name two stars from the film *Four Weddings and a Funeral*.
6. Who played the lead role in the TV series *The Fugitive*?
7. What was the historic film about William Wallace, starring Mel Gibson and Patrick McGoohan?
8. Who played 'Harry Callahan' in such movies as *Magnum Force*?
9. Actress Mira Sorvino won an Oscar for her role in which film?
10. Who has received the most actor or actress Oscar nominations?
11. Five known criminals are put in a police line-up for a crime they didn't do. Can you name the title of the film?
12. What was the purpose of Schindler's List?
13. Who played 'Adenoid Hynkel' in *The Great Dictator*?
14. Name the film starring Gene Hackman and Clint Eastwood in a story of an ageing desperado returning for one last gunfight?
15. Who starred in the 1991 movie *The Silence of the Lambs*?

ANSWERS

1. Laurel and Hardy. 2. Audrey Hepburn, George Peppard. 3. *Ben Hur*. 4. *Legends of the Fall*. 5. Hugh Grant, Andie McDowell, Simon Callow, Rowan Atkinson. 6. David Jansen. 7. *Braveheart*. 8. Clint Eastwood. 9. *Mighty Aphrodite*. 10. Katherine Hepburn. 11. *The Usual Suspects*. 12. To save the lives of some 1,000 Jews in Nazi Europe. 13. Charlie Chaplin. 14. *Unforgiven*. 15. Jodie Foster and Anthony Hopkins.

SESSION 44
QUIZ 6

• •

1. Ex Happy Monday's frontman, Shaun Ryder, went on to further success with which band?
2. Which major U.S. city is home to 'Fun Loving Criminals'?
3. Who was 'Going for Gold' in 1996?
4. Name the 1992 Manic Street Preachers album featuring 'You Love Us' and 'Motorcycle Emptiness'.
5. Billy MacKenzie was the lead singer of which 1980's group?
6. Which group's first hit was 'What you need' in 1985?
7. Which 1980's three piece group had hits including 'Doctor, Doctor' and 'Hold me now'?
8. 'Dub be good to me' was a hit for which group featuring Norman Cook?
9. Stuart Adamson of Big Country was formerly a member of which late 1970's band?
10. What is the name of the original drummer in the super group The Who?
11. Who had hits with 'White lines (Don't do it) with Melle Mel and 'The message' with The Furious Fire?
12. Which group had a hit with 'The only one I know' in 1990?
13. David McAlmont teamed up with which ex-Suede member on the 1995 hit 'Yes'?
14. Who had a hit in 1993 with 'Boom Shack-a-lak'?
15. What was the B-side to Neil, from the Young one's, hit 'Hole in my shoe'?

ANSWERS

1. Black Grape. 2. New York. 3. Shed Seven. 4. Generation Terrorists. 5. The Associates. 6. INXS. 7. Thompson Twins. 8. Beats International. 9. The Skids. 10. Keith Moon. 11. Grandmaster Flash. 12. The Charlatans. 13. BernardButler. 14. Apache Indian. 15. Hurdy Gurdy Mushroom Man.

SESSION 44
QUIZ 7

. . . .

1. Which author dropped the Onions when he changed his name?
2. Who wrote the early play, *Every Man in His Humour*, performed with Shakespeare in the cast?
3. Which early writer compiled *Chronicles of Britain* in 1577?
4. Who wrote the novel *Porgy*, which was later dramatised into the musical, *Porgy and Bess*?
5. Who were Gilbert and Pamela Frankau?
6. Which pop music singer and songwriter published a collection of his words with the title *Tarantula*?
7. Whose epic poem, *Endymion* was published when he was only 23 years old?
8. Which author and novelist named Korzeniowski became famed as a writer of English novels under another name?
9. Which newspaper correspondent, taken prisoner during the Boer War, became British Prime Minister?
10. Who wrote *The Pit And The Pendulum*?
11. What was Arnold Bennett's first name?
12. Who wrote the novel *Gentlemen Prefer Blondes*?
13. Which Poet Laureate started life as a sailor and only took up writing due to ill-health?
14. Which daily newspaper formerly bore the slogan on its masthead, 'Forward with the People'?
15. Which 'Goon' wrote *Puckoon* and a series of autobiographies about his time in the Second World War and after?

ANSWERS

1. George Oliver Onions, who became plain George Oliver. 2. Ben Jonson in 1598. 3. Hollinshed. 4. Du Bose Heywood. 5. Novelists, father and daughter. 6. Stephen Foster. 7. John Keats. 8. Josef Conrad. 9. Winston Churchill. 10. Edgar Allen Poe. 11. Enoch. 12. Anita Loos. 13. John Masefield. 14. *The Mirror*. 15. Spike Milligan.

SESSION 44
QUIZ 8

1. What does 'naff' mean?
2. If someone sent you an invitation marked R.S.V.P., what should you do?
3. Why were the first London policemen called 'peelers'?
4. What does AWOL stand for?
5. What does 'schmaltz' mean?
6. What was nicknamed 'The Thunderer'?
7. What did the Owl and the Pussycat go to sea in?
8. What is The Observer?
9. By what name is Robert Louis Stevenson's novel, *The Sea Cook* better known?
10. In the 1930s, a child could buy *The Rainbow*. What was it?
11. Who was the first author to have his novels serialised?
12. Who wrote *Kane and Abel*?
13. Who was Hans Christian Andersen?
14. What famous character did Richmal Crompton create?
15. Who has written well over 500 romantic novels?

ANSWERS

1. It describes something inferior or below standard. 2. Make sure you reply! 3. They were first organised by Sir Robert Peel. 4. Absent Without Leave. 5. Sickly sweet, sentiment. 6. *The Times* newspaper. 7. A beautiful pea green boat. 8. A long-established Sunday newspaper. 9. *Treasure Island.* 10. A weekly children's comic. 11. Charles Dickens. 12. Jeffrey Archer. 13. Danish author of fairy stories. 14. William Brown – Just William. 15. Barbara Cartland.

447

SESSION 44
QUIZ 9

• •

1. In diving, what does the acronym 'scuba' stand for?
2. Which home entertainment system needs woofers and tweeters?
3. What does the chemical symbol C signify?
4. What are hydraulic machines driven by?
5. How many lines does a British television set use?
6. Nacre is another name for what?
7. What was tested for the first time by a Dutchman on the Thames in 1620?
8. What does a compositor do?
9. How many units in a score?
10. What colour does litmus paper become when immersed in acid?
11. What is the difference between a 'corpse' and a 'carcass'?
12. What was Betamax?
13. Which electronic systems use hardware and software?
14. As a measurement, how many links are there in a chain?
15. What proportion of air is nitrogen?

ANSWERS

• •

1. What is the name for the nostril of a whale?
2. Which animal may defend itself by squirting blood from its eyes?
3. How fast can a mallard duck fly?
4. What is the present name for what used to be called the camelopard?
5. For how many days is a cow pregnant?
6. What is the true name of the bird called the 'laughing jackass'?
7. The dragonfly has one sense better developed than any other insect. Which?
8. Which tree is sometimes called the 'Scots mahogany'?
9. How much of an egg's weight is taken up by shell?
10. Which fruit has the largest amount of calories?
11. 'White ants' is another name for what creatures?
12. Dogs are canine, cats are feline. What are bears?
13. Nowadays 'Chinese gooseberries' are better known as what?
14. What colour is a cornflower?
15. What to a British person is what an American would call a 'chickadee'?

ANSWERS

1. Blowhole. 2. The American horned toad. 3. 65mph. 4. The giraffe.
5. About 280. 6. The kookaburra. 7. Its eyesight. 8. The alder. 9. Twelve
percent. 10. The avocado. 11. Termites. 12. Ursine. 13. Kiwi fruit.
14. Blue. 15. The bird called a 'tit' or 'titmouse'.

SESSION 45
QUIZ 1

1. What is a 'salto'?
2. What does the latin, *'ad valorem'* mean?
3. What is an 'alcazar'?
4. What is a caricature?
5. If something is cooked 'à la king' what does it mean?
6. How many items are in a gross?
7. How long is a league?
8. What is phagomania a fear of?
9. What is a testator?
10. What is a psalter?
11. What is georgette?
12. What do the initials, BAA stand for?
13. What is a 'parapet'?
14. Can you give two meanings for the word, 'sorrel'?
15. What is 'bran'?

ANSWERS

1. A daring or dangerous leap. 2. In proportion to the estimated value. 3. A Spanish castle. 4. A drawing which exaggerates features to make fun of them. 5. In mushrooms with a cream sauce and pimentos. 6. 144. 7. Three miles. 8. Food. 9. Someone who makes a will. 10. A book of psalms. 11. A crepe-like fabric similar to chiffon. 12. British Airports Authority. 13. A long wall along a balcony. 14. (a) an acid-tasting plant (b) a reddish-brown colour. 15. The husks of grain.

SESSION 45
QUIZ 2

• •

1. When England and Australia play for the Ashes, the contents of the urn are reputed to be what?
2. How many crew are there in a Tornado Sailing Boat?
3. In Judo, which is the higher grade, White Belt, Yellow Belt or Blue Belt?
4. Which sport usually uses the larger pitch, Rugby League or Rugby Union?
5. What is the maximum number of players permitted in a Rounders Team?
6. Who won the 1996/97 Carling Premiership?
7. Which of Horse racing's classics is the oldest?
8. Who was John Mcenroe's normal doubles partner?
9. Which one of these golf courses is the odd one out : Birkdale, Troon, Gleneagles, Carnoustrie?
10. In what sport might you catch a crab?
11. Who was Britain's first million pound footballer?
12. What was Billy Jean Kings maiden name?
13. With which team did James Hunt begin his career?
14. With which sport would you associate Jens Weissflog?
15. In which U.S. city would you see the Sea Hawks play?

ANSWERS

1. Ashes of a burnt cricket ball 2. Two. 3. Blue Belt. 4. Rugby Union. 5. Nine 6. Manchester United. 7. St. Leger. 8. Peter Fleming. 9. Birkdale - others are in Scotland. 10. Rowing 11. Trevor Francis 12. Moffat. 13. Hesketh. 14. Ski-jumping. 15. Seattle.

451

SESSION 45

QUIZ 3

- -

1. King Edward III defeated which fleet at Winchelsea in 1350?
2. Henry Cecil Booth patented which household appliance in 1901?
3. Who was found dead in Whitechapel, London, in 1888?
4. What was the Cape of Good Hope first to issue in 1853?
5. What did Flight-Lieut. W. Leefe Robinson achieve following an air raid on London in 1916?
6. What youth organisation held its first rally at Crystal Palace, London, in 1909?
7. Which European Queen abdicated in 1948 in favour of her daughter?
8. King Carol of Romania abdicated in 1940 in favour of whom?
9. Brazil became independent of whom in 1822?
10. Which large South African city was founded in 1886?
11. What aerial menace first reached London in 1944?
12. What object was erected on the Thames Embankment in 1878?
13. What status did New York achieve in 1788?
14. Alexander Kerensky, in 1917, proclaimed what status for Russia?
15. The Commonwealth of Australia was formed from how many colonies?

ANSWERS

1. The Spaniards. 2. The vacuum cleaner. 3. The first victim of Jack the Ripper. 4. The world's first triangular postage stamps. 5. He was the first to shoot down a Zeppelin airship. 6. The Boy Scouts. 7. Queen Wilhelmina of the Netherlands. 8. His son, Michael. 9. Portugal. 10. Johannesburg. 11. The V2 flying bombs. 12. 'Cleopatra's Needle'. 13. It became the capital of the newly-formed United States. 14. A republic. 15. Six.

452

SESSION 45
QUIZ 4

• •

1. 'Hi-yo Silver, Away!' was the catchphrase of which TV hero?
2. 'Mary the Mole' from *Thumbelina*, received what award in 1994?
3. What 1994 father-and-son story starred Jeff Bridges and Edward Furlong?
4. Who's first feature film was *Take The Money And Run*?
5. Peter O'Toole starred as the sympathetic Scot advising a very young Chinese ruler in what film?
6 Sophia Abuza was an American vaudeville star famed in Britain as a popular singer. By what name was she better known as?
7. Who starred in the cop shows, *The Sweeney* and *Inspector Morse*?
8. What was missing from the series of Batman films in the 1980s and 1990s?
9. Which Hungarian-born US pioneer founded the company which became Paramount Pictures?
10. Which sexy, bawdy American woman wrote and performed her own material in the 1930s?
11. Who directed the 1951 film *A Streetcar Named Desire*?
12. Dino and Pebbles are characters in which popular cartoon series?
13. Who wrote the play *Chicken Soup with Barley* in 1959?
14. For what production was music lyricist Alan Jay Lerner mainly famed?
15. Laszlo Loewenstein, and actor who played 'Mr Moto', is better known as what?

ANSWERS

1. The Lone Ranger. 2. Worst Song Of The Year. 3. *American Heart*. 4. Woody Allen. 5. *The Last Emperor*. 6 Sophie Tucker. 7. John Thaw. 8. Batman's sidekick, Robin, the boy wonder. 9. Adolph Zukor. 10. Mae West. 11. Elia Kazan. 12. *The Flintstones*. 13. Arnold Wesker. 14. *My Fair Lady*. 15. Peter Lorre.

453

SESSION 45
QUIZ 5

• •

1. Which American four piece band had a hit album called 'Pocket full of kryptonite'?
2. Which Seventies Bond singer joined fellow Welshmen, Propellorheads in their 1998 hit?
3. What made the 'Magical mystery tour' different from the other Beatles' films.
4. What was the inspiration for Midnight Oil's 'Beds are burning'?
5. How much cash did the KLF burn?
6. Who is the link between The Bangles, Chakka Khan and Sinead O'Connor.
7. What's the name of Kid Creole's backing singers?
8. Name the 1980's TV pop show hosted by Jools Holland?
9 Where is Massive Attack's home town?
10. Who recommended that the BBC should ban the Frankie Goes To Hollywood hit 'Relax'?
11. Who was dancing on the ceiling?
12. Which female artist guested on Massive Attack's hit 'Protection'?
13. Who was the mastermind behind the hit singles by the Wombles?
14. Which star of the movie 'Armaggedon' sang 'Under the boardwalk'?
15. Puff Daddy's 1998 hit featured a guitarist from which 1970's super group?

ANSWERS

1. Spin Doctors. 2. Shirley Bassey. 3. It was made for TV. 4. The fight for Aboriginal rights in Australia. 5. One million pounds. 6. Prince. 7. The Coconuts. 8. The Tube. 9. Bristol. 10. Mike Reed. 11. Lionel Ritchie. 12. Tracey Thorn. 13. Mike Batt. 14. Bruce Willis. 15. Led Zeppelin.

SESSION 45

QUIZ 6

1. Which famous book by a famous Irish author, was described by a critic as 'the foulest book ever printed?
2. Who was Sir Henry Morton Stanley?
3. Which American author wrote *Of Mice and Men*?
4. Who wrote a series of essays called *Virginibus Puerisque*?
5. Which Ancient Greek thinker wrote *Republic* and *Phaedo*?
6. Which famous thriller writer died in debt, but paid this off after his death?
7. Who wrote the novel *My Brother Jonathan* in 1928?
8. Who was Israel Zangwill?
9. Who was Daisy Ashford?
10. What was very unusual about the book, *The Young Visitors*?
11. Who wrote *Moll Flanders*?
12. Who wrote *The Tenant of Wildfell Hall* in 1848?
13. Under what name was Manfred Bennington Lee better known?
14. For which great historical work was Edward Gibbon famed?
15. Who wrote *Erewhon* and *Erewhon Revisited*?

ANSWERS

1. *Ulysses* by James Joyce. 2. The explorer and journalist who went to Africa in search of David Livingstone. 3. John Steinbeck. 4. Robert Louis Stevenson. 5. Plato. 6. Edgar Wallace, whose huge royalties only accrued after he died. 7. Francis Brett Young. 8. Novelist and playwright, son of Russian-Jewish refugees, but born in London, 1864. 9. An author at the age of nine, she wrote *The Young Visitors*. 10. It was printed exactly as she wrote it, spelling and grammatical errors and all. 11. Daniel Defoe. 12. Anne Brontë. 13. As 'Ellery Queen' with his cousin, Frederic Dannay. 14. *The Decline and Fall of the Roman Empire*. 15. Samuel Butler, in 1872 and 1901.

455

• •

1. Who, or what, is Stanley Gibbons?
2. Where and what was Dixieland?
3. What was a 'Tin Lizzie'?
4. What does 'carry coals to Newcastle' mean?
5. What is the *Reader's Digest*?
6. Who created 'Tarzan'?
7. What is *Private Eye*?
8. What is the *Frankfurter Allgemeine Zeitung*? Is it (a) a newpaper (b) a sausage (c) a secret society?
9. What famous book did A.A. Milne write?
10. Which country was the home of Dracula?
11. Who was Robert Browning?
12. What is the *Melody Maker*?
13. Who was Geoffrey Chaucer?
14. What was the surname of the family of writers whose first names were Osbert, Sacheverell and Edith?
15. Who was the author of the Noddy books?

ANSWERS

1. A famous London stamp dealer. 2. The Southern States of America. 3. An early Ford car. 4. To do a pointless, useless task. 5. A monthly magazine specialising in extracts from other sources. 6. Edgar Rice Burroughs. 7. A weekly satirical newspaper. 8. (a) A newspaper. 9. *Winnie the Pooh*. 10. Transylvania. 11. Poet, and husband of Elizabeth Barret Browning. 12. A weekly newspaper dealing with pop, rock and dance music. 13. English poet and author of The Canterbury Tales. 14. Sitwell. 15. Enid Blyton.

SESSION 45
QUIZ 8

• •

1. How many lines does an American television set use; 325, 525, 625 or 675?
2. How many hundredweights are there in a ton?
3. What did Sir Frederick Banting and and J.J.R. MacLeod discover in 1922?
4. What is the chemical symbol for Zinc?
5. When did the first cable car come into use?
6. What was the name given in early times, to people who thought they could transmute base metals into gold?
7. The first commercial typewriter was made by an armaments firm. True or false?
8. How many pecks are there in a bushel?
9. Geometrically speaking, how many surfaces does a cone have?
10. If you had a cutaneous infection, what would be troubling you?
11. What is your oesophagus?
12. What was the name of the space-traveller aboard Sputnik 2 in 1967?
13. What do veins do in the human body?
14. What do arteries do in the human body?
15. What day was known to the Romans as *Dies Mercurii*?

ANSWERS

1. 525. 2. 20. 3. Insulin. 4. Zn. 5. On 27th July, 1908, in Switzerland. 6. An alchemist. 7. True. Remingtons were gunmakers. 8. Four. 9. Two. 10. Your skin. 11. The gullet. 12. Laika, the dog. 13. Carry blood to the heart. 14. Carry blood from the heart. 15. Wednesday.

457

SESSION 45

QUIZ 9

. . . .

1. Which bird is able to swim fastest?
2. Which monkey has the longest nose?
3. The old word emmet meant which insect?
4. What can substances called 'gums' do which 'resins' can't?
5. Why is the pilot fish so called?
6. Why would you have difficulty in identifying a female blackbird?
7. What sort of fruit would you find on an arbutus?
8. Rabies has another name, too. What is it?
9. On which part of the body would you find your tarsus?
10. What is a fingerling?
11. Which is fastest, a greyhound, a red deer or a bluefish tuna?
12. What is a pangolin?
13. The budgerigar is an Australian parakeet. True or false?
14. Which is the tallest and thickest kind of grass?
15. What exactly is a poult?

ANSWERS

1. The penguin. 2. The proboscis monkey. 3. The ant. 4. Dissolve in water. 5. Because it tends to swim alongside ships and even with sharks. 6. Because it's brown, not black. 7. Strawberries. 8. Hydrophobia. 9. On your foot. It's the ankle-bone. 10. A very small fish, such as a baby salmon. 11. Bluefish tuna, with a top speed of 44mph. 12. Another name for the scaly anteater. 13. True. 14. Bamboo. 15. A young turkey or other domestic fowl.

SESSION 45
QUIZ 10

• •

1. At which London cemetery is Karl Marx buried?
2. Which city is to host the 2000 Olympic Games?
3. In which island would you find Montego Bay?
4. Where would you find the lost city of Machu Picchu?
5. What region includes the islands Tahiti and Bora-Bora?
6. What does ACT stand for?
7. Which country is the greatest consumer of baked beans ahead of Sweden, in second place?
8. Which island is split into contested Greek and Turkish areas?
9. What is the largest lake in Africa?
10. What two continents does the Drake Passage separate?
11. Name three of North America's Great Lakes?
12. Which country has a larger population; Indonesia, Brazil or Japan?
13. How many provinces are in Canada?
14. Which African country has Mogadishu as its capital city?
15. Which country, bordering India and China, contains much of the Himalaya range of mountains?

ANSWERS

1. Highgate. 2. Sydney. 3. Jamaica. 4. Peru. 5. French Polynesia. 6. Australian Capital Territory. 7. United Kingdom. 8. Cyprus. 9. Lake Victoria. 10. South America and Antarctica. 11. Lake Ontario, Lake Huron, Lake Superior, Lake Michigan, Lake Erie. 12. Indonesia. 13. Ten. 14. Somalia. 15. Nepal.

459

CHILDREN'S
SECTION

QUIZ 1

1. Are there any bees without stings?
2. What do we mean when we say someone is like a cat on hot bricks?
3. Which is the longest and narrowest country?
4. Which French leader was defeated at the battle of Waterloo?
5. Who was the last American president to be assassinated? (1963)
6. Who sang the song Yellow Submarine?
7. Which animal lives on the seabed and has tentacles but looks like a flower?
8. For how long does a baby grow inside its mother?
9. What is an ellipse?
10. What is an oasis?
11. What is a space probe?
12. Cox and Golden Delicious are the names of what kind of fruit?
13. Which of these is not a reptile: tortoise, alligator, octopus, snake?
14. What does the proverb the pen is mightier than the sword mean?
15. What do 25, 16 and 9 have in common?

ANSWERS

1. Yes 2. The person is restless 3. Chile 4. Napoleon Bonaparte 5. John F. Kennedy 6. The Beatles 7. A sea anemone 8. 9 months 9. A flattened circle 10. A fertile place in a desert 11. An unmanned spacecraft 12. The apple 13. Octopus 14. Words are stronger than force 15. They are all square numbers

QUIZ 2

1. Is the Earth completely round?
2. What does the proverb you can't get a quart into a pint pot mean?
3. How deep is the deepest part of the ocean: 1 mile, 3 miles, or 7 miles?
4. Can the world's largest bird fly?
5. Who was the British prime minister during World War II?
6. What do we mean when we say that someone has a sweet tooth?
7. Do lines of latitude go from north to south or from east to west?
8. Is there more of an iceberg under or over the water?
9. Which is the largest bone in the human body – the shin bone, the thigh bone, or the hip bone?
10. Which animal builds a dam?
11. What divides the Northern hemisphere from the Southern hemisphere?
12. What causes the tides?
13. What is the name of the war that took place between 1914 and 1918?
14. What does an anaesthetic do?
15. Which is the world's smallest country?

ANSWERS

1. No. It is slightly flattened at the Poles 2. You can't do the impossible 3. 7 miles (11,000 m) 4. No. The ostrich is too big to fly 5. Winston Churchill 6. The person likes eating sweet things 7. East to west, parallel to the Equator 8. Under 9. The thigh bone or femur 10. The beaver 11. The Equator 12. The pull of the Moon and of the Sun 13. World War I or the First World War 14. It stops you feeling pain 15. Vatican City in Rome

QUIZ 3

1. Which sport is the most popular worldwide?
2. What is the capital of Belgium?
3. What is minting?
4. What is the name of the most famous tower in Paris?
5. Why do hot air balloons float in the air?
6. Who lives in the White House?
7. Which two countries is Mont Blanc on the border of?
8. What is veal?
9. Of what were the houses of the Three Little Pigs made?
10. What is the name of the musical instrument made of rows of bars that are struck with a hammer?
11. Which town did the Pied Piper rid of rats?
12. How does a marsupial carry its young?
13. How were Viking longboats powered?
14. What is a young swan called?
15. What is the name of the famous British queen who fought against the Romans?

ANSWERS

1. Football (soccer) 2. Brussels 3. The craft of making coins 4. The Eiffel Tower 5. Because hot air is lighter than cold air 6. The president of the United States 7. France and Italy 8. Calf meat 9. Straw, sticks and bricks 10. A xylophone 11. Hamelin 12. In its pouch 13. By a sail and oars 14. A cygnet 15. Boudica

464

QUIZ 4

1. Give another name for a hog?
2. What do we call the disorder many people feel when they travel by boat?
3. On which tree do acorns grow?
4. Which is the world's longest river – the Amazon, the Nile, or the Mississippi?
5. Which day occurs only once every 4 years?
6. How many planets in our solar system support living things?
7. Where are the Tropics?
8. What is a volunteer?
9. Are people animals?
10. What are twins?
11. What do we mean when we say that someone is in hot water?
12. Do we have a drum in our ear?
13. Where did the Vikings come from?
14. What is a lathe?
15. What did Johannes Gutenberg invent?

ANSWERS

1. A pig 2. Sea sickness 3. The oak 4. The Nile 5. February 29 (in a leap year) 6. Only the Earth 7. On or near the Equator 8. Someone who offers to do something 9. Yes, they are animals with complex brains 10. Two babies born at one birth 11. The person is in trouble 12. Yes – the eardrum 13. From Scandinavia 14. A machine to shape wood or metal 15. Printing with movable type

QUIZ 5

1. What is paper made from?
2. What does the proverb don't count your chickens before they're hatched mean?
3. Which pop group has sold more records and tapes than any other?
4. How many bones do adults have: 56, 106, 206?
5. Where is Kennedy airport?
6. Can a doctor cure a cold?
7. Which ancient civilization invented paper, gunpowder, and silk-making?
8. What is the capital of Scotland?
9. What do we mean when we say that someone is under the weather?
10. Which country's flag is called the Star Spangled Banner?
11. Who were the first people to live in New Zealand?
12. Where do we have lenses in our head?
13. Which is the fastest land animal – the hare, the gazelle, or the cheetah?
14. What did suffragettes fight for?
15. Who was Tutankhamun?

ANSWERS

1. Wood or cloth that is pulped and pressed 2. Don't assume things until you're sure 3. The Beatles 4. 206 bones 5. New York 6. No. No cure for the cold has been found 7. The ancient Chinese 8. Edinburgh 9. The person is unwell 10. The United States of America 11. The Maoris 12. In our eyes 13. The cheetah 14. Votes for women 15. An Egyptian pharaoh

QUIZ 6

1. What does a doctor use a stethoscope for?
2. What does it mean to have forty winks?
3. How many muscles do we have in our bodies – 69, 239, or 639?
4. Which was the first supersonic airliner?
5. What is a Great Dane?
6. What is albumen?
7. Do the continents move?
8. What is braille?
9. What does take the bull by the horns mean?
10. How many sides does a triangle have?
11. When were the Middle Ages?
12. Which animal has the longest nose?
13. What is the capital of Spain?
14. What does sugar come from?
15. What do Americans celebrate on July 4th?

ANSWERS

1. To listen to your breathing and heart 2. It means to have a nap 3. 639 muscles 4. Concorde 5. A large dog 6. The white of an egg 7. Yes, but very slowly 8. A system of dots read by the blind 9. Tackle a problem without fear 10. 3 11. From about the years 500 to 1460 12. The elephant (its trunk) 13. Madrid 14. Sugar cane and sugar beet 15. Independence day

467

QUIZ 7

1. Which food substance most damages your teeth?
2. In which city could you ride in a gondola?
3. What is formed when two lines meet?
4. Which are warmer – black clothes or white clothes?
5. Which mountain range contains the 13 highest mountains?
6. What is at the centre of our solar system?
7. Which American city suffered a huge earthquake in 1906?
8. What is the capital of Australia?
9. Where is a rattlesnake's rattle?
10. What did George's marvellous medicine do?
11. Which animal is sometimes called a river horse?
12. Which game has smashes, rallies and lobs?
13. Who was the president of the United States during World War II?
14. What is deer meat called?
15. Who built an ark to survive a great flood?

ANSWERS

1. Sugar 2. Venice in Italy 3. An angle 4. Black clothes because black absorbs heat 5. The Himalayas 6. The Sun 7. San Francisco 8. Canberra 9. At the end of its tail 10. It made Grandma very tall 11. The hippopotamus 12. Tennis 13. Franklin D. Roosevelt 14. Venison 15. Noah

QUIZ 8

1. Where does a guinea pig store its food?
2. What does a carnivore eat?
3. How many senses have we got?
4. Which mythical creature is supposed to be half woman and half fish?
5. Which tree produces conkers?
6. What is another name for a shooting star?
7. Where is the spinal cord?
8. Whose court was at Camelot?
9. What are pedal pushers?
10. Which line on the map divides east from west?
11. What kind of animals are the most intelligent?
12. What is a chronometer used for?
13. What kind of land covers most of Australia?
14. What does blow your top mean?
15. Where is Hong Kong?

ANSWERS

1. In its cheeks 2. Meat 3. Five: sight, hearing, smell, taste, touch 4. A mermaid 5. The horse chestnut 6. A meteor 7. In your backbone 8. King Arthur's 9. A type of trouser 10. The Greenwich meridian 11. People 12. Navigation 13. Desert 14. To be very angry 15. Off the coast of China

QUIZ 9

1. Which elephants have larger ears: African or Indian?
2. What do viruses cause?
3. What is ju-jitsu?
4. Could you jump higher on the Moon or on Earth?
5. What do people receive Oscars for?
6. Why do spiders build webs?
7. Which countries make up Scandinavia?
8. When do eclipses of the Sun occur?
9. What does to throw in the towel mean?
10. Who led the Roundheads in the English Civil War?
11. Who wrote The Twits?
12. In which sport can you make a hole-in-one?
13. What was the code name for the day the Allied forces landed in Normandy during World War II?
14. Which dinosaur had spiky plates along its back and ate plants?
15. What is the collective name for knives, forks and spoons?

ANSWERS

1. African 2. Diseases such as colds and measles 3. A form of wrestling developed in Japan 4. On the Moon 5. Achievements in films 6. To catch their prey 7. Norway, Sweden and Denmark 8. If the Moon hides the Sun from the Earth 9. To admit defeat 10. Oliver Cromwell 11. Roald Dahl 12. Golf 13. D-Day 14. Stegosaurus 15. Cutlery

QUIZ 10

1. What is the difference between amateurs and professionals in sport?
2. What is the difference between hail and hale?
3. What was a blunderbuss?
4. Ding dong bell – where's pussy?
5. What is the name for a tube which carries blood to the heart?
6. Why do we have seasons every year?
7. What is cheese made from?
8. What happens if a football player gets a red card?
9. What does a bud grow into?
10. Which country produces Camembert cheese?
11. Who is remembered for the Gunpowder Plot?
12. Do female reindeer have antlers?
13. Which countries make up Great Britain?
14. Which melon has pink flesh and black seeds?
15. What is 25 percent of 16?

ANSWERS

1. Amateurs aren't paid professionals are. 2. 'Hail' is frozen rain; 'hale' means healthy 3. A kind of gun 4. In the well 5. A vein 6. Because the Earth is tilted on its axis 7. Milk 8. The player is sent off 9. A flower or a leaf 10. France 11. Guy Fawkes 12. Yes 13. England, Scotland and Wales 14. A water melon 15. 4

471

QUIZ 11

1. Why do some desert plants have very long roots?
2. Which airport handles more international aircraft than any other airport in the world?
3. Which is the only mammal that flies?
4. What does CD stand for?
5. Which famous painting by Leonardo da Vinci is known for its smile?
6. What is biology the science of?
7. What is produced in a blast furnace?
8. What is the target ball in a game of bowls called?
9. Why do astronauts on the Moon need to take oxygen with them?
10. Which is the highest mountain in Britain?
11. Shakespeare wrote a play about which Roman general?
12. The Carribean Sea is part of which ocean?
13. Who said: Never in the field of human conflict was so much owed by so many to so few?
14. How would you measure a perimeter?
15. In which war did the Roundheads fight the Cavaliers?

ANSWERS

1. To reach water deep underground 2. London Heathrow 3. The bat 4. Compact Disk 5. The Mona Lisa 6. Life 7. Iron 8. The jack 9. Because there is no air on the Moon 10. Ben Nevis in Scotland 11. Julius Caesar 12. The Atlantic 13. Winston Churchill 14. By adding the lengths of the sides 15. The English Civil War

QUIZ 12

1. What is a hangar?
2. What is 50 percent of 50?
3. John Lennon, Ringo Starr and George Harrison were three of the Beatles. Who was the fourth?
4. What is the study of plants called?
5. Who founded the Boy Scouts movement?
6. Which are you most likely to see at night: a butterfly or a moth?
7. In which sea is the island of Crete?
8. Who wrote Robinson Crusoe?
9. What is chlorophyll?
10. What does a disinfectant do?
11. Which city were the Crusaders fighting for control of?
12. What is the name for a small explosive charge that sets off a bomb?
13. Who was the only ruler of Britain who ruled instead of a king or a queen?
14. Which is the world's largest country?
15. Which spiny plants grow in deserts?

ANSWERS

QUIZ 13

1. What are young goats called?
2. How many holes are there on a golf course?
3. Currants, raisins and sultanas are all dried what?
4. What is the force that pulls everything towards the Earth?
5. Which German brothers wrote a famous collection of fairy tales?
6. How many humps does a Bactrian camel have?
7. What is the capital of Denmark?
8. What happens at the Edinburgh Festival?
9. Which English monarch led the defeat of the Spanish Armada?
10. Which is the longest river entirely in England?
11. What is a private eye?
12. Who pioneered the Theory of Evolution?
13. Early pens were made from birds' feathers. What were they called?
14. If someone has a nest egg, what do they have?
15. In which year did England and Wales unite with Scotland; 1607, 1707 or 1807?

ANSWERS

1. Kids 2. 18 3. Grapes 4. Gravity 5. The brothers Grimm 6. 2 7. Copenhagen 8. Arts events such as drama, music, dance 9. Queen Elizabeth I 10. The Severn 11. A private detective 12. Charles Darwin 13. Quill pens 14. Savings put aside 15. 1707

QUIZ 14

1. Where is the biggest and busiest McDonald's – New York, Paris, Moscow or London?
2. What are the White Cliffs of Dover made from?
3. What do you call a curved stick used by the Aborigines in Australia for hunting?
4. Which kind of cat is fawn-coloured and has blue eyes?
5. What is the capital of Egypt?
6. Are dolphins a kind of whale?
7. Pines, cedars and yews are all what kind of tree?
8. Who wrote David Copperfield?
9. Which precious stone is green?
10. Who is Mickey Mouse's girlfriend?
11. Which river flows through Paris?
12. Who led Britain for much of World War I?
13. Do like magnetic poles attract each other or push each other apart?
14. Which battle did William the Conqueror win in 1066?
15. What do you call a toy with mirrors that creates random regular patterns?

ANSWERS

1. In Moscow! 2. Chalk 3. A boomerang 4. A Siamese cat 5. Cairo 6. Yes 7. Conifers 8. Charles Dickens 9. Emerald 10. Minnie Mouse 11. The Seine 12. Lloyd George 13. They push each apart. 14. The battle of Hastings 15. A kaleidoscope

QUIZ 15

1. Which insect transmits malaria?
2. What does smell a rat mean?
3. How long is a leap year?
4. If a person is short-sighted, do they have trouble seeing nearby objects or objects at a distance?
5. What is the capital of Japan?
6. Which parts of a tree trap sunlight and make food for the tree?
7. What is a loom used for?
8. Which American president vowed to put men on the Moon before 1970?
9. What is the word fax short for?
10. What is the main religion of India?
11. How did Adolf Hitler die?
12. Where is Cape Horn?
13. What is economic inflation?
14. What vegetable keeps away vampires?
15. Which English king established the Church of England?

ANSWERS

1. The mosquito 2. To suspect that something is wrong 3. 366 days 4. Objects at a distance 5. Tokyo 6. The leaves 7. Weaving cloth 8. John F. Kennedy 9. Facsimile 10. Hinduism 11. He committed suicide 12. At the southern tip of South America 13. A period of rising prices 14. Garlic 15. Henry VIII

QUIZ 16

1. Which rodent is covered with long, sharp, black and white spikes called quills?
2. What kind of boats have rigging?
3. Does a whale breathe air?
4. What is another name for pingpong?
5. What do Milton, Wordsworth and Roger McGough have in common?
6. What is the device for showing the movement of stars and planets on a curved ceiling?
7. What were Henry Morgan and Captain Kidd?
8. When did King Wenceslas last look out?
9. Who invented radio?
10. Which queen was called Bloody Mary?
11. Which strait connects the Mediterranean to the Atlantic Ocean?
12. Which prehistoric reptiles died out 65 million years ago?
13. Why is a mocking bird so called?
14. Who founded the Muslim religion?
15. Which is the highest mountain in Europe?

ANSWERS

1. The porcupine 2. Sailing boats 3. Yes 4. Table tennis 5. They are all poets 6. A planetarium 7. Pirates 8. On the feast of St Stephen 9. Guglielmo Marconi 10. Queen Mary I 11. The Strait of Gibraltar 12. Dinosaurs 13. Because it mimics other creatures' cries 14. Muhammad 15. Mt Elbrus (in the Russian Federation)

QUIZ 17

1. Which missionary organization is structured like an army with ranks and uniforms?
2. It is the smallest fish of the herring family and we usually buy it in tins. What is it?
3. What is the headquarters of London's Metropolitan Police called?
4. Which small fish hangs upright in the water, holding on to seaweed stems with its tail?
5. Which plant is the emblem of Ireland?
6. Which language is spoken in Rome?
7. A cricket ball and a tennis ball are dropped from the top of a building: which hits the ground first?
8. In which continent is the Zambezi River?
9. The average roomful of air weighs 15, 25, 35, or 45 kg?
10. Which is the largest of the apes?
11. How many degrees are there in a right angle?
12. In which building in central Rome did the Romans hold contests between gladiators
13. What is the capital of Canada?
14. Who was Prince Albert married to?
15. What was dropped on Hiroshima?

ANSWERS

1. The Salvation Army 2. The sardine 3. Scotland Yard 4. The sea horse 5. The shamrock 6. Italian 7. They hit the ground at the same time 8. Africa 9. 45 kg 10. The gorilla 11. 90 degrees 12. The Colosseum 13. Ottawa 14. Queen Victoria 15. The first atom bomb

QUIZ 18

1. Which group of sea mammals have flippers for swimming, live in herds and bark?
2. What do we mean when we say curiosity killed the cat?
3. Who was Moses' brother?
4. Which Scottish doctor explored Africa in the nineteenth century?
5. Which tall plant has huge, yellow flowers and has seeds that are rich in oil?
6. The litre is the metric measure of what?
7. Who were Pavlova, Nijinsky, and Fonteyn?
8. As time goes on the human brain is getting bigger. True or false?
9. Which country produces the most coffee?
10. The beam, the arch, and the suspension are three kinds of what?
11. Which river do the Great Lakes flow into?
12. What type of insect is a Red Admiral?
13. Where is Jesus said to have been born?
14. What did Hitler, Mussolini, and Stalin have in common?
15. Which mammals use echoes?'

ANSWERS

1. Seals 2. Being curious can lead you into trouble 3. Aaron 4. David Livingstone 5. The sunflower 6. Capacity 7. Famous ballet stars 8. True 9. Brazil 10. Bridges 11. The St Lawrence River 12. A butterfly 13. Bethlehem 14. They were all dictators 15. Bats to fly in the dark

479

QUIZ 19

1. The dove returned to Noah with what?
2. Who were the first people to grow potatoes, maize, tomatoes, and tobacco?
3. What were V1s?
4. Which country is New Mexico in?
5. Who wrote Pride and Prejudice?
6. Where is Fiji?
7. If someone's bank account is in the red what does it mean?
8. If the length of a cube's side is 2 cm, what is its volume?
9. Which fish can fly?
10. What are cirrus, cumulus and cirrostratus examples of?
11. Which country did Britain fight in 1982 for the Falkland Islands?
12. What does a bird have that no other animal has?
13. Which cereal crop grows under water?
14. Where did Horatio Nelson die?
15. What do we mean when we say that people are as thick as thieves?

ANSWERS

1. An olive branch 2. The Native Americans 3. German guided missiles 4. The USA 5. Jane Austen 6. In the Pacific Ocean 7. The person owes the bank 8. 8 cubic cm 9. Flying fish 10. Clouds 11. Argentina 12. Feathers 13. Rice 14. Trafalgar 15. They are very friendly

QUIZ 20

1. What is the name for twins joined together at some part of their bodies?
2. What does your bladder do?
3. Does a flea have wings?
4. Which country does the island of Corsica belong to?
5. How did Mahatma Gandhi die?
6. What are rings, parallel bars and the pommel horse?
7. What do you call small flakes of dead skin in the hair caused by a disorder of the scalp glands?
8. Who was Robinson Crusoe's companion?
9. What is the Tour de France?
10. Which country was at war with Iran for 8 years from 1980?
11. What is the currency of Japan?
12. In which disease do some of the body's cells go out of control and multiply?
13. What are hock, withers, muzzle, and pattern?
14. What are Orion, Leo, Lyra, and Gemini?
15. How many people dance a pas de deux?

ANSWERS

1. Siamese twins 2. Collects and stores urine 3. No 4. France 5. He was shot by a fellow Hindu 6. Gymnastic exercises for men 7. Dandruff 8. Man Friday 9. A cycle race 10. Iraq 11. The yen 12. Cancer 13. They are all parts of a horse 14. They are constellations of stars 15. 2

QUIZ 21

1. Algebra, calculus and geometry are three branches of which subject?
2. Which city do Muslims face when they pray?
3. How does a dog cool itself down?
4. What two colours do you mix to make green?
5. Which are the three most important fuels?
6. What does a flag raised at half-mast mean?
7. What do ants, bees and termites have in common?
8. What is the difference between maps and charts?
9. What is theology?
10. Where are British monarchs crowned?
11. What was the mass killings of Jews in Nazi Germany called?
12. What is copper mostly used for?
13. Which brass instrument has a slide section?
14. To whom was Anne Hathaway married?
15. What are the horns of a stag called?

ANSWERS

1. Mathematics 2. Mecca in Saudi Arabia 3. By panting 4. Blue and yellow 5. Coal, oil, and natural gas 6. People are mourning someone's death 7. They live in highly organized groups 8. Maps show the land, charts cover the sea 9. The study of religion 10. Westminster Abbey 11. The Holocaust 12. To make electrical wires 13. The trombone 14. William Shakespeare 15. Antlers

QUIZ 22

1. How many sides are there on the base of a square?
2. What is the name for the Hindu festival of lights?
3. What is the world's population? More than 3 billion, 4 billion, 5 billion, or 6 billion?
4. What is three-quarters of 16?
5. What is the name for the masses of tiny plants and animals that drift in the sea?
6. Manhattan Island is at the centre of which city?
7. What is the Earth's closest neighbour in space?
8. Which Roman god of war had a month named after him?
9. Who was the Führer?
10. What is the long digestive tube which begins at the stomach and ends at the anus called?
11. Red sky at night is whose delight?
12. Which current UK coin has a diameter of 3 cm?
13. What is called the ship of the desert?
14. What was Aesop famous for writing?
15. Which country was Lenin leader of?

ANSWERS

1. Four sides, making a pyramid 2. Divali 3. More than 5 billion 4. 12 5. Plankton 6. New York 7. The Moon 8. Mars – March 9. Adolf Hitler 10. The intestine 11. Shepherds' 12. The 50-pence piece 13. The camel 14. Fables 15. The USSR

QUIZ 23

1. How many strings does a violin have?
2. Where do people pay in deutschmarks?
3. Which are your incisors?
4. How many sides has a twenty-pence piece?
5. Do butterflies or moths rest with their wings spread out flat?
6. Which Hollywood actor became president of the United States?
7. A rowing eight has a ninth member. What is he or she called?
8. Is a baboon an ape or a monkey?
9. What did Prohibition ban in America?
10. Which is the smallest stringed instrument in the modern orchestra?
11. In which ocean is the island of St Helena?
12. Which country did Hitler invade in 1939?
13. What are the words of a song called?
14. What is the commonest produce of insects that we eat?
15. What is an Islamic place of worship called?

ANSWERS

1. 4 2. In Germany 3. The flat front teeth 4. 7 5. Moths. Butterflies hold theirs upright 6. Ronald Reagan 7. The cox or coxwain 8. A monkey 9. The sale of alcohol 10. The violin 11. The Atlantic 12. Poland 13. The lyrics 14. Honey 15. A mosque

QUIZ 24

1. What are the vault, beam, floor and asymmetric bars?
2. Which creatures have a head, a thorax, and an abdomen?
3. What are the three states of matter?
4. What are Pravda, Le Monde, and the Washington Post?
5. What are barnacles?
6. What is 0.75 of 24?
7. Who is Jayne Torvill's partner?
8. Who was the first Danish king of England?
9. What is another name for gypsies?
10. What kind of plane was a Lancaster?
11. When is the best time to see badgers?
12. How do Americans spell grey?
13. Where do people pay with pesetas?
14. Who created Jeremy Fisher and Peter Rabbit?
15. Where would you find a retina, cornea, and iris?

ANSWERS

1. Gymnastic exercises for women 2. Insects 3. Solids, liquids, and gases 4. Newspapers 5. A kind of shellfish 6. 18 7. Christopher Dean 8. Canute 9. Romanies or travellers 10. A bomber 11. After sunset 12. Gray 13. Spain 14. Beatrix Potter 15. In the eye

QUIZ 25

1. What is a gaucho?
2. In which sport is the Davis Cup awarded?
3. Which statue is at the centre of Piccadilly Circus in London?
4. Who ate Turkey Lurkey?
5. Which food is eaten by most of the world's people?
6. Pneumonia affects which part of the body?
7. What is the opposite of honest?
8. Where in your body would you find your adenoids?
9. What is 0.2 x 10?
10. Who was Al Capone?
11. The Secretary-General is the head of which organization?
12. Which German city was divided by a wall?
13. Who went to sea in a beautiful pea-green boat?
14. In which country is the ski resort of St Moritz?
15. Which is Islam's most holy city?

ANSWERS

1. A South American cowboy 2. Tennis 3. Eros 4. Foxy Loxy 5. Rice 6. The lungs 7. Dishonest 8. At the back of the nose and throat 9. 2 10. An American gangster 11. The United Nations 12. Berlin 13. The owl and the pussy-cat 14. Switzerland 15. Mecca

QUIZ 26

1. Which country is known for its mountains, watches and chocolate?
2. How is plywood made?
3. In which sport was Rocky Marciano unbeatable?
4. Which of these is not an African country: Gambia, Ghana, Guyana, Congo?
5. Which metal costs three times as much as gold?
6. How does the possum try to avoid capture?
7. How many spots are on a six-sided dice?
8. Which is the highest numbered segment on a dart board?
9. Which is the only bird that can fly backwards and hover?
10. In which country is the Algarve?
11. There are no such things as Vampire bats. True or false?
12. What do Americans call a sweet shop?
13. If I have 14 sweets and give 3 to one friend and 2 to another. How many do I have left?
14. How many years are there between 15 bc and ad 15 ?
15. Julius Caesar sailed from Gaul to England. What is Gaul now called?

ANSWERS

1. Switzerland 2. By gluing thin layers of wood together 3. Boxing 4. Guyana 5. Platinum 6. By pretending to be dead 7. 21 8. 20 9. The humming bird 10. Portugal 11. False 12. A candy store 13. 9 14. 30 15. France

487

QUIZ 27

1. Which musical instrument consists of a long pipe and is played by Aborigines?
2. What do you dry to get a prune?
3. Who were the greatest road-builders of the ancient world?
4. Which substance makes fireworks explode?
5. Which black and white seabird has a red, blue, and yellow bill?
6. What are your sinuses?
7. Which famous New York skyscraper was for some time the world's highest building?
8. When used for lighting, what colour does neon gas give out?
9. Six nations produce two-thirds of the world's oranges. Name three of them.
10. What does it mean to take the plunge?
11. In which American state is Disneyland?
12. What does it mean to nip something in the bud?
13. Which big bird has long legs, a graceful neck, and pink plumage?
14. Which religion did the Romans adopt in the ad 300s?
15. Is an egress a kind of bird?

ANSWERS

1. The didgeridoo 2. A plum 3. The Romans 4. Gunpowder 5. The puffin 6. Four cavities in the bones of your skull 7. The Empire State Building 8. A brilliant orange-red 9. US, Brazil, Mexico, Spain, Italy, Israel 10. Decide to do something risky 11. California 12. Stop something before it begins 13. The flamingo 14. Christianity 15. No – it's an exit!

488

QUIZ 28

1. Which group of animals has hair and feeds its young on the mother's milk?
2. What is our galaxy called?
3. What is the mongoose famed for killing?
4. Who was Henry Moore?
5. What do three dots represent in the Morse Code?
6. What is noise measured in?
7. Who was Juliet's lover in Shakespeare's play?
8. Tibet is ruled by which country?
9. Which brightly-coloured tropical bird has an enormous orange beak?
10. What is the capital of Turkey?
11. Where is urine made in your body?
12. Which naval hero won the battles of Cape St Vincent, the Nile, and Copenhagen?
13. Which ocean lies between Africa, Asia, Australia, and Antarctica?
14. What is the masculine of goose?
15. Which ancient people invented paper?

ANSWERS

1. The mammals 2. The Milky Way 3. Snakes 4. A great British sculptor 5. The letter S 6. Decibels 7. Romeo 8. China 9. The toucan 10. Istanbul 11. In your kidneys 12. Horatio Nelson 13. The Indian Ocean 14. Gander 15. The Chinese

QUIZ 29

1. In the US, pumpkin pie is a traditional dish on which day?
2. In which city is the Louvre?
3. On which day of the week does Pancake Day fall?
4. Which rodent spread the Plague?
5. Alligators, crocodiles, and snakes are all what?
6. Which rock is formed from grains of sand?
7. Which is the most common animal in Australia?
8. Sinking the black ball in snooker scores how many points?
9. What does supersonic mean?
10. What are your biceps?
11. What are you doing if you are doing the quick-step?
12. How many sides has a cube?
13. What does you scratch my back and I'll scratch yours mean?
14. Which of the Seven Wonders of the World still stands?
15. Which Houses fought the Wars of the Roses?

ANSWERS

QUIZ 30

1. What is a census?
2. What is special about a catamaran?
3. Which edible blue-black mollusc is found in clusters on coastal rocks?
4. What is the capital of Israel?
5. Which animal is yellow with black spots and is called a panther in India?
6. What colour is jade?
7. What do we call the technique of creating a sleep-like trance in people?
8. What is a dromedary?
9. What does make a clean breast of it mean?
10. Who built the famous Model T car?
11. What were seagoing galleys?
12. What is the French city of Chartres famous for?
13. Stockholm is the capital of which country?
14. What do you call someone who comes from Sweden?
15. What is horse sense?

ANSWERS

1. An official count of the population 2. It is a boat with two hulls 3. The mussel 4. Jerusalem 5. A leopard 6. Usually green 7. Hypnosis 8. A one-humped camel bred for riding 9. Confess everything 10. Henry Ford 11. Roman long boats powered by rowers 12. Its cathedral 13. Sweden 14. A Swede 15. Common sense

QUIZ 31

1. Where is the Grand National run?
2. Why are ladybirds useful to gardeners?
3. Where might you find the Abominable snowman?
4. What are secateurs?
5. Which mountains divide Spain from France?
6. Howard Carter discovered which Egyptian pharaoh's tomb in 1922?
7. How many players are there in an ice hockey team?
8. What is a French castle or large mansion called?
9. What is a bream?
10. Which instrument did Chopin play?
11. What is the crown of a tooth?
12. Elementary, my dear Watson? Who said that?
13. Which colours make up the Irish flag?
14. Which dictator ruled Iraq during the 1980s and 1990s?
15. Which speckled freshwater fish belongs to the salmon family?

ANSWERS

1. Aintree, near Liverpool 2. They eat insects, especially greenfly 3. In the Himalaya Mountains 4. Pruning shears 5. The Pyrenees 6. Tutankhamun 7. Six and the goalkeeper 8. A château 9. A fish 10. The piano 11. The part above the gum 12. Sherlock Holmes 13. Orange, green and white 14. Saddam Hussein 15. The trout

QUIZ 32

1. Which is the largest seaport in northwest England?
2. Who led the Israelites out of captivity in Egypt?
3. What is the correct term for ancient Egyptian picture-writing?
4. Which process for preserving food was named after Louis Pasteur?
5. Which fungus is used to make bread, beer, and wine?
6. How many people are in a quintet?
7. Who was Saladin?
8. Which Indian and African dog-like animal makes an uncanny laughing noise?
9. What is the main ingredient in sauerkraut?
10. Which animals shed their antlers and grow new ones every year?
11. What proportion of the air is oxygen – one fifth, one eighth, or one tenth?
12. What is to practise what you preach?
13. Which age came after the Stone Age?
14. What, according to the nursery rhyme, are little girls made of?
15. What is 20 percent of 100?

ANSWERS

1. Liverpool 2. Moses 3. Hieroglyphic script 4. Pasteurization 5. Yeast 6. 5 7. A Muslim leader who fought the Crusaders 8. The hyena 9. Cabbage 10. Deer 11. One fifth 12. To behave as you tell others to behave 13. Bronze Age 14. Sugar and spice and all things nice 15. 20

QUIZ 33

1. Why is pain useful?
2. Dates, coconuts, and raffia all come from what?
3. What does the Jewish Passover commemorate?
4. Which large bear-like animal has black and white fur and eats bamboo shoots?
5. Who wrote the operas Don Giovanni and the Magic Flute?
6. Where is the volcano Mount Etna?
7. Which game has knights, castles, and bishops?
8. Which sea creature squirts out an inky fluid to escape from an enemy?
9. What have taken the place of glass valves?
10. Which large sea-mammal has two long tusks?
11. Which cereal grain is grown in paddy fields?
12. What does ask no questions and you'll hear no lies mean?
13. How often in 24 hours does the tide rise and fall?
14. What does ecstatic mean?
15. When did World War I begin?

ANSWERS

1. To warn us when something is wrong 2. Palm trees 3. The escape from Egypt under Moses 4. The Giant panda 5. Mozart 6. Italy (on the island of Sicily) 7. Chess 8. The octopus 9. Transistors in radios 10. The walrus 11. Rice 12. Don't show curiosity 13. Twice 14. Happy 15. 1914

QUIZ 34

1. What are a clove hitch and a reef?
2. The world's fourth largest island lies off the east coast of Africa. What is it called?
3. What made the craters on the Moon?
4. What kind of music did Louis Armstrong and Duke Ellington play?
5. Which boy didn't want to grow up?
6. Who were the Boers?
7. Which is Britain's only poisonous snake?
8. Why does water flow downhill?
9. Is the Sun an unusual kind of star?
10. What are the citrus fruits?
11. Which country was led by General de Gaulle?
12. Why are flowers coloured?
13. What do Americans call a car-park?
14. What was remarkable about Matilda?
15. What is a male chicken called?

ANSWERS

1. Types of knot 2. Madagascar 3. Meteorites 4. Jazz 5. Peter Pan 6. Dutch settlers in South Africa 7. The adder 8. Because it is pulled by gravity 9. No, it is quite ordinary 10. Oranges, lemons, grapefruits, limes 11. France 12. To attract insects which transfer pollen 13. A parking lot 14. She had magical powers 15. A cockerel

QUIZ 35

1. Woodwind, percussion and brass are three sections of an orchestra. What is the fourth?
2. What do we call a tropical fruit with yellow skin, yellow flesh, and spiky leaves out of the top?
3. What does eccentric mean?
4. What happened to Anne Boleyn?
5. Which one of these materials will a magnet pick up: paper, iron, aluminium, wood?
6. If you go aft in a boat, where do you go?
7. What is an extinct volcano?
8. A geriatric ward in a hospital takes care of what kind of people?
9. What breed are Eskimo dogs?
10. What garment, worn mainly by Hindu women, is made by wrapping cloth?
11. Which part of the body is affected by conjunctivitis?
12. Which harbour did the Japanese attack on December 7, 1941?
13. Which sport is Le Mans famous for?
14. Which king of England was called The Lionheart?
15. What is the name of Moscow's chief square?

ANSWERS

1. Strings 2. The pineapple 3. Different from most others 4. She was beheaded 5. Iron 6. To the stern – the back 7. A volcano that no longer erupts 8. Old people 9. Huskies 10. The sari 11. The eye 12. Pearl Harbor, Hawaii 13. Motor racing 14. Richard I 15. Red Square

QUIZ 36

1. Which English king reigned from 1660 to 1685?
2. What is the minimum school-leaving age in Britain?
3. Which dwarf could spin straw into gold?
4. What is one third of 51?
5. Which is the lee side of a boat?
6. Which country's national symbol is a thistle?
7. What is a Jewish place of worship called?
8. What crop does sweet corn come from?
9. Who saw Cock Robin die?
10. What colour are cornflowers?
11. Did the Crusades take place in the Middle Ages, the Dark Ages, or the Renaissance?
12. What is the climate like in a tropical forest – hot and dry or hot and wet?
13. Which famous London museum is named after a queen of England and her husband?
14. How many millilitres are in half a litre?
15. Which fish makes spectacular leaps to return to its birthplace?

ANSWERS

1. Charles II 2. 16 3. Rumpelstiltskin 4. 17 5. The side away from the wind 6. Scotland 7. A synagogue 8. Maize 9. The fly, with his little eye 10. Blue 11. The Middle Ages 12. Hot and wet 13. The Victoria and Albert Museum 14. 500 15. The salmon

497

QUIZ 37

1. Who are the Harlem Globe Trotters?
2. What is 15 divided by 2.5?
3. What is the study of history through objects called?
4. What is the singular of dice?
5. Which title is given to the eldest son of an English sovereign?
6. What man-made objects orbit the Earth and help with communication?
7. Does a west wind blow from the west or to the west?
8. Who was the Roman god of the sea?
9. How many minutes are there between 10.15 and 11.05?
10. Which of these words is a noun: hopped, laughing, road, because?
11. Which is nearer to London – Glasgow or Paris?
12. What kind of creature can unhinge its jaws to swallow its prey?
13. Who was Benjamin Disraeli?
14. Which rogue had a hook instead of a hand?
15. How many legs has a quadruped?

ANSWERS

1. An all-black basketball team 2. 6 3. Archaeology 4. Die 5. Prince of Wales 6. Satellites 7. It blows from the west 8. Neptune 9. 50 minutes 10. Road 11. Paris 12. The snake 13. A British prime minister 14. Captain Hook in Peter Pan 15. 4

QUIZ 38

1. What is curious about a Manx cat's tail?
2. Who are the Wallabies?
3. Which country is the largest consumer of tea in the world?
4. Is a bird an animal?
5. For what does GMT stand?
6. What kind of person was Scrooge?
7. How many noughts has a million?
8. Which animal faded away, leaving only its grin?
9. What is the highest number on a playing card?
10. What might you find in an oyster?
11. In what sport do you butterfly or crawl?
12. Who was William Gladstone?
13. What is a Camberwell Beauty?
14. In photography, what is a negative?
15. Which American civil rights leader was assassinated in 1968?

ANSWERS

1. It doesn't have one 2. The Australian rugby union team 3. Ireland 4. Yes 5. Greenwich Mean Time 6. Mean 7. 6 8. The Cheshire Cat 9. 10 10. A pearl 11. Swimming 12. A British prime minister 13. A butterfly 14. Developed, unprinted film 15. Martin Luther King

QUIZ 39

1. What is the name for a straight line that joins one corner of a square to the opposite corner?
2. Looking towards a ship's bow, is the port side on left or the right?
3. People drink the fermented juice of apples. What is it called?
4. Who was Sherlock Holmes's assistant?
5. Is the Sun mainly solid, like the Earth, or liquid or gas?
6. What is the name for a large, slow-moving mass of ice on the surface of the land?
7. What is the national bird of New Zealand?
8. What word means a family or species of animals that has died out?
9. Who was Good Queen Bess?
10. Which tree is the most massive?
11. Which reptiles ruled the world for over 160 million years?
12. What do you call people who study animals?
13. Who wrote the music for The Lion King?
14. Which is the Red Planet?
15. Where is the Grand Canyon, the world's longest gorge?

ANSWERS

QUIZ 40

1. What country's flag is a red circle on a white background?
2. What does RSVP mean on an invitation?
3. What is the capital of India?
4. Which planet is named after the Roman god of water?
5. How many corners does a cube have?
6. What is a vertebrate?
7. Where are the lands of the midnight sun?
8. Who is the patron saint of Wales?
9. Who was the first man on the Moon?
10. Who reached America in 1492?
11. What does an entomologist study?
12. How many limbs has an octopus?
13. Which is the noun in this sentence: The bird is black?
14. What is another name for a cupola?
15. What is the square root of 64?

ANSWERS

1. Japan 2. Please reply 3. New Delhi 4. Neptune 5. 8 6. An animal which has a backbone 7. The Arctic and Antarctic 8. Saint David 9. Neil Armstrong 10. Christopher Columbus 11. Insects 12. 8 13. Bird 14. A dome 15. 8

SCORE SHEET

....

SCORE SHEET

. . . .

SCORE SHEET

....